# Self, Situations, and Social Behavior

# Self, Situations, and Social Behavior

## REVIEW of PERSONALITY and SOCIAL PSYCHOLOGY

### Edited by
## PHILLIP SHAVER

——————— **6** ———————

Published in cooperation with the Society for Personality and Social
Psychology (Division 8 of the American Psychological Association)

 **SAGE** PUBLICATIONS Beverly Hills London New Delhi

*For information address:*

SAGE Publications, Inc.
275 South Beverly Drive
Beverly Hills, California 90212

SAGE Publications India Pvt. Ltd.
M-32 Market
Greater Kailash I
New Delhi 110 048 India

SAGE Publications Ltd
28 Banner Street
London EC1Y 8QE
England

Printed in the United States of America

**Library of Congress Cataloging in Publication Data**

International Standard Book Number 0-8039-2507-7
0-8039-2508-5 (pbk.)

International Standard Series Number 0270-1987

FIRST PRINTING

# Contents

# Editor's Introduction

This volume of the *Review* is concerned with the relationship between personality and social behavior, and in particular with ways in which the self and situational forces interact to produce emotions and social outcomes. Along the way, questions are raised about the nature of personality, self, and social situations; the forms and reliability of self-knowledge; and such diverse outcomes of person-situation interactions as life choices, altruistic behavior, perceptions and evaluations of others, and health.

One might think, given the phrase "Personality and Social Psychology" in the title of the *Review* and the name of the APA Divison that sponsors it, that it could hardly deal with anything other than the relationship between personality and social behavior. But that would be underestimating the tendency of subgroups in an organization to fear each other and remain separate as long as they fail to perceive common goals and interests. Ironically, the very psychologists who have most carefully documented humans' readiness to distrust and oppose each other when divided into arbitrarily labeled groups (Eagles and Rattlers in one famous study, As and Bs in another) find themselves just as burdened by their A and B (personality and social) title as any other group would be. Division 8's As, as research leads us to expect, have called the Bs disparaging names: "situationists," "superficial social learning theorists," and "specialists in concocting artificial laboratory paradigms." The Bs, naturally enough, have retaliated with "dispositionists," "connoisseurs of .20 correlations," and "outmoded trait theorists." The major periodical in the field, the *Journal of Personality and Social Psychology*, is partitioned into sections that are walled off from each other like zones of a militarily divided city. Suggestions have been made that the *Review* be partitioned along similar lines. I have opposed these suggestions, and hope that the chapters in this volume show why.

Most of the chapters, even those written by people thought to be associated with a particular section of the divided city, meander back and forth across the supposed boundaries as if there were no walls. In Chapter 1, Nancy Cantor and John F. Kihlstrom propose an approach to personality based on recent discoveries in the field of social cognition. Earlier theorists, notably George Kelly (working in the 1950s), had suggested that individual differences are primarily cognitive, but the nature of human cognition remained a mystery. As Cantor and Kihlstrom demonstrate: "The social cognition literature is now in a better position to specify the idiographic content and organization of individuals' personal constructs." In particular, concepts and procedures have been developed that allow us to portray the complexity and situationally attuned flexibility of human problem-solving efforts (in social and personal as well as purely cognitive domains) while also capturing some of the major individual differences.

Lest Chapter 1 seems to make a convincing case for discarding the trait approach to personality (and the authors do make a strong case), the next two chapters show why traits continue to capture researchers' attention. In Chapter 2, Stephen R. Briggs reviews the literature on shyness, a trait of interest to both personality and social psychologists. He finds that observers, whether thoroughly or only casually acquainted with a particular group of people, readily agree about which members of the group are shy and which are not. Moreover, these observers' ratings agree substantially with group members' self-ratings, and both kinds of ratings remain stable over time. In other words, it makes sense—as nonpsychologists have always known—to label certain individuals as shy. Briggs goes further and defends traits in general, not just as descriptive labels, but also as causal concepts, arguing that if certain people are persistently and recognizably shy there must be reasons for it. He considers biological, learning, and cognitive explanations, showing how each might provide part of the answer.

In Chapter 3, Steve Gangestad and Mark Snyder offer a conceptually related analysis of individual differences in self-monitoring. Extensive research has established that high and low scorers on Snyder's Self-Monitoring Scale differ in their values, friendship patterns, social-cognitive orientations, and sexual behavior. Snyder and his students have sometimes written about these differences as if the world were populated by just two kinds of people: high and low scorers on the Self-Monitoring Scale. Most readers have probably regarded this as a mere expository shortcut, because it was known that many people's scores fell in the scale's middle range. Now, however, Gangestad and Synder explicitly propose that (1) when it comes to self-monitoring, at the genotypic level there really are just two kinds of people; (2) the distinction between these two kinds is fundamentally biological; and (3) the distinction reveals itself phenotypically as early as the first few years of life, when children tackle language in one of two ways that seem similar to high and low self-monitoring.

Chapters 2 and 3 indicate, I believe, that although many aspects of personality may best be characterized in social-cognitive terms, it would be a mistake to abandon traits as either descriptive or explanatory concepts. Shyness is probably not simply a cognitive matter, for example, even though interesting studies (reviewed by Briggs) have revealed some of its cognitive components; and self-montoring is not only (maybe not even largely) a cognitive matter, unless innate temperament somehow determines social cognition. One of the goals of personality research should be to provide dynamic, processual explanations of the regularities designated by trait labels. Of course, as Cantor and Kihlstrom argue, it will also be important to identify and illuminate individual differences in social cognition for which there are no common or useful trait names. The two approaches to personality—trait-oriented and social-cognitive—seem complementary and mutually supportive rather than opposed.

The next three chapters bring to center stage a concept that makes brief appearances in the first three: *the self*. Cantor and Kihlstrom touch briefly on self-conceptions and self-schemas; Briggs talks indirectly about self-presentation and fear of the consequences of self-assertion; and, of course, the very term *self*-monitoring implicitly characterizes the self as something that can be strategically monitored and managed. But what, exactly, is this thing called self? In Chapter 4, Seymour Rosenberg and Michael A. Gara show that the self can be represented as a hierarchical structure, using statistical techniques previously developed for "idiographic representations of a person's beliefs about *others*, as gleaned from various kinds of free-response data." In other words, an integrated portrait of a particular person's multiple identities can be extracted from that person's conversations, self-descriptions, and fantasies; and one person's self need not contain identities, concepts, or elements common to anyone else's. Idiographic self-portraits can be used in a variety of ways, including the study of developmental changes. (Interestingly, some of these changes are the same ones being studied by Cantor and Kihlstrom under the rubric "life transitions," as can be seen by comparing Chapters 1 and 4.)

In Chapter 5, Dan P. McAdams explores the related possibility that the self comprises several "imagoes"—characters in a person's life story. His is a literary approach to the multiple identity issue, one compatible with much existing work in psychoanalysis and clinical, personality, and social psychology. Particularly interesting, considering the walled-city image of personality-social psychology, is McAdams's integration of concepts as diverse as Jungian archetypes, internalized object relations, scripts, and self-schemas. "The two major thematic lines around which the content of identity can be organized," says McAdams, "are *agency* (power/mastery/separation) and *communion* (intimacy/surrender/union)." Working in the Murray-McClelland tradition, McAdams assesses these themes via the Thematic Apperception Test, a method that seems ultimately compatible with the procedures used by Rosenberg and Gara to extract themes from Thomas Wolfe's novel, *Look Homeward Angel* (see Chapter 4).

Chapter 6, by Peter Salovey and Judith Rodin, proposes an explanation in terms of self-related cognitions of the link between emotions and moods, on the one hand, and certain kinds of social behavior (e.g., altruism) on the other. Emotions and moods are hypothesized to affect the availability of certain kinds of cognitions about the self, which in turn affect social behavior. In exploring this elegant and appealing hypothesis, Salovey and Rodin review a heterogeneous set of literatures, showing that data from studies conducted under the rubrics of personality, social, cognitive, and clinical psychology fit together to support it. One section of the chapter suggests possible links with Rosenberg and Gara's structural analysis of the self: "When one experiences [a particular] mood or emotion, one should represent the self more simply. . . . It is difficult to call to mind aspects of the self that are inconsistent with the mood state." In another section, Salovey and Rodin use the concept of self-involvement to clarify the elusive distinction between moods and emotions.

Taken together, the three "self" chapters point to a future psychology of personality whose handling of structure and dynamics will rely heavily, as Cantor and Kihlstrom advocate, on research in the areas of social cognition and social interaction.

Chapter 7, by Timothy D. Wilson and Julie I. Stone, sounds a warning for researchers doing dynamically oriented studies of personality and the self. Progress in understanding personality processes would be enhanced if researchers could rely on people's self-reports to provide valid insights into the causes of behavior. These reports have been challenged for decades, however, because of contamination by response sets and self-serving biases. In 1977, Richard Nisbett and Timothy Wilson argued in a highly controversial article that even if such biases could be set aside, human beings simply do not have privileged access to their own mental processes. In Chapter 7, Wilson and Stone revise this claim on the basis of subsequent experiments, but without rendering it less troublesome or provocative. They argue that although people *do* have privileged access to some information about their mental processes, they are not very good at using it to construct correct explanations of their behavior.

The remaining chapters explore interrelations of personality and social processes in particular content domains. Chapter 8, by Victor Battistich, Avi Assor, Lawrence A. Messé, and Joel Aronoff, deals with personality and person perception. The authors reconsider the intellectually exciting but empirically disappointing "new look in perception" of the 1940s and explain why, in terms of contemporary person-situation interaction theory, it failed. In brief, insufficient consideration was given to matching the personality and situational variables studied; situations presented to subjects were not real or personally significant enough to engage subjects' motives; the stages of information-processing were poorly understood, and consequently experimental effects were often sought in the wrong place; the perceptual variables studied typically involved general description of a target person rather than interaction-relevant evaluation, hence subjects' motives and goals remained irrelevant to the perceptual process. Battistich et al.'s literature review culminates in a summary of two successful studies supporting their approach and pointing the way to a productive new era of research on personality and person perception.

Chapters 9 and 10, dealing with love and jealousy, are inherently connected. In the first, Karen and Kenneth Dion review the literature on personality, gender, and romantic love—a literature containing several influential studies by the Dions themselves. The experience, or phenomenology, of love is shown to depend on the experiencer's locus of control orientation, self-esteem, self-actualization, defensiveness, and gender; and love itself is revealed to be a complex phenomenon, consisting of feelings, defenses, attitudes, and ideology. At the end of the chapter, Dion and Dion suggest that "*responses to intimacy* underlie the relation between personality and the experience of romantic love," a suggestion that links romantic love research with studies of mother-infant attachment, gender differences in self-disclosure, and adult interaction styles. In Chapter 10, Robert G. Bringle and Bram Buunk review the rapidly expanding literature on jealousy—a common, emotionally painful concomitant of intimacy and romantic love. Like all new areas of social-personality research, the study of jealousy has spawned what at first might seem a bewildering array of measures, concepts, and findings. Bringle and Buunk do an excellent job of organizing and evaluating what has been discovered to date, showing that jealousy is partly a matter of personality, partly a matter of situation, and partly a function of particular kinds of relationships.

The final chapters, 11 and 12, deal with personality, stress, and health. In the first, Stevan E. Hobfoll critically reviews recent research on stress resistance, focusing on both personal and social stress-resistance resources. He shows that extant research has generally failed to consider the issue of *fit* between resources and situationally based needs, a fit he calls "ecological congruence." Hobfoll, living in Israel and writing his chapter while serving in the military, is accustomed to extreme situations—war, rampant inflation, severe political and ethnic strife. This seems to have colored his reaction to American research on stress, with its emphasis on accumulated life events (as if all kinds of life events could be tallied on a single scale), fairly mild daily hassles, and the stresses and strains of well-paid corporate executives. Part of Hobfoll's criticism is directed specifically at Suzanne C. Kobasa, conceptualizer of the personality variable "hardiness." In the final chapter, Kobasa offers a personal, forward-looking overview of the gains and shortcomings of existing studies of personality and health, including her own innovative research.

Although I deliberately kept Hobfoll and Kobasa in the dark concerning the contents of each other's chapters, Kobasa concurs with Hobfoll on a number of important points. For example, she is critical of single-variable studies and desirous of a person-situation interaction approach to the study of personality and health. She also suggests that the scope of personality and health research be expanded to include not just illness but also illness-related behaviors, behaviors that may evolve and change over a considerable period of time—a suggestion in line with the time dimension of Hobfoll's ecological congruence model. Kobasa makes unique points as well, emphasizing, for example, the need for some researchers to work from a more global, theoretical, "persono-logical" stance. Her own perspective is drawn, as she explains, from Henry Murray and existential theorists. Together, Chapters 11 and 12 convey the excitement, tension, and forward movement characteristic of contemporary research on personality, stress, and health.

In addition to providing excellent reviews of various specific research literatures and in every case offering promising new directions for future study, the chapters in this volume highlight some of the larger themes in contemporary personality-social psychology. I have space to list only three: (1) The hybrid discipline of "personality and social psychology," despite the hazards of its A and B name, is producing a single, remarkably (and increasingly) coherent body of knowledge. It would be a shame to place artifical barriers between its subdisciplines. (2) The call for a person-situation interactionist approach to human social behavior, sounded in recent years in abstract-looking books and articles of the kind that often go unheeded, has been heard. The interactionist theme is woven natually, fundamentally, and fruitfully into most of the chapters in this book, without any prompting from me. It seems likely that before long there will be no personality psychology that is not interactionist. (3) The social self, and the conviction that self-involvement is an important issue in all research aimed at illuminating human emotions, have quietly taken their place at the center of today's personality-social theorizing. The self appears, again without editorial prompting, in every single chapter. These are signs, I believe, of an emerging theoretical core shared by personality and social psychology, a core around which an integrative and cooperative discipline can be built. With such a center securely in place, walls between subdisciplines should become unnecessary and obsolete.

I am deeply grateful to the authors for their creativity, speed, cooperativeness, and good humor. It is indeed a challenge to do justice to one's own ideas and the related literature in only 35 type-written pages, write clearly and interestingly so that students as well as colleagues will find the result enticing, and finish several drafts within a few months—all without attacking one's demanding, cajoling editor. All of the authors did a beautiful job without complaining or unduly slowing down the process. I am also very grateful to the associate editors and members of the editorial board who reviewed proposals and manuscripts, and to several members of my department who offered useful advice, support, and wise criticism: Susan Harter, Cindy Hazan, Harry Gollob, Gail Goodman, Cary O'Conner, Robbie Rossman, and Judith Schwartz. Without their help the volume would have been later in getting to the publisher, less well-organized and up-to-date, and considerably less readable.

—Phillip Shaver

# 1

# Social Intelligence

## THE COGNITIVE BASIS OF PERSONALITY

NANCY CANTOR
JOHN F. KIHLSTROM

**Nancy Cantor** is Associate Professor in the Department of Psychology, affiliated with the Institute for Social Research, and Chair of the Personality Area at the University of Michigan. She received her Ph.D. (1978) from Stanford, where she worked with Walter Mischel, and she was on the faculty of Princeton University from 1978-1982.

**John F. Kihlstrom** is Professor in the Department of Psychology at the University of Wisconsin and Chair of the Area Group in Social Psychology and Personality. He received his Ph.D. (1975) from the University of Pennsylvania, where he worked with Martin Orne, and was on the faculty of Harvard University from 1975-1980. His collaboration with Nancy Cantor has produced an edited book, *Personality, Cognition, and Social Interaction* (Erlbaum, 1981); several chapters, including a recent one in *Advances in Experimental Social Psychology* (Academic, 1984); and a book on personality theory and research, currently in preparation.

The present chapter outlines a cognitive theory of personality based on the social intelligence that individuals bring to bear in solving personal life tasks. Our argument is derived from earlier cognitive approaches to personality, including the personal-construct theory of Kelly (1955) and the social learning theories of Rotter (1954), Mischel (1968, 1973), and Bandura (1977). Like these, it attempts to account for both constancy and change in social behavior with a single set of principles. As Allport (1937) put it, individuals are not all *consistent in*

AUTHORS' NOTE: This chapter is based on joint invited addresses presented at the 56th annual meeting of the Midwestern Psychological Association, Chicago, May 1984. The point of view represented here is based on research supported in part by grants #BNS8022253 and #BNS8411778 from the National Science Foundation, grant #MH-35856 from the National Institute of Mental Health, and an H. I. Romnes Faculty Fellowship from the University of Wisconsin. An expanded version of this chapter appeared as Technical Report 60 from the Center for Cognitive Science, University of Michigan (June 1983). We thank Marjorie H. Cantor, Nancy W. Denney, Marvin L. Goldfried, Patricia Gurin, Sarah E. Hampson, Judith M. Harackiewicz, Reid Hastie, William Heindel, Irene P. Hoyt, Rebecca Laird, Hazel Markus, Walter Mischel, Richard Nisbett, Patricia A. Register, Carol A. Ryff, Robert J. Sternberg, Jeanne Sumi, William B. Swann, Camille Wortman, and Robert Zajonc for their very helpful comments on earlier drafts.

*the same way;* rather, individuals are *consistent with themselves.* People's actions are predictable from our knowledge of the *meaning* they ascribe to the situations in which they are located and the *solutions* they have favored in the past.

Although placing cognition at the center of a theory of personality is by no means new, the present approach seeks to extend earlier work by drawing on developments in the literature on social cognition (Showers & Cantor, 1985) and intelligence (Sternberg, 1982). The social cognition literature is now in a better position to specify the idiographic content and organization of individuals' personal constructs. Meanwhile, the intelligence literature has also been moving toward a more contextualist perspective, one that emphasizes the unique ways in which individuals frame problems and shape solutions to fit personal and cultural agendas. In both instances, attention is directed less toward characterizing primary abilities and commonly shared tasks and more toward capturing the particulars of individuals' problem solving in different life-task domains. The objective is no longer simply to show stability in the rank order of individuals on a select set of ability or style dimensions across standardized testing formats. Rather, investigators seek to demonstrate flexibility in the ways people approach the problems of everyday life.

Even with substantial improvements in the sophistication of our psychometric technology, many questions remain concerning the ontological status of personality traits and cognitive styles (Pervin, 1985). If the doctrine of traits is not entirely wrong, at least traits are not the powerful determinants and organizers of personality that we once thought them to be. However, there is also no reason to conclude that the dominant determinants of social behavior are situational in nature. Rather, the available evidence suggests that people are able to make even very subtle discriminations among their life situations, to give meaning to these situations through the operation of their cognitive processes, and to respond flexibly in terms of their goals to the constraints they encounter. Traditional trait theories of personality have little or nothing to say about this sort of behavioral variance. Yet it would seem that a complete theory of personality must be able to account for both *inter*individual and *intra*individual variance in behavior.

Lawful intraindividual variability, especially across situations, is precisely the characteristic that we ascribe to intelligence. Intelligent action, as contrasted with the instinctual or the reflexive, is flexible rather than rigidly stereotyped, discriminative rather than indiscriminate, and optional rather than obligatory. It follows then—or so it seems to us—that a theory of personality may reasonably be centered on human intelligence, and especially on the intelligence that people bring to bear on their social interactions. As Gould reminds us (1981, p. 331): "What is intelligence, if not the ability to face problems in an unprogrammed (or, as we often say, creative) manner?" The task for the personality psychologist is to demonstrate that two individuals are often prepared to see the same situation as presenting different problems to be solved, and even more important, that the same individual is prepared to construe two situations in very different ways.

In this chapter, we take an unabashedly mentalist position that places mental contents and processes at the center of social interaction. Expressed in terms of a problem-solving analogy, individual differences in social behavior reflect individual differences in people's interpretations of, and solutions for, their current life tasks. In formulating solutions to their problems, people draw on their repertoires of social intelligence. The organization and content of social intelligence includes much that is unique to each person. Thus, social intelligence can form the cognitive basis for personality.

## SOCIAL INTERACTIONS AS PROBLEMS

We begin with an analogy between the thinking and problem solving that goes on in social interaction and that studied by mainstream cognitive psychologists (Newell & Simon, 1973). Every social interaction, whether mundane or monumental, can be represented as a problem—or rather a series of problems—to be solved. The social actor, who enters the problem situation with many prior conceptions about himself or herself, others in the interaction, and the event itself, works to set goals and find procedures that can achieve the desired endpoint. This is, of course, not so much a sequence as it is a cycle, with each element in the interaction influencing the other elements (Darley & Fazio, 1980). At each stage, however implicitly, the person must ask such questions as "What do I want here?" "What are the likely consequences of my actions?" "How can I get what I want here?" As he or she works to make sense of the social problem at hand, cognitive structures and processes are central: The actor's impressions, actions, and interpretations are influenced by the body of social knowledge and the repertoire of social interaction strategies he or she possesses.

Some social interactions present very well-defined problems, and people draw on consensually shared knowledge to arrive at similar interpretations of the best solution. For example, when meeting a stranger in our own country we all adopt relatively uniform conventions of greeting. These well-defined problems are the social equivalent of simple arithmetic, and their solutions involve highly scripted, seemingly thoughtless behavior. Ill defined problems, by contrast, require the thoughtful application of social intelligence. How do you greet someone in a foreign country when the normative rules are unclear to you? We suspect that many social interactions pose problems of this kind, and that an individual's personality is revealed through the way in which these problems are represented and solved. In fact, we purposely concentrate our empirical analyses on a set of social problems that are typically ill-defined, allowing for considerable variation in construal and solution from one person to the next. For example, when we ask college students about their pressing concerns, there is considerable uniformity at the abstract level of academic and social problems, but there is much diversity at the level of specific thoughts, feelings, and plans for working on these current life tasks (Cantor, Brower, & Korn, 1984). Even in the face of strong environmental demands, as in the life transition period from high school to college, people make these problems their own by drawing on social intelligence.

## THE STRUCTURES OF PERSONALITY: CONCEPTS, EPISODES, AND RULES

Although there are a number of different viewpoints within cognitive psychology (Hastie, 1985), all share a focus on internal, mental representations of the environment, and transformations applied to these representations in the course of thought and action. From a cognitive viewpoint, personality may be construed in terms of individual differences in the mental structures and processes that guide social interaction. This repertoire of *social intelligence* is stored in memory as organized knowledge. This knowledge, in turn, forms the structural basis for personality.

In attempting to characterize this knowledge, we follow the practice in cognitive psychology and artificial intelligence of distinquishing between declarative and procedural knowledge, and between episodic and semantic knowledge (Anderson, 1983; Hastie & Carlston, 1980; Tulving, 1983). Declarative knowledge consists of facts concerning the nature of the physical and social world; procedural knowledge consists of the skills, strategies, and rules by which we manipulate and transform declarative knowledge. Within declarative knowledge, a further distinction may be drawn between episodic and semantic knowledge. Semantic knowledge is the mental lexicon of abstract, categorical information. Episodic knowledge consists of autobiographical memory—specific events encoded in the context of the self as agent or experiencer, and of the particular place and time in which they occurred. These

TABLE 1.1
Taxonomy of Social-Cognitive Structures and Processes

| Declarative-Semantic | Declarative-Episodic | Procedural |
|---|---|---|
| Implicit personality theory | Person memory | Categorization |
| Social categories: | Autobiographical | Causal attribution |
| Self | memory | Information integration |
| Other persons | | Judgmental heuristics |
| Social behaviors | | Hypothesis testing |
| Situations | | Encoding and retrieval |
| Scripts | | Impression management |
| | | Scripts |

considerations yield a taxonomy of the mental structures and processes involved in social cognition: concepts, events, and rules (see Table 1.1).

Declarative-semantic knowledge in the social domain comprises what is called implicit personality theory (Schneider, 1973) intuitive knowledge concerning the causes of human behavior, population norms for various attributes of personality, and the relationships among these attributes. More particularly, implicit personality theory consists of the categories we use to classify social stimuli: other people, ourselves, interpersonal actions, and the situations in which social interaction takes place (Cantor & Mischel, 1979; Cantor, Mischel, & Schwartz, 1982a; Hampson, 1982).

These social concepts contain a wealth of information about the typical behavior of particular types of people in their habitual social contexts—for instance, the behavior of "frat types at parties" and "nerds during classes." Embedded within these concepts is information about our evaluative reactions to such people and contexts (e.g., Fiske, 1982), and the actions and interaction scripts that characterize such events (e.g., Abelson, 1981). Some of us cringe at the mere thought of a frat type dressed in pink and green playing out a script from *Animal House*. Similarly, the self-concept—rather than being a monolithic, unitary mental representation of our personality—comprises the many "selves," past, present, and hoped for, that emerge in different social contexts (Kihlstrom & Cantor, 1984). Our current "yuppie self" may be far from the future "iconoclast self" we hope to attain. These self-conceptions record likes and dislikes, goals and aspirations, often in detail in very self-defining domains (Markus, 1983).

Declarative-episodic knowledge comes in two forms: our knowledge of the experiences, thoughts, and actions of other people, and our personal autobiographical record. In the study of social cognition, a great deal of attention has been given to the principles governing the encoding, organization, retrieval, and use of memory for other persons (Hastie, Park, & Weber, 1984). However, relatively little is known about these principles as they apply to autobiographical memory per se (Kihlstrom, 1981; Neisser, 1978). Autobiographical memory is important because it provides the basis for personal unity and coherence amidst flexibility and change. Through such knowledge we are reminded that the awkward adolescent of the past is not altogether gone in the suave urban professional of the present. Autobiographical memory is a continuous record of experience, thought, and action, the stream of consciousness linking what is happening now to what has gone before, and what will occur in the future (see Kihlstrom & Harackiewicz, 1982). It keeps track not only of specific events, but also of the individual's subjective impression of success and failure and affective reactions. These features serve to distinguish what is important from what is trivial. It is probably largely from such records that particular approach-avoidance tendencies become associated with aspects of the self, people, and situations. These evaluative associations can serve as the basis for future planning, channeling one's efforts in some directions and away from others. The subjective record of successes and failures may also contribute to the experiential basis of self-esteem and self-efficacy (see Harter, 1984).

The other component in the social intelligence repertoire, procedural social knowledge, consists of the social competencies, strategies, and rules by which we interpret situations and plan action. These are the rules that enable us to form impressions of others, make causal attributions, encode and retrieve social memories, and predict social behaviors (Smith, 1984). For example, recent research has identified some of the rules we follow in assigning people to social categories (see Buss & Craik, 1983; Cantor, Smith, French, & Mezzich, 1980). Studies of attribution show how we employ various kinds of information in order to assess the probable causes of events occurring in the social world (Jones, Kanouse, Kelley, Valins, & Weiner, 1974). More recently, there has been a great deal of attention given to the biases and shortcomings that influence memories and judgments about social events (Nisbett & Ross, 1980).

Procedural knowledge can also shape a person's plan of action in a social situation. People possess a great deal of knowledge about how to inculcate particular impressions of themselves in the minds of other people (Jones & Pittman, 1982). And, as Robert Abelson (1981) has suggested, we also possess scripts that govern our behavior in various kinds of social interactions. Scripts are especially interesting knowledge

structures because the information in them is organized both conceptually and sequentially, in terms of a canonical order in which the
various exchanges occur. As semantic knowledge structures, they are
used to help categorize the situations in which people find themselves,
and to make inferences about what has happened in the past and will
happen in the future; as procedural knowledge structures, they help to
guide the behavior in the situation from start to finish.

Individuals act intelligently by using the concepts and procedures in
their social intelligence repertoire to appraise problems, shape intentions, monitor actions, and evaluate outcomes (Baron, 1982). These
executive skills enable the individual to see problems as they emerge and
plan actions that are consonant with personal goals (as reflected in the
concept repertoire). For example, a successful individual with underlying qualms about her "true abilities" in a domain may shy away from a
diagnostic test of those capacities by engaging in self-handicapping
(Jones & Berglas, 1978). The individual may decide to risk a less than
optimal performance in favor of the safety provided by creating an
ambiguous attributional environment. The effort involved in this
"decision" is minimal, as the skills of goal-setting, means-end analysis,
playing through potential outcomes and attributions operate quite
naturally in these familiar achievement settings. However, the personal
benefits of this intelligence can be substantial. The self-handicapper,
highly attuned to the self-esteem implications of a poor performance,
uses his or her knowledge intelligently to serve a self-protective end.

## INDIVIDUAL DIFFERENCES IN
## SOCIAL-COGNITIVE STRUCTURES AND PROCESSES

From a cognitive point of view, individual differences in social
interaction reflect individual differences in social intelligence. These
individual differences take two general forms: in the base of declarative
social knowledge in a particular domain and in procedural social
knowledge in that domain. Although some work on these individual
differences has been done in the personal construct tradition of George
Kelly (Pervin, 1976; Rosenberg, 1977), comparatively little attention
has been devoted to individual differences by social cognition researchers (Kihlstrom, 1981). Elsewhere, Kihlstrom and Nasby (1981;
Nasby & Kihlstrom, 1985) have offered suggestions for the adaptation
of contemporary social-cognitive experimental paradigms for the
purposes of clinically assessing the maladaptive declarative and procedural knowledge presumed to underlie abnormal social behavior.
Such techniques offer a means for mapping the individual's perceptions

of his or her social life, and for uncovering the cognitive processes that may guide the individual's social judgments and interactions. Along the same lines, a number of recent studies illustrate how individual differences in social cognition can be explored within the domain of normal personality.

Variation in the structure and content of semantic and episodic social knowledge provides a basis for individual differences in social problem-solving. For example, people have different domains of expertise about the social world (e.g., Fiske & Kinder, 1981), as well as specially elaborate conceptions of self in selected domains (e.g., Markus, 1977). Individual differences in the *elaboration* of knowledge in a particular domain are reflected in people's interpretations of situations. When a certain domain, such as extroversion or anxiety, is very self-defining for an individual, there is a strong tendency to turn a social interaction into a test of skills in that domain (Fong & Markus, 1982; Riggs & Cantor, 1984). Experts seem to see things that novices miss or find unimportant. And, as our expertise varies considerably across different domains of social life, we are each quite likely to give relatively superficial attention to some social problems while working on others in depth. Rather than rank order individuals as to degree of attentiveness to social stimulation (Witkin & Goodenough, 1977) or focus on a generalized reflective or impulsive problem-solving style (Baron, 1982), it may be more useful to look at each individual's activity in domains of relative "expertise" and "ignorance."

The *evaluative content* of these social concepts and memories also varies from person to person, providing another basis for different reactions to social events. For example, whereas one person has very positive feelings about family dinners, another views the same situation with anxiety derived from fierce sibling rivalry (Pervin, 1976). These two people are working to solve very different problems as they confront the occasion of a family dinner: One is concerned with affiliative goals and the other is striving to protect self-esteem. Their concepts of self-at-family-dinners may differ in other ways as well. The former may feel very close to reaching his or her ideal "affiliative self" in such contexts, whereas the latter individual perceives a substantial gap between expectations for self-with-family and the reality of his or her actions, feelings, and reactions in that context. *Self-ideal discrepancy* provides another basis for individuals' unique interpretations of social situations (Higgins, Klein & Strauman, in press). In fact, individuals may be motivated to find situations in which the match between the self-concept and an ideal standard is a close one.

A study by Niedenthal reveals how individual differences in choice—preferences for choice of a living unit among college students—are related to individual differences in declarative social knowledge, knowledge about oneself and others (Niedenthal, Cantor, & Kihlstrom, in press). At the time that they were deciding where to live for the next year, college freshmen completed an adjective checklist describing themselves, and then completed the same checklist describing their impressions of the kind of person who is happy and comfortable living in each of seven classes of housing generally available to undergraduates. For the subjects as a whole, but especially for those individuals who defined themselves in extremely narrow terms and who approached the choice of housing with interpersonal goals in mind, choice was associated with the degree of match between the self and prototypical others. Prototype-matching may be a general strategy for social decision making. When making important choices, people often seem to approach the problem by asking, "Am I the kind of person who . . . ?" If so, this is a strategy that people have in common. Individual differences in choice behavior reflect individual differences in the specific structure and content of the self-concept, and in the declarative knowledge about other people on which this common procedural knowledge operates.

Another set of studies illustrates individual differences in procedural knowledge used to achieve similar personal outcomes (Norem & Cantor, in press; Showers & Cantor, 1985). College undergraduates with histories of academic success reported on their performance expectations for forthcoming achievement tasks. Later, in preparing for achievement tasks, "optimists"—those students who set expectations in line with their prior record of academic success—used a strategy of playing through best-case outcomes ("How I'll feel when I do really well") and focusing upon positive attributes of their self-concepts ("I'm cool, calm, and confident"). This optimistic strategy contrasted sharply with the preparatory cognitive activity of other successful students, the "defensive pessimists." Despite an acknowledged history of success, the pessimists set low expectations for personal performance on forthcoming tasks, played through worst-case outcomes, and focused upon negative aspects of their self-concepts. Although their characteristic cognitive strategies differed, both the optimists and the pessimists worked hard at achievement tasks and performed equally well. Different procedures, serving to "psych-up" the optimists and calm the anxious pessimists, enabled them to reach common endpoints and feel happy about their records of achievement. These students quite intelligently developed cognitive strategies for preparation that were uniquely well-suited to motivate their own best performances.

## THE DYNAMICS OF PERSONALITY:
## LIFE-TASK PROBLEM-SOLVING

Having examined the structure of social intelligence, and some ways of characterizing individual differences in terms of social intelligence, it is appropriate to examine the manner in which it is utilized in actual problem solving. What are the relevant problems on which individuals work? And how can we study people as they work on them? In this regard we take our lead from some recent work on intelligence in which the objective is to find tasks that have functional significance for the individual in his or her current life environment (Baltes, Ditmann-Kohli, & Dixon, 1984; Sternberg, 1984). Actually, both the contextualist position, with its focus on tasks that reflect the everyday ecology of the individual's life, and emphasis on the pragmatics of intelligence have precedents within the literature on personality development. The contextualist position is represented in the personality literature by the nomothetic analyses of age-graded and history-graded life tasks that emerge over the course of the life span (Baltes, Reese, Lipsitt, 1980), whereas analyses of individuals' idiosyncratic projects and concerns explicitly focus upon the functional significance of personal life tasks (e.g., Klinger, 1975; Little, 1983). Our approach seeks to meet both the contextualist and pragmatist objectives by concentrating on the life tasks that individuals perceive to be central and important during a specified period of life transition.

*Life tasks* are the problems that individuals explicitly see themselves as devoting energy to solving at a particular period in life. At one time we may be obsessed with finding a career direction, only to find ourselves facing the dilemmas of a two-career marriage some years later. Life tasks reflect both the social demands of a period of life transition, as from college to professional life, and the idiographic meaning of each normative task. Often, when major transitions take place, people can articulate the way in which their attention has shifted from the old life tasks to new ones. (One of our single-minded colleagues once remarked: "Now that I have tenure, I want to get married.")

Imagine, for example, a quite nervous but excited high-school graduate embarking on the first year of college life. As part of a longitudinal analysis of the transition to college life, Cantor, Brower, and Korn (1984) questioned 44 such individuals about the life tasks they were facing during this period of transition. The inquiry began by asking subjects to describe their first-year experience: their expectations, hopes, fears, and plans. Then the subjects generated a list of their most pressing life tasks and subsequently narrowed the list to the two tasks they perceived to be most important. Each student provided descriptions of the situations that tapped these life concerns; their affective reactions in these situations, plans for handling the situations, and the projected ease or difficulty of successfully carrying out these plans. Inspection of these freeform responses and structured ratings revealed some striking features of life tasks during a period of transition.

Periods of life transition, as in moving from high school and home to college and dormitory, seem to make life tasks very salient. The students clearly felt motivated to tackle demands presented by the new environment. They saw themselves working on new tasks, such as living without their families, and on old tasks in new ways, such as handling academic competition from other "ex-high school stars." They had no trouble generating these life tasks: An average of 8 to 9 such tasks came to each subject without much apparent effort. Nor was it difficult for them to place these tasks in the context of their everyday life activities at college. The students concentrated on a familiar set of basic interpersonal themes of identity, intimacy, achievement, and power, portrayed in the light of their college experiences. As we had expected, life tasks considered during a period of transition often have the interesting feature of tapping into old concerns situated in new contexts. They seem to constitute the "nonentrenched" yet personally involving tasks that intelligence theorists seek to study (Sternberg, 1984).

The life tasks themselves, at least for this particular period of transition, tended to be fairly uniform when viewed at a high level of abstraction. Fully 85 percent of the tasks selected as most important were easily categorizable in terms of five broad categories—the social tasks of making friends and living without family, the academic tasks of being successful at their studies and shaping their future careers, and the time-management task of balancing academic and social activities and priorities. At the same time, the situations or personal projects associated with these consensual life tasks were quite idiosyncratic. One student considered living without family to involve learning to handle the stress of personal failure without "dad's hugs," whereas another concentrated on the practical side of independence—"managing money, doing laundry, eating well." Life-task analyses reflect on the personal meaning of age-graded normative demands, thus encompassing the contextualists' desire for ecological validity and the pragmatists' focus on the functional significance of intelligent activity.

How then do we study social intelligence in life tasks? First, we choose a life period, preferably at the onset of a life transition—when individuals are motivated to tackle new life tasks or old ones in new ways, and when there is likely to be some uniformity in the salient life tasks facing the research participants. (Although our analyses concentrate on the transition to college, others have worked productively with life tasks that characterize later stages of adult development; such as Ryff, 1982.) Second, we document the life-task issues relevant to this group and the unique construals of the members. Such data allow one to see how a common life task maps onto different activities, and elicits different patterns of affective reactions and coping strategies for different participants. The next step is to assess the self-concepts and social concepts, relevant past episodes, and rules of the individual, and to connect them with the problem-solving strategies that he or she employs to work on life tasks. Here it is important to include analyses of at least two life-task domains in order to see the flexibility of participants' problem-solving strategies.

For example, we designed our longitudinal study of the transition to college with these goals in mind. Based upon the earlier work described above, we chose to focus on academic and social life tasks that were likely to elicit different appraisals from the students and enable us to see the evolution of a variety of problem-solving strategies. At least half of the initial student sample had chosen one academic and one social life task when describing their most pressing concerns. These students uniformly described the academic task in harsh, pessimistic terms and the social one in a more positive light. Appraisals of the social life tasks indicated that the students typically felt in control of the likely outcomes in that domain; they didn't expect any great surprises. By contrast, most students seemed to anticipate feeling "out of control" and "over their heads" in the academic domain. Their plans reflected this difference in life-task appraisal. They showed a firm commitment to one (often familiar) course of action in the social domain and more experimentation and even wavering between options in the academic task situations. They seemed to think, for example, that well-established scripts from high school would work for the task of making friends, whereas getting good grades in college demanded a new set of procedures for studying, monitoring anxiety, setting goals, and so forth. Comparison of the students' plans and activities in academic and social life task domains over the course of their first few years at college should reveal *intraindividual* variation in problem-solving strategies across life task domains.

These differences in problem-solving approaches to social and academic life tasks derive, presumably, from differences in declarative and procedural knowledge. This assumption, a central one in the social intelligence analysis, must be tested. In the longitudinal study we include measures of self-ideal discrepancy and plan complexity for each domain. These measures should be useful as predictors of problem-solving strategy and eventual satisfaction in the two life-task domains. Furthermore, as we know that students also differ among themselves in appraisals of each life task, it should follow that *interindividual* differences in appraisal, strategies, and performance will also be predicted from profiles of declarative and procedural knowledge.

There is another side to the social intelligence analysis. Although we expect to see consistency between an individual's declarative and procedural knowledge in a life-task domain and his or her appraisals and strategies in that domain, we also predict that the base of knowledge will change with experience. Life-task activities should feed back to the individual and elicit change in his or her concepts and rules. Interviews with older students, for example, suggest that the first-year novices will be in for some suprises as they work on social and academic life tasks. Those optimistic appraisals and highly scripted plans for social life activities may shift considerably in the face of the realities of college existence. And, if our assumptions are correct, students may increasingly reflect on a gap between their actual and ideal self in the social domain; their skills and plans may no longer seem so well-elaborated or well-suited to the demands of this pressing task. Fortunately, in the case of these college students, there is clearly much room for growth in their ability to handle the tasks they set for themselves in college life. Tracking that growth is the crux of a social intelligence analysis at the level of individual development.

When we follow individuals' progress in problem-solving about life tasks, the goal is to demonstrate some central features of intelligent action. Intelligent problem-solving should be flexible. An individual should approach each life task differently because he or she has different goals derived from concepts and rules in the relevant domains. This focus on intraindividual variation in problem-solving sets the present model somewhat apart from theories of cognitive styles in personality (see Baron, 1982, for a review). We do not posit a few basic styles of problem solving, with each style utilized fairly consistently by individuals across tasks. We suggest instead that variation in the content and complexity of a person's repertoire across domains of social life encourages flexibility in his or her style of problem solving on different life tasks.

Intelligent behavior should also be malleable with training. Therefore, people's social intelligence for life tasks ought to evolve as they encounter new opportunities for social learning. The expectation for growth sets the present approach apart from the doctrine of trait stability over time. Although this may seem to fly in the face of evidence for long-term stability of temperamental and stylistic traits (Costa & McCrae, 1980), it is more consistent with recent analyses of the development of social expertise and "wisdom on the pragmatics of life" over the life span (Baltes et al., 1984, p. 64). Changes in the array of social experience fostered by involvement in different social institutions may well be reflected in developments in social intelligence. We await the results of our own longitudinal study in order to provide one empirical test of these propositions. Yet, even as we wait, it should be clear that this perspective asks a slightly different set of questions about personality than has been characteristic of the cognitive style and trait traditions.

## POTENTIAL MISUNDERSTANDINGS

At this point, it seems prudent to anticipate some potential misunderstandings. It is most important to understand that social intelligence is not social IQ. We have no interest in rating people on a single dimension from social moron to social genius. We are persuaded that human intelligence, both social and nonsocial, is too complex and multifaceted to permit ranking of individuals in terms of a single score. Moreover, the tasks of social life are far too ill-defined to permit a single ordering from good to poor solution. Rather, we label the cognitive repertoire for working on life tasks as social intelligence in order to underscore the flexibility and malleability also implied by the term "intelligent."

Nor do we have any interest in developing a taxonomy of people. In this respect, we depart from classic approaches to personality. People are too rich, too multifaceted to be captured by such classificatory schemes, except at a highly abstract level that obscures the flexibility and discriminativeness of experience, thought, and action that is central to human life. We assume, by direct analogy to language, that an infinite variety of individual differences can be produced by the interactions among a finite set of general principles of social learning, social cognition, and social interaction. The first task of a cognitive personology then, from our point of view, is to describe the general processes out of which individual differences are constructed.

The cognitive point of view is not a disguised situationism. A true interactionism, it acknowledges that people are creatures of the social environment—but also insists that people have a hand in actively creating these environments. People respond to the meaning of the social situation, not the situation itself. This meaning, contra Skinner, is not determined wholly by the individual's past environmental history.

In discussing the role of cognitive processes in social interaction, we do not wish to imply that these processes are always conscious, deliberate, or rational. The literature on social cognition provides many demonstrations of heuristics, biases, and other shortcomings that lead to inaccuracies in social judgment. Many cognitive processes run off automatically and unconsciously; and the direction of thought can be influenced by priming effects and other processes that operate outside of awareness (Bargh, 1982). Along these same lines, investigations of hypnotic phenomena, such as amnesia and posthypnotic suggestion, appear to reveal a set of dissociative processes that can disrupt access to self-knowledge, limiting one's awareness of what one has done in the past, is doing now, or intends to do in the future (Kihlstrom, 1984). However, regardless of the effects of cognitive heuristics, the limitations on conscious control of behavior, or the barriers to introspective awareness, there is little reason to abandon a cognitive theory of personality (Kihlstrom, 1984; Showers & Cantor, 1985). The most routine and "mindless" social activity (Langer, 1978) is not devoid of cognitive work (Cantor, Mischel, & Schwartz, 1982b). Social intelligence is brought to bear even when people engage in behavior uncritically, without conscious reflection (Smith, 1984).

Although the social intelligence view emphasizes cognitive and social processes as determinants of individual differences, it does not ignore the role of other factors. People are creatures in a biological world, and are subject to that world's demands and constraints. There are certainly individual differences in temperament observed in neonates, and there are certainly psychological consequences of hormonal endowments that are correlated with such factors as sex and age. From our perspective, the interesting aspect of these biological predisposing agents rests in the variety of patterns of growth that emerge when cognitive, environmental, and biological factors interact—as illustrated by the experimental and clinical literature on gender dimorphism in identity and role (e.g., Money & Ehrhardt, 1974).

Similar considerations apply to affect. We do not wish to enter the debate on the primacy of affect or cognition (Lazarus, 1984; Zajonc, 1984). Nevertheless, it is clear that a great deal of social cognition is *hot* cognition. Problem-solving about life tasks is, by definition, a motivated cognitive activity. Emotional and motivational processes influence social cognition and social interaction; but we want to underscore the reciprocal role of cognitive and social processes in the construction and control of emotional states (Showers & Cantor, 1985).

Finally, in leaving the consistency debate behind, we do not intend to shirk the responsibility of personologists to search for coherence in individuals' social behavior. We find much consistency in the ways in which individuals cognitively represent and behaviorally attempt to solve currently salient life tasks. Yet the search must be for "appropriate consistency," not rigid constancy. Neither the life tasks nor the strategies for working on them are likely to be powerfully fixed for one person over time or for different persons within a task domain.

## SOCIAL INTELLIGENCE AND PERSONALITY THEORIES

We began this essay with the assertion that the study of personality is as much a study of learning and change as a testament to behavioral consistency. Individuals can change even their favored modes of problem-solving by learning new concepts and rules. After all, social intelligence is acquired through social learning, with the potential for change through direct experience, precept, and example. Given that the earliest developments in personality emerge from a complex interactive process, there is little reason to believe that the important outcomes are set in stone at the outset. Individuals, at least in principle, can use their minds to effect change in themselves as well as in their social and biological environments. Gould (1981, p. 324) made the argument at the species level: "Human uniqueness resides primarily in our brains. It is expressed in the culture built upon our intelligence and the power it gives us to manipulate the world. Human societies change by cultural evolution, not as a result of biological alteration." We will continue to try to make the argument at the level of individual social intelligence and personality development.

For too long, personality psychology has concentrated on debating the merits and demerits of the doctrine of traits. In so doing, positions have become dangerously polarized around the single issue of consistency versus change. This debate has perseverated without sufficient attention being paid to construction and testing of alternative conceptualizations. Now, through efforts at theory building, it may be possible to see whether other viable candidates can stand the test of empirical scrutiny and serve as centerpieces for a comprehensive theory of personality. New theories may better capture *both* coherence and change in individuals' social behavior. It is time to do more than hand-waving about alternatives. By taking cognitive-social psychology seriously, we hope to develop understanding of general principles from which human individuality can be constructed, and achieve a modern personology that is both idiographic and nomothetic in nature.

## REFERENCES

Abelson, R. P. (1981). Psychological status of the script concept. *American Psychologist, 36,* 715-729.

Allport, G. W. (1937). *Personality: A psychological interpretation.* New York: Holt.

Anderson, J. R. (1983). *The architecture of cognition.* Cambridge: Harvard University Press.

Baltes, P. B., Dittman-Kohli, F., & Dixon, R. A. (1984). New perspectives on the development of intelligence in adulthood. In P. B. Baltes & O. G. Brim, Jr. (Eds.), *Life-span development and behavior.* New York: Academic Press.

Baltes, P. B., Reese, H. W., & Lipsitt, L. P. (1980). Life-span developmental psychology. *Annual Review of Psychology, 31,* 65-100.

Bandura, A. (1977). *Social learning theory.* Englewood Cliffs, NJ: Prentice-Hall.

Bargh, J. A. (1982). Attention and automaticity in the processing of self-relevant information. *Journal of Personality and Social Psychology, 43,* 425-436.

Baron, J. (1982). Personality and intelligence. In R. Sternberg (Ed.), *Handbook of human intelligence* (pp. 308-352). Cambridge: Cambridge University Press.

Buss, D., & Craik, K. (1983). The act frequency approach to personality. *Psychological Review, 90,* 105-126.

Cantor, N., Brower, A., & Korn, H. (1984). Cognitive bases of personality in a life transition. Paper presented at the 23rd International Congress of Psychology, Acapulco.

Cantor, N., & Mischel, W. (1979). Prototypes in person perception. In L. Berkowitz (Ed.), *Advances in experimental social psychology* (Vol. 12, pp. 4-51). New York: Academic Press.

Cantor, N., Mischel, W., & Schwartz, J. (1982a). A prototype analysis of psychological situations. *Cognitive Psychology, 14,* 45-77.

Cantor, N., Mischel, W., & Schwartz, J. (1982b). Social knowledge: Structure, content, use, and abuse. in A. Hastorf & A. Isen (Eds.), *Cognitive social psychology.* New York: Elsevier-North Holland.

Cantor, N., Smith, E. E., French, R., & Mezzich, J. (1980). Psychiatric diagnosis as prototype categorization. *Journal of Abormal Psychology, 89,* 181-193.

Costa, P. T., & McCrae, R. R. (1980). Still stable after all these years: Personality as a key to some issues in adulthood and old age. In P. Baltes & O. Brim, Jr. (Eds.), *Life-span development and behavior.* New York: Academic Press.

Darley, J. M., & Fazio, R. H. (1980). Expectancy confirmation processes arising in the social interaction sequence. *American Psychologist, 28,* 404-416.

Fiske, S. (1982). Schema-triggered affect: Applications to social perception. In M. Clark & S. Fiske (Eds.), *Affect and cognition: The 17th annual Carnegie symposium.* Hillsdale, NJ: Lawrence Erlbaum.

Fiske, S., & Kinder, D. R. (1981). Involvement, expertise, and schema use: Evidence from political cognition. In N. Cantor & J. Kihlstrom (Eds.), *Personality, cognition, and social interaction.* Hillsdale, NJ: Lawrence Erlbaum.

Fong, G., & Markus, H. (1982). Self-schemas and judgments about others. *Social Cognition, 1,* 191-204.

Gould, S. J. (1981). *The mismeasure of man.* New York: Norton.

Hampson, S. E. (1982). Person memory: A semantic category model of personality traits. *British Journal of Psychology, 73,* 1-11.

Harter, S. (1984). Developmental perspectives on the self-system. In M. Hetherington (Ed.), *Carmichael's manual of child psychology: Social and personality development.* New York: John Wiley.

Hastie, R. (1985). A primer of information-processing theory for the political scientist. In R. Lau (Ed.), *Political psychology.* Hillsdale, NJ: Lawrence Erlbaum.

Hastie, R., & Carlston, D. C. (1980). Theoretical issues in person memory. In R. Hastie, T. Ostrom, E. Ebbesen, R. Wyer, D. Hamilton, & D. Carlston (Eds.), *Person memory: The cognitive basis of social perception.* Hillsdale, NJ: Lawrence Erlbaum.

Hastie, R., Park, B., & Weber, R. (1984). Social memory. In R. Wyer & T. K. Srull (Eds.), *Handbook of social cognition* (Vol. 2). Hillsdale, NJ: Lawrence Erlbaum.

Higgins, E. T., Klein, R., & Strauman, T. (in press). Self-concept discrepancy theory: A psychological model for distinguishing between different aspects of depression and anxiety. *Social Cognition.*

Jones, E. E., & Berglas, S. (1978). Control of attributions about the self through self-handicapping strategies: The appeal of alcohol and the role of underachievement. *Personality and Social Psychology Bulletin, 4,* 200-206.

Jones, E. E., Kanouse, D. E., Kelley, H. H., Valins, S., & Weiner, B. (Eds.). (1972). *Attribution: Perceiving the causes of behavior.* Morristown, NJ: General Learning Press.

Jones, E. E., & Pittman, T. S. (1982). Toward a general theory of strategic self-presentation. In J. Suls (Ed.), *Psychological perspectives on the self.* Hillsdale, NJ: Lawrence Erlbaum.

Kelly, G. (1955). *The psychology of personal constructs.* New York: Norton.

Kihlstrom, J. F. (1981). On personality and memory. In N. Cantor & J. F. Kihlstrom (Eds.), *Personality, cognition, and social interaction.* Hillsdale, NJ: Lawrence Erlbaum.

Kihlstrom, J. F. (1984). Conscious, subconscious, unconscious: A cognitive perspective. In K. Bowers & D. Meichenbaum (Eds.), *The unconscious reconsidered.* New York: John Wiley.

Kihlstrom, J. F., & Cantor, N. (1984). Mental representations of the self. In L. Berkowitz (Ed.), *Advances in experimental social psychology* (Vol. 17). New York: Academic Press.

Kihlstrom, J. F., & Harackiewicz, J. M. (1982). The earliest recollection: A new survey. *Journal of Personality, 50,* 134-148.

Kihlstrom, J. F., & Nasby, W. (1981). Cognitive tasks in clinical assessment: An exercise in applied psychology. In P. C. Kendall & S. D. Hollon (Eds.), *Cognitive-behavioral interventions: Assessment methods.* New York: Academic Press.

Klinger, E. (1975). Consequences of commitment to and disengagement from incentives. *Psychological Review, 82* (1), 1-25.

Langer, E. (1978). Rethinking the role of thought in social interaction. In J. Harvey, W. Ickes., & R. Kidd (Eds.), *New directions in attribution research* (Vol. 2). Hillsdale, NJ: Lawrence Erlbaum.

Lazarus, R. (1984). On the primacy of cognition. *American Psychologist, 39* (2), 124-130.

Little, B. (1983). Personal projects: A rationale and method for investigation. *Environment and Behavior, 15,* 273-309.

Markus, H. (1977). Self-schemata and processing information about the self. *Journal of Personality and Social Psychology, 35,* 63-78.

Markus, H. (1983). Self-knowledge: An expanded view. *Journal of Personality, 51,* 543-565.

Mischel, W. (1968). *Personality and assessment.* New York: John Wiley.

Mischel, W. (1973). Towards a cognitive social learning and reconceptualization of personality. *Psychological Review, 80,* 252-283.

Money, J., & Ehrhardt, A. (1974). *Man and woman, boy and girl: Differentiation and dimorphism of gender identity from conception to maturity.* Baltimore: Johns Hopkins Press.

Nasby, W., & Kihlstrom, J. F. (1985). Cognitive assessment of personality and psychopathology. In R. E. Ingram (Ed.), *Information-processing approaches to psychopathology and clinical psychology.* New York: Academic Press.

Neisser, U. (1978). Memory: What are the important questions? In M. M. Gruneberg, P. E. Morris, & R. N. Sykes (Eds.), *Practical aspects of memory.* New York: Academic Press.

Newell, A., & Simon, H. A. (1973). *Human problem-solving.* Englewood Cliffs, NJ: Prentice-Hall.

Niedenthal, P., Cantor, N., & Kihlstrom, J. F. (in press). Prototype-matching: A strategy for social decision-making. *Journal of Personality and Social Psychology.*

Nisbett, R., & Ross, L. (1980). *Human inference: Strategies and shortcomings of social judgment.* Englewood Cliffs, NJ: Prentice-Hall.

Norem, J., & Cantor, N. (in press). Anticipatory and post-hoc cushioning strategies: Optimism and defensive pessimism in risky situations. *Cognitive Therapy and Research.*

Pervin, L. (1976). A free-response description approach to the analysis of person-situation interactions. *Journal of Personality and Social Psychology, 34,* 465-474.

Pervin, L. (1985). Personality: Current controversies, issues, and directions. *Annual Review of Psychology, 36*, 83-114.

Riggs, J., & Cantor, N. (1984). Getting acquainted: The role of the self-concept and preconceptions. *Personality and Social Psychology Bulletin, 10*(3), 432-445.

Rosenberg, S. (1976). New approaches to the analysis of personal constructs in person perception. In A. W. Landfield (Ed.), *Nebraska symposium on motivation* (Vol. 23). Lincoln: University of Nebraska Press.

Rotter, J. (1954). *Social learning and clinical psychology.* Englewood Cliffs, NJ: Prentice-Hall.

Ryff, C. (1982). Successful aging: A developmental approach. *The Gerontologist, 22*, 209-214.

Schneider, D. (1973). Implicit personality theory: A review. *Psychological Bulletin, 79*, 294-309.

Showers, C., & Cantor, N. (1985). Social cognition: A look at motivated strategies. *Annual Review of Psychology, 36*, 275-305.

Smith, E. R. (1984). A model of social inference processes. *Psychological Review, 91*, 392-413.

Sternberg, R. (Ed.). (1982). *Handbook of human intelligence.* Cambridge: Cambridge University Press.

Sternberg, R. (1984). Toward a triarchic theory of human intelligence. *Behavioral and Brain Sciences, 7*, 269-315.

Tulving, E. (1983). *Elements of episodic memory.* Oxford: Oxford University Press.

Witkin, H., & Goodenough, O. (1977). Field dependence and interpersonal behavior. *Psychological Bulletin, 84*, 662-689.

Zajonc, R. (1984). On the primacy of affect. *American Psychologist, 39*(2), 117-123.

# 2

# A Trait Account of
# Social Shyness

## STEPHEN R. BRIGGS

**Stephen R. Briggs,** Assistant Professor of Psychology at the University of Tulsa, is co-editor of *A Sourcebook on Shyness: Research and Treatment.* His other research interests include self-monitoring and the self in social interaction. He completed his doctoral work in personality psychology at the University of Texas at Austin in 1982.

Including the term "trait" in the title of a chapter may seem foolhardy, for the term embodies what many see as the worst tendency of personality psychology. Indeed, so provocative is the term that in recent years it has become fashionable to hide trait notions behind apparently more acceptable synonyms such as personal attributes, dispositions, and enduring tendencies. I am comfortable with these other terms and have used them before, so why insist now on the more hazardous course? Why the term "trait"?

No other word epitomizes the core of personality psychology as well; trait is the essential concept, the sine qua non of the field. Yet, criticisms of the trait concept are hardly new. For example, chapter 11 of Allport's classic work *Personality* (1937) outlines a number of criticisms, including that traits are only "*forms of perception* for an observer to use" (p. 287), "that a man's personality seems to vary with the expectations and prejudices of his associates" (p. 288), and that traits exist only in the context of an interpersonal encounter (p. 289). A recent text suggests that the controversy over traits is in fact simply a warmed-over version of a centuries-old philosophical debate (Pervin, 1984). The issues that now divide the person camp from the situation camp are some of the same issues that separated Aristotle from Plato and Leibniz from Locke. Is the person a product of forces internal or external? Should we emphasize stability or change in our scientific accounts of human behavior?

**AUTHOR'S NOTE:** I gratefully acknowledge the thoughtful comments provided by Robert Hansson, Robert Hogan, William Ickes, Harry Reis, Phillip Shaver, and Tod Sloan, as well as the excellent clerical help provided by Lucy Mylar and Vicki Booth.

The current campaign against traits can be traced specifically to the publication of Mischel's (1968) monograph *Personality and Assessment*. Others offered similar arguments, claims, and evidence, but Mischel's book initiated the present struggle and polarized the field into its current camps. Mischel's position has to be taken seriously, not so much because he raised new and insurmountable issues, but because he stands within the ranks of personality psychologists. His attack was, in effect, an attempted coup. In subsequent writings, Mischel (1978, 1984) has protested that he never sought to deliver a fatal blow to personality; rather he attempted only to shore up the inherent weaknesses of the traditional trait position by redefining the goals, tasks, and strategies of personality psychology. For many, however, Mischel's approach involved more than just an ambitious reformulation. In attacking traits, he was striking at the heart of the field. Stalwart defenders leapt into the fray to keep the standard of traits aloft. The volleys and salvos of that clash have filled several volumes already (e.g., Endler & Magnusson, 1976; London, 1978; Magnusson & Endler, 1977; Page, 1983; Zucker, Aronoff, & Rabin, 1984), and the various arguments are much too detailed to be recounted here.

My goal in this chapter is considerably more focused. I want to persuade the reader of three pairs of points: (1) that traits must be regarded as the quintessential stuff of personality, and that the concept of traits has been vilified unfairly; (2) that trait notions are empirically justifiable, and that *shyness* provides a good example of what a trait approach has to offer; and (3) that other approaches to the study of personality can supplement a trait approach but can in no way serve as a replacement for it.

The chapter consists of four parts. The first section briefly examines the concept of traits, drawing a distinction between traits as descriptive concepts and traits as explanatory constructs. The second section takes an extended look at social shyness as an example of a trait concept used descriptively. The third section examines some of the issues involved in the trait controversy, focusing particularly on what constitutes good evidence of a trait concept. The final section considers various explanations of how a stable disposition such as shyness might be acquired.

## THE MEANINGS OF TRAIT

The term "trait" means different things to different writers. In fact, as Hogan, DeSoto, and Solano (1977, p. 256) point out, "Most recent writers, particularly those in the 'empirical tradition' of personality research . . . rarely attempt to define the term *trait* in a formal way." Logical analyses of the trait construct have been offered by a number of authors (e.g., Alston, 1975; Brandt, 1970; Cochran, 1984; Hirschberg, 1978; Stagner, in press; and Wiggins, 1974). For our purposes, however, it is sufficient to distinguish between two uses of the term.

First, trait can be used as a *descriptive concept*. Although the term is rich in connotations, almost everyone seems to agree that it refers to aspects of an individual that are distinctive, general, and enduring (Levy, in press). Trait terms are used in ordinary language to describe the regularities and pecularities that we observe in the actions and expressions of others, as well as in our own actions, thoughts, feelings, and goals. McClelland (1951) writes:

> It is for such consistencies that we need the concept of trait. We need terms which will cover the fact that a person consistently, in a variety of situations, produces a lot of words per unit time, or the fact that a person introduces a lot of empathic movement into static situations, or the fact that a person generally performs well in a new situation. These are the kind of observations on which the trait term is based. (p. 215-216)

Trait words can serve, then, as "categorical-summary" accounts (Wiggins, 1974). They presumably describe what has been observed empirically—behavioral regularities that are both lasting (temporal stability) and general (cross-situational consistency). Some recurrent pattern emerges that points to attributes that are distinctive or peculiar. This fundamental insight leads to a systematic simplification of what is known, thereby enabling us to process, analyze, and communicate vast amounts of information with considerable efficiency. Recent studies have in fact shown that observers prefer to use trait terms when describing others, particularly those who are well known (e.g., Hampson, 1983).

The term "trait" has also been used in a second way, as an *explanatory construct*. In this use of the word, traits are not just labels for observed patterns of regularity. They refer to properties of an individual that are real and that exist internally. According to Allport (1937, p. 289), "A trait . . . has more than nominal existence; it is independent of the observer, it is really there." The argument is straightforward. If regularity characterizes a person, something must produce that regularity. If the source of the regularity is intrinsic to the person—something that is carried about from place to place and not situationally prescribed—then what can that something be other than a property or process that really exists? It seems reasonable to locate such an entity in the brain, hence Allport's (1937) notions of "neuropsychic systems" and "bona fide mental structures."

Of course, to the extent that such systems exist, they function in a causal fashion. Regularities in behavior, then, can be traced back to properties of the brain. Two additional points are important. First, it is in this sense that a trait "structure" can be said to underlie trait behavior. The structure is genotypic, whereas trait behavior is phenotypic (Allport, 1937); the structure is the deep source, and the behavior is on the surface (Cattell, 1946). The second point is that the underlying structure or processes need not be seen as a direct reflection of the observed regularity (see Mischel, 1968; Wiggins, 1974, p. 33). Allport himself pointed to a "deeper metaphysical problem concerning the relation of any name to the unit-structures of nature" (1937, p. 310). He proposed that "trait-names are symbols socially devised . . . for the naming and evaluation of human qualities" but went on to clarify:

> Although in some respects this theory follows the position of the Nominalists it does not at all agree with those extremists who in denying perfect correspondence between names and traits think they must also deny the very existence of traits. Traits exist in exactly the same sense in which any mental disposition or readiness-for-response exists. The naming of such intangible mental states is hazardous, but it is also unfortunately necessary. It would be absurd to allow the difficulties involved to lead us into the wholly untenable nihilistic position of denying mental organization and readiness altogether. (Allport & Odbert, 1936, pp. 20-21)

The term "trait," therefore, can be used either as a descriptive concept (a categorical summary account) or as a real, and therefore explanatory, construct. Both uses of the term are important, and both are controversial. As a descriptive concept, at issue is whether trait terms are misleading insofar as they refer to behavioral regularities that cannot be demonstrated. As an explanatory construct, the issue is whether traits are real entities that can explain behavioral regularities. Both uses of the term assume, however, that there is some regularity to people's actions, thoughts, and feelings. It is precisely this assumption that has been roundly criticized in recent years. The next section deals with this issue by examining the evidence for one specific trait.

### THE CASE OF SHYNESS

Psychologists often work with concepts that are borrowed from the common language. Shyness is a case in point. The term is familiar, one that we have often used to describe and explain the actions and feelings of others, and one that we may have applied to ourselves as well. As a psychological construct, its origin in ordinary language is a mixed blessing. On one hand, personal characteristics that facilitate or hamper appropriate interpersonal functioning tend to be salient features of our experience. Hence, they are noticed and labeled. On the other hand, common language terms tend to be imprecise. The same breadth that makes them descriptively useful may also blur important distinctions and promote misleading connotative associations. Thus, when translating these terms into psychological constructs, we must define them more exactly, and we must identify crucial distinctions. In the case of shyness, several distinctions are important.

## DISTINCTIONS AND DEFINITIONS

### State Versus Trait

In exploring the logic of trait concepts, Wiggins (1974, p. 13) points out that although trait terms probably "were coined to express the lawlike relations that have been observed between certain kinds of human actions and particular classes of social outcomes" these same terms can also be used to identify people who routinely display such actions. In a similar fashion, the term "shy" can be used to describe an individual's behavior in a particular situation ("The girl glanced at him and he looked away shyly"), or to describe the individual ("The shy boy stood off by himself"). In the first instance, the term characterizes the boy's momentary behavior or current state—he looked away shyly, not defiantly, nonchalantly, or angrily—but does not characterize the boy himself. In the second example, the term implies a typified way of responding, a *trait* of shyness. Many people who occasionally experience the state of shyness would not be well characterized by the trait of shyness. In fact, survey research shows that most people report having felt shy at one time or another (more than 80 percent), whereas a much smaller number (about 25 percent) report feeling chronically shy (Zimbardo, 1977). Other research suggests that although many individuals experience some shyness during early adolescence, this shyness is usually just a passing phase and does not persist into adulthood (Cheek, Carpentieri, Smith, Rierdan, & Koff, in press). The state experience is an integral part of the trait of shyness, but for present purposes can be set aside until later when we deal with explanations of shyness.

### Syness Versus Related Constructs

Our understanding of shyness has benefited greatly from investigations into various related topics such as introversion-extraversion, assertiveness, and social skills, as well as topics that can be grouped under the general heading of social anxiety including speech anxiety, evaluation apprehension, and communication apprehension. It would be a mistake, however, to assume that these constructs are equivalent to shyness. In particular, it is important to distinguish shyness from the well-known constructs of introversion and social anxiety.

## Introversion

Shyness is not introversion, although the two constructs overlap statistically and conceptually. Shyness does not necessarily involve the inward focus and intellectual orientation of the Jungian introvert, nor is it as heterogeneous as Eysenck's dimension of introversion-extraversion, which includes such disparate elements as sociability, impulsivity, and sensation-seeking. Eysenck (1956) himself alludes to a distinction between introversion and shyness in positing two types of shyness: an *introverted social shyness* (individuals who prefer to be alone but have little difficulty interacting with others when it is necessary or to their advantage to do so) and *neurotic social shyness* (those who are self-conscious, lonely, and feel inadequate with superiors). A similar distinction is drawn by Cheek and Buss (1981) who differentiate sociability from shyness. They define sociability as a preference for being with others rather than alone; thus, a lack of sociability resembles Eysenck's notion of introverted social shyness. Cheek and Buss define shyness as self-consciousness, tension, and inhibition in the presence of others; this definition seems similar to Eysenck's notion of neurotic social shyness. Shyness in general, therefore, may be as closely linked to Eysenck's superfactor of Neuroticism as to his Extraversion dimension, which may explain why the item "Do you suddenly feel shy when you want to talk to an attractive stranger?" is scored on the Neuroticism scale rather than the Extraversion scale of the Eysenck Personality Questionnaire (Eysenck & Eysenck, 1975).

## Social Anxiety

Shyness is also not synonymous with social anxiety. Depending on how the terms are defined, either shyness can be one type of social anxiety or social anxiety can be an aspect of shyness. Buss (1980) argues that social anxiety can be decomposed into four varieties—shyness, audience anxiety, embarrassment, and shame—with shyness and audience anxiety sharing certain causes (novelty and conspicuousness) and reactions (fear and sympathetic arousal), and embarrassment and shame sharing a different set of characteristics. In this scheme, then, shyness is one type of social anxiety.

From a different perspective, Leary defines social anxiety as anxiety that results from "the prospect or presence of interpersonal evaluation in real or imagined social settings" (1984, p. 14). Leary argues that social anxiety should be defined only in terms of the subjective experience of nervousness and dread and should not be confounded with any behavioral referents. He suggests that we reserve the term "shyness" for those instances where the subjective experience of social anxiety occurs in conjunction with certain behavioral manifestations. A similar distinction is made by McCroskey and Richmond (1982), who distinguish the subjective experience of communication apprehension from behavioral inhibition and quietness. From this perspective, then, social anxiety may be an element of one's shyness but need not always result in behavioral indicants.

With these basic distinctions in mind, we can turn next to the evidence for shyness as a descriptive concept. To what extent does it serve as a useful summary account for describing the actions, thoughts, and feelings of individuals?

## THE EVIDENCE

Block (1977) suggests that three kinds of data are germane to the study of traits:

(1) R data—observers' *ratings* of individuals that typically take the form of global assessments of personality.
(2) T data—information derived from standardized, objective laboratory *tests* where the emphasis is on discrete behaviors that can be counted or clocked.
(3) S data—*self*-observations of behaviors, feelings, and cognitions that also are assessed at a global level.

The next three sections review some of the research on shyness and are organized around these three modes of measurement.

## Observers' Ratings

If shyness is a trait—a recurring pattern of behavior that characterizes an individual—then with proper opportunity, independent observers should be able to distinguish reliably those who are shy from those who are not. Studies that bear on this issue vary according to who does the rating and what is being rated (Briggs & Smith, in press).

### Informed Observers

One type of study uses raters who know the target well (e.g., relatives or friends), but who for this very reason are more susceptible to certain biases (e.g., "leniency" error). These raters have observed the target in a variety of situations over an extended period of time and can therefore be called knowledgeable observers. They may also, however, be unable to provide impartial ratings, for by definition they are not disinterested onlookers.

An excellent example of this approach is Kenrick and Stringfield's (1980) study of moderator variables and trait ratings. The investigators collected self-, peer (friend), and parental ratings on 16 adjective scales (derived from Cattell's 16 personality factors). One of these scales was the dimension of shy/timid versus venturesome. In addition to rating themselves on the adjective scales, target participants also rated each dimension in terms of how much they varied on that attribute from one situation to another and how publicly observable their behavior was on that dimension.

The authors reported a number of analyses, but for the moment only one is relevant. (We will consider their study in more detail in a later section.) The correlation between the ratings by parent and peer for the shy/timid-venturesome dimension was .41 (n = 64, p < .01). This correlation is remarkable for three reasons. First, each rater judged only one target participant. Ratings were made relative to some personal image or prototype of the shy person, not in comparison to the behavior of other targets. Thus, no two targets were rated from a common frame of reference. Second, the correlation is based on only two data points; most tests do not have pairs of items that correlate this strongly (Fiske, 1966). We can predict confidently that this correlation would increase with more observers (e.g., other friends or a second parent; Cheek, 1982; Epstein, 1984). Third, this correlation is based on the full sample, and it is clear from other findings in the study that the correlation would be substantially higher among individuals who perceived themselves as consistent and observable on this dimension. Thus, this correlation represents the low end of the range of possible correlations, not the ceiling.

My colleagues and I recently collected similar data as part of a large project (Jones, Briggs, & Smith, 1985). One group of participants provided us with the names of two or three friends who in turn rated the participants on a short adjective checklist. The participants themselves completed the same set of adjectives, which assessed six broad dimensions of personality. Two of the adjective pairs are relevant: reserved-outgoing and shy-showoff. Ratings by two peers were available for 60 of our participants, and these pairs of ratings correlated .23 for reserved-outgoing and .54 for shy-showoff. For a small set of participants (n = 15), we obtained ratings from three peers. The average correlation for these ratings improved to .59 for reserved-outgoing and remained the same (r = .53) for shy-showoff.

In general, then, friends and relatives agree in their assessment of an individual's shyness, even though this judgment is made relative to some vague, unsystematic standard. Of course, it is possible that this agreement is simply the product of some tacit collusion whereby an individual (the target person) negotiates an identity with friends and family. Presumably, the other parties play along because such acquiescence is normal and necessary for harmonious social functioning (Goffman, 1959).

## Objective Observers

A second type of rating study emphasizes "objectivity." Raters observe the targets in a standard setting (e.g., a laboratory task or structured interview) or have available to them some permanent record of information (e.g., written files or video recordings). The ratings are objective in the sense that raters are unacquainted with the targets. In addition, these ratings are generally more systematic than those made by friends or relatives, for two reasons. First, these raters typically are trained before they make their assessments. Second, each rater usually sees all (or a large number) of the target participants and is therefore able to judge each target relative to the rest of the sample. Hence, the frame of reference is relatively uniform.

At the same time, however, the external validity of such ratings is constrained by the sparseness of the information available. Ratings based on a single period of observation in a specific setting can hardly reflect the richness of an individual's behavior, nor can this limited opportunity provide substantial insight into behavioral regularities. Nevertheless, ratings by independent observers ensure that any agreement is not simply the product of a negotiated identity.

The extent to which observers agree is often reported in terms of an interrater reliability coefficient. This index is more than just another psychometric detail; a high coefficient implies that the independent observers agree on both the definition of the attribute being rated and the extent to which a specific individual manifests it. The first type of agreement reveals something about the observers (that they employ a similar semantic network), whereas the second type of agreement reveals something about the targets (that they exhibit a recognizable pattern of behavior).

Considerable agreement among observers as to who is shy seems to be the rule rather than the exception. In one recent study, we asked 39 participants to talk about themselves for two minutes in front of a video camera (Jones et al., 1985). Eight observers rated the participants on shyness and on several other dimensions as well. We calculated all possible correlations between pairs of observers (28 pairs); the correlations ranged from .21 to .88 with an average of .51. This corresponds to an alpha coefficient of .89. We have found this same level of interobserver agreement in other studies (e.g., Briggs, 1985), as have other investigators (e.g., see Cheek & Buss, 1981; Gough & Thorne, in press; Pilkonis, 1977).

Perhaps the most convincing rating study to date combines elements from both types of rating studies. Backteman and Magnusson (1981) examined the stability of certain traits over a three-year period in a large sample of school-aged children (445 girls and 413 boys) in the Swedish town of Orebro. Swedish children complete a nine-year compulsory program of education that consists of three levels; students in level 1 are from 7 to 10 years of age, and students in level 2 are from ages 10 to 13. Students generally have one teacher for all three years of each of the first two levels, and these teachers give lessons across all subjects. Classes stay essentially intact when they pass from one level to the next, and the only form of written record passed along is their grades. There is no formal mechanism by which personal remarks about the pupils are passed from one teacher to the next.

Teachers in the study rated the children in their classes when they were about to pass to the next level. At this point, the teachers had instructed the students for three years and were extremely familiar with their individual characteristics. Ratings were made on seven dimensions, one of which was timidity (shy versus open). In filling out the ratings, teachers were instructed to use the class as a frame of reference. The most extreme pupils were to be given the most extreme ratings, and the final distribution of scores was to be as normal as possible. The correlation (stability coefficient) between different teachers' ratings at age 10 and age 13 was .42 for girls and .44 for boys. These correlations compare with an average off-diagonal correlation (the relationship between two different trait dimensions across the 3-year time period) of .09 for girls and .04 for boys.

The implications of this study should be apparent. Pairs of informed observers, rating children independently and three years apart, showed considerable agreement. As Backteman and Magnusson suggest (p. 159), "Whatever it is that is reflected in the ratings, it is rated in a significantly similar way by the raters observing the children on two occasions. Thus it represents, in a rather stable and reliable way, characteristics of the ratees."

## Behavioral Indices

The studies reported so far clearly demonstrate that observers agree as to who is shy and who is not. Insofar as trait concepts are based on observed regularities in behavior, we also ought to be able to demonstrate that certain behavioral measures covary reliably. Response measures of this sort often involve a physical dimension of behavior that can be counted or timed. In the study of shyness, researchers have used video recordings of interactions to examine a variety of social behaviors including measures of frequency (number of gestures, head nods, smiles, utterances, and questions), measures of duration (amount of time spent talking to and looking at one's partner, and time spent touching self), and measures of latency (amount of time needed to initiate conversation initially and after a period of silence) (see Cheek & Buss, 1981; Daly, 1978; Mandel & Shrauger, 1980; Orchard, Schallow, & Perlman, 1983; Pilkonis, 1977). Unfortunately, the coding of videotapes is tedious and time consuming. Most researchers, therefore, are willing to examine only a limited number of measures. In addition, shyness researchers often collect behavioral measures to serve primarily as criteria for validating self-report instruments. Consequently, researchers typically do not report the correlations among their behavioral measures.

A set of intercorrelations of this sort was reported, however, by Cheek (1980, Appendix 2; see also Cheek & Buss, 1981). He surreptitiously videotaped five-minute dyadic interactions between pairs of women (n = 40) and then scored these video recordings using five behavioral measures: amount of time spent talking to and looking at the interacting partner, and the number of distracting comments, self-manipulations, and head nods. A pair of observers rated each dimension; the average correlation between the observers was high, .89, so their ratings were combined.

Of the ten possible correlations among the behavioral measures, only three were significant. The amount of time spent looking was positively correlated with the number of head nods (r = .37), and both of these measures correlated negatively (as expected) with the number of distracting comments (r = −.58 for time looking and −.40 for head nods). All ten intercorrelations were in the expected direction, and the mean intercorrelation was .22.

The modest and inconsistent set of relationships among these various behavioral indices is consistent with other research in the area of nonverbal communication. As a rule, behavioral measures of this sort are highly reliable in the sense of interobserver agreement, but they do not hang together tightly as a group. Moreover, behavioral measures are only imperfectly related to global ratings of shyness. In the study reported above (Cheek, 1980), global ratings on a composite measure (consisting of the adjective pairs tense versus relaxed, inhibited versus expressive, and unfriendly versus friendly) correlated significantly with two of the five behavioral dimensions (r = .62 for time talking and .31 for time looking). The other behavior-global rating correlations were all above .20, with a mean correlation of .37.

Thus, whereas the correlations among the various behavioral ratings tends to be modest at best, the correlations among global ratings is substantially higher, even though in some cases the two sets of ratings were derived from the same videotape. This finding suggests that we need to examine more closely what cues observers attend to when making global ratings and whether they attend to the same cues in different targets.

## Self-Ratings

In our efforts to study and understand recurrent patterns of behavior, it is important not to neglect self-generated information. Some researchers seem ready to reject this source of data without exception as too self-serving and self-deceiving, but as Mischel (1978 p. 8) correctly comments:

> It would be wise to allow our subjects to slip out of their roles as passive assessees or testees and to enroll them, at least sometimes, as active colleagues who are the best experts on themselves and are eminently qualified to participate in the development of descriptions and predictions, not to mention decisions, about themselves. Of course, if we want individuals to tell us about themselves directly, we have to ask questions that they can answer . . . applications would require conditions in which people's accurate self-reports and honest choices could not be used against them.

### Types of Measures

Self-generated information about shyness can be assessed using a variety of formats (Briggs & Smith, in press). For example, Russell, Cutrona, and Jones (in press) have introduced a scale that measures how an individual reacts to specific shyness-eliciting situations, and Zimbardo (1977) developed a checklist for assessing symptoms that accompany the experience of shyness. Gough and Thorne (in press) have developed separate scales containing positive and negative indicators of shyness using the item pool of the Adjective Check List (Gough & Heilbrun, 1965).

Undoubtedly, however, the best-known and most widely used method for self-appraisal remains the traditional personality inventory or the tried and true "trait" measure. But it should be apparent from what has been said already that so-called trait or scale measures in no way represent the only (or even the chief) means by which trait concepts can be assessed. Although testing has always played an important role in the applied field of personality assessment (Goldberg, 1981), those who use tests are not necessarily trait theorists (Hogan et al., 1977), and tests—however valid—cannot magically reveal an individual's trait characteristics.

## Inventory Measures

A number of scale measures of shyness have been used in published research reports. In addition to measures included on large omnibus inventories (such as Cattell's threctia, and shyness scales by Comrey and Guilford), there are measures that focus specifically on the limited domain of shyness. They assess the extent to which individuals regard themselves as shy (e.g., Cheek & Buss, 1981; Jones & Russell, 1982; McCroskey, Anderson, Richmond, & Wheeless, 1982; Morris, 1982; and Watson & Friend, 1969) or socially anxious (e.g., Dixon et al., 1957; Fenigstein et al., 1975; Leary, 1983; Sears, 1967).

In recent years, my colleagues and I have studied various shyness scales in an effort to understand and document their psychometric characteristics, interrelationships, and external correlates. In one recent paper (Briggs & Smith, in press), we reviewed seven of the limited-domain measures, concentrating specifically on reliability and behavioral validity evidence for each. In a second paper (Jones et al., 1985), we reported the primary findings from a comprehensive study in which we compared five of the shyness measures in a single, large sample (n = 1213; 718 women and 495 men). The results of this study can be summarized in terms of two points.

First, all five scales exceeded the conventional standards for internal consistency. Alpha coefficients ranged from .82 to .92, and the means of the interitem correlations varied from .25 to .36 [The mean interitem correlation coefficient is the average correlation of all possible pairs of items. It provides an unadulterated index of scale homogeneity (Fiske, 1971). Unlike Cronbach's alpha coefficient, the mean interitem correlation is not a function of the number of items on a test and therefore provides an index of homogeneity that can be used to compare tests of different lengths.] Thus, each of the scales seems to be tapping into some specific construct in a relatively pure fashion.

The second point is that the five scales all appear to measure more or less the same construct despite differences in conceptual orientation and scale development. Evidence for this conclusion comes from three sources:

(1) The five scales are highly intercorrelated; the pairwise correlations ranged from a low of .70 to a high of .86, with a mean of .77. These correlations are only slightly smaller than the estimates of internal consistency, suggesting that the scales are virtually interchangeable.

(2) All five scales showed a remarkably similar pattern of correlations with other self-report measures (such as self-esteem, fearfulness, loneliness, and assertiveness) and with a set of peer-rated adjectives.

(3) All five scales correlated positively with objective ratings of shyness from a video recording. Participants were videotaped while talking about themselves for two minutes. Eight observers rated the participants, and the average of these ratings correlated significantly with the scores on three of the five shyness scales. Only one of the scales differed noticeably from the rest.

As the previous section illustrates, it is often useful to compare self-report data with both global and behavioral ratings by others. Comparing self-generated information with other sources does not imply, however, that the self-reports must be validated against some "higher" standard (Golding, 1977). Self-report measures are not validated by observational or behavioral data any more than observations or measures of behavior are validated by test scores. Nevertheless, it is always advantageous to compare different modes of measurement because no single perspective can ever provide a complete view of a multifaceted construct (Fiske, 1971).

A number of studies have examined the relationship between self-reported shyness and shyness as rated by observers. These studies can again be divided into two groups: those that rely on friends or family as observers and those that use "objective" observers.

### With Informed Observers

In a study discussed earlier, Kenrick and Stringfield (1979) obtained self-, peer (friend), and parental ratings for a group of students. We have already noted the .41 correlation between peer and parental ratings. In addition, self-rated shyness correlated .45 with parental ratings and .33 with ratings by friends. Recall that target participants also rated their shyness behavior in terms of its public observability and cross-situational consistency. Two sets of findings are worth noting with regard to these moderator variables. First, the average correlation across the three data sources (i.e., the average of the self-parent, self-peer, and parent-peer correlations) was higher for participants who were above rather than below the median on either observability (.55 versus .18) or cross-situational consistency (.44 versus .33). Furthermore, the average correlation was remarkably higher for individuals who were above the median on both observability and consistency as compared to those below the median on both (.70 and .25, respectively). Thus, individuals generally concurred with informed observers about their relative standing on the dimension of shyness; this agreement was particularly impressive  with respect to those individuals for whom shyness was an apt and salient dimension. These findings lend some credence to the Allportian notion that shyness may be a *central trait* for some individuals but not for others.

The second noteworthy finding has to do with the observability and cross-situational consistency of shyness relative to the other dimensions assessed. Of the sixteen personality dimensions included in the study, shyness was rated (a) as the dimension on which the average participant was most consistent across situations, and (b) as the second most observable of the dimensions (following only sober/serious versus happy-go-lucky). Thus, shyness would appear to occupy a well-defined and central position in the universe of trait dimensions.

Two other studies have reported correlations between self-ratings of shyness and ratings by an informed other. One study correlated scores on a 14-item Shyness Scale with ratings made by friends using a third-person version of the same scale (McCroskey & Richmond, 1982). Observer reports correlated .53 with self-reports in a large sample (n = 295) of elementary and secondary school teachers. In another study (Jones & Briggs, 1984), college students completed five different shyness scales. Ratings by several acquaintances (from one to three) were also obtained. The others' ratings were combined for each participant and correlated with the average of the participant's five shyness scores. Others' ratings correlated .59 with the adjective pair of reserved versus outgoing and .53 with the adjective pair shy versus showoff.

Taken together, these studies show rather substantial agreement between self-ratings of shyness and ratings obtained from relatives or friends. Again, however, it is important to replicate this finding in studies using impartial observers.

*With Objective Observers*

Several studies have compared self-reported shyness with ratings made by impartial observers. In one investigation, participants inter-acted with an opposite-sex stanger (a confederate) for five minutes, then interacted with an experimenter for a brief period, and finally delivered a short speech after a brief period of preparation (Pilkonis, 1977). Self-ratings of shyness correlated substantially (r = .58) with the combined ratings of the interaction partner, the experimenter, and an independent observer. (However, this correlation may overestimate the actual relationship between these two sets of ratings because participants in the study were selected on the basis of extreme scores on shyness—see Briggs & Underwood, 1982).

In a recent study (Jones et al., 1985), we found reasonably strong correlations between scores on a shyness scale and judges' ratings in two separate samples. In both cases, a group of judges rated the participants after watching 2-minute videotaped monologues in which participants talked informally about themselves. Shyness scores correlated .50 and .39 with the average ratings by judges in these two samples. These findings are also consistent with data reported by Cheek and Buss (1981), and show that the agreement between ratings of shyness by self and others is not just a function of the closeness of the relationship between self and other.

### With Behavioral Indices

A number of studies have examined the behavioral correlates of self-reported shyness. Most of the studies compare one of the limited domain measures of shyness with a group of behavioral indices. In general, these studies demonstrate that self-reported shyness is linked to quieter, less responsive conversational styles. Several researchers have shown that individuals who score high on shyness scales—compared to those who score low—talk less, initiate conversations less, and are less likely to break periods of silence when they interact with others (Cheek & Buss, 1981; Daly, 1978; Mandel & Shrauger, 1980; and Pilkonis, 1977). Similarly, high as compared to low socially anxious persons differ in the number and type of utterances used (Leary, Knight, & Johnson, 1984). High as compared to low scores also show more signs of anxiety such as nervous gestures and self-touching, and they tend to avert their gaze more often and exhibit less facial expressivity (Cheek & Buss, 1981; Mandel & Shrauger, 1980).

### With Interpersonal Measures

In the previous few sections, I have reviewed briefly the relationship between self-report measures of shyness and global or behavioral ratings of shyness. A much larger literature on shyness also exists in which self-report measures are correlated with a variety of affective, personality, relational, and laboratory measures. Much of this research is reviewed in recent volumes by Jones et al. (in press), Daly and McCroskey (1984), and Leary (1984). Space limitations allow mention of only a few of the findings here.

Individuals who score high on shyness scales are generally rated as *less* friendly, assertive, talented, and poised in unstructured dyadic conversations and monologues than their non-shy counterparts (Cheek & Buss, 1981; Jones & Briggs, 1984; Pilkonis, 1977). Shyness also seems to have consequences for romantic and intimate relationships. For example, among college students, shyness scores are inversely related to number of dating partners, number of friends, dating frequency, and dating satisfaction (Jones & Russell, 1982). In addition, self-reported shyness is related to various aspects of sexual behavior including less sexual experience and fewer sexual partners, but to greater apprehension about sex and sexual dysfunction (Leary, 1984).

Shyness scores also show modest negative correlations with both quantitative measures of social support (e.g., number of persons in one's social network) and qualitative measures of social support (e.g., satisfaction with the degree of support received). In general, however, shyness is more strongly related to qualitative than to quantitative measures (Jones, 1984). A recent field study also found that unemployed older workers scoring high on shyness were more troubled by their unemployment experience than those scoring low, and were more likely to feel helpless and to lower their expectations in the absence of social support mechanisms (Hansson, Briggs, & Rule, 1985). Finally, shyness scores have implications for various social-psychological processes. Laboratory studies have shown, for example, that shyness scores are associated with conformity (Santee & Maslach, 1982), reduced helping behavior (McGovern, 1976), a preference for greater interpersonal distance (Carducci & Webber, 1979), and an inability to judge how one is being perceived by others (Jones & Briggs, 1984).

### Summary

Five points are worth noting from this limited review of the shyness literature. First, observers agree as to who is shy and who is not, and they seem to agree even when given only a brief opportunity to observe the target persons. Second, observers' ratings of shyness correlate substantially with self-ratings of shyness. Third, ratings of shyness are stable over time. Fourth, self-ascribed shyness correlates negatively with a variety of measures of effective interpersonal functioning, thereby attesting to the usefulness of the construct. Finally, the various behavioral indices correlate with each other only modestly, and do not correlate much higher with ratings by self or others.

## THE TRAIT CONTROVERSY

Psychology prides itself on its empirical orientation. Controversies revolve around data—that which can be demonstrated or observed—even though the disagreements are often rooted in a priori assumptions and assertions. To the extent that theorists differ in their fundamental assumptions, they are also likely to disagree about the facts. Perhaps the most important issue in the study of traits has to do with what will be admitted as evidence.

Our discussion of shyness was oriented toward examining the evidence for it as a trait construct. The pattern of findings that emerged is similar to what has been reported for other personality characteristics (e.g., Block, 1977; Emler, 1983). Interestingly, trait advocates and critics seem to concur on what types of data are relevant (R-data, T-data, and S-data), and they even seem to agree about the state of the evidence. Whereas R-data and S-data generally support trait notions, T-data do not (e.g., see Block, 1977; Mischel, 1968, chaps. 2-4). Advocates and critics part company, however, in their *interpretations* of these data.

## THE CASE AGAINST TRAITS

For Mischel, T-data provide the primary exhibit in the case against traits. In his 1968 review of the literature he argues that "with the possible exception of intelligence, highly generalized behavioral consistencies have not been demonstrated, and the concept of personality traits as broad response dispositions is thus untenable"(p. 146). He says much the same elsewhere: "I am more and more convinced . . . hopefully by data as well as on theoretical grounds that the observed inconsistency so regularly found in studies of noncognitive personality dimensions often reflects the state of nature and not merely the noise of measurement" (1969, p. 1014).

At the same time, Mischel acknowledges that the other two modes of measurement yield results apparently in support of a trait position:

> Appreciable continuity over long periods of time is found in well-done studies using R-data (personality ratings by observers) and S-data (self-ratings); moreover, these two types of data may be (and often are) significantly related. . . . Temporal consistency and agreement among judges in personality ratings—by self and by others—is not and has not been in dispute. (1977, p. 333)

In interpreting such findings, however, he chooses to emphasize how cognitive constructions accentuate the consistencies we observe in ourselves and others. In his earlier work he made this point rather provocatively: "Traits are categories of the observer who perceives and describes behavior and not necessarily properties of the observed behavior itself" (1968, p. 68) and "research on person perception has led to the conclusion that the results depend far more on the person than on the person perceived" (p. 48). In subsequent writings Mischel has made the same point in a more conciliatory manner:

I am not dismissing perceived consistencies in human qualities as artifacts or fictions by emphasizing their cognitive, constructive nature. . . . It may not be possible to assign the residence of dispositions exclusively either to the actor or to the perceivers; we may have to settle . . . for a reality that is constructed and cognitively created but not fictitious. (1977, p. 334)

Nevertheless, it seems apparent that when choosing between kinds of evidence, Mischel sides with T-data. As he puts it:

Unless R and S data predict T data appreciably, the links between trait impressions and specific behavior in situations remain tenuous. Although traditional trait ratings may serve as summaries in everyday language of the gist of our impressions of each other . . . they certainly do not illuminate the causes of behavior. (1977, p. 335)

Mischel's position is based on several assumptions. First, he holds that traits, however defined, must exhibit considerable consistency across situations:

Data that demonstrate strong generality in the behavior of the same person across many situations are critical for trait and state personality theories; the construct of personality itself rests on the belief that individual behavioral consistencies exist widely and account for much of the variance in behavior. (Mischel, 1968, p. 13)

The chief problem with this statement is its ambiguity (Golding, 1977). What does "strong generality" mean? How are we to know if "behavioral consistencies exist widely" or not? How much is "much of the variance in behavior"? Not only does this statement misrepresent the position of most trait adherents (who believe only that traits contribute a reasonable amount to an understanding of behavior), it also stacks the deck in favor of the critics. Even if traits accounted for as much of the variance as any other predictor, they could be faulted for not being sufficiently strong, wide, or big.

Mischel's preference for T-data also follows from his assumption that "the value of trait and state approaches depends on how well they facilitate the prediction and modification of individual behavior"

(Mischel, 1968, p. 9). This assumption is characteristic of an *instrumentalist* view of science in which explanation and prediction are seen as symmetrical. The prediction and control of individual behavior are important elements of an applied discipline, but they need not be the primary goals of a basic science. For instance, Manicas and Secord (1983, pp. 404-405) have endorsed a *realist* approach to scientific inquiry. From this perspective,

> laboratory psychology should not be aimed at explaining behavior . . . ; its purpose is far more circumscribed. The explanation of behavior . . . is properly a multidisciplinary effort and, though based on the behavioral sciences, necessarily transcends them to involve both biology and the social sciences. . . . science aims at discovering lawful processes, but such laws are not about events, but about the causal powers of those structures which exist and operate in the world.

Thus, the value of trait concepts depends first and foremost on how much they contribute to an understanding of human behavior, rather than whether they facilitate "point predictions" of the behavior of specific individuals in specific situations (T-data).

## THE DEFENSE

Not surprisingly, trait advocates interpret the evidence for traits somewhat differently from the position described above. Whereas many of us would agree that "putatively equivalent or related measures in the T-data domain do not manifest their conceptually required correspondence" (Block, 1977, p. 60), by no means do we accept this deficiency as a cogent proof that the notion of personality traits is untenable. Instead, we take a closer look at the evidence, and ask specifically, "How much confidence should we put in T-data?"

T-data often involve single, discrete acts, and frankly we should be surprised to find much evidence of continuity at this level of analysis. The trait notion implies regularity in behavior but not in the superficial sense of high intercorrelations among single units of behavior. Rather, it suggests that an individual typically acts so as to produce a certain social outcome or impression; this outcome is a tendency, not an immutable fact (Wiggins, 1974). More important, a given outcome or impression can be expressed by way of a whole class of actions. The particular mode of expression will probably differ from person to person, and it will often vary even within a person over time and across situations.

Thus, trait advocates by and large will agree with Mischel's arguments about behavioral specificity when the units of measurement are discrete acts or microbehaviors. Searching for traits by focusing on specific behaviors is like trying to view a Monet painting from a distance of six inches. The details are plain but you miss the picture. Blindness due to this sort of behavioral specificity no more invalidates the trait notion than putting one's nose to a painting rules out the possibility that there is a coherent picture waiting to be appreciated. One need only step back and the pattern emerges.

Trait advocates often seem willing to rely heavily on R- and S-domain measures. This confidence is based in part on the assumption that a sophisticated information processor is necessary to detect the regularities in human behavior. Human observers are able to integrate information using heuristic rules in a way that is difficult to achieve otherwise. The fallibility of human observers is a well-known fact both in clinical psychology and the cognitive sciences, yet human observers still provide the single best means by which to gain insight into the complex and subtle regularities that characterize interpersonal behavior.

A number of trait critics have dismissed R-data as reflecting little more than shared semantic categories (e.g., Jones & Nisbett, 1972; Mischel, 1968; Schweder and D'Andrade, 1980). They argue that trait ratings reflect "implicit personality theories" more than actual observations of an individual's behavior. Certainly we do have implicit personality theories, and certainly these theories sometimes lead us to incorrect generalizations. For instance, from the shyness literature we know that shy people's fears of being misinterpreted are well-founded. Their reticence often elicits gratuitous attributions on the part of others—specifically that shy individuals are aloof and disinterested in social interaction and are untalented.

Furthermore, we know that the factor structure of peer ratings remains essentially the same whether based on ratings of friends or total strangers (e.g., Passini & Norman, 1966). To suggest, however, that traits primarily reflect categories of the observer rather than characteristics of the person being observed is to blunder. It ignores, for instance, an important study by Norman and Goldberg (1966) showing that ratings made by acquaintances result in much greater interrater reliabilities than those made by strangers (see Weiss, 1979, for a conceptual replication of this finding). It also fails to explain how observers come to agree on the relative standing of specific individuals in a group. Several important studies have demonstrated convincingly that independent observers agree as to the characteristics of specific individuals (e.g., Magnusson & Heffler, 1969; Koretzky, Kohn, & Jeger, 1978; and the studies reported earlier by Backteman & Magnusson, 1981, and Kenrick & Stringfield, 1980). The semantic distortion hypothesis may account in part for the taxonomic structure of trait ratings, but it is difficult to conceive of how it can account for the fact that *independent* observers agree that one person scores high on a dimension whereas another scores low. Correspondence of this sort must derive from characteristics of the individuals being observed.

## EXPLANATORY NOTIONS

McDougall (1938) once suggested that *tendencies* are the essential elements of psychology. My contention so far in this chapter has been that a belief in trait tendencies is requisite to the study of personality. According to Wiggins (1974, p. 6), "If persons are not more or less prone to behave in certain ways on certain occasions, then the psychometric approach is out of business at the outset; as are all approaches to personality study." Now I want to take the argument one step further and contend that traits are useful not only as summary accounts of behavior, but as a kind of explanatory construct. This point is considerably more controversial than the first point, but just as straightforward.

### Traits as Explanations

Traits can serve as explanations in two related ways. First, a single event can be understood as an instance of a chronic tendency. (Why was John acting anxious around Sue? Because John always acts anxious around attractive women.) This answer tells us that John's anxiousness in this context is typical and not due to some irregular circumstance (e.g., her having been a former girlfriend or his having been caught in a lie). As Hirschberg (1978, p. 52) put it: "Knowing this much does not allow us to give a unique reconstruction of the agent's reasons and intentions, but it sets limits on the sort of detailed story that is possible." In the first sense, then, traits serve as explanations insofar as they rule out other possible causes, although in this sense they provide only partial explanations (Wiggins, 1974).

Traits, however, can also serve as explanations in a second and more profound sense. When we explain an action by pointing to a recurring behavioral pattern (traits as summary concepts), we also point to the individual as the locus of causality. As I pointed out earlier, insofar as behavioral regularity is the product of a person—and something that the person carries around from place to place—that something must be registered internally. However and wherever preserved, this trait provides a second kind of explanation:

> By means of it, we can refer to a hypothetical state or mechanism that we do not yet understand, or to any of various such states or mechanisms, while merely specifying one of its characteristic effects. . . . There are dispositions, such as intelligence, whose physical workings we can scarcely conjecture; the dispositional characterization is all we have to go on. Intelligence is the disposition to learn quickly, if I may oversimplify. By intelligence I still mean some attribute of the body, despite our ignorance concerning it; some durable physical state. (Quine, 1974, p. 10)

In a similar fashion, Allport said, "Traits are cortical, subcortical, or postural dispositions having the capacity to gate or guide specific phasic reactions. It is only the phasic aspect that is visible; the tonic is carried somehow in the still mysterious realm of neurodynamic structure" (1966, p. 3).

Here, then, is the point of difference. On one side are those who view trait explanations as "lost causes" (Wiggins, 1974). Like mythical creatures, homunculi, and supernatural forces, traits are what we posit when an explanation is beyond our grasp. We invent traits as causal entities out of our ignorance. On the other side are those (myself included) who view traits as "a promissory note for an eventual description in mechanical terms" (Quine, 1974, p. 14). Of course, a deep understanding of behavioral regularities in terms of underlying processes (whether neurodynamic, biochemical, or cognitive) is still well beyond our grasp. This should not discourage us, however. Other causal agents (e.g., genes and germs) proved to be useful constructs long before they were identified physically. Moreover, they would have remained useful and would have existed physically regardless of whether they had ever been isolated by researchers. In the same way, traits can serve as useful causal entities even if the underlying processes or structures cannot be clearly identified, and even if we doubt whether objects or actions at one level can ever be totally reduced to or explained in terms of objects and actions at another level.

In a sense, then, I agree with Mischel's view that traits are not the unit of explanation. I view traits not as *the* unit of explanation but as *a* unit of explanation. Traits remind us that the individual actually possesses something substantive, whether it be preserved as a cognitive or mental property (e.g., a self-image), or a neurological, biochemical property (e.g., a neuropsychic entity). And yet, traits themselves require further explanation; they are, after all, only promissory notes. Simply stated, then, how do we acquire whatever it is that regularizes our behavior, and how do such structures and processes change over time?

## EXPLANATIONS OF SHYNESS

To return to the case of shyness for a moment, two of our goals should be (1) to understand the nature of the mechanisms that produce the affective, behavioral, cognitive, and somatic experiences that characterize shyness, and (2) to understand how these mechanisms (structures and processes) come about. Current explanations for the trait of shyness fall into one (or more) of three categories: biological, learning, and cognitive.

Biological explanations involve three main points. First, shyness is in part an emotional experience, and there is considerable evidence that the fundamental human emotions are "wired in" (Izard & Malatesta, in press). Second, although the fundamental emotions are universal, we know that there are inherited individual differences in the extent to which emotionality is experienced and expressed (Buss & Plomin, 1984; Goldsmith, 1983). More specifically, there is good evidence that some (early developing) forms of shyness have an inherited component (Buss, in press; Plomin & Daniels, in press). The third point is that inherited differences in shyness probably involve the sympathetic division of the autonomic nervous system (Buss, 1980). Consistent with this suggestion is the recent program of research by Kagan and his colleagues (e.g., Kagan & Rezneck, in press), which links behavioral inhibition in children with several physiological indices (e.g., heart rate variability and pupillary dilation) and demonstrates longitudinal stability for each. These impressive findings complement earlier work on the biological underpinings of extraversion (Eysenck, 1981) and anxiety (Gray, 1982).

Learning explanations help us to understand how certain behavioral regularities and affective associations are acquired. Presumably, learning reflects changes in neural structure or material although the substance of the "engram" remains elusive. All of the classical forms of learning are relevant. Emotional reactions to certain types of social stimuli could be acquired through classical conditioning. Alternatively, shyness could occur because a child is repeatedly punished for attempting to communicate, or because the pattern of reinforcements is inconsistent and upredictable (Arkin, Lake, & Baumgardner, in press; McCroskey & Beatty, in press). Finally, modeling theory suggests that children may acquire shy behaviors by emulating parents or significant others.

A third way to explain the trait of shyness emphasizes the cognitive-perceptual strategies of an individual, although these strategies are also partly learned and (perhaps) partly influenced by genes. One form of the cognitive approach suggests that people act and feel shy primarily because they have been labeled as shy and believe the label to be true (Brodt & Zimbardo, 1981). Another type of cognitive explanation suggests that one kind of shyness involves excessive public self-consciousness (Buss, 1980). This preoccupation with self may be rooted in certain parental child-rearing practices or a reaction to some stigmatizing event. A third type of cognitive explanation holds that shyness arises out of doubts about one's self-presentational abilities. In this approach, shyness is a function of (a) how much one is motivated to give a certain impression, and (b) the perceived probablity of achieving that end (Leary, 1984).

Notice that each of these explanations rests on some element that is thought to be real: genes and the sympathetic nervous system for the biological explanations, some change in the neurochemical substrate of memory for the learning explanations, and for the cognitive explanations, an enduring self-image or nonconscious "internal processing algorithm" (Lewicki, in press). From a trait perspective, then, there is no inherent incompatibility among these three types of explanation. In fact, though these explanations represent different intellectual traditions, with respect to any one individual they all apply. Behavior is multiply determined and thus requires multiple explanations.

## CONCLUSION

The trait approach emphasizes the orderliness of a person's behavior. It recognizes the continuities that exist in the lives of individuals and assumes that this coherence reflects an underlying arrangement or process that is both real and enduring.

In recent years, we have begun to understand some of the mechanisms that might produce behavioral regularities. For instance, genetic and biochemical factors have now been reliably linked to a number of personality characteristics (e.g., Goldsmith, 1983; Zuckerman, 1983). The existence of such factors underscores the reality of traits and strongly suggests that there may be something to Allport's notions of neuropsychic entities. Furthermore, there is growing evidence that nonconscious cognitive processes play a pervasive role in structuring one's perceptions and responses (Lewicki, in press) and may initiate and guide behavior in a manner that is consistent with the concept of traits as espoused by Allport (1937) and Stagner (in press). Thus, I contend that there is good reason to believe that traits actually exist, and with respect to this claim, I would like to suggest three final points.

First, the reality of traits does not imply a rigid determinism. Mischel's objections to the trait approach—as reflected in the last paragraph of his 1968 book (see also 1984, pp. 278-282)—seem to derive as much from a moral stance as from a careful analysis of the evidence. However, trait accounts are no more deterministic than social learning accounts (whether cognitive or situational). Allport's writings clearly demonstrate that a trait position is not incompatible with an interest in individual behavior. Even a genetic or biological basis does not presume a fixed and unalterable trait, but rather suggests that a person has a propensity to operate within certain bounds.

The second point is that the reality of traits helps us to define the central goals of personality psychology. Our mission is to understand what produces continuity in individual lives and to discover how and why trait characteristics develop and endure. In the preceding chapter of this volume, Cantor and Kihlstrom elaborate a cognitive-social approach to personality that emphasizes categorization processes and conscious problem-solving strategies in the service of life plans. Insofar as this approach acknowledges that individuals act coherently, I agree that it addresses a fundamental concern of personality psychologists. Of course, for this reason I would argue that it also implies a trait account.

The final point has to do with what might serve as a profitable agenda for the future. Throughout this chapter, I have defined the concept of traits broadly. As Cochran (1983) correctly points out, however, the trait concept is not monolithic. We can identify many kinds of traits. They differ in terms of their origin: Some may have clear biological foundations whereas others may be grounded in nonconscious cognitive processes and still others in rational strategies. Traits may also differ in content. McClelland (1951), for instance, distinguished among expressive, performance, and social norm traits. And traits may also differ in terms of their centrality and relevance for a particular individual (Allport, 1937; Kenrick & Stringfield, 1980).

Although the trait concept has been out of vogue for some time now, the present analysis suggests that it was abandoned prematurely. Traits are still the fundamental unit of analysis in personality psychology, and an understanding of the nature of traits remains as the discipline's most challenging research topic.

# REFERENCES

Allport, G. W. (1937). *Personality: A psychological interpretation.* New York: Holt, Rinehart & Winston.

Allport, G. W., & Odbert, H. S. (1936). Trait-names: a psycho-lexical study. *Psychological Monographs: General and Applied, 47* (1, Whole No. 211).

Alston, W. P. (1975). Traits, consistency, and conceptual alternatives for personality theory. *Journal for the Theory of Social Behavior, 5,* 17-47.

Arkin, R. M., Lake, E. A., & Baumgardner, A. H. (in press). In W. H. Jones, J. M. Cheek, & S. R. Briggs (Eds.), *Shyness: Perspectives on research and treatment.* New York: Plenum.

Beckteman, G., & Magnusson, D. (1981). Longitudinal stability of personality characteristics. *Journal of Personality, 49,* 148-160.

Block, J. (1977). Advancing the study of personality: Paradigmatic shift or improving the quality of research? In D. Magnusson & N. S. Endler (Eds.), *Personality at the crossroads: Current issues in interactional psychology.* Hillsdale, NJ: Lawrence Erlbaum.

Brandt, R. B. (1970). Traits of character: A conceptual analysis. *American Philosophical Quarterly, 7,* 23-37.

Briggs, S. R. (1985). *Shyness and the evaluation of self and others.* Paper presented at the meeting of the Eastern Psychological Association, Boston.

Briggs, S. R., & Smith, T. G. (in press). The measurement of shyness. In W. H. Jones, J. M. Cheek, & S. R. Briggs (Eds.), *Shyness: Perspectives on research and treatment.* New York: Plenum.

Briggs, S. R., & Underwood, B. (1982). *Selecting extremes: Alternative methods of data analysis.* Unpublished manuscript.

Brodt, S. E., & Zimbardo, P. G. (1981). Modifying shyness-related social behavior through symptom misattribution. *Journal of Personality and Social Psychology, 41,* 437-449.

Buss, A. H. (1980). *Self-consciousness & social anxiety.* San Francisco: Freeman.

Buss, A. H. (in press). A theory of shyness. In W. H. Jones, J. M. Cheek, & S. R. Briggs (Eds.) *Shyness: Perspectives on research and treatment.* New York: Plenum.

Buss, A. H., & Plomin, R. (1984). *Temperament: Early developing personality traits.* Hillsdale, NJ: Lawrence Erlbaum.

Carducci, B. J., & Webber, A. W. (1979). Shyness as a determinant of interpersonal distance, *Psychological Reports, 44,* 1075-1078.

Cattell, R. B. (1946). *Description and measurement of personality.* New York: World Books.

Cochran, L. (1984). On the categorization of traits. *Journal for the Theory of Social Behavior, 14,* 183-209.

Cheek, J. M. (1980). *Shyness and sociability.* Unpublished master's thesis, University of Texas at Austin.

Cheek, J. M. (1982). Aggregation, moderator variables, and the validity of personality tests: A peer-rating study. *Journal of Personality and Social Psychology, 43,* 1254-1269.

Cheek, J. M., & Buss, A. H. (1981). Shyness & sociability. *Journal of Personality and Social Psychology, 41,* 330-339.

Cheek, J. M., Carpentieri, A. M., Smith, T. G., Rierdan, J., & Goff, E. (in press). Adolescent shyness. In W. H. Jones, J. M. Cheek, & S. R. Briggs (Eds.), *Shyness: Perspectives on research and treatment.* New York: Plenum.

Daly, J. A., & McCroskey, J. C. (Eds.). (1984). *Avoiding communication: Shyness, reticence, and communication apprehension.* Beverly Hills, CA: Sage.

Daly, S. (1978). Behavioral correlates of social anxiety. *British Journal of Social and Clinical Psychology, 18,* 121-128.

Dixon, J. J., de Monchaux, C., & Sandler, J. (1957). Patterns of anxiety: An analysis of social anxieties. *British Journal of Medical Psychology, 30,* 102-112.

Emler, N. (1983). Moral character. In H. Weinreich-Haste & D. Locke (Eds.), *Morality in the making.* New York: John Wiley.

Endler, N. S., & Magnusson, D. (1976). *Interactional psychology and personality.* Washington, DC: Hemisphere.

Epstein, S. (1984). The stability of behavior across time and situations. In R. A. Zucker, J. Aronoff, & A. I. Rabin (Eds.), *Personality and the prediction of behavior.* Orlando, FL: Academic.

Eysenck, H. J. (1956). The questionnaire measurement of neuroticism and extraversion. *Revista de Psicologia, 50,* 113-140.

Eysenck, H. J. (Ed.). (1981). *A model for personality.* New York: Springer-Verlag.

Eysenck, S.B.G., & Eysenck, H. J. (1975). *Manual of the Eysenck Personality Questionnaire.* London: Hodder & Stoughton.

Fenigstein, A., Scheier, M. F., & Buss, A. H. (1975). Public and private self-consciousness: Assessment and theory. *Journal of Consulting and Clinical Psychology, 43,* 522-527.

Fiske, D. W. (1966). Some hypotheses concerning test adequacy. *Educational and Psychological Measurement, 26,* 69-88.

Fiske, D. W. (1971). *Measuring the concepts of personality.* Chicago: Aldine.

Goldberg, L. R. (1981). A historical survey of personality scales and inventories. In P. McReynolds (Ed.), *Advances in psychological assessment* (Vol. 2). Palo Alto: Science and Behavior Books.

Golding, S. L. (1977). Toward a more adequate theory of personality: Psychological organizing principles. In H. London (Ed.), *Personality.* New York: Hemisphere.

Goldsmith, H. H. (1983). Genetic influences on personality from infancy to adulthood. *Child Development, 54,* 331-355.

Goffman, E. (1959). *The presentation of self in everyday life.* Garden City, NY: Doubleday.

Gough, H. G., & Heilbrun, A. B. (1965). *Adjective Check List manual.* Palo Alto, CA: Consulting Psychologists Press.

Gough, H. G., & Thorne, A. (in press). Positive, negative and balanced shyness: Self-definitions and the reactions of others. In W. H. Jones, J. M. Cheek, & S. R. Briggs (Eds.), *Shyness: Perspectives on research and treatment.* New York: Plenum.

Gray, J. A. (1982). *The neuropsychology of anxiety: An enquiry into the functions of the septo-hippocampal system.* Oxford: Oxford University Press.

Hampson, S. E. (1983). Trait ascription and depth of acquaintanceship: The preference for traits in personality descriptions and its relation to target familiarity. *Journal of Research in Personality, 17,* 398-411.

Hannson, R. O., Briggs, S. R., & Rule, B. (1985). *Shyness and coping among older unemployed workers.* Manuscript submitted for publication.

Hirschberg, N. (1978). A correct treatment of traits. In H. London (Ed.), *Personality: A new look at metatheories.* Washington, DC: Hemisphere.

Hogan, R., DeSoto, C. B., & Solano, C. (1977). Traits, tests, and personality research. *American Psychologist, 32,* 255-264.

Izard, C. E., & Hyson, M. C. (in press). Shyness as a discrete emotion. In W. H. Jones, J. M. Cheek, & S. R. Briggs (Eds.), *Shyness: Perspectives on research and treatment.* New York: Plenum.

Izard, C. E., & Malatesta, C. Z. (in press). A developmental theory of emotions. *The Behavioral and Brain Sciences.*

Jones, E. E., & Nisbett, R. (1972). The actor and the observer: Divergent perceptions of the causes of behavior. In E. E. Jones et al. (Eds.), *Attribution: Perceiving the causes of behavior.* Morristown, NJ: General Learning Press.

Jones, W. H. (1984). Relational competence in loneliness and social support. In B. H. Gottlieb (Chair), *Social support and loneliness.* Symposium conducted at the meeting of the American Psychological Association, Toronto.

Jones, W. H., & Briggs, S. R. (1984). The self-other discrepancy in social shyness. In R. Schwarzer (Ed.), *The self in anxiety, stress, and depression.* Amsterdam: North Holland.

Jones, W. H., Briggs, S. R. & Smith, T. G. (1985). *Shyness: Conceptualization and measurement.* Unpublished manuscript, University of Tulsa.

Jones, W. H., & Russell, D. (1982). The social reticence scale: An objective instrument to measure shyness. *Journal of Personality Assessment, 46,* 629-631.

Kagan, J., & Rezneck, J. S. (in press). Shyness and temperament. In W. H. Jones, J. M. Cheek, & S. R. Briggs (Eds.), *Shyness: Perspectives on research and treatment.* New York: Plenum.

Kenrick, D. T., & Stringfield, D. O. (1980). Personality traits and the eye of the beholder: Crossing some traditional philosophical boundaries in the search for consistency in all of the people. *Psychological Review, 87,* 88-104.

Koretzky, M. B., Kohn, M., & Jeger, A. M. (1978). Cross-situational consistency among problem adolescents: An application of the two-factor model. *Journal of Personality and Social Psychology, 36,* 1054-1059.

Leary, M. R. (1983). Social anxiousness: The construct and its measurement. *Journal of Personality Assessment, 47,* 66-75.

Leary, M. R. (1984). *Understanding social anxiety: Social, personality, and clinical perspectives.* Beverly Hills, CA: Sage.

Leary, M. R., Knight, P. D., & Johnson, K. A. (1984). *Social anxiety and dyadic conversation: A verbal response analysis.* Unpublished manuscript.

Levy, L. (in press). Trait approaches. In M. Hersen, A. E. Kazden, and A. S. Bellack (Eds.), *The clinical psychology handbook.* New York: Pergamon.

Lewicki, P. (in press). *Nonconscious social information processing.* New York: Academic.

London, H. (1978). *Personality: A new look at metatheories.* Washington, DC: Hemisphere.

Magnusson, D. & Endler, N. S. (Eds.). (1977). *Personality at the crossroads: Current issues in interactional psychology.* Hillsdale, NJ: Lawrence Erlbaum.

Magnusson, D., & Heffler, B. (1969). The generality of behavioral data: III. Generalization potential as a function of the number of observation instances. *Multivariate Behavioral Research, 4,* 29-42.

Mandel, N. M., & Shrauger, J. S. (1980). The effects of self-evaluation statements on heterosocial approach in shy and nonshy males. *Cognitive Therapy and Research, 4,* 369-381.

Manicas, P. T., & Secord, P. F. (1983). Implications for psychology of the new philosophy of science. *American Psychologist, 38,* 399-413.

McClelland, D. C. (1951). *Personality.* New York: Holt, Rinehart & Winston.

McCroskey, J. C., Anderson, J. F., Richmond, V. P., & Wheeless, L. R. (1981). Communication apprehension of elementary and secondary students and their teachers. *Communication Education, 30,* 122-132.

McCroskey, J. C., & Beatty, M. (in press). Oral communication apprehension. In W. H. Jones, J. M. Cheek, & S. R. Briggs (Eds.), *Shyness: Perspectives on research and treatment.* New York: Plenum.

McCroskey, J. C., & Richmond, V. P. (1982). Communication apprehension and shyness: Conceptual and operational distinctions. *Central States Speech Journal, 33,* 458-468.

McDougall, W. (1938). Tendencies as indispensable postulates of all psychology. *Proceedings of the XI International Congress on Psychology: 1937* (pp. 157-170). Paris: Alcan.

McGovern, L. P. (1976). Dispositional social anxiety and helping under three conditions of threat. *Journal of Personality, 44,* 84-97.

Mischel, W. (1968). *Personality and assessment.* New York: John Wiley.

Mischel, W. (1969). Continuity and change in personality. *American Psychologist, 24,* 1012-1018.

Mischel, W. (1977). The interaction of person and situation. In D. Magnusson & N. S. Endler (Eds.), *Personality at the crossroads: Current issues in interactional psychology.* Hillsdale, NJ: Lawrence Erlbaum.

Mischel, W. (1978). Personality research: A look at the future. In H. London (Ed.), *Personality: A new look at metatheories.* Washington, DC: Hemisphere.

Mischel, W. (1984). On the predictability of behavior and the structure of personality. In R. A. Zucker, J. Aronoff, & A. I. Rabin (Eds.), *Personality and the prediction of behavior.* Orlando, FL: Academic.

Morris, C. G. (1982). *Assessment of shyness.* Unpublished manuscript, University of Michigan.

Norman, W. T., & Goldberg, L. R. (1966). Raters, ratees, and randomness in personality structure. *Journal of Personality and Social Psychology, 4,* 681-691.

Orchard, J., Schallow, J., & Perlman, D. (1983). *The behavioral consequences of shyness and responses of others to the shy.* Unpublished manuscript.

Page, M. M. (Ed.). (1983). *Nebraska symposium on motivation: Personality—Current theory and research.* Lincoln: University of Nebraska Press.

Passini, F. T., & Norman, W. T. (1966). A universal conception of personality structure? *Journal of Personality and Social Psychology, 4,* 44-49.

Pervin, L. A. (1984). *Current controversies and issues in personality* (2nd ed.). New York: John Wiley.

Pilkonis, P. A. (1977). The behavioral consequences of shyness. *Journal of Personality, 45,* 566-611.

Plomin, R., & Daniels, D. (in press). Genetics and shyness. In W. H. Jones, J. M. Cheek, & S. R. Briggs (Eds.), *Shyness: Perspectives on research and treatment.* New York: Plenum.

Quine, W. V. (1974). *The roots of reference.* LaSalle, IL: Open Court.

Russell, D., Cutrona, C. E., & Jones, W. H. (in press). A trait-situational analysis of shyness. In W. H. Jones, J. M. Cheek, & S. R. Briggs (Eds.), *Shyness: Perspectives on research and treatment.* New York: Plenum.

Santee, R. T., & Maslach, C. (1982). To agree or not to agree: Personal dissent amid social pressure to conform. *Journal of Personality and Social Psychology, 42,* 690-700.

Shweder, R. A., & D'Andrade, R. G. (1980). The systematic distortion hypothesis. In R. Shweder (Ed.), *New directions for methodology of social and behavioral science* (Vol. 4, pp. 37-58). San Francisco: Jossey-Bass.

Sears, D. O. (1967). Social anxiety, opinion structure and opinion change. *Journal of Personality and Social Psychology, 7,* 142-151.

Stagner, R. (in press). Trait psychology. In N. S. Endler & J. Hunt (Eds.), *Personality and behavioral disorders.*

Watson, D., & Friend, R. (1969). Measurement of social-evaluative anxiety. *Journal of Consulting and Clinical Psychology, 33,* 448-457.

Weiss, D. S. (1979). The effects of systematic variations in information on judge's descriptions of personality. *Journal of Personality and Social Psychology, 37,* 2121-2136.

Wiggins, J. S. (1974). *In defense of traits.* Invited address at the Ninth Annual Symposium on Recent Developments in the Use of the MMPI, Los Angeles.

Zimbardo, P. G. (1977). *Shyness: What it is, what to do about it.* Reading, MA: Addison-Wesley.

Zucker, R. A., Aronoff, J., & Rabin, A. I. (Eds.). (1984). *Personality and the prediction of behavior.* Orlando, FL: Academic.

Zuckerman, M. (Ed.). (1983). *Biological bases of sensation seeking, impulsivity, and anxiety.* Hillsdale, NJ: Lawrence Erlbaum.

# 3

# On the Nature of
# Self-Monitoring

## AN EXAMINATION OF
## LATENT CAUSAL STRUCTURE

STEVE GANGESTAD
MARK SNYDER

**Steve Gangestad** is a postdoctoral fellow at the Institute of Child Development, the University of Minnesota. He received his doctoral degree from the University of Minnesota in 1984. His current research interests include conceptual and methodological issues surrounding inquiry into the nature of causal structures underlying personality.

**Mark Snyder** is Professor of Psychology at the University of Minnesota. He received his doctoral degree from Stanford University in 1972. His research interests include theoretical and empirical issues associated with the study of personality and social behavior.

According to theoretical analyses of self-monitoring, individuals differ in the extent to which they can and do monitor, through self-observation and self-control, their expressive behavior and self-presentation (e.g., Snyder, 1979a). Some people—those high in self-monitoring—are thought to regulate their expressive self-presentation for the sake of desired public appearances, and thus are thought to act in ways that are highly sensitive to social and interpersonal cues to situationally appropriate performances. Other people—those low in self-monitoring—are thought to lack either the ability or the motivation to regulate their expressive self-presentational behaviors. Instead, they are thought to display expressive behaviors that truly reflect their own attitudes, traits, feelings, and other enduring and momentary inner states.

A number of hypotheses follow from these basic propositions. According to self-monitoring theory, high self-monitoring individuals should be better able than low self-monitoring individuals to display

**AUTHORS' NOTE:** This research and the preparation of this manuscript were supported in part by National Science Foundation grant BSN 82-07632 to Mark Snyder, in part by an NIMH National Research Council postdoctoral traineeship to Steve Gangestad, and in part by a grant from the University of Minnesota Computer Center.

convincingly a wide variety of emotions without actually experiencing them. Furthermore, the behavior of high self-monitoring individuals should be more sensitive than that of low self-monitoring individuals to shifts in what constitutes "good" performance in a social situation. And in behavioral domains where cross-situational variation in the definition of social appropriateness is substantial, high self-monitoring individuals should exhibit and report greater behavioral variability than low self-monitoring individuals. By contrast, low self-monitoring individuals should exhibit greater consistency of behavioral expressions of feelings and thoughts, and thus should show greater correspondence between self-report measures of attitudes and preferences and nontest behavioral indicators of these attitudes and preferences.

Research involving a measure of self-monitoring propensities (the Self-Monitoring Scale; for information on its reliability and validity, see Snyder, 1974) has provided empirical support for all of these—and many more—hypotheses about the cognitive, behavioral, and interpersonal consequences of self-monitoring.[1] For reviews of these validations of the self-monitoring construct, see Snyder (1979a, 1979b) and Shaw and Costanzo (1982).

Furthermore, these empirical relations have led to elaborations of the self-monitoring construct that extend beyond the initial propositions. Thus, individuals high in self-monitoring tend to adopt a "pragmatic" interpersonal orientation, being able strategically to create social interaction patterns that facilitate situationally appropriate interaction outcomes. Conversely, those low in self-monitoring tend to adopt a "principled" interpersonal orientation, reflected in correspondence between feelings and attitudes on the one hand and social behavior on the other (Snyder & Campbell, 1982).

Empirical and theoretical investigations of self-monitoring continue, often drawing the self-monitoring construct into new domains of applicability. At times, these new explorations have led to conceptual elaborations, extensions, and clarifications of the self-monitoring construct. For example, investigations of self-monitoring and friendship have suggested that, whereas high self-monitoring individuals tend to have different and varied friends for different and varied occasions, low self-monitoring individuals tend to have a set of exclusive friendships that are, in a sense, good for all occasions (Snyder, Gangestad, & Simpson, 1983). Moreover, low self-monitoring individuals appear to be more committed to their dating partners than are high self-monitoring individuals (Snyder & Simpson, 1984). These findings indicate that low self-monitoring individuals place a higher premium on affective closeness and attachment than do high self-monitoring individuals (Snyder & Smith, in press). Indeed, when it comes to that particularly intimate form of social interaction, the sexual relationship, low self-monitoring individuals tend to insist on mutual affective closeness and commitment as prerequisites; by contrast, high self-monitoring individuals are substantially more likely to engage in casual sexual relations (Snyder, Simpson, & Gangestad, 1985).

### A LATENT CAUSAL STRUCTURE FOR SELF-MONITORING

Presumably, there is a latent causal structure, perhaps involving a single major causal variable, that accounts for the network of empirical relations that are observed in studies of the many and varied manifestations of self-monitoring propensities. Of course, we have not yet observed this causal structure directly, and so are not able to define it *explicitly*. Nevertheless, in the spirit of construct validation (Cronbach & Meehl, 1955), we can postulate the existence of a latent causal structure understood *implicitly* in terms of its role in a theoretical network designed to explain the empirical relations between behavioral variables. That is, even though we do not know exactly what the "something" is, the latent causal structure *is* that "something" postulated to explain empirical relations between behavioral manifestations observed in self-monitoring studies.

Recently we have been led to ask questions whose answers may make our knowledge of this causal structure more explicit. These questions can be placed in the larger theoretical context of the nature of individual differences in personality. In personality theories, the features thought to distinguish people from one another have typically been treated as comparative individual differences, on the assumption that one can meaningfully compare any two people in terms of the same variables. These personality variables, in principle, may be of at least two varieties—*dimensions* and *class variables*. Dimensions are characteristics thought to be possessed in some degree by all individuals; as a result, the distributions of such characteristics are continuous. For example, dominance is thought to be a dimension of personality, and it is assumed to be continuously distributed and measured by a scale on Jackson's Personality Research Form (1974). On the other hand, certain units of personality may not be dimensions, but rather class variables, which are expressed not continuously but as differences distributed into discrete categories. Class variables can be introduced by the colloquial expression "There are two [or for that matter any finite number of] types of people in the world . . ."

If comparative individual differences can be distributed either as continuous dimensions or as discrete classes, we may ask whether any specific difference between individuals is properly conceptualized as a dimension or as a class variable. In the context of our current concerns with self-monitoring, we may ask: Is self-monitoring a continuous dimension, possessed in some degree by all people, or is it a class variable, with people belonging either to the discrete class of high self-monitoring individuals or to the discrete class of low self-monitoring individuals?

To answer this fundamental question requires that it first be phrased in sufficiently specific terms; the answer to any question of this form may depend upon the kind of classification to which the question refers. At a *phenotypic* level, of course, self-monitoring tendencies are distributed continuously. That is, the extent to which individuals actually exercise self-control over their overt expressive behavior exists in all degrees and thus is continuously distributed. Nevertheless, at a *genotypic* level there may exist one *latent causal entity* or structure that is discretely distributed, and thus is a class variable. Consider, for example, that individuals possess, in varying degrees, masculine and feminine characteristics that, on the average, discriminate between the sexes. At the phenotypic level, masculinity and femininity are continuously distributed dispositions; yet, at the latent level, there exists a discretely distributed variable—biological sex itself—that plays a role in the causal network giving rise to the visible expressions of masculinity and feminity.

## A CLASS MODEL OF SELF-MONITORING PROPENSITIES

To rephrase the question more specifically in light of these considerations, we may ask: Does there exist a latent causal factor underlying self-monitoring differences that is a class variable? Recently, on the basis of some relatively strong intuitive hunches bolstered by theoretical considerations, we have addressed this question and gathered evidence that strongly suggests that the answer is affirmative. Specifically, psychometric analyses indicate that, underlying the responses to items on the Self-Monitoring Scale, there exists a latent causal factor that is not distributed continuously, but rather is distributed discretely into two latent cases.

Let us consider this evidence more precisely by asking, first: How can one distinguish variables that entail discrete classes from ones that involve continuous dimensions? Generally speaking, if a class variable exerts a strong influence on some domain of behavioral characteristics, then individuals will be discontinuously distributed in the multi-dimensional space defined by these behavioral characteristics. To the extent that unusual clustering of individuals (or in extreme cases, multi-modality) can be detected in this multidimensional space, we have evidence consistent with a class model. Further evidence for a latent factor conjectured to be a class variable can be found in the network of empirical relations between a measure of the latent factor and nontest behaviors. That is, the construct validity of any classification scheme purported to measure a class variable can be evaluated in terms of the consistency between theoretically defined and empirically observed relations between test behavior and nontest behavior (see Cronbach & Meehl, 1955).

Our efforts to test the class model of self-monitoring propensities included two components: (1) a *structural component*, involving examination of responses to items on the Self-Monitoring Scale for discontinuities consistent with a class model, and (2) an *external component*, involving examination of the relation between a classification scheme based on the observed discontinuities and nontest criterion behaviors relevant to self-monitoring. For details of the psychometric aspects of these studies, see Gangestad and Snyder (1985).

## The Structural Component of the Class Model

Over the years, Meehl and his colleagues have developed taxometric models to detect latent class structures in sets of empirical data. These methods can be applied when one has conjectured the existence of a dichotomous class variable and can supply a list of indicators believed to discriminate between the two classes. In the context of self-monitoring, previous research and theorizing permitted conjectures about the status of self-monitoring as a class variable, and the items of the Self-Monitoring Scale constituted a set of indicators believed to discriminate between the two classes.

The taxometric methods we employed are based on a maximum covariance model (Meehl & Golden, 1982), one that has been shown in extensive Monte Carlo simulations as well as empirical trials to detect real class structures effectively and not to spuriously detect class structures where none exist (e.g., Meehl, 1978). In essence, what these methods assess are deviations from multivariate normality of the conjectured indicators, deviations consistent with a model stipulating that two latent classes underlie the indicators. Indeed, when we applied these methods to an appropriate set of self-monitoring indicators (specifically, a subset of items on the Self-Monitoring Scale chosen to meet the assumptions and requirements of the taxometric procedures), they indicated that a class model is an appropriate model for self-monitoring propensities.

Moreover, additional analyses provided further evidence consistent with the class model. For instance, if a dichotomous class variable underlies responses to a set of purported indicators of this variable, then two values—the proportion of the population belonging to one class and the proportion belonging to the other class—define the distribution of the class variable. If real classes exist, these base rates are fixed within a given sample, and different mathematical formulae derived from the class model ought to yield consistent estimates of these base rates. In the case of self-monitoring, six quasi-independent methods of base-rate estimation yielded remarkably consistent estimates of the proportion of the population belonging to the class of high self-monitoring individuals (.41) and the proportion belonging to the class of low self-monitoring individuals (.59). In addition, it was possible to calculate for each individual the probability of his or her belonging to the latent class of high self-monitoring individuals or alternatively to the latent class of low self-monitoring individuals. When individuals were assigned to latent classes on the basis of these calculations, it was estimated that 89 percent of the classifications were correct.

These taxometric analyses, then, have provided considerable corroboration for the conjecture that a major latent causal factor underlying responses to the self-monitoring measure is a class variable. To further corroborate the model we conducted two series of control analyses, each of which demonstrated that in addition to being able to detect a real class structure when they should detect one, the taxometric methods fail to detect a latent class structure when no such structure is present. These control analyses add to our confidence that a latent discrete causal factor underlies responses to the self-monitoring measure.

**Factor Analysis and the Class Model**

If a class variable is a major source of covariation in responses to items on the self-monitoring measure, it ought to be possible to find this variable in the factor structure of the Self-Monitoring Scale. There are several published factor analyses of the scale (e.g., Briggs, Cheek & Buss, 1980; Furnham & Capon, 1983; Gabrenya & Arkin, 1980; Sparacino, Ronchi, Bagley, Flesch, & Kuhn, 1983; Tobey & Tunnell, 1981); all of them have indicated that multiple factors may underlie responses to the self-monitoring items. Sparacino et al. (1983) have suggested that the factor space is two dimensional. Gabrenya and Arkin

(1980) and Furnham and Capon (1983) have claimed that four reliable factors exist. Briggs et al. (1980) found three factors. None of these analyses, however, has yielded a factor that the authors have interpreted as a "self-monitoring" factor. Consider, for instance, Briggs et al. (1980). They have interpreted their three factors as "extraversion," "other-directedness," and "acting." If a self-monitoring class variable actually exists and underlies responses to items on the measure, why doesn't it appear in these factor analyses? Perhaps it fails to appear because, quite simply, the self-monitoring class variable identified by the taxometric analyses is *not* a major source of variation underlying responses to the items of the Self-Monitoring Scale.

Although this conclusion may seem to follow from the results of published factor analyses, it is not yet justified. The identification of a factor space is, for a given factoring method, unique, but the precise identification of the axes defining that factor space is not unique. In order to identify the axes, factor analysts typically have relied upon simple structure, and in fact, all of the factor analyses cited here involved factor rotation in accordance with simple structure criteria. Unfortunately, there is no indisputable justification for believing that a rotated factor structure identifies the "real" sources of variation underlying the responses (e.g., Eysenck, 1950; Guilford & Zimmerman, 1963; Overall, 1964).

Accordingly, one need not expect the self-monitoring class variable to appear as one of the axes in a factor solution involving rotation to simple structure. Where, then, should it appear? If the assumption of local independence holds such that, within latent classes, items do not intercorrelate highly relative to their correlations in the mixed sample, then the class variable should emerge as a general factor accounting for a relatively large proportion of the common variance shared across items. That is, the class variable should emerge as the first *unrotated* factor extracted in a principal components analysis of variance (the first unrotated factor being the inferred variable that maximally accounts for the variation in the items; Rummel, 1970).

Indeed, when we performed a principal axes factor analysis on the items of the Self-Monitoring Scale, the first unrotated factor did, as conjectured, correspond closely to the self-monitoring class variable. Specifically, the factor loading for a given item was an excellent estimate of that particular item's ability to predict individuals' latent class membership, these two variables rank-order correlating .97. Thus, it appears that the self-monitoring class variable is expressed as a factor that lies very near the first unrotated factor within the factor structure of the measure. That is, the self-monitoring class variable seems to be virtually identical to the variable that accounts for the maximal amount of variance in responses to self-monitoring items.

What meaning, then, should be attributed to the *rotated* factors? In our analysis, an oblique rotation yielded three factors (not, incidentally, dissimilar to those reported by Briggs et al., 1980), all positively correlated with the first unrotated factor. These factors appear to define three content domains (in order of importance to the self-monitoring class variable—as reflected in correlations with the first unrotated factor—these domains are "expressive self-control," "social stage presence," and "other-directed self-presentation") that discriminate between the classes of high self-monitoring and low self-monitoring individuals.

We may speculate that the three rotated factors correspond to three dimensional variables that discriminate between the high and low self-monitoring classes and yet are, in part, independent of the latent class variable. With respect to these dimensional variables, then, the self-monitoring class variable may be a higher-order disposition that potentiates the expression of lower-order dispositions corresponding to the three dimensions. Thus, the self-monitoring class variable may potentiate the development of the ability to control expressive behavior, the ability to maintain a social stage presence, and a propensity to present oneself with others' reactions in mind, all phenomena that in addition to being potentiated by the self-monitoring class variable are influenced by other factors in the course of their development. Hence, at the same time that the self-monitoring class variable may be strongly reflected in the phenomena of expressive self-control, social stage presence, and other-directed self-presentation, there may also exist reliable differences between individuals in these phenomena that exist even when the self-monitoring class variable is held constant.

## The External Component of the Class Model

Clearly, the taxometric analyses indicate that a dichotomous class model is highly consistent with the internal structure of the items of the Self-Monitoring Scale. To validate the class model further, we examined empirical relations, derived from self-monitoring theory, between the self-monitoring class variable and relevant behavioral criterion variables observed in empirical investigations covering a wide range of self-monitoring phenomena. The results demonstrate the ability of the self-monitoring class variable to account successfully for relations between the Self-Monitoring Scale and behavioral criteria predicted by the theory of self-monitoring. For each of six self-monitoring studies, we calculated the effect size achieved by, or the percentage of variance accounted for by, first, the classification scheme that emerged from the taxometric analyses, and second, the full Self-Monitoring Scale treated as a continuous dimension. If the class model is appropriate, the classification scheme should have outperformed the full Self-Monitoring Scale. If a conventional dimensional model is appropriate, however, the full Self-Monitoring Scale should have outperformed the classification scheme (Gangestad & Snyder, 1985). As Table 3.1 shows, the classification scheme outperformed the full Self-Monitoring Scale by approximately 50 percent across the six studies. These relative performances are very near those expected if the class variable were the *sole* source of covariance between the Self-Monitoring Scale and the external behavioral criteria.

We should note in this regard that in these assessments of criterion-oriented validity, individual factors within the Self-Monitoring Scale (such as those reported by Briggs et al., 1980) were, in general, more weakly related to the criterion variables than were either the taxometrically-derived classification scheme or the Self-Monitoring Scale itself. It appears, then, that a measure of the class variable detected by the taxometric procedures can effectively stand in for the entire Self-Monitoring Scale and can account successfully for relations between the Self-Monitoring Scale and behavioral criteria predicted by the theory of self-monitoring. Factors obtained by other procedures cannot.

### IMPLICATIONS OF THE CLASS MODEL

What does it mean to assert that there exists a latent causal factor underlying self-monitoring phenomena that is a discretely distributed class variable rather than a continuously distributed dimensional variable? First of all, it should be acknowledged that the very act of asking this question is unusual. In inquiries about personality and social behavior, the question of whether a comparative difference between individuals is properly conceptualized and investigated as a dimension or as a class variable rarely get asked, let alone answered. Indeed, the appropriate roles of continuous dimensions and discrete classes in personality rarely surface as issues for theoretical or empirical inquiry.

### The Role of Continuous Dimensions and Discrete Classes in Personality

The question rarely surfaces, it appears, because the answer is almost universally prejudged. With few exceptions, it has been widely presumed

TABLE 3.1

Effect Size Achieved by or Percentage of Variance Accounted for
by the Classification Scheme Relative to the Full Self-Monitoring
Scale:  Empirical Results and Class Model Predictions

|  | Empirical Results | Class Model Predictions[a] |
|---|---|---|
| Snyder & Cantor (1980) | | |
| Investigation 2 | 1.49 | 1.32 |
| Snyder & Gangestad (1982) | | |
| Investigation 1 | 2.70 | 1.62 |
| Investigation 2 | 1.75 | 2.44 |
| Snyder & Kendzierski (1982) | | |
| Investigation 1 | 1.14 | 2.20 |
| Snyder, Gangestad, & Simpson (1983) | | |
| Investigation 1 | .88 | 1.11 |
| Investigation 2 | 1.51 | 1.35 |
| Average | 1.58 | 1.67 |

a. These values are the reciprocal of the percentage of variance the full scale shares
with the class variable, and reflect corrections for the fallibility of the classification
scheme; uncorrected values are not highly dissimilar.

that the basic units of personality are continuous dimensions. This
pervasive assumption is bolstered by an enduring prejudice against the
viability of class models in personality, a prejudice rooted in part in
claims that class variables constitute oversimplifications of reality or
arbitrary fictions (e.g., Mendelsohn, Weiss, & Feimer, 1982; Mischel,
1976).

As statements of the possible underpinnings of the prejudice against
class variables, consider the following:

> Simplicity limits their [class variables'] value. Generally, an individual's behaviors
> are so complex, diverse, and variable that he cannot be sorted into a simplistic
> category or slot. (Mischel, 1976, p. 16)

> Because personality variables are distributed continuously and are inevitably
> subject to consensual definitions, personality types are bound to be arbitrary
> constructions rather than discoveries of how to "carve nature at its joints."
> (Mendelsohn et al., 1982, pp. 1131-1132)

But just how legitimate are these arguments? We suggest that the
answer may depend on what form of classification system is under
scrutiny. As we have noted, phenetic classifications, which are undertaken primarily for descriptive convenience with no underlying meaning
ascribed to the classes so constructed, are vulnerable to criticisms of

oversimplification and arbitrariness. We simply doubt that there exist discrete classes manifested at a phenotypic level of behavior. Thus, we suspect that phenetic classification schemes are what critics have had in mind when arguing against class variables.

By contrast, genotypic approaches to classification are not vulnerable to being labeled as, at best, oversimplifications and, at worst, arbitrary fictions. These class variables are purported to correspond to real causal entities, latent entities that actually exist and exercise genuine influences upon phenotypic behavioral characteristics.

Such a genotypic approach to the explication of class variables ought to be particularly appealing to personality researchers. It identifies the class variable as a causal-dispositional construct that refers to an underlying attribute or structure within the person thought to account for some domain of behavioral events. Yet, as appealing as genotypically explicated class variables ought to be to personality researchers concerned with causal-dispositional constructs that underlie, organize, and structure behavior, until now at least, no genotypically-explicated class variable (with the exception of biological sex) had been shown to exert substantial influence on human social behavior. With one exception now substantially corroborated, we may turn to implications of the class model for our further understanding of the explicit nature of the causal structure underlying individual differences in self-monitoring.

## Origins of the Class Variable

Perhaps the most immediate and important questions raised by the existence of a latent class variable concern the issues of etiology and development of individual differences. If a discrete factor underlies individual differences in self-monitoring, we would like to know the following: What is this discrete factor? What are its origins? How do its manifestations develop?

Let us consider first the question of etiology. What *is* the latent class variable? Although self-monitoring is a variable most evident in social and interpersonal settings—and thus, perhaps a variable that might be considered likely to emerge from differential exposure to social learning environments—there are reasons to entertain very seriously the possibility that the latent class variable underlying self-monitoring has biological origins. Specifically, the fact that the latent factor *is* a discrete factor is in itself one good reason to suspect a strong role played by genetics. Although in principle, at least, it is not impossible that an environmental factor could be discrete, environmental parameters nevertheless generally are considered to be continuously distributed;

biological genetic systems, in contrast, are widely recognized to produce, at times, discrete or quasi-continuous forms (see Falconer, 1981). Although it seems unlikely that a single Mendelizing gene has substantial effects on a biological parameter with wide-ranging psychological effects, it may be that more complex epistatic and polygenic threshold models (e.g., Carter, 1969; Falconer, 1967) account for discretely distributed psychobiological parameters having wide-ranging effects on individual and social behavior.

Could, then, the latent discrete factor underlying self-monitoring be a genetic factor? Fortunately, this is a highly testable possibility. Monozygotic (MZ) twins share all of their genetic material; they are, truly, genetically identical. Dizygotic (DZ) twins share, on average, half their genetic material, the same proportion shared by single-birth siblings. Under the hypothesis that the class variable has genetic origins, then, the true concordance rate on this latent factor for MZ twins must equal 1.00—MZ twins must *always* belong to the same latent class. The true concordance rate for DZ twins, by contrast, should be substantially less than 1.00.

To test the hypothesis that the class variable has genetic origins, Gangestad (1984) estimated the latent concordance rates for a set of 149 pairs of MZ twins and 76 pairs of DZ twins through a series of "bootstrasping" operations involving latent structure modeling. The resultant values emerging from the analyses were, it should be noted, estimates and not actually observed concordance rates, given that one cannot examine a pair of twins and directly "see" whether they belong to the same latent class. A set of consistency tests (Meehl, 1979) indicated, however, that the estimates are reasonably trustworthy.

Consistent with the genetic hypothesis, the estimated concordance rate for the sample of MZ twins was very near 1.00 (.95). For a subsample of these MZ twins whose zygosity determination was known to be error-free, the concordance rate was even higher (.99). Also consistent with this hypothesis, the estimated latent concordance rate for DZ twins was substantially lower (.74). (Randomly pairing individuals would yield an expected concordance rate of .55.) It appears, then, that genetic factors are—if not exclusively—heavily implicated in the operation of the latent class variable underlying individual differences in self-monitoring. Whether these genetic factors operate through a *specific* biochemical pathway or are implicated in a number of *nonspecific* and independent biochemical pathways is at this time unknown (although, for one suggested candidate for a specific biochemical pathway, see Gangestad, 1984).

**Emergence of the Class Variable**

Let us now consider the behavioral emergence of the latent class variable underlying self-monitoring. If a genetic factor determines class membership, across what parameters of psychological functioning are initial differences produced, and what are their behavioral manifestations? Research on individual differences in children's symbolic styles offers one intriguing possibility. Nelson (1973, 1981) and others (e.g., Horgan, 1981; Ramer, 1976; Starr, 1974) have observed two relatively distinct patterns in the acquisition of language by children at ages 2 to 3. Some children, referred to as *referential,* tend to learn first to use language as a referential system that allows them to communicate actual happenings in the world. For instance, they develop a large vocabularly of referential nouns. Other children, referred to as *expressive*, tend early on to acquire the social uses of language. That is, they learn that the pattern, structure, and intonation of linguistic expressions are dependent upon social context, and that language is a means to obtain attention from others.

Wolf and Gardner (1979) have provided reasons to believe that these differences in language acquisition are associated with differences in general symbolic activities. Thus, expressive children (whom Wolf and Gardner call dramatists) focus in general on the social structure of events, learning at an early age that different persons on different occasions can play the same role in the same social situation, and that persons can exchange roles in play. Dramatists also like to tell dramatic stories and display elaborate forms of imitation.

The behavioral overlap between the referential-expressive distinction and the adult manifestations of self-monitoring is striking. Both expressive children and high self-monitoring adults are relatively sensitive to considerations of social context and are "dramatists" in their social performances, being both sensitive to the attention dramatic performances gain and skilled at imitating others. In contrast, both referential children and low self-monitoring individuals tend to be relatively insensitive to social context and nondramatic. On the basis of content validity, then, we can speculate that the two sets of individual differences are manifestations of the *same* latent factor expressed at different ages.

Whatever the initial manifestations of the self-monitoring class variable, they are probably a more circumscribed set than we observe in adult behavior. For instance, there may exist initial cognitive differences that facilitate learning in different domains, foster different global orientations to the social world, or produce differences in domains of skill acquisition (as expressed in the referential-expressive distinction), but there may initially be no motivational differences, such as differences in the concern for social appropriateness, which presumably mediate the use of self-monitoring skills. These and other differences may develop through a process of *divergent causality*.

## Divergent Causality and the Class Variable

Divergent causality occurs when an initially restricted range of differences between individuals becomes amplified or extended over time, producing larger differences between individuals in similar or additional domains (Langmuir, 1943; London, 1946; Meehl, 1978; compare Waddington's, 1957 discussion of the epigenetic landscape). Initial differences may involve propensities to attend to different features of the social world and later be expressed as actual differences in social knowledge. Similarly, initial differences in potential to acquire dramatic role-playing skills may later be expressed as actual differences in these skills. Yet later, as the child who possesses these skills learns that they may be used toward instrumental ends, possession of these skills may become associated with a motive to use them in social situations to obtain social attention and approval. Over time, then, the network of manifestations of the latent factor may expand through normal processes of knowledge, skill, and motive acquisition.

Further, this network of manifestations may be expanded through people's choices of situations. It has been demonstrated, for instance, that individuals high and low in self-monitoring tend to enter situations and choose friends in ways that are conducive to the expression of their own behavioral orientations (e.g., Snyder & Gangestad, 1982; Snyder et al., 1983; Snyder & Simpson, 1984). High self-monitoring individuals tend to develop a wide network of friendships that are activity specific. With different friends, high self-monitoring individuals choose to do different activities, activities for which the friends are relatively well-suited as partners. Low self-monitoring individuals, by contrast, tend to develop more exclusive friendships that span many activities. Furthermore, these exclusive friendships are apparently based on perceived similarity between low self-monitoring individuals and their friends (Snyder et al., 1983).

As a consequence of these friendship choices, high self-monitoring individuals may have the opportunity to develop further their role-playing skills in many domains, and low self-monitoring individuals may have the opportunity to develop behavioral repertoires consistent with their dispositional tendencies. In other words, people may develop behavioral repertoires and skills increasingly consistent with their initial orientations, and thereby the initial manifestations may become increasingly amplified over time (for further discussion of the nature of such developmental sequences, see Snyder, 1981, 1983; compare Plomin, DeFries, & Loehlin, 1977; Scarr & McCartney, 1983).

In sum, the identification of a class variable underlying self-monitoring phenomena has raised intriguing and researchable issues concerning the etiology and development of propensities to control one's expressive behavior. First, the class variable may correspond to a specific dichotomous etiological factor or threshold effect, one that research strongly suggests is biological in nature. Second, this specific etiological factor may have a circumcribed and, in principle, identifiable domain of manifestations early in childhood. Through processes of divergent causality, this initial domain of manifestations may become amplified and extended over time to the full range of effects attributable to the variable in adult behavior.

Clearly, to the extent that these issues raised by the class model can be addressed effectively, our understanding of self-monitoring phenomena will accrue substantially. Our understanding of the roots of self-monitoring will accrue to the extent that a specific biological etiology or threshold effect determining class membership becomes identified. Our understanding of the emergence of self-monitoring will accrue to the extent that early manifestations are identified. Our understanding of the development of self-monitoring will accrue to the extent that increased differentiation of the classes over time becomes identified. We believe that these potential increases in knowledge can be actualized because the issues we have discussed not only involve questions whose answers would be highly informative; they are also, in principle, quite researchable.

## ON THE EXISTENCE OF
## LATENT STRUCTURES IN PERSONALITY

Finally, let us consider briefly our attempts to understand the latent structure of self-monitoring in the broader context of personality theory, research, and assessment. We began these attempts by postulating that there *does* exist some latent causal structure underlying responses to the Self-Monitoring Scale and its relations to external criterion variables. We hoped that, through empirical research, we could come to understand the nature of this latent causal structure more explicitly.

As such, we regarded the items on the Self-Monitoring Scale as representing more than representative *samples* of behavior selected from some semantically coherent behavioral domain defined by the investigator. Rather, we regarded responses to these items as *signs* of an underlying latent reality that we sought to explicate (see Goodenough, 1952). That is, we interpreted the responses to the measure as more than summary descriptions of past behavior; we interpreted them as a set of coherences that could be understood more fully at an underlying level.

These presumptions on our part are, by the standards of many contemporary personality theorists, quite risky. Indeed, it is typically assumed today that one postulates "real" latent structures underlying psychological assessment devices only with great trepidation. According to this view, responses to personality items should be interpreted as summary statements of behavior, behaviors whose nature may be maintained tenuously by a readily changeable social learning regime. Thus, assessment devices should *not* be viewed as measuring causal structures that exist as properties of the person making the responses and that can explain the person's actions. Although this view that assessment devices do not measure causal theoretical structures is most prototypically characterized by the statements of social learning theorists (e.g., Bandura, 1971; Mischel, 1968, 1973; Nicholls, Licht, & Pearl, 1982), it is certainly not limited to these theorists. Even many defenders of trait theory reject the claim that personality scales measure real latent structures that can be invoked in explanatory accounts (e.g., Hogan, 1976; Wiggins, 1974; see also Hogan et al., 1977).

Under the influence of this view, some researchers have explicitly acknowledged the descriptive—rather than causal-theoretical—role of assessment, and have attempted to devise assessment procedures that more accurately summarize behavior (e.g., Buss & Craik, 1983a, 1983b). In this approach, self-statement personality measures may still serve a function, but their value is merely descriptive, lying "in part in their often impressive efficiency in serving as brief surrogates for the long-term observation and acquaintance process entailed by the monitoring of act-trends" (Buss & Craik, 1983b, p. 407).

We agree that the researcher does well to keep in mind the possibility that personality scales may represent only summary statements of behavior maintained by environmental circumstances and not signs of underlying latent structures. Indeed, to reify traits such as "dominance," "nurturance," and "aggressivity," and thus to ascribe to them a real causal role, the researcher must bear a substantial burden of proof (see

Cronbach & Meehl, 1955). Nevertheless, despite our acknowledgment of these considerations, the arguments against attempts to identify real causal structures underlying personality scales do not persuade us to believe that no such attempts should be undertaken. Underlying *some* personality scales there may exist real latent causal structures that *are* tractable to empirical investigation. Thus, through empirical investigation it may be possible to identify and explicate the nature of major causal variables underlying personality.

Of course, attempts to identify real causal structures will continue to involve risk, in the sense that underlying many phenotypic domains there may exist no real causal structures that *are* tractable to study. To the extent that formal criteria—or even rough guidelines—can be developed for evaluating whether, in any instance, major latent causal structures exist, the hazards of reifying traits that do not implicate major latent causal structures may be avoided.

We believe that our investigations of the latent causal structure underlying self-monitoring represents one instance of the successful identification and explication of latent causal structure. The taxonomic analyses and reevaluation of self-monitoring studies appear to provide strong evidence for the existence of a latent causal variable that is discrete or quasi-discrete. Furthermore, the evaluation of twin concordances on this discrete latent factor indicates that the factor may be biological-genetic in nature. We believe that additional investigations— possibly ones identifying a specific biological pathway through which the latent factor operates, as well as ones identifying the developmental trajectories influenced by the latent causal factor—will further explicate the true nature of the structure underlying self-monitoring. To the extent that these investigations do successfully explicate the latent causal structure underlying self-monitoring, we will have at least one instance of a latent causal structure for a phenomenon of importance to personality.

Perhaps this one instance will serve as a model for the identification of additional latent structures of personality. Indeed, the identification of latent structures underlying personality may serve a larger and more fundamental goal—that of shoring up the foundations of the construct of traits in personality. For if traits are to remain one of the core constructs (if not *the* core construct) of personality theory, one would hope that traits are real entities. Identification of latent causal structures constitutes one means of going beyond hoping that traits are real to demonstrating that, at least in some cases, they actually are real.

# NOTE

1. For example, Ajzen, Timko, and White (1982); Becherer and Richard (1978); Caldwell and O'Reilly (1982); Danheiser and Graziano (1982); Ickes, Layden, and Barnes (1978); Krauss, Geller, and Olson (1976); Kulik and Taylor (1981); Lippa (1976, 1978a, 1978b); Lippa and Mash (1979); Lippa, Valdez, and Jolly (1979); Lutsky, Woodworth, and Clayton (1980); McCann and Hancock (1983); Paulhus (1982); Rarick, Soldow, and Geiser (1976); Ross, McFarland, and Fletcher (1981); Shaffer, Smith, and Tomarelli (1982); Snyder (1974); Snyder, Berscheid, and Glick (1985); Snyder and Cantor (1980); Snyder and Gangestad (1982); Snyder, Gangestad, and Simpson (1983); Snyder and Kendzierski (1982a, 1982b); Snyder and Monson (1975); Snyder and Swann (1976); Snyder and Tanke (1976); Tunnell (1980); Tybout and Scott, (1983); Zanna, Olson, and Fazio (1980).

# REFERENCES

Ajzen, I., Timko, C., & White, J. B. (1982). Self-monitoring and the attitude-behavior relation. *Journal of Personality and Social Psychology, 43,* 426-435.

Bandura, A. (1971). *Social learning theory.* Morristown, NJ: General Learning Press.

Becherer, R. C., & Richard, L. M. (1978). Self-monitoring as a moderator of consumer behavior. *Journal of Consumer Research, 5,* 159-162.

Briggs, S. R., Cheek, J. M., & Buss, A. H. (1980). An analysis of the Self-Monitoring Scale. *Journal of Personality and Social Psychology, 38,* 679-686.

Buss, D. M., & Craik, K. H. (1983a). The act frequency approach to personality. *Psychological Review, 90,* 105-126.

Buss, D. M., & Craik, K. H. (1983b). The dispositional analysis of everyday conduct. *Journal of Personality, 51,* 393-412.

Caldwell, D. F., & O'Reilly, C. A. (1982). Responses to failure: The effects of choice and responsibility on impression management. *Academy of Management Journal, 25,* 121-136.

Carter, C. O. (1969). Genetics of common disorders. *British Medical Bulletin, 25,* 52-57.

Cronbach, L. J., & Meehl, P. E. (1955). Construct validity in psychological tests. *Psychological Bulletin, 52,* 281-302.

Danheiser, P. R., & Graziano, W. G. (1982). Self-monitoring and cooperation as a self-presentational strategy. *Journal of Personality and Social Psychology, 42,* 497-505.

Eysenck, H. J. (1950). Criterion analysis: An application of the hypothetico-deductive method of factor analysis. *Psychological Review, 57,* 38-53.

Falconer, D. S. (1967). The inheritance of liability to diseases with variable ages of onset, with particular reference to diabetes melitus. *Annals of Human Genetics, 31,* 1-20.

Falconer, D. S. (1981). *Introduction to quantitative genetics*(2nd ed.). London: Longman.

Furnham, A., & Capon, M. (1983). Social skills and self-monitoring processes. *Personality and Individual Differences, 4,* 171-178.

Gabrenya, W. K., Jr., & Arkin, R. M. (1980). Factor structure and factor correlates of the Self-Monitoring Scale. *Personality and Social Psychology Bulletin, 6,* 13-22.

Gangestad, S. (1984). *On the etiology of individual differences in self-monitoring and expressive self-control: Testing the case of strong genetic influence.* Unpublished doctoral dissertation, University of Minnesota.

Gangestad, S., & Snyder, M. (1985). To carve nature at its joints: On the existence of discrete classes in personality. *Psychological Review, 92,* 317-349.

Goodenough, F. L. (1952). *Mental testing: Its history, principles, and applications.* New York: Rinehart.

Guilford, J. P., & Zimmerman, W. S. (1963). Some variable-sampling problems in the rotation of axes in factor analysis. *Psychological Bulletin, 60,* 289-301.

Hogan, R. (1976). *Personality theory.* Englewood Cliffs, NJ: Prentice-Hall.

Hogan, R., DeSoto, C. B., & Solano, C. (1977). Traits, tests, and personality research. *American Psychologist, 32,* 255-264.

Horgan, D. (1981). Rate of language acquisition and noun emphasis. *Journal of Psycholinguistic Research, 10,* 629-640.

Ickes, W. J., Layden, M. A., & Barnes, R. D. (1978). Objective self-awareness and individuation: An empirical link. *Journal of Personality, 46,* 146-161.

Jackson, D. N. (1971). Structured personality tests: 1971. *Psychological Review, 78,* 229-248.

Jackson, D. N. (1974). *Personality Research Form manual.* New York: Research Psychologists Press.

Krauss, R. M., Geller, V., & Olson, C. (1976, September). *Modalities and cues in perceiving deception.* Paper presented at the meeting of the American Psychological Association, Washington, DC.

Kulik, J. A., & Taylor, S. E. (1981). Self-monitoring and the use of consensus information. *Journal of Personality, 49,* 75-84.

Langmuir, I. (1943). Science, common sense, and decency. *Science, 97,* 1-7.

Lippa, R. (1976). Expressive control and the leakage of dispositional introversion-extraversion during role-played teaching. *Journal of Personality, 44,* 541-559.

Lippa, R. (1978a). Expressive control, expressive consistency, and the correspondence between behavior and personality. *Journal of Personality, 46,* 438-461.

Lippa, R. (1978b, September). *Self-presentation and expressive display of personality.* Paper presented at the annual meeting of the American Psychological Association, Toronto.

Lippa, R., & Mash, M. (1979). *The effects of self-monitoring and self-reported consistency of personality statements made by strangers and intimates.* Unpublished manuscript, California State University, Fullerton.

Lippa, R., Valdez, E., & Jolly, A. (1979, September). *Self-monitoring and the consistency of masculinity-femininity cues.* Paper presented at the annual meeting of the American Psychological Association, New York.

London, I. D. (1946). Some consequences for history and psychology of Langmuir's concepts of convergence and divergence of phenomena. *Psychological Review, 53,* 170-188.

Lutsky, N., Woodworth, W., & Clayton, S. (1980, May). *Actions-attitudes-actions: A multivariate, longitudinal study of attitude-behavior consistency.* Paper presented at the annual meeting of the Midwestern Psychological Association, St. Louis.

McCann, D., & Hancock, R. D. (1983). Self-monitoring in communicative interactions: Social cognitive consequences of goal-directed message modification. *Journal of Experimental Social Psychology, 19,* 109-121.

Meehl, P. E. (1978). Theoretical risks and tabular asterisks: Sir Karl, Sir Ronald, and the slow progress of soft psychology. *Journal of Consulting and Clinical Psychology, 46,* 806-834.

Meehl, P. E. (1979). A funny thing happened on the way to the latent entities. *Journal of Personality Assessment, 43,* 563-581.

Meehl, P. E., & Golden, R. R. (1982). Taxometric methods. In J. N. Butcher & P. C. Kendall (Eds.), *The handbook of research methods in clinical psychology* (pp. 127-181). New York: John Wiley.

Mendelsohn, G. A., Weiss, D. S., & Feimer, N. R. (1982). Conceptual and empirical analysis of the typological implications of patterns of socialization and femininity. *Journal of Personality and Social Psychology, 42,* 1157-1170.

Mischel, W. (1968). *Personality and assessment.* New York: John Wiley.

Mischel, W. (1973). Toward a cognitive social learning reconceptualization of personality. *Psychological Review, 80,* 252-283.

Mischel, W. (1976). *Introduction to personality* (2nd ed.). New York: Holt, Rinehart & Winston.

Nelson, K. (1973). Structure and strategy in learning how to talk. *Monographs of the Society for Research in Child Development, 38,* (1-2, Serial No. 149).

Nelson, K. (1981). Individual differences in language development: Implications for development and language. *Developmental Psychology, 17,* 170-187.

Nicholls, J. G., Licht, B. G., & Pearl, R. A. (1982). Some dangers of using personality questionnaires to study personality. *Psychological Bulletin,* 572-580.

Overall, J. (1964). Note on the scientific status of factors. *Psychological Bulletin, 61,* 270-276.

Paulhus, D. (1982). Individual differences, self-perception, and cognitive dissonance: Their concurrent operation in forced compliance. *Journal of Personality and Social Psychology, 43,* 838-852.

Plomin, R., DeFries, J. C., & Loehlin, J. C. (1977). Genotype-environment interaction and correlation in the analysis of human behavior. *Psychological Bulletin, 84,* 309-322.

Ramer, A. (1976). Syntactic styles in emerging language. *Journal of Child Languages, 3*, 49-62.

Rarick, D. L., Soldow, G. F., & Geiser, R. S. (1976). Self-monitoring as a mediator of conformity. *Central States Speech Journal, 27*, 267-271.

Ross, M., McFarland, C., & Fletcher, G.J.O. (1981). The effect of attitude on the recall of personal histories. *Journal of Personality and Social Psychology, 40*, 627-634.

Rummel, R. J. (1970). *Applied factor analysis.* Evanston, IL: Northwestern University Press.

Scarr, S., & McCartney, K. (1983). How people make their own environments: A theory of genotype-environment effects. *Child Development, 54*, 424-435.

Shaffer, D. R., Smith, J. E., & Tomarelli, M. (1982). Self-monitoring as a determinant of self-disclosure reciprocity during the acquaintance process. *Journal of Personality and Social Psychology, 43*, 163-175.

Shaw, M. E., & Costanzo, P. R. (1982). *Theories of social psychology* (2nd ed.). New York: McGraw-Hill.

Snyder, M. (1974). Self-monitoring of expressive behavior. *Journal of Personality and Social Psychology, 30*, 526-537.

Snyder, M. (1979a). Cognitive, behavioral, and interpersonal consequences of self-monitoring. In P. Pliner et al. (Eds.), *Advances in the study of communication and affect: Vol. 5. Perception of emotion in self and others* (pp. 181-201). New York: Plenum.

Snyder, M. (1979b). Self-monitoring processes. In L. Berkowitz (Ed.), *Advances in experimental social psychology* (Vol. 12, pp. 85-128). New York: Academic.

Snyder, M. (1981). On the influence of individuals on situations. In N. Cantor & J. F. Kihlstrom (Eds.), *Personality, cognition, and social interaction* (pp. 309-329). Hillsdale, NJ: Lawrence Erlbaum.

Snyder, M. (1983). The influence of individuals on situations: Implications for understanding the links between personality and social behavior. *Journal of Personality, 51*, 497-516.

Snyder, M., Berscheid, E., & Glick, P. (1985). Focusing on the exterior and the interior: Two investigations of the initiation of personal relationships. *Journal of Personality and Social Psychology, 48*, 1427-1439.

Snyder, M., & Campbell, B. (1982). Self-monitoring: The self in action. In J. Suls (Ed.), *Psychological perspectives on the self* (Vol. 1, pp. 185-207). Hillsdale, NJ: Lawrence Erlbaum.

Snyder, M., & Cantor, N. (1980). Thinking about ourselves and others: Self-monitoring and social knowledge. *Journal of Personality and Social Psychology, 39*, 222-234.

Snyder, M., & Gangestad, S. (1982). Choosing social situations: Two investigations of self-monitoring processes. *Journal of Personality and Social Psychology, 43*, 123-135.

Snyder, M., Gangestad, S., & Simpson, J. A. (1983). Choosing friends as activity partners: The role of self-monitoring. *Journal of Personality and Social Psychology, 45*, 1061-1072.

Snyder, M., & Kendzierski, D. (1982a). Acting on one's attitudes: Procedures for linking attitude and behavior. *Journal of Experimental Social Psychology, 18*, 165-183.

Snyder, M., & Kendzierski, D. (1982b). Choosing social situations: A strategy for generating correspondence between attitudes and behavior. *Journal of Personality, 50*, 280-295.

Snyder, M., & Monson, T. C. (1975). Persons, situations, and the control of social behavior. *Journal of Personality and Social Psychology, 32*, 637-644.

Snyder, M., & Simpson, J. A. (1984). Self-monitoring and dating relationships. *Journal of Personality and Social Psychology, 47*, 1281-1291.

Snyder, M., Simpson, J. A., & Gangestad, S. (1985). *Personality and sexual relations.* Unpublished manuscript, University of Minnesota.

Snyder, M., & Smith, D. (in press). Personality and friendship: The friendship worlds of self-monitoring. In V. Derlaga & B. Winstead (Eds.), *Friendship and social interaction.* New York: Springer-Verlag.

Snyder, M., & Swann, W. B. (1976). When actions reflect attitudes: The politics of impression management. *Journal of Personality and Social Psychology, 34*, 1034-1042.

Snyder, M., & Tanke, E. D. (1976). Behavior and attitude: Some people are more consistent than others. *Journal of Personality, 44*, 510-517.

Sparacino, J., Ronchi, D., Bagley, T. K., Flesch, A. L., & Kuhn, J. W. (1983). Self-monitoring and blood pressure. *Journal of Personality and Social Psychology, 44*, 365-375.

Starr, S. (1974). The relationship of single words to two-word sentences. *Child Development, 45*, 701-708.

Tobey, E. L., & Tunnell, G. (1981). Predicting our impressions on others: Effects of public self-consciousness and acting, a Self-Monitoring subscale. *Personality and Social Psychology Bulletin, 7*, 661-669.

Tunnell, G. (1980). Intraindividual consistency in personality assessment: The effect of self-monitoring. *Journal of Personality, 48*, 220-232.

Tybout, A. M., & Scott, C. A. (1983). Availability of well-defined internal knowledge and the attitude formation process: Information aggregation versus self-perception. *Journal of Personality and Social Psychology, 44*, 474-491.

Waddington, C. H. (1957). *The strategy of the genes.* New York: Macmillan.

Wiggins, J. S. (1974). *In defense of traits.* Paper presented at the Ninth Annual Symposium of the MMPI, Los Angeles.

Wolf, D., & Gardner, H. (1979). Style and sequence in early symbolic play. In N. Smith & M. Franklin (Eds.), *Symbolic functioning in childhood* (pp. 117-138). Hillsdale, NJ: Lawrence Erlbaum.

Zanna, M. P., Olson, J. M., & Fazio, R. H. (1980). Attitude-behavior consistency: An individual difference perspective. *Journal of Personality and Social Psychology, 38*, 432-440

# The Multiplicity of Personal Identity

**4**

## SEYMOUR ROSENBERG
## MICHAEL A. GARA

**Seymour Rosenberg** received his Ph.D. in clinical psychology from Indiana University in 1952 and is now Professor of Psychology at Rutgers University. He also identifies himself as a personality and social psychologist with research interests in personal identity, person perception, history of psychology, and psychopathology.

**Michael A. Gara** received his Ph.D. in personality and social psychology from Rutgers University in 1980 and is currently a research psychologist at UMDNJ-Community Mental Health Center of Rutgers Medical School. Prominent among his identities are research interests in personal identity, schizophrenia, and program planning and evaluation.

Personal identity, like a number of important topics in psychology, has its historical antecedents in philosophy. Acceptance among scholars of the idea that the individual is an important object of study occurred during the Renaissance, and Locke was the first of the post-Renaissance philosophers to provide a systematic analysis of the nature of personal identity and diversity (Locke, 1694/1959, chap. 27). Disputations on the definition and psychological nature of personal identity became traditional issues in philosophy, much of them grounded in eighteenth and nineteenth century dualism, the "naturalized" offspring of the theological soul-body distinction.

A second major transition in the conception of self and personal identity occurred at about the turn of the century, best marked perhaps by James's extensive chapter on the self in his *Principles of Psychology*

**AUTHORS' NOTE:** The writing of this chapter was supported in part by NSF grant BNS-83-01027 to Seymour Rosenberg. We wish to acknowledge Bertram Cohen's collaboration in the development of the ideas presented in this chapter, particularly those on identity functioning and dysfunctioning. We thank Paul Grubb, Christine Joseph, and Ranana Rosoff, student members of our research group, for their contributions to the research and for their comments on an earlier draft, and Stephanie Micale for her patience, care, and good humor in preparing the manuscript. Our thanks to Rae Carlson, Paul DeBoeck, Susan Harter, James Mancuso, Colin Martindale, Jill Morawski, and Louis Zurcher for their comments—and especially Phillip Shaver, a most diligent and supportive editor.

(1890). The shift in the view of self stems from his elaboration of the empirical self as consisting of "the material Self, the social Self, and the spiritual Self." Each of these constituents of the empirical self is, in turn, a set of multiple selves. Of particular interest to us in this historical overview is James's conception of the social selves, because it placed the phenomena in a social psychological framework and ushered in empirical inquiry into self and identity by twentieth-century social psychologists and sociologists.

Within a decade, Baldwin published his *Social and Ethical Interpretations in Mental Development* (1897)—apparently the first social psychology text in English—in which he proposed that the self is essentially a product of social process. For Baldwin, the self—or "socius," as he frequently referred to it—is the person's social and cultural milieu individualized. Cooley (1902), the sociologist, and Mead (1934), the pragmatist philosopher, continued to emphasize the relationship between self and social environment.

Within sociology, the notion of multiple social identities has become common. The individual is seen as having positions within a system of interpersonal relationships, and attached to each of these positions is a set of psychological characteristics and enactments—or roles. Any given social identity of an individual obtains when she or he conforms to the characteristics and enactments attached to the given position within the social system.

Social pressures to conform to role expectations are not consistent and are not always obeyed, as some sociological writers readily acknowledge. Thus, idiosyncratic patterns emerge for most, if not all, of a person's social identities. That is, although a person may refer to role identities in terms of culturally conventional labels—mother, pilot, manager—there is considerable variation among individuals in the felt characteristics and enactments associated with such social identities. There are, of course, shared beliefs about the characteristics and enactments associated with the roles. Nevertheless, at the psychological level, social identities are, in essence, identities elaborated by the individual within seemingly broad societal constraints. Moreover, these role-derived identities do not exhaust the multiplicity of a person's identities because personal identities may also consist of clusters of characteristics and enactments not associated with any particular social positions.

The assumption that a person has multiple identities, social or personal, led naturally to questions about how they are related to one another; that is, to their organization or structure. James (1890) ventured the notion that the empirical selves are arranged in a _"hierarchical scale"_ in terms of the person's self-regard. Mead also differentiated among a person's selves in terms of their importance; or "identity salience," as symbolic interactionists sometimes refer to the notion (e.g., Stryker & Serpe, 1982). Somewhat more intricate conceptions of identity structure were outlined by McCall and Simmons (1966) who conjectured that role-identities seem to cluster into sub-patterns and that "these clusters may themselves be linked more or less closely with other clusters or may be quite rigidly 'compartmentalized' or dissociated from others," and finally, that "identities are also loosely patterned in a somewhat plastic hierarchy of _prominence_" (p. 77).

These various structural ideas have not stimulated a coherent line of empirical research on identity structure, nor have they been further developed, although writers continue to refer to the multiplicity of personal identity and to its structure (Gergen, 1971; Kihlstrom & Cantor, 1983; Mair, 1977; Martindale, 1980; Rowan, 1983—to name but a few!). Morris Rosenberg (1979), an empirical sociologist, recently wrote a comprehensive and critical overview of self-concept research in which he characterized the study of structure as a "neglected area," while according it considerable importance. In his overview of self-concept research, Rosenberg also argued that the idiographic nature of identity content within a hierarchical structure has generally been ignored by "investigators [who] ask their respondents how intelligent, good-looking, likeable, moral, or neurotic they are without ever bothering to determine how much the respondent cares about these characteristics" (Rosenberg, 1979, p. 282).

We would argue that the development of a cohesive, detailed theory of identity structure has been limited until recently by the lack of systematic empirical methods for studying a person's identities and analytic methods for representing the idiographic content and organization of these identities. Without such research tools, theoretical ideas of structure have remained rudimentary. Naturalistic and other free-response methods are being developed by us and other investigators (e.g., Hermans, 1976; Zavalloni, 1971, 1975) to study the multiplicity of personal identity at the idiographic level, along with a structural theory that is intended to be general in applicability. Our own methods for studying personal identity evolved from a line of research on implicit personality theory that focused on idiographic representations of a person's beliefs about others, as gleaned from various kinds of free-response data (Gara & Rosenberg, 1979; Kim & Rosenberg, 1980; Rosenberg, 1977; Rosenberg, & Jones, 1972).

In this chapter we present a theory of identity structure and function developed primarily from our empirical work on person perception and identity structure. In the process of looking for nomothetic properties of identity structure, we have also developed the notion of "elaboration"—somewhat akin to Kelly's (1955) "elaborative choice"—which plays a central role in identity function and dysfunction. Empirical and data-analytic methods for the study of identity will be outlined along with examples of identity structures that illustrate their application. The concluding section contains a critique of the theory and methods, a discussion of their implications for the study of identity and personality, and reexamination of the age-old issue of unity versus multiplicity of self.

## A THEORY OF IDENTITY

An identity is defined in this chapter as an amalgam of features—personal characteristics, feelings, values, intentions, and images—experienced by the individual. Focusing on experience does not imply reification of this amalgam within the person, although an identity—particularly a prominent one—may, like any strong belief, be experienced as a compelling reality. The set of identities, their content, and their interrelationships will be called an identity structure. In our exposition of a theory of identity we first take up its formal structural aspects. This is followed by a description of the functional relations between identities and their enactments, and among the identities themselves.

The concatenation of three basic structural relations—*subset-superset, disjunction,* and *equivalence*—forms an identity structure, or more generally, a belief system (D'Andrade, 1976). The particular structural relation that holds between any two identities is based on their features. In order to illustrate these relations in terms of features, we present Table 4.1, a matrix of professional identities (rows) by features (columns) for a hypothetical academic psychologist. The features shared by Psychologist and Researcher in Table 4.1 show that Psychologist is a superset of Researcher, because the features and enactments attributed to Psychologist include those attributed to Researcher. On the other hand, Psychologist and Occultist are disjunctive as there is absolutely no overlap in their features. There are no examples of equivalent identities in Table 4.1 because no two identities share the same features. Given that real feature data are not error-free, algorithms for representing structure may represent some identities as "equivalent" and treat the small number of features that fail to overlap as error.

Two alternative models of identity structure will be outlined here. The first is a model in which the three structural relationships are

**TABLE 4.1**
Hypothetical Identities × Features Matrix
for an Academic Psychologist

| Identities | Witty | Extroverted | Precise | Curious | Speculative | Prescient |
|---|---|---|---|---|---|---|
| | | | *Features* | | | |
| Undergraduate teacher | 1 | 1 | 0 | 0 | 0 | 0 |
| Graduate teacher | 1 | 0 | 1 | 0 | 0 | 0 |
| Professional in community | 1 | 1 | 1 | 0 | 0 | 1 |
| Professor | 1 | 1 | 1 | 0 | 0 | 0 |
| Scholar | 0 | 0 | 1 | 1 | 0 | 0 |
| Reviewer | 0 | 0 | 1 | 0 | 1 | 0 |
| Meditator | 0 | 0 | 0 | 1 | 1 | 1 |
| Researcher | 0 | 0 | 1 | 1 | 1 | 0 |
| Psychologist | 1 | 1 | 1 | 1 | 1 | 0 |
| Occultist | 0 | 0 | 0 | 0 | 0 | 1 |

specified for every pair of identities. The second model is based on the idea that certain classes of features serve as the "building blocks" for the various identities. Thus, any given identity is a composite of one or more building blocks. As a consequence, the overlap between any two identities in the model is not restricted to superset-subset, equivalence, and disjunction, although these basic relations still hold among subgroups of identities.

In the first model, the three relations yield a hierarchical organization, with the most superordinate identities at the top and disjunctive relationships forming different branchings of the hierarchy. This model parallels a hierarchical model proposed for person perception (Gara & Rosenberg, 1979). The most superordinate identity, when it exists in a given domain (e.g., work, recreation, personal relationships), is defined as a *major identity*. There can be more than one major identity in a person's belief system: For example, a major identity in the work domain and another major identity in the family domain.

Figure 4.1A is an example of the application of this model to the data in Table 4.1 (De Boeck, 1983; Rosenberg, 1982). The figure shows Psychologist as the major identity, Occultist as disjunctive with Psychologist, and various subidentities of Psychologist. One can imagine a more complete structure formed by including nonprofessional identities; for instance, personal relationships and their features.

In the second model, certain features of identity are assumed to be organized into discrete classes, the basic "self-categories" of identity structure. An identity is a combination of one or more of these basic categories. The second model has more parameters than the first. In fact, the first model is a special case of the second and, hence, more parsimonious. Nevertheless, most of our recent thinking centers on the building-block model because it frames structure in terms of basic categories of features rather than in terms of identities. These basic categories presumably correspond to the less mutable characterological aspects of personality.

Figure 4.1B exemplifies the building-block model for the hypothetical psychologist; that is, it is based on the matrix in Table 4.1. Each basic category in Figure 4.1B is represented by the features shown in parentheses. Some basic categories have clear identity exemplars; other categories do not. For example, Undergraduate Teacher is the exemplar of the leftmost basic category in the figure, which consists of Witty and Extroverted. On the other hand, the category consisting of Curious and Speculative contains no identity exemplars, although this category is important in forming other identities, such as Researcher, Psychologist, and Meditator. As in the structural model exemplified in Figure 4.1A, Psychologist is the most superordinate or major identity in Figure 4.1B, and Occultist is the only identity disjunctively related to Psychologist.

In constructing this model, we have made use of the concept of category exemplar, which is similar to the notion of prototype in conceptualizations of person perception (Cantor & Mischel, 1979), situation perception (Cantor, Mischel, & Schwartz, 1982), and self-perception (Rogers, Kuiper, & Kirker, 1977). Some readers may also recognize that the building block model is formally analogous to ones proposed for cognitive categories (Rosch, 1978). However, self-categories may not have the same psychological status as object categories—the former are typically more affectively charged and less culturally shared. (See also McAdams, this volume.)

We now turn to the functional relations between identities and their overt enactments. We assume that an identity serves to select and filter specific situations or settings for its enactment. The selection of identity enactments does not necessarily require conscious deliberation but may instead involve features directly linked to a repertoire of habits. For example, a person who identities himself or herself as a "traditional"

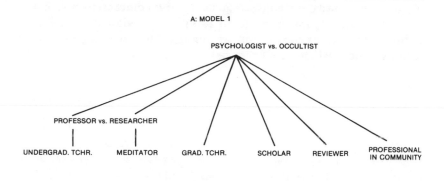

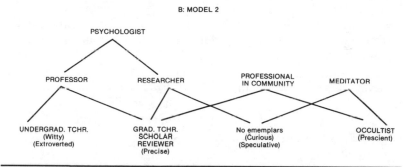

Figure 4.1   Structural representations of hypothetical academic psychologist.

corporate executive may routinely and without thinking wear conservative suits and adopt a certain frame of mind and posture for the office. On the other hand, identities can also be accessed or constructed from the "bottom up": When a person dresses up for the evening in tight jeans, open shirt, high heels, heavy cologne or perfume, she or he begins to feel like a "night self," whether or not this identity is otherwise elaborated. Advertising is often predicated on selling the tangible props of certain identities, and a consumer often buys such products—many of which end up in the closet or attic—to construct such identities.

When fixed routines develop in identity enactment, individuals may "break out" of them by creating new enactments. If we assume that features of identity serve as blueprints for action (Carver, 1979; Mancuso & Ceely, 1980; Martindale, 1980), then new enactments for an identity can be derived by recruiting features from other identities and possibly dismissing features from the identity in question. However, the capacity in identity structure to generate new combinations of basic categories and their associated features is determined to some extent by the degree of identity elaboration, an important nomothetic property of identity structure that we take up next.

## Elaboration and Contrast
## in Personal Identity

The elaboration of an identity refers to the full set of ways in which an identity is experienced and enacted. Identities vary considerably in the degree to which they are elaborated. One index of elaboration is the level of the identity in the hierarchy. The validity of this index is based on the assumption that a superset-subset relation in the structure implies a functional relation as well. Thus, Psychologist (in Figure 4.1) is highly elaborated in that it subsumes a number of other identities and is dependent on some of these subidentities for its meaning to the person and for its enactment. Another index of elaboration is the number of features associated with the identity. This index can be different from the level in the hierarchy, in that an identity of low prominence may have many features. Both of these indices of elaboration are assumed to be related to the number and diversity of the enactments associated with an identity. (See also Stryker & Serpe, 1982a).

Another important nomothetic property of identity structure and function is *contrast*. In the first model, contrast is represented among the identities themselves, and is reflected in the structure by certain disjunctive or partially disjunctive relations, although a disjunctive relation does not by itself indicate contrast. A general evaluative dimension typically underlies a major identity and its contrast.

The algorithm used to produce Figure 4.1A identified two contrasts: Psychologist versus Occultist and Professor versus Researcher. A major identity is usually more elaborated than its contrast; in the example, Psychologist subsumes several identities, whereas its contrast, Occultist, subsumes no other identities. Moreover, an identity is fully explicated when its contrast is also specified. For example, Psychologist means something different in the person's identity structure when its contrast is Occultist than when its contrast is Business Executive.

In the second model (Figure 4.1B), the notion of contrast is in general more applicable to the basic self-categories than it is to the identities themselves. The most superordinate contrast among the categories usually aligns them along nonorthogonal evaluative dimensions, each dimension referring to specific content such as competence, sociability, potency (Kim & Rosenberg, 1980). Typically, it is the case that positive categories are more elaborated than negative ones, possibly because people tend to avoid proliferating and connecting enactments to negative identities. Even when this is not the case, a major identity is highly elaborated in that it subsumes many of the basic self-categories in a given content domain.

Elaboration and contrast are critical properties of identity function and dysfunction. An event in one's life takes on crisis proportions to the extent that it disrupts the more superordinate identities in a person's structure. Given that a person's identities can be experienced as compelling realities, the loss or threat of loss of superordinate identities can be experienced by the individual as endangering those realities as well as threatening his or her very sense of continuity. What follows are our current conjectures on likely responses to loss or threat of loss from the standpoint of our identity theory.

One response is to shift to another superordinate identity. If the individual has several major identities—for example, a professional identity, a family identity, and a hobby—the disruption of one still permits a shift to and emphasis of another, if only for a transitional period of time. This kind of response allows the individual to maintain some elaborated sense of self while resolving the crisis.

If the person has only one major identity, the disruption of that identity can be a strong threat to the person's sense of reality. If the disruption persists, the person may shift to the contrasting identity. The reasoning involved here is similar to Kelly's (1955): "When he is under pressure, he is not likely to develop new channels [identities]; instead he will tend to reverse himself along the dimensional lines which have already been established" (p. 128). If the contrast is unelaborated, a less conceptually organized mode of experience will predominate, making it difficult for the person to find validation and social support during the crisis (Gara, Rosenberg, & Cohen, 1984).

Another kind of response to the disruption of a major identity, or any elaborated identity, is suggested by Zurcher's (1977) recent findings. He found that college students are more likely now than in the past to define themselves in terms of "statements which are abstract enough to transcend specific social situations" (p. 46)—in our terms, features of basic self-categories—rather than in terms of "positions which depend upon performance in defined social contexts for their establishment and maintenance" (p. 45). Thus, for individuals in contemporary American society, a likely response to a disruption of an elaborated identity is to regroup features of basic categories into a new identity and to do so "habitually"; that is, to have an identity structure more oriented to change than to stability. If true, this "mutable self" represents an important cultural shift in the nature of identity.

Zurcher's findings point up the importance of not detaching identity structure and function from the cultural context in which they are embedded. That is, the cultural support for fixed identities may be less secure now than in the past. Identities are also embedded in a person's interpersonal relationships and require validation from an actual or imagined audience (Goffman, 1959), with the patterning of interactions between actor and audience working not only to validate identity, but to shape it as well. In addition, actors and their targeted audiences are frequently in the process of negotiating with one another about which identities will be assumed by whom during any given interaction (Swann, 1984).

## METHODOLOGICAL APPROACHES AND ISSUES

### Data Gathering

Given the variety of ways in which individuals describe their personal identities, data-gathering methods should include a free-response option. Personality and social psychologists are becoming increasingly aware of the importance of this option. (See, for example, Gordon, 1968; Hastorf, Richardson, & Dornbusch, 1958; Kelly, 1955; Kim & Rosenberg, 1980; Rosenberg, 1977; and Zavalloni, 1971, 1975.)

The free-response method most widely used in the study of self-concept and identity is one in which people are asked to respond to the question "Who am I?" with a number of brief answers. Variations exist both in the wording of the prompt (e.g., "Who are you?," "Tell us about yourself") and in the constraints placed on the answers (Wylie, 1974).

One of the major concerns with the "Who am I?" instrument is that it may yield superficial responses; that is, it may encourage respondents to list items that come readily to mind rather than the more important, "deeper" aspects of identity and the negative or embarrassing components that tend to be suppressed. Stated more generally, this is a concern about the comprehensiveness of the set of identities given in response to the "Who am I?" instrument. This limitation, if true, may also be due partly to the brief and superficial relationship usually established between researchers and subjects.

The methods we use to increase the comprehensiveness of the identities obtained combine both open-ended and more structured approaches, and parallel methods well established in the study of person perception (Gara & Rosenberg, 1979; Rosenberg, 1977). In the application of these methods to the study of identity, people are asked to describe, in their own terms, each of from 20 to 50 personal identities, one at a time, and to list as exhaustively as possible the characteristics and feelings (features) associated with each of these. They are asked to formulate identity features in the form of discrete units, but not necessarily single words; while doing this, they cumulate a feature list—that is, when a person uses a feature to describe one identity, he or she is asked to judge the presence of this feature for *all* his or her identities.

These various tasks—listing identities, listing features, and judging the presence of each feature in each identity—require several hours to complete and are divided into several sittings. The result is an identities X features matrix for the person, Table 4.1 being a miniature example. The structural analysis of this matrix provides a representation of the person's identity structure. The high redundancy in the protocol that we obtain from a person guards against the possibility that such structural representations will be unduly influenced by random responding due to occasional boredom, fatigue, or inattention.

An important methodological issue arises in one of the tasks described above: the elicitation of a person's multiple identities. Because identities are assumed to be tagged with a potpourri of concepts such as the person's physical and psychological traits ("handsome person," "smart person"), activities and habits ("gourmet cook," "heavy smoker"), achievements ("college graduate"), and ideals or fantasies ("I am going to be a great artist"), there are few empirical or theoretical guidelines to assure the researcher that the person's multiplicity has been adequately represented. Not to be neglected as a part of this potpourri are the negative identities: roles, traits, habits, and emotional ties with certain people that a person would like to get rid of, stop, or break, but cannot seem to. The candor required of a person to reveal these negative identities requires, in turn, considerable care on the part of the researcher in creating a safe and confidential relationship.

There are several ways of eliciting identities. One is a structured interview in which a person is guided to examine several sources of identity such as religious affiliation, kinship roles (e.g., sister, daughter), occupational roles, group memberships (e.g., union member), intellectual concerns (e.g., reader), activities (e.g., hiking), and possessions (e.g., car owner) (see Gordon, 1968). The person is also guided in exploring important relationships, such as relationships with lovers, friends, co-workers, relatives, and so on (Gara & Rosenberg, 1979). Also included in the interview is a parallel coverage of the negative (disliked) identities. And, finally, the person is encouraged to add identities, liked or disliked, that are not explicitly covered by the various categories in the structured interview.

During the course of the interview, a person sometimes labels an identity or a set of related identities with a personality characteristic, for example, "I am a curious person" (Zurcher, 1977). In our framework, the person is probably referring to a key feature in a basic self-category. In line with this framework, a personality trait is added to the person's feature list and not to the list of identities. At this point an option is to ask the person to articulate, if possible, another identity associated with the feature and not previously mentioned. For example, "I am a curious person" may describe the person's experience in an identity such as Meditator.

When the range of identities in a given population becomes relatively well-known, it is often possible to streamline identity elicitation considerably by narrowing the focus to the known range. In some instances one can bypass the interview entirely by designing a structured questionnaire that covers the range of identity domains but is still open-ended.

There are several advantages to the various free-response tasks described above. First, they are naturalistic in the sense that aspects of self are simply described in everyday terms. Second, although identity structure is implicit in these descriptions and can be extracted via structural analyses, the person is unlikely to be completely aware of this structure, if asked directly. Third, because the person is *never* asked to arrange identities in ways that reflect an assessment of identity structure, distortions such as those designed to create a socially desirable impression are excluded from the method. For example, if asked *directly*, a person might place a relatively minor identity in a super-ordinate position in the structure, simply because that particular identity is socially desirable. Social desirability effects can still occur, of course, in the features that a person selects to describe identities. To reduce these effects, the methods deliberately call for negative identities, which, in turn, elicit socially undesirable features.

The representation of an identity structure can often be made more complete by eliciting descriptions of other people in the individual's life and including these descriptions as additional rows in the matrix. Other people personify elaborated and unelaborated contrasts of self that the person cannot readily articulate as identities (Zavalloni, 1975). An example of the value of including others in the structure will be presented later in this chapter, in an analysis of Thomas Wolfe. This analysis also illustrates the use of naturalistic materials as a data source for the study of identity.

## Structural Representations

One approach to extracting structure from an identities X features matrix involves the use of clustering or multidimensional scaling (Rosenberg, 1977; Rosenberg & Sedlak, 1972a, 1972b). Unfortunately, superset/subset relations *among identities* are not represented by hierarchical clustering and multidimensional scaling methods, although these methods may be adequate for portraying basic relations among the features of identities.

A study by Gara and Rosenberg (1979) demonstrated the feasibility and validity of applying set-theoretical concepts to the structural analysis of belief systems about self and others. Since that study, several more powerful and sophisticated algorithms have been developed by DeBoeck (1983) within a set-theoretical framework. Applied to identity data, the first of these represents one or more identities as supersets of others, based on the pattern of feature sharing in the two-way matrix. This algorithm also identifies major and minor identity contrasts and thus can be used to represent input data in terms of the model of identity structure exemplified in Figure 4.1A. In fact, the structure shown in the figure was derived from the application of this algorithm to the two-way matrix in Table 4.1.

A second set of algorithms developed by DeBoeck (1983) represents identity data in terms of the building block model. Boolean factor analysis (Mickey, Mundle, & Engelman, 1983) is still another algorithm for this model. All these algorithms optimize the number and combination of basic categories to form an identity structure. Output from those algorithms includes two goodness-of-fit measures, one for each identity separately and one for the overall structural representation. The former measure is used to index the extent to which a given identity is an exemplar of its associated basic or superordinate category. Not included, but currently under development (P. DeBoeck, personal communication, September 14, 1984) in the output of the Boolean factor analysis, is an explicit identification of contrasts.

In order to obtain more interpretable output, we typically constrain the Boolean analysis with an initial configuration. This initial configuration is obtained by performing a hierarchical clustering of the features based on their pattern of co-occurrence in the identities (see Rosenberg, 1977, for details on the co-occurrence measure and clustering analysis), and then choosing the level of the hierarchical tree that results in $n$ nonoverlapping clusters of the features, where $n$ is the number of basic categories desired in the Boolean output configuration. Figure 4.1B is based on an application of this "constrained" Boolean factor analysis. Identity structures discussed in the next section are also based on this analysis.

## APPLICATIONS

### A Sample of Professional Women

Previous applications of these methods by us and by some of our colleagues (Corijn, 1982; De Boeck & Corijn, 1982) to samples of college students demonstrated the feasibility of the methods for a population with which we are familiar and one that is accustomed to participating in psychology experiments. The necessity for going beyond college students—even though their identity structure and functioning can be very illuminating about process—is obvious. We have, in fact, also begun empirical work on schizophrenic patients, not only to demonstrate the general applicability of the methods but also to understand the role of identity in the schizophrenic process and in other forms of psychopathology (Gara et al., 1984).

An in-depth study of professional women provided still another opportunity to examine the applicability of these methods in a population that had evolved rather complex identity structures (Joseph, 1985). For purposes of this chapter, we will limit ourselves to the structural aspects of the results. A sample of 12 volunteers was recruited from an organization whose membership consists almost exclusively of women scholars. The organization, which is located in a university community, is an active forum for intellectual exchange among its members on a wide variety of topics. In general, the women in the organization have maintained an active involvement in their discipline from college days and have also married and raised a family; a minority have developed a full-time career in academia, industry, or consulting, and some hold part-time appointments.

The women in the sample are representative of the total membership in age, education, professional interests, and marital status. The women in the sample range from 36 to 60 years of age; ten have a Ph.D. and two an M.A. degree, almost evenly split between the social sciences and humanities; all have one or more children. A semistructured interview was used to obtain their identities and the features associated with each of them, resulting in features X identities matrix for each woman. Each two-way matrix was subjected to a constrained Boolean factor analysis in order to obtain an identity structure for each woman.

The identity structures of two of the women are shown in Figure 4.2. In order to assure complete anonymity, some of the identities have been relabeled with more general terms than those used by the women themselves: for example, identity labels such as "psychologist," "sociologist," and "historian" are replaced in the figure with "professional title"; unwanted identities such as "bad girl" and "overeater" with "negative identity"; and so on. The structures depicted in Figure 4.2 are representative of the sample in both the types of identities listed and described and the variation among the women in the content of their superordinate identities. The two structures exemplify some of the variation in identity organization; woman F does not have any overarching identities, for example, whereas woman G does, in the professional domain.

After completing their descriptions of each of their identities, the women were asked to judge the importance of each identity in their lives. Two seven-point scales were used to assess importance, one direct and the other somewhat indirect. The direct question was "How important is this identity to you?"; the indirect, "If you were to wake up one morning and find that this identity had been taken away or lost its significance, to what extent would your life be affected?" (Hermans, 1976, p. 110).

These subjective ratings, combined with the hierarchical representation of a person's identity structure, provide the first opportunity to test empirically the positive, monotone relationship hypothesized by a number of writers (see the introduction) between subjective importance and prominence in the identity hierarchy. The obtained relationship is summarized in Figure 4.3 for each of the 12 women, identified in the figure as A through L. For either set of importance ratings, the

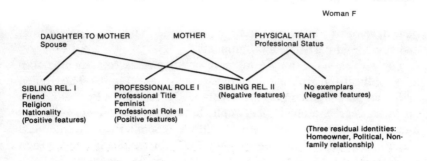

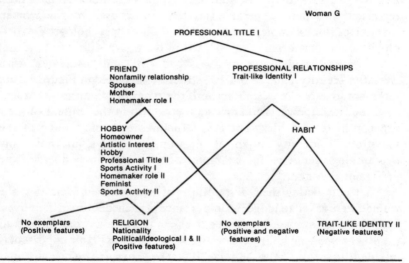

Figure 4.2  Identity structure of two professional women. The best exemplar in a
          group of identities is shown in all capital letters. Remaining identities in
          a group are listed in descending order of inclusiveness.

relationship is clearly present for the majority of women, and provides
an empirical verification of the hypothesized relationship.

One might view this finding as a validation of the empirical and
analytic methods that we are developing for obtaining a person's
identity structure. Conversely, one could also view the hierarchical

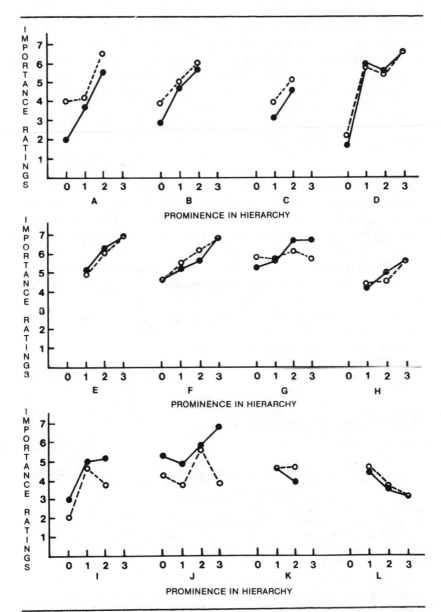

Figure 4.3 Relation between subjective importance and prominence in the hierarchy. Dotted lines are ratings from direct question and solid lines are ratings from indirect question. Women in the sample are referred to as A, B, . . . L.

structure, which is richer in information and theoretical underpinning, as a context for understanding subjective judgments of importance. Thus, where the relationship in Figure 4.3 is weak or, in two cases (K and L) slightly reversed, our inclination is to look to factors other than prominence that might affect subjective judgments of importance. We know from the interviews that women K and L are undergoing a reexamination of their professional identities, which are prominent in their hierarchies; and as a consequence, they may have started discounting the importance of these identities—a process that decreases the positive relationship between subjective importance and prominence. The identity structure seems much less vulnerable in the short run to such discounting of a major identity. We conjecture that if these women continue to discount the importance of their major identity, they have much "psychological work" to do to dimish the structural prominence of a highly elaborated identity.

The indirect question about "possible loss" appears to be as good as, and in some cases superior to, the direct question about "importance" in yielding a positive relationship between subjective importance and prominence. After the interview each woman also rated each of her identities on a satisfaction scale. The correlation within subjects between the satisfaction rating and the direct rating of importance is somewhat greater than that between satisfaction and the indirect rating, and may reflect, in part, a confounding by some people of direct importance judgments with satisfaction. Moreover, the relationships between satisfaction and prominence varies considerably for the different women, showing that the most satisfying identities are not necessarily the most prominent.

## Identity Development: A Naturalistic Study

We now turn to the use of naturalistic data such as diaries, ordinary conversation, letters, and literary material to study identity. Here, the *selection* of an appropriate corpus substitutes for the laboratory-based self-description methods discussed earlier. However, the analytic tools we have described for representing structure are applicable to naturalistic materials, and the theory continues to serve as an orienting framework for extracting the relevant data from such material and for understanding the results.

A study of the autobiographical novel, *Look Homeward, Angel (LHA)* by Thomas Wolfe (1929), illustrates the application of the theory and structural analyses to naturalistic materials. *LHA* describes Wolfe's childhood and adolescence, the members of his family, and many others in the community in which he grew up—most of them readily identifiable even with their fictional aliases. The book was written when Wolfe was in his late twenties. Wolfe's strong determination to tell the story of his early life as he experienced it (Kennedy, 1962), his dedication to recovering these experiences by scribbling a voluminous chronology of his early life before writing *LHA*, and his stream-of-consciousness writing style all support the characterization of *LHA* as a highly personal document. (Would that it were feasible to recreate such conditions in a sample of subjects!)

Wolfe's extensive descriptions of his childhood and adolescence make it possible to represent his identity development within a hierarchical structure. This was done by treating, as separate selves, Wolfe's description of himself at each of five chronological periods: 0-2, 3-5, 6-11, 12-15, 16-early 20s. Wolfe wrote the book in a chronological order and divided it into three parts; our last two chronological periods correspond to Parts II and III, respectively. Part I covers his life from birth through age 11, which we further partitioned into 0-2, 3-5, and 6-11.

Every term or phrase in *LHA* that referred to a stable characteristic of a person or age-related self was recorded verbatim and listed according to the character or self to whom it was attributed. The terms and phrases extracted from *LHA* were grouped into trait categories (features) that preserved Wolfe's linguistic categories, following rules developed in a previous study of Theodore Dreiser (Rosenberg & Jones, 1972). In forming these traits categories, no judgments were made about the possible synonymity of trait terms with different morphemes; for example, *pretty* and *beautiful* were treated as two different categories. On the other hand, a range of qualification was permitted within a category; for example, *awkward, awkward bulk of puberty,* and *awkward muscles* were assigned to the same trait category, *awkward.*

A sample of 91 high-frequency trait categories was selected for the structural analyses. Wolfe's attributions of these traits variously to characters and selves in *LHA* were summarized by us in a matrix of persons and selves (rows) by trait categories (columns), with a cell entry of one when any given person or self was described by an instance of any given trait category, and zero otherwise. Formally, this is the same kind of matrix as the one shown in Table 4.1 for the academic psychologist, and as such lends itself to the same structural analyses.

A constrained Boolean analysis that yielded eight factors was selected as the most interpretable solution. The traits associated with each factor

(A through H) are listed at the bottom of Figure 4.4. There are also traits associated with certain combinations of factors. These traits are listed with the character or characters who are the best exemplars of them. Thus, FATHER is the best exemplar of *confused life, sad, savage*; MABEL is the best exemplar of *humor(ous), vitality*; and so on. Such traits are also associated with any character who is a subset of the named character. For example *humor(ous)* and *vitality* are associated with Fred, Mrs. Roberts, and a minor character because they are subsets of Mabel (as shown in the lower half of the structure). Traits with no discernible pattern of attribution among characters are listed as RESIDUAL in Figure 4.4.

The structure shown in Figure 4.4 does not include Wolfe's infancy period (age 0-2), in which he described himself primarily with a few unique traits (e.g., "shiny," "tiny acorn," "imp") and not in terms of any of the basic clusters in the figure—understandable for someone describing his infancy. *LHA* does not contain explicit descriptions of each of Wolfe's multiple identities in any given time period but the structure does identify the basic building blocks of each time period.

The figure shows that in characterizing his preadolescent development, Wolfe emphasizes one cluster of traits at 3-5 and another at 6-11. It is in the adolescent period that he first attributes the main family cluster, category B, *alone*, and so forth, to himself. During this entire period (ages 3-15) he is always like his father (a subset) and only somewhat like his mother. It is only in the postadolescent period that his identity shifts away from the father to some degree, both in the traits he sees in his father and not in himself and in traits he sees in himself and not in his father. Also interesting is the increasing superordinancy of self with age: A younger self is generally subsumed by an older self. This result is a consequence of the way he described himself and not an artifact of the analysis.

The figure also strongly suggests a contrast between Thomas (self), his father, Ben, and other members of the family. Although there is considerable overlap among family members, Mabel and Fred are not characterized by category B, *alone*, and so on, but do share category E, *kind*, not attributed to any of the other family members. Also, the mother has a set of traits not shared by Thomas or any other member of the family.

A striking feature of the structure extracted from *LHA* is that there are almost no nonfamily characters in the structure, even for the basic

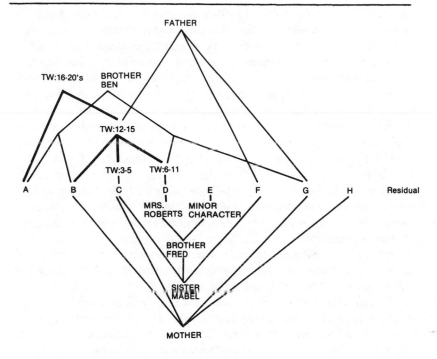

TRAITS IN EACH CATEGORY

A: bitter; dark (complexion); thin face
B: alone; desperate; dark fantasies; long (body frame); lonely; life of pain; proud; sensual; shame; stranger
C: big (body frame); brooding; desires (various); fantasized; fear(ful); (filled with) terror
D: nervous; passion(ate); thin; wild
E: kind
F: big (body parts); drank; eager; needs (various); sensitive; straight (body frame); vulgar
G: grey eyes; old; red (complexion); sallow; shaven; small eyes; yellow (complexion)
H: black hair; bright; heavy (build); loose lips; scarred; scotch; triumphant

FATHER: confused life; sad; savage. FATHER AND MOTHER: intense; hunger (various).

MABEL: humor(ous); vitality. BEN: lost; powerful (strength); sick; white(complexion).

FAMILY TRAITS WITH NO SPECIFIC FAMILY EXEMPLAR: gaunt; liked money; superstitious; quiet; generous; mad(ness); strange; hard.

RESIDUAL: gentle; soft; elegant; shy; beautiful; young; wise; country manner; (plus 19 physical trait categories)

**Figure 4.4   Identity structure of Thomas Wolfe as extracted from *Look Homeward, Angel*.**

factors. Almost all of the nonfamily characters and their associated sets of traits were represented as "Residuals." That is, Wolfe created no clear trait *patterns* in his description of most of the characters in *LHA*. However, according to a multidimensional scaling of the *traits*, the most salient dimension—that is, the superordinate contrast—is family versus nonfamily traits. This contrast is highly asymmetric in elaboration and one pole is highly fragmented. The asymmetric elaboration is reflected in the fact that nonfamily traits are scattered over a large number of characters, whereas the family trait clusters are concentrated on a few people and are intricately related in the structure. Traits ascribed to nonfamily characters refer primarily to physical features, whereas the family traits include a large proportion of psychological traits. Moreover, the few psychological traits attributed to nonfamily, such as *gentle, soft, elegant*, and *shy*, also contrast in content with the more disturbing family traits.

As we have already noted in the section on theory, asymmetric elaboration of contrasts is probably not an unusual feature of identity organization. What is noteworthy about *LHA* is that the degree of elaboration corresponds so closely to a family-nonfamily distinction. Such a close correspondence between an asymmetrically elaborated contrast and the relationship to the person described would seem to have important implications for the way Wolfe related to people. In particular, it fits with the fact that he rarely developed close relationships during his adult life, in spite of the numerous and diverse social contacts available to him when *LHA* catapulted him into fame.

Snyder (1971), in his psychobiography of Wolfe, traced Wolfe's self-imposed social isolation to early childhood when his mother divided the family household by buying a boarding house and moving into it with Thomas and his brother Ben, leaving his father and sister Mabel in the family home. Snyder also cited Wolfe's own acknowledged discomfort with people, as expressed in his numerous letters. For example, he wrote to Mabel in 1933: "The habit of loneliness, once formed, grows on a man from year to year and he wanders across the face of the earth and has no home and is an exile, and he is never able to break out of the prison of his own loneliness again, no matter how much he wants to" (Nowell, 1956, p. 371). (The compelling reality of an elaborated major identity!) Snyder (1971) also remarked, in this context, that "neither of his parents was competent enough socially to teach Tom the good manners and etiquette which might lead to easy social relationships" (p.

72). Note that these are the kind of traits Wolfe attributed to nonfamily members—the unelaborated side of himself. Synder's analysis and Wolfe's own explanation of his loneliness are very much in accord with the literature on the relation between childhood experiences and adult loneliness (Shaver & Rubenstein, 1980).

## CRITIQUE AND IMPLICATIONS

The empirical applications described in the previous section are illustrative of the window that the theory and methodology can provide for observing, representing, and interpreting basic characteristics of identity structure. Further theoretical and methodological developments are proceeding apace with substantive studies of the phenomena. Although this is not the place to dwell in detail on these developments, certain general directions can be outlined.

Concerning methodology, the study of Wolfe has demonstrated the value of including descriptions of other people as well as self for a more comprehensive picture of identity structure than that obtained from self-description alone. That is, there are certain categories that may be exemplified by other people ("alters") and these categories may not be psychologically accessible to, or acknowledged by, the person in the context of self-description, because the categories are unelaborated, extremely negative, or represent identity ideals. The representation of identity structure with a person's view of self and others is a special case of a commonplace notion in the study of personality through literature. That is, the literary work as a whole, not just the author's characterization of the hero or self, represents the personality of the author. Such a representation is also consonant with a social psychological approach to self, and in the case of Wolfe's fictionalized autobiography, displays the development of his "socius" in the context of family and community.

Comprehensive pictures of a person's identity structure may or may not be necessary, depending on the nature of the substantive research question. Where it is necessary, laboratory-based free-response methods are available for the simultaneous study of self-perception and the perception of others. Relative to naturalistic materials as a data source, laboratory-based methods are efficient, and the fidelity with which they portray a person's identity structure depends on the person's willingness to go beyond superficial descriptions of self and others. The same consideration applies in the selection of naturalistic materials, that is, a consideration about the commitment of the writer or speaker to express experience deeply and in detail and how the medium, such as literary form, facilitates and hinders this expression. No data source is perfect!

Coupled with the creation or selection of a corpus of data is the development and selection of analytic methods for representing structure. The algorithms now available are either of recent development or of recent application to this domain. Future empirical application will undoubtedly suggest certain refinements by revealing more of what the algorithms are and are not doing and perhaps inspire the development of new, more powerful algorithms. It would seem inappropriate at this point to fixate on any one or two algorithms, not only because they may have shortcomings, but because theoretical insights may render them obsolete. Also, a structural algorithm, like any analytic and statistical tool, conceals as well as reveals. Intimacy with the data, from several vantage points, serves as a way of separating the phenomenon (here, personal identity) from a particular methodology. Finally, structural representation hardens category boundaries that are perhaps more fuzzy in an organically functioning self.

In our outline of a theory of identity structure and function, we limited our discussion of the nomothetic properties of an identity primarily to two structurally derived properties: prominence and elaboration. These two properties are defined in terms of the location of an identity in the overall structure, although elaboration also refers to the enactments associated with an identity. There are other culturally important nomothetic properties that are not structural but subjective, such as satisfaction and commitment. Still other subjective properties that can be associated with individual identities are achievement, crisis, and moratorium; and with pairs of identities, conflict.

Investigators have, with little exception, measured these nomothetic features of identity as global features of individuals. Such global measures are of interest because of their potential value for assessing a person's general functioning. A theory of personal identity as a multiplicity suggests, however, that although global measures may have heuristic value, their theoretical value is questionable and even misleading. At any given time in one's life, some identities may be satisfying and others not; some may be in crisis whereas others are quite stable; some identities may dominate in the thoughts and actions of a person although they are not hierarchically the most prominent; and so on.

The idea of associating certain nomothetic properties with each identity opens up a line of research on the psychological relations among these properties at the individual level. The possibilities for discovering these psychological relations and their connection with an individual's identity structure and functioning are at hand, and such discovery would put the assessment of the general functioning of a person on a sounder theoretical footing.

The general approach advocated here for the study of identity may also find use in the study of personality generally. Supplanting general trait theory would be a more differentiated view of the person, perhaps in terms of identities. In an identity framework, the issue of behavioral ("situational") consistency, for example, might be resolved by the notion that any given identity can subsume a wide variety of enactments, even in the same situation, and that the same "situation" may be the locus for enactment of different identities at different times. Extreme behavioral consistency would actually seem to imply a poorly elaborated or severely limiting identity (structure).

Finally, we turn to the issue of unity versus multiplicity of self. To a great extent, it is an inherited question stripped of its historical context, a vestige of the way Locke and his successors in philosophy framed the concept of self and identity. Within our theoretical framework, we view the identity structure as a whole as the unity of self, and would not look to just the superordinate identity as the source of unity—at unity as an "individual difference variable" measured perhaps in terms of the fragmentation of identity structure—and certainly not to the continuity of consciousness—the last being a three-century regression. This is not to underestimate the psychological importance of these various features of identity structure and functioning, or of a person's "sense of identity," an experience characterized by Erikson (1968), for example, as "a *subjective sense* of an *invigorating sameness* and *continuity*" (p. 19). However, it would be a mistake to confuse a phenomenological sense of unity with the structural and functional features of self that create an organizational unity. Phenomenologically, but not formally, it may seem paradoxical that a person's view of people, groups, or whatever else he or she rejects or does not "identify with" is an aspect of self and as such participates in the organizational unity of self; that is, that the dichotomy is essential to the unity. Even more paradoxical perhaps is the notion that the more intense the rejection of the "not me," the more evident it is that the "not me" is part of the "me."

This absolute determinability of our mind by abstractions is one of the cardinal facts in our human constitution. Polarizing and magnetizing us as they do, we turn towards them and from them, we seek them, hold them, hate them, bless them, just as if they were so many concrete beings. And beings they are, beings as real in the realm they inhabit as changing things of sense are in the realm of space. (James, 1902/1958)

# REFERENCES

Baldwin, J. M. (1897). *Social and ethical interpretations in mental development.* New York: Macmillan.

Cantor, N., & Mischel, W. (1979). Prototypes in person perception. In L. Berkowitz (Ed.), *Advances in experimental social psychology* (Vol. 12). New York: Academic.

Cantor, N., Mischel, W., & Schwartz, J. C. (1982). A prototype analysis of psychological situations. *Cognitive Psychology, 14,* 45-57.

Carver, C. S. (1979). A cybernetic model of self-attention processes. *Journal of Personality and Social Psychology, 37,* 1251-1281.

Cooley, C. H. (1902). *Human nature and the social order.* New York: Scribners.

Corijn, M. (1982). *Structuring self-experience: Implicit self theory.* Paper presented at the European Conference on Personality, Tilburg, The Netherlands.

D'Andrade, R. G. (1976). A propositional analysis of U.S. American beliefs about illness. In K. H. Basso & H. A. Selby (Eds.), *Meaning in anthropology* (pp. 155-180). Albuquerque: University of New Mexico Press.

DeBoeck, P. (1983, July). *Prototype analysis.* Paper presented at the joint meeting of the Classification and Pyschometric Societies, Jouy-en-josas, France.

DeBoeck, P., & Corijn, M. (1982). Zelfbeleving. *De Psycoloog, 18,* 604-610.

Erikson, E. H. (1968). *Identity: Youth and crisis.* New York: Norton.

Gara, M. A., & Rosenberg, S. (1979). The identification of persons as supersets and subsets in free-response personality descriptions. *Journal of Personality and Social Psychology, 37,* 2161-2170.

Gara, M. A., Rosenberg, S., & Cohen, B. D. (1984). *Personal identity and the schizophrenic process: An integration.* Unpublished manuscript submitted for publication.

Gergen, K. J. (1971). *The concept of self.* New York: Holt.

Goffman, E. (1959). *The presentation of self in everyday life.* Garden City, NY: Doubleday.

Gordon, C. (1968). Self-conceptions: Configurations of content. In C. Gordon & K. J. Gergen (Eds.), *The self in social interaction* (pp. 115-136). New York: John Wiley.

Hastorf, A. H., Richardson, S. A., & Dornbusch, S. M. (1958). The problem of relevance in the study of person perception. In R. Tagiuri & L. Petrullo (Eds.), *Person perception and interpersonal behavior* (pp. 54-62). Stanford: Stanford University Press.

Hermans, H. J. (1976). *Value areas and their development.* Amsterdam: Swets & Zeitlinger.

James, W. (1890). *The principles of psychology.* New York: Holt.

James, W. (1958). *The varieties of religious experience.* New York: New American Library. (Original work published 1902)

Joseph, C. (1985). *Identity patterns of professional women.* Unpublished master's thesis. Rutgers University, New Brunswick, NJ

Kelly, G. A. (1955). *The psychology of personal constructs.* New York: Norton.

Kennedy, R. (1962). *The window of memory: The literary career of Thomas Wolfe.* Chapel Hill: University of North Carolina Press.

Kihlstrom, J. F., & Cantor, N. (1983). Mental representations of the self. In L. Berkowitz (Ed.), *Advances in experimental social psychology* (Vol. 15). New York: Academic.

Kim, M. P., & Rosenberg, S. (1980). Comparison of two structural models of implicit personality theory. *Journal of Personality and Social Psychology, 38,* 375-389.

Locke, J. (1959). *An essay concerning human understanding.* New York: Dover. (Original work published 1694)

Mair, J.M.M. (1977). The community of self. In D. Bannister (Ed.), *New perspectives in personal construct theory* (pp. 125-149). London: Academic.

Mancuso, J. C., & Ceely, S. G. (1980). The self as memory processing. *Cognitive Therapy and Research, 4,* 1-25.

Martindale, C. (1980). Subselves: The internal representation of situational and personal dispositions. In L. Wheeler (Ed.), *Review of personality and social psychology* (Vol. 1, pp. 193-218). Beverly Hills, CA: Sage.

McCall, G. J., & Simmons, J. L. (1966). *Identities and interactions.* New York: Free Press.

Mead, G. H. (1934). *Mind, self, and society.* Chicago: University of Chicago Press.

Mickey, M. R., Mundle, P., & Engelman, L. (1983). Boolean factor analysis. In W. J. Dixon (Ed.), *BMDP statistical software.* Berkeley: University of California Press.

Nowell, E. (Ed.) (1956). *The letters of Thomas Wolfe.* New York: Scribners.

Rogers, T. B., Kuiper, N. A., & Kirker, W. S. (1977). Self-reference and the encoding of personal information. *Journal of Personality and Social Psychology, 35,* 677-688.

Rosch, E. (1978). Principles of categorization. In E. Rosch & B. B. Lloyd (Eds.), *Cognition and categorization* (pp. 27-48). Hillsdale, NJ: Lawrence Erlbaum.

Rosenberg, M. (1979). *Conceiving the self.* New York: Basic Books.

Rosenberg, S. (1977). New approaches to the analysis of personal constructs in person perception. *Nebraska symposium on motivation* (Vol. 24, pp. 174-242). Lincoln: University of Nebraska Press.

Rosenberg, S. (1982, October). *The role of prototypes in a person's belief system about self and others.* Paper presented at the meeting of the Society of Experimental Social Psychology, Nashville, IN.

Rosenberg, S., & Jones, R. A. (1972). A method for investigating and representing a person's implicit personality theory: Theodore Dreiser's view of people. *Journal of Personality and Social Psychology, 22,* 372-386.

Rosenberg, S., & Sedlak, A. (1972a). Structural representations of implicit personality theory. In L. Berkowitz (Ed.), *Advances in experimental social psychology* (Vol. 6, pp. 235-297). New York: Academic.

Rosenberg, S., & Sedlak, A. (1972b). Structural representations of perceived personality trait relationships. In A. K. Romney, R. N. Shepard, & S. B. Nerlove (Eds.), *Multidimensional scaling: Theory and applications in the behavioral sciences* (Vol. 2, pp. 134-162). New York: Seminar.

Rowan, J. (1983). Person as group. In H. H. Blumberg, A. P. Hare, V. Kent, & M. Davies (Eds.), *Small groups and social interaction* (Vol. 2, pp. 253-264). London: John Wiley.

Shaver, P., & Rubenstein, C. (1980). Childhood attachment experience and adult loneliness. In L. Wheeler (Ed.), *Review of personality and social psychology* (Vol. 1, pp. 42-73). Beverly Hills, CA: Sage.

Synder, W. U. (1971). *Thomas Wolfe: Ulyssess and Narcissus.* Athens: Ohio University Press.

Stryker, S., & Serpe, R. T. (1982). Commitment, identity salience, and role behavior: Theory and research example. In W. Ickes & E. Knowles (Eds.), *Personality, roles and social behavior* (pp. 199-218). New York: Springer-Verlag.

Swann, W. B. (1984). Quest for accuracy in person perception: A matter of pragmatics. *Psychological Review, 91,* 457-477.

Wolfe, T. (1929). *Look homeward, angel.* New York: Scribners.

Wylie, R. C. (1974). *The self-concept.* Lincoln: University of Nebraska Press.

Zavalloni, M. (1971). Cognitive processes and social identity through focused introspection. *Eurpoean Journal of Social Psychology, 1,* 235-260.

Zavalloni, M. (1975). Social identity and the recoding of reality: Its relevance for cross-cultural psychology. *International Journal of Psychology, 10,* 197-217.

Zurcher, L. A. (1977). *The mutable self: A self-concept for social change.* Beverly Hills, CA: Sage.

# 5

# The "Imago"

## A KEY NARRATIVE
## COMPONENT OF IDENTITY

### DAN P. McADAMS

**Dan P. McAdams** is Associate Professor of Psychology at Loyola University of Chicago. He received his Ph.D. from Harvard University in 1979 and is the author most recently of *Power, Intimacy, and the Life Story: Personological Inquiries into Identity.* His research interests include identity, intimacy, human motivation, and biographical approaches to personality.

To understand the development of ego identity in the life of George Bernard Shaw, writes Erik Erikson (1959), one must appreciate the nature and interactions of three central protagonists in Shaw's life story. These are "the Snob," "the Noisemaker," and "the Diabolical One," and each is a personified part or facet of Shaw himself. The young George Bernard Shaw saw himself as a snob raised in a family of snobs; an inveterate elitist who, after learning that one of his ancestors was an Earl of Fife, decided that that was almost as good as being a direct descendant of Shakespeare, whom the young Shaw "had unconsciously resolved to reincarnate from my cradle" (in Erikson, 1959, p. 107). In the identity guise of the Noisemaker, Shaw the child tormented his mother by banging out on the piano his favorite selections from Wagner, in essentially the same way, according to Shaw himself, that he was later to torment conductors and composers as the strident music critic writing under the pseudonym Corno di Basseto—a critic who made a prodigious amount of noise. And Shaw the Diabolical One teased the Almighty by composing, as a "little devil of a child," literary prayers that bordered on the scandalous. Erikson writes that Shaw the child "did not feel identical with himself when he was good: 'Even when I was a good boy, I was so only theatrically.'" The "upgrowing moustaches and eyebrows" and the "sarcastic nostrils" of the young Shaw were, in Shaw's own mind, bodily reflections of the attitudes of the Diabolical One, which "I had sung as a child" and which were to continue to manifest themselves as significant identity elements throughout Shaw's adult years (Erikson, 1959, p. 108).

The Snob, the Noisemaker, and the Diabolical One are three idealized and personified images of self that appear to function as main characters in the life story of the young George Bernard Shaw. Each of these internalized identity structures is associated with characteristic roles, recurrent behavioral scripts, consistent attitudes, hopes, fears, and goals. Each, moreover, appears to be "born" in a specific biographical episode in Shaw's life, generally an episode from childhood. More encompassing than the mere "roles" that Shaw plays in daily living, these images of self cut across a host of identity domains while integrating essential information about the self to be found in Shaw's past, his present situation, and his expectations for the future. According to Erikson, the young Shaw's maturation in adulthood is signified by an integration of the three images of self within a larger, superordinate image of the self as "Actor." The emergence of the Actor image created "for myself a fantastic personality fit and apt for dealing with men, and adaptable for the various parts I had to play as author, journalist, orator, politician, committee man, man of the world, and so forth" (p. 109, Shaw speaking in Erikson, 1959).

The Snob, the Noisemaker, the Diabolical One, and the Actor are examples of what I have termed *imagoes*. An imago is an idealized and personified image of self that functions as a main character in an adult's life story (McAdams, 1984a, 1985a). Imagoes are essential constituents of identity. They are created by the individual to aid in defining the self. Once created, they serve to orient the individual in interpersonal relationships, suggesting characteristic modes and manners of social interaction. In this chapter I first trace some essential ideas concerning the imago embedded within related theoretical formulations to be found in the literatures of psychoanalysis and clinical, personality, and social psychology. This survey is highly selective, as I delineate common themes in certain theories while passing over a number of associated propositions and claims from these same theories. Secondly, I briefly outline my own work on the imago as a critical component of identity and highlight an initial taxonomy of imagoes delineated from an exploration of life stories in midlife adults. Finally, I propose a number of linkages between personified images of self and characteristic orientations toward significant interpersonal relationships.

## INSIGHTS FROM PSYCHOANALYSIS AND CLINICAL PSYCHOLOGY

### The Self is Composed of Personified and Idealized Internal Images, or "Imagoes," That Are Affect-Laden

The term "imago" was sometimes used by Jung (1943) when referring to the *archetype*. According to Jung, archetypes are emotionally charged templates for human experience existing within the collective unconscious of all men and women. Residual products of human phylogeny, archetypes encode universal patterns inherent in the natural life cycle of humans:

> Being mothered, exploring the environment, playing in the peer group, adolescence, being initiated, establishing a place in the social hierarchy, courting, marrying, child rearing, hunting, gathering, fighting, participating in religious rituals, assuming the social responsibilities of advanced maturity, and preparation for death. (Stevens, 1983, p. 40)

Thus, every individual is endowed with an archetype of the "earth mother"—an unconscious template that gives rise to a conscious image of what a mother should be, which in turn influences and is influenced by one's experiences with mothers. Normally outside the bounds of everyday awareness, archetypes are best discerned in the creative productions of humans, such as dreams, art, myths, folklore, and religion.

In the Jungian view of human ontogeny, every person is mandated to explore the archetypes within the unconscious and to employ the archetypes' creative energies in ways that benefit the self and society as a whole. Such an exploration is a life-long process, according to Jung (1961), and some of the most significant breakthroughs in understanding the self may await midlife and beyond. Along the journey, one encounters such archetypes as the *anima* (the suppressed feminine side of the man), the *animus* (the suppressed masculine side of the woman), and the *shadow* (the embodiment of socially reprehensible thoughts, desires, and feelings). Other important archetypes to be explored include the hero, the wise old man, the earth mother, the demon, the child, birth, rebirth, death, power, and magic. Note that the first five of these are expressly personified, but the latter five are more abstract or conceptual: The wise old man is a person; death is a concept.

An idea that bears some resemblance to Jung's archetype, even though it is premised on a radically different view of human nature, is Sullivan's (1953) *personification*. Sullivan proposed that personified images of self such as the "good me," the "bad me," and the "not me" and personified images of others such as the "good mother" and the "bad mother" are organized within the child's *self-system*. The self-system enables the child to construct and orchestrate interactions with the environment in such a way as to minimize anxiety, which in the early years is the paramount threat to psychological well-being. As the child grows older, personifications fuse into large configurations; for example, when the individual blends the good mother and the bad mother into an integrative representation of mother *in toto*. Thus, human beings tend to organize information about the self and others within categories that are inherently personified.

Sullivan's view of the self is much closer to contemporary "cognitive" views within personality and social psychology than is Jung's. Yet, both Sullivan and Jung agree that the self is at least partially composed of idealized and personified images that serve to organize human experience. Further, these images of self are charged with emotion—in Jung's case as a result of their origins in universal challenges in human phylogeny and in Sullivan's case because of their origins in childhood experiences that are rich with pleasure and anxiety.

### The Origins of a Particular Imago Lie in the Internalization of Loved (and Hated) "Objects" in the Person's World

Neither Jung nor Sullivan provide a satisfactory explanation for the origins of idealized and personified images of self. Jung's belief that archetypes are remnants of the phylogenetic past has been tossed off by many as a kind of biological mysticism, and Sullivan's cursory explanation for the development of personifications seems disconcertingly vague. It is rather in the writings of Freud and the object-relations theorists such as Fairbairn that a more detailed account of imago ontogenesis can be found.

In "Mourning and Melancholia," Freud (1917/1957) proposed that chronic depression is often a result of the internalization of a lost object with whom one hitherto had a highly ambivalent relationship. In a literal sense, depression is self-hatred (in Freud's view) in that the object (the person whom the individual both loved and hated) that is now lost (through death, separation, or any perceived parting) becomes *internalized* to function as a personified part of the self. The hatred and the love of the other are now displaced onto the self, in that the other is now part of the self. The dynamics of melancholia are exactly those of the Oedipus complex, which exists as the life cycle's prototypical experience of object loss followed by internalization. In the Oedipus complex, the unconscious desire *to have* the other (what Freud termed *cathexis*) gives way, under threat of loss, to the unconscious desire *to be like* the other (what Freud termed *identification*). In both melancholia and the Oedipus complex, therefore, "cathexis regresses to identification" (Freud, 1933/1964, p. 63), and a new personified part of the ego is formed via the internalization of (identification with) the other. Therefore, "the ego is a precipitate of abandoned object-cathexes," and "it contains the history of those object-choices" (Freud, 1923/1961, p.

19). In the case of the Oedipus complex, the internalized other splits off from the rest of the ego to form what Freud variously termed the *superego* or *ego-ideal*. It thus functions as a personified representation of the loved and hated parents within the self. Recent developments in superego theory suggest that this component of the self may emerge gradually through a succession of internalizations occurring both before and after the Oedipus complex (Arlow, 1982).

Freud's writings on internalization of loved and hated objects in the wake of loss paved the way for the *object-relations* approach to personality theory, represented in its various versions in the writings of Klein (1948), Fairbairn (1952), Jacobson (1964), and Guntrip (1971). Central to this general approach is the argument that internalization of significant objects is a sine qua non of interpersonal relationships. According to Fairbairn, the ego is object-seeking from birth, and as it gains experience in interpersonal relationships, it acquires a structuring whereby external objects are invariably internalized to become personified parts of the self. In infancy, even momentary "losses" of the object (e.g., the mother) result in internalization such that the ego comes to be inhabited, as it were, by a host of *internalized objects*. These include the "good and exciting mother who meets my needs" and "the bad and frustrating mother who does not." In a slightly different vein, Jacobson (1964) writes of the *wished-for self-image* as an internalized personification that emerges from emotionally-charged interactions with others who embody qualities and attributes that the individual longs to make his or her own. Fairbairn's internalized objects and Jacobson's wished-for self-images are but two types of idealized and personified self-images that, object-relations theorists argue, are born from significant interpersonal relationships and, once formed, come to influence those same relationships.

## A Person's Most Significant Interpersonal Relationships Are Profoundly Influenced by Imagoes

Beginning with Klein (1948), object-relations theorists have tended to take a rather negative view of the influence of internalized objects upon external interpersonal relationships. According to Klein, the infant projects its death instinct (Freud, 1920/1955) upon certain objects (mother) or part-objects (breast) and then incorporates these so that they become internal personifications of the child's aggressive urges. The internalization of objects and part-objects creates an internal stage of fantasy upon which a variety of introjected personifications act and interact. For Klein, the internal drama overshadows external relationships, and an internal "pattern world is created into which the child's experience of the external world is fitted" (Guntrip, 1971, p. 57).

The same idea, stripped of its associations with the death instinct, is found in Fairbairn (1952). From birth onward, the individual repeatedly internalizes significant objects in the interpersonal world. The internalized objects become personifications within the ego that, like Freud's superego, carve out their own territory in order to do battle with other internalized objects. The battles are waged in unconscious fantasy, and the fantasized battleground serves as a template for ordering relationships in the real world. In other words, the internal drama creates an unconscious *schema* to which external relationships are assimilated.

Many problems in external relationships are a result, argues Fairbairn, of the distorting influence of the subjective inner world upon the outer. A goal of development (and therapy) is the freeing of oneself from the internal drama in order to experience real-world relationships "objectively." Fairbairn terms this a developmental move from *immature* to *mature dependency*, but he does not appear very sanguine about its likelihood. The grip of the internal is difficult to loosen, especially in the not uncommon case of the *schizoid personality*. Traumatic interpersonal experiences in the early years of life create for the schizoid a host of internalized bad (frustrating) objects. Narcissistic and delusional, incapable of investing affect in external relationships, the schizoid withdraws from external reality and retreats to a fantasy kingdom of internalized objects, a safe haven from the frustration and loss that have haunted past relationships. To the extent that the schizoid is capable of engaging in interpersonal relationships, he or she generally appears narcissistic and highly dependent.

Coming from the very different theoretical perspective of *transactional analysis,* clinicians such as Berne (1972) and Steiner (1974) have posited internal *ego states* and *scripts* that influence interpersonal relationships in ways highly reminiscent of Fairbairn's internalized objects. Berne's three ego states—the "parent," "adult," and "child"— are personified structures of the self associated with characteristic patterns of interpersonal interaction. Problems of relationships typically involve recurrent mismatches of partners' ego states, as when one partner adopts a parent-child mode of interaction and the other acts according to an adult-adult scenario. More personalized than Berne's ego states are the personified scripts described by Steiner. These include (for men) "Big Daddy," "Playboy," and "Jock," and (for women) "Mother Hubbard," "Poor Little Me," and "Queen Bee." Much of interpersonal behavior, according to Steiner, is "scripted," causing participants to substitute playacting for authentic and spontaneous interpersonal exchange.

Although the object-relations theorists and the transactional-analysts tend to view the internal personified world as a dysfunctional distorter of external relationships, their shared belief that an emancipation from the internal is the key to healthy relationships may be somewhat naive. It is acceptable, on the one hand, to assert that bad objects and banal scripts get in the way of adaptive relationships, but it may be going too far to conclude that internal personified images of all sorts invariably wield a negative influence. Pure objectivity in relationships is probably a myth, and the best that human beings may be able to do on this score is to gain awareness of their own internal images of self and others and, perhaps, work toward the construction of more adaptive ones—in Steiner's terms, to substitute better scripts for banal scripts. In any case, the perspective on imagoes adopted here shares with Fairbairn, Berne, and Steiner the belief that internal personified images *do* inform interpersonal behavior in important ways—ways, however, that are both positive and negative.

## Imagoes Are Often Arranged in the Self as Dialectical Opposites

A number of theorists couch their conceptualizations of personified images of self and others in dialectical terms. In these cases, a particular imago implies its opposite, the two existing in a dialectical tension of thesis and antithesis. For instance, Fairbairn writes of the conflict between internalized good (need-fulfilling) objects and bad (need-frustrating) objects. Sullivan suggests that personifications are frequently split into pairs: the good mother versus the bad mother, the good me versus the bad me (though there also exists the not me). Berne points to the parent and child as two opposing, though complementary, ego states and implies that the third ego state—the adult—is a kind of reconciliation or synthesis of the two. Even Steiner posits latent *counterscripts* that serve as opposites to manifest scripts. A therapist's goal, in Steiner's view, should be to understand both script and counterscript in attempting to facilitate the client's replacement of scripted behavior with spontaneity.

Of all the viewpoints surveyed thus far, Jung's is probably the most explicitly dialectical. Confrontation of paired opposites is a central theme throughout Jungian psychology. The conscious ego stands in opposition to the unconscious; the individual unconscious stands in opposition to the collective unconscious; the attitude of extraversion is opposed to introversion; the rational functions of thinking and feeling oppose the irrational functions of sensing and intuiting; and so on. For Jung, the strong manifest expression of one characteristic always implies the equally strong latent expression of its opposite. Many archetypes, too, appear to be arranged in dreams and myths as opposites: the anima and animus, the wise old man and the child, the earth mother and the sky father. The reconciliation of opposites is, according to Jung, a coveted goal of human development and a cardinal sign of maturity.

## The Synthesis of Opposing Imagoes Is a Hallmark of the Mature Self

Jung's term for maturation of the self is *individuation*. Individuation involves an attentional shift from everyday consciousness to the unconscious, which is replete with some psychic material that one shares with all others (the collective unconscious) and other material that is unique to the person (the individual unconscious). More explicitly, one must dare to explore one's archetypes if one is to be mature, and this exploration invariably leads to confrontations of opposites. Through individuation, opposites come to be reconciled. This involves an integration of the conscious and the unconscious and a blending of antithetical archetypal images of self. The mandala was Jung's symbol for the unity of the self—an accomplishment usually saved for midlife— in which all dualities are dissolved in psychic harmony.

Sullivan, too, pointed to the integration of personifications as an accomplishment of the maturing self-system, though he spoke about a developmental phenomenon much less grand than Jung's individuation. For Sullivan, the development of language in children is mainly responsible for the ultimate fusion of personifications such as the good and bad mother and the good and bad me. In speaking of wished-for self-images, Jacobson states that over time the most desirable images of who one would like to be become more differentiated and ultimately integrated within larger and more coherent images of who one is likely to be. In addition to the theories already surveyed, a host of clinicians and other students of human nature have argued that maturity of the self involves a reconciliation of opposites. For Bakan (1966) this means finding a balance between *agency* and *communion;* for Angyal (1941), a balance between the *need for autonomy* and the *need for surrender;* for Loevinger (1976), the reconciliation of autonomy and interdependence at the highest (*integrated*) state of ego development; for Gutmann (1980), a blending of *masculinity* and *femininity* after midlife; and for

Fowler (1981), a rapprochement of the mysterious and the empirical, the ecstatic and the rational at the highest stage of human *faith*.

## INSIGHTS FROM PERSONALITY AND SOCIAL PSYCHOLOGY

### Imagoes Are Superordinate Schemata for Organizing and Evaluating Information About the Self

The recent "cognitivization" of personality and social psychology has made the study of the self a respectable endeavor in academic circles. Freed from the stultifying stimulus-response models of American behaviorism, contemporary students of the self have formulated models and theories that bear interesting resemblances to ideas about the self to be found in the psychoanalytic/clinical literature. Though one would be remiss to push these similarities too far, the concept of the imago as an idealized and personified image of self can be profitably characterized as a product of just such a theoretical confluence.

A substantial number of cognitively-oriented scholars have proposed that the self is a *system of schemata* that provides a general frame of reference for construing experience (Epstein, 1973; Kelly, 1955; Markus & Sentis, 1982). Schemata are abstract knowledge structures that guide the processing of information. Schemata go beyond the information given by (a) simplifying information when there is too much for the organism to handle efficiently and (b) filling in gaps when information is missing. Furthermore, schemata function both as *structures* to which information can be fitted and *processes* by which the information is fitted. As Neisser (1976) puts it, a "schema is not only the plan but also the executor of the plan" (p. 56).

According to Markus and Sentis (1982), self-schemata are

> generalizations about the self derived from the repeated categorizations and evaluations of behavior by oneself and by others. The result is a well-differentiated idea of the kind of person one is with respect to a variety of domains of behavior. Individuals only develop schemata about those aspects of their behavior that are important to them in some ways. Over the life course, we become increasingly aware of the distinctive characteristics of our appearance, temperament, abilities, and preferences. (p. 45)

A self-schema can be distinguished from all other kinds of schemata on at least four points: (a) it is larger and more complex than other schemata; (b) it manifests a richer network of relationships among its associated elements; (c) it is more frequently "activated" in daily information processing; and (d) it is suffused with affect (Markus &

Sentis, 1982). On the later point, a self-schema is a particularly "hot" cognition, intricately associated with highly emotional issues and experiences.

Schemata can be organized in a variety of ways, but one prevalent form appears to be that of the *prototype* (Cantor & Mischel, 1979). A particular prototype is defined not by necessary or sufficient attributes but by family resemblances among category members. Categories represented by prototypes, therefore, are characterized by "fuzzy sets" of overlapping instances, such as is the case in defining the natural category of "fruits." In everyday cognition, different kinds of fruits appear to share subsets of the defining features rather than any central defining attribute, and some fruits appear to be more prototypical of the class than others (e.g., apples as compared with tomatoes). Fuzzy sets are organized such that more prototypical *exemplars* of the class—like apples—occupy a central position in the knowledge structure, whereas tomatoes are situated on the periphery.

Rogers (1981) has proposed that the system of schemata constituting the self takes the form of a prototype. The "elements of the prototype are self-descriptive terms such as traits, values, and possibly even memories of specific behaviors and events" (Rogers, 1981, p. 196). Cantor and Mischel (1979) have shown that people are quite adept at organizing information about others with reference to prototypes such as "jock," "genius," "extravert," and "phobic." Each of these prototypes contains a host of exemplary and peripheral features and attributes. Rogers suggests that information about the self may also be organized in this fashion. A personified and idealized image of self, or imago, would appear to qualify as a self prototype in Rogers's terms. Imagoes, therefore, may function as superordinate schemata that are structured like prototypes and that are utilized by the person to organize and evaluate self-relevant information. As such, imagoes reduce the multitude of motley information about the self to manageable personified categories and fill in the gaps when self information is occasionally missing or deficient.

### Imagoes Specify Recurrent Behavioral Plans

As superordinate schemata guiding the processing of information about the self, imagoes specify characteristic action strategies or recurrent *plans* for behavior. Rogers's self-prototype organizes "memories of specific behaviors and events," suggesting that recurrent action sequences are contained within self-schemata organized as prototypes. A number of other theorists have agreed that characteristic action plans are significant components of self-schemata (Cohen, 1981; Kuiper & Derry, 1981; Markus & Sentis, 1982).

Martindale (1980) has elaborated upon this theme in his theory of *subselves*. According to Martindale, personality is a hierarchical bureaucracy in which cognitive units of varying levels of abstraction and complexity receive input and send output to each other with the ultimate aim of guiding social behavior. At the lowest (most concrete) level of the system, numerous *action units* code discrete and recurrent behaviors. These action units are nested within larger *plans*—akin to Abelson's (1981) *scripts*—that specify sequences of discrete behavior organized to accomplish a particular end. Plans are maidservants to larger and more encompassing *dispositional units,* which code consistent personality trends. Murray's (1938) taxonomy of *needs* provides a representative listing of many important dispositions coded at this level. Finally, dispositional units are subsumed within larger subselves or systems of related dispositions. According to Martindale, subselves are akin to what Murray (1938) termed *complexes.*

Subselves, therefore, are high level abstractions about self within which are nested (in descending order) cognitive units for dispositions, plans, and behavior. Thus, plans are specified by subselves via the intervening level of dispositions. Carrying this line of reasoning to the imago, one could argue that idealized and personified images of self provide the individual with a repertoire of action plans or scripts, which can be activated in behavior in the service of important personality dispositions, especially those dispositions identified by Murray as psychogenic needs, or *motives.* Imagoes give cognitive form to basic human motives by personifying them and thereby specifying particular behavioral plans for the fulfillment of these motives.

## Imagoes Give Cognitive Form to
## Personal Goals, Fears, and Desires

The link between motivation and imagoes is addressed directly in the work of Markus (1984) on *possible selves.* Aligning herself with the many theorists who have emphasized the multifaceted nature of self, Markus argues that most adults function in accordance with a wide range of well-articulated possible selves, each of which carries a great deal of affect. Possible selves are ideas we have about who we might become, who we would like to become, and who we fear becoming. These include various good selves, bad selves, hoped-for selves, feared selves, not-me selves, ideal selves, and ought selves. Using one of Markus's examples, the assistant professor up for tenure doubtlessly has articulated not only a scenario of self as tenured professor—secure, prestigious, influential, addressing august audiences—but also an equally convincing scenario of self as failing to get tenure—anxious, without a job, writing trashy novels, and so on. These possible selves, therefore, give cognitive form, meaning, and direction to personal hopes, fears, goals, and threats. Not only do they function as schemata to promote interpretation and evaluation of incoming information about the self, but they also serve as incentives for future behavior by giving form to personal ends to be approached or avoided.

James (1892/1963) appears to have had in mind the crucial interplay of various possible selves when he wrote of the "rivalry and conflict of the different mes." Various motivational trends and their accompanying affects are given cognitive form in the many empirical mes that each of us constructs. Inevitably a few of the mes must win out, argues James, as the person is forced by circumstances to make choices among different appealing possible selves. The process, akin to what Erikson has described as the formation of identity, was described by James as follows:

> With most objects of desire, physical nature restricts our choice to but one of many represented goods, and even so it is here. I am often confronted by the necessity of standing by one of my empirical selves and relinquishing the rest. Not that I would not, if I could, be both handsome and fat and well dressed, and a great athlete, and make a million a year, be a wit, a bon-vivant, and a lady-killer, as well as a philosopher; a philanthropist, statesman, warrior, and African explorer, as well as a "tone-poet" and saint. But the thing is simply impossible. The millionaire's work would run counter to the saint's; the bon-vivant and the philanthropist would trip each other up; the philosopher and the lady-killer could not well keep house in the same tenement of clay. Such different *characters* may conceivably at the outset of life be alike possible to a man. But to make any one of them actual, the rest must more or less be suppressed. So the seeker of his truest, strongest, deepest self must review the list carefully, and pick out the one on which to stake his salvation. All other selves thereupon become unreal, but the fortunes of this self are real. Its failures are real failures, its triumphs real triumphs, carrying shame and gladness with them. This is as strong an example as there is of that selective industry of the mind. . . . Our thought, incessantly deciding, among many things of a kind, which ones for it shall be realities, here chooses one of many *possible selves or characters,* and forthwith reckons it no shame to fail in any of those not adopted expressly as its own. (James, 1892/1963, p. 174, italics added)

## IMAGOES AS "MAIN CHARACTERS" IN IDENTITY

### Identity as a Life Story

When James states that each of us must pick out a possible self upon which to "stake our salvation," he is referring to what Erikson has described as the quest for ego identity. And when James twice terms these possible selves from which we choose "characters," he is hinting at a powerful metaphor for the understanding of identity formation. This is the metaphor of the *story*. My own work on identity proceeds from this narrative metaphor (McAdams, 1984a, 1985a, in press). In what follows, I shall introduce this approach by proposing that the structure of identity is a story complete with setting, scenes, characters, plot, and recurrent themes. Identity formation is the process of constructing a self-defining *life story*. The main characters in the story arc imagoes.

With the onset of genital sexuality, the advent of formal operational thinking (Inhelder & Piaget, 1958), and the rising expectations from one's social environment that it is now time to find one's place in the adult world, the late adolescent or young adult enters a period in the life cycle in which he or she is confronted with the two key questions of identity: Who am I? How do I fit into the adult world? Erikson has argued that the process of answering these questions involves putting together a personalized *configuration* that integrates a panoply of diverse identity elements, such as ideological beliefs and values, instrumental and interpersonal roles, talents and abilities, identifications from the past, and expectations for the future. The consolidation of identity brings with it a pervasive personal sense of "inner sameness and continuity" (Erikson, 1963, p. 261)—the reassuring sense that I am essentially the same person from one situation to another and that there is a continuity to my life between past, present, and an anticipated future. I have argued that Erikson's use of the term "sameness" suggests a *synchronic* dimension to identity in that the person seeks a contemporaneous harmony between self and external environment, a personalized niche in the here-and-now world of adults that specifies exactly how the individual is the same as and different from other aspects of the environment. The term "continuity," on the other hand, suggests a *diachronic* dimension to identity—identity as an integration of temporally-ordered elements such that the understanding of self makes sense in terms of one's personal past and anticipated future (McAdams, in press).

Beginning in late adolescence, each of us constructs a self-defining narrative—a life story—that promises to consolidate the synchronic and diachronic dimensions of identity in order to answer the twin identity questions and to provide our lives with a sense of inner sameness and continuity. This is precisely what the formation of identity means. A process akin to this has been described by a number of other psychologists in terms of a "mythological rearranging" of one's life attempted in young adulthood (Hankiss, 1981), the creation of a "personal fable" in adolescence (Elkind, 1981), the construction of a personal "myth" that draws upon a "library of scripts" offered by one's embedding society (Bruner, 1960), the coalescence of "nuclear scenes" within life "scripts" (Carlson, 1981; Tomkins, 1978), and the creation of a "fictional finalism" that orients one's reconstruction of the past and one's present situation to an envisioned future (Adler, 1927).

I have proposed a life-story model of identity in which one's identity is conceived as a narrative construction embodying salient *content* clusterings (termed *thematic lines*) and a particular *structural* complexity (termed *narrative complexity*; McAdams, 1985a, in press). The two major thematic lines around which the content of identity can be organized are *agency* (power/mastery/separation) and *communion* (intimacy/surrender/union; Bakan, 1966). Initial investigations of life stories of college students and men and women at midlife suggest that the power motive (Winter, 1973) and the intimacy motive (McAdams, 1980) are two independent personality dispositions—both assessed via the Thematic Apperception Test or TAT—that serve as significant *predictors* of the salience in life stories of thematic lines of agency and communion, respectively. Loevinger's (1976) ego development—assessed via a sentence-completion test—has served as a significant predictor of the level of narrative complexity in life stories, with individuals scoring at higher ego stages constructing more differentiated and integrated self-defining narratives (McAdams, 1985a).

Life stories, furthermore, are made up of at least four identifiable components: an *ideological setting, nuclear episodes, generativity script,* and *imagoes.* An ideological setting is the backdrop of personal belief and value established by the late adolescent or young adult as an ontological, epistemological, and ethical "time and place" within which the story's action unfolds. Established early in the identity-making process, the ideological setting is fairly resistant to change in adulthood, for to transform it in any fundamental way is to undermine the basic setting within which the story has hitherto made sense. Nuclear episodes are highlighted scenes from one's past, happenings in the story that stand out and are thus given a privileged status in the narrative. They include narrative high points, low points, and turning points. A generativity script extends the narrative into the future by providing a plot outline of what the individual plans to do so that he or she can "leave something behind" for the next generation (and thereby extend the story beyond one's own lifetime). Finally, imagoes, as personified and idealized images of the self, function as main characters in identity. Like Shaw's Snob, Noisemaker, Diabolical One, and Actor, they are semiautonomous guises of the self whose exploits and conflicts provide some of the most illuminating identity material in the life story.

## The Meaning and Measurement of Imagoes

The first systematic exploration of imagoes is described in detail in McAdams (1985a). In this study, my colleagues and I collected questionnaire and interview data from 20 men and 30 women between the ages of 35 and 50 years. Most of the subjects were recruited from evening classes taught at a large, private university in the midwestern United States. The sample was predominantly white (94 percent) and middle class, with 70 percent of the subjects having obtained at least a bachelor's-level degree. At the time of initial assessment, 58 percent of the subjects were married. Median family income (1981-1982) was between $30,000 and $40,000.

All 50 subjects participated in two sessions. A number of personality tests and questionnaires were administered in the first session. In the second session, each subject was interviewed concerning his or her life story. The subjects were asked to think about their lives as books, dividing them into chapters and describing the content of each chapter. Other questions in the interview concerned significant life experiences and turning points, one's plans for the future, heroes and role models, philosophy of life, and the underlying theme of the person's life story. The life-story interviews lasted between one and two hours.

My colleagues and I listened to the taped interviews for evidence of personified and idealized images of self, using a number of theoretical formulations described above as guides for our exploration. After composing detailed case interpretations for the first 25 subjects, we delineated a set of features that might serve as criteria for the presence of a given imago in a life-story interview. A prototypical imago, therefore, would be an idealized and personified image of self reflected in all the following:

(1) an *origin myth* or biographical event to which the perceived genesis of the imago could be traced;

(2) a *significant other person* in the individual's life who served as an exemplar or incarnation of the imago;

(3) a *set of personality traits* attributed to the self by the subject and associated with a particular imago;

(4) a set of personal *goals* and *wishes* associated with a particular imago;

(5) *behavioral incidents* drawn from the individual's biography suggesting a particular imago;

(6) supporting evidence from the subject's description of his or her *philosophy of life* or his or her account of the *underlying theme of the life story;* and

(7) an opposite image of self—or *anti-imago*—embodying evidence from the six categories described above and existing in conflict or tension with the primary imago.

In the first 25 cases, no interview provided consistent evidence in all
seven of these categories for a single imago, but most of the cases could
be adequately depicted as portraying one, two, or three imagoes for
which considerable evidence in four or five of the categories could be
garnered (see McAdams, 1985a, pp. 183-191, for a full discussion). In a
number of cases, two imagoes appeared to be in conflict with each other.
Our case discussions for the first 25 subjects resulted in a tentative
classification scheme for imagoes that attempts to capture some of the
more prominent images of self observed in our data.

## A Taxonomy of Imagoes

As can be seen in Table 5.1, the taxonomy of imagoes proposed is
grounded in the mythology of ancient Greece. The Greek pantheon
seemed an appropriate model for imagoes in that its gods and goddesses
represent, on at least one level, projected *personifications* of what the
Greeks understood as fundamental human propensities and strivings.
Though they were larger and stronger than their mortal counterparts,
the heroes and heroines of Olympus made love and war, experienced
rage, envy, and joy, and performed acts of altruism and ignominy in
ways that were remarkably human. Each of the major deities, furthermore, personified a distinctive set of personality traits that were
repeatedly manifested in the myths and legends in which his or her
behavior can be observed. We chose 12 major gods and goddesses for
our prototypes of imagoes. Taken together, the group embodies most of
the idealized and personified self-images we observed in the initial 25
cases.

The taxonomy is also organized along the thematic lines of agency
and communion (Bakan, 1966). Class 1 imagoes are purely agentic—
idealized and personified images of self as strong and powerful agents
who have significant impact on the environment. These include various
images of self under the heading of Zeus: the sage, judge, and almighty
source. Hermes subsumes a host of diverse images of self, imagoes of the
explorer, trickster, athlete, and entrepreneur. Hermes is forever on the
move, traveling from one place or experience to another. The third
purely agentic imago is Ares, the god of war. In our data, Ares appeared
as the soldier or fighter. Impetuous but generally well intentioned, Ares
finds himself or herself in the midst of warfare time and time again. Life
is seen as a series of battles, and one must be strong if one is to emerge
victorious.

Class 3 imagoes, on the other hand, are purely communal. Demeter is
the consummate caregiver who must often suffer in order to promote the

# TABLE 5.1

## A Taxonomy of Imagoes

*Class 1:* (High Agency)

(1) *Zeus: The Omnipotent Source.*
Patriarch, judge, sovereign, conqueror, seducer, creator, provider, sage, wise one, celebrity, star.

(2) *Hermes: The Swift Traveller.*
Explorer, adventurer, trickster, thief, rabble-rouser, persuader, spokesman, athlete, gameplayer, gambler, entrepreneur.

(3) *Ares: The Warrior.*
Fighter, soldier, policeman, strongman.

*Class 2:* (High Agency and High Communion)

(1) *Apollo. The Healer.*
Doctor, shaman, prophet, artist, shepherd, protector, organizer, legislator.

(2) *Athene: The Peacemaker.*
Arbiter, counselor, therapist, teacher, guide.

(3) *Prometheus: The Humanist.*
Mentor, defender of the weak, scientist, revolutionary, evangelist.

*Class 3:* (High Communion)

(1) *Demeter: The Caregiver.*
Altruist, sufferer, martyr.

(2) *Hera: The Loyal Friend.*
Spouse, helpmate, chum, confidante, sibling, servant, subordinate, assistant.

(3) *Aphrodite: The Lover.*
Charmer, enchanter.

*Class 4:* Low Agency and Low Communion)

(1) *Hestia: Feminine Stereotype.*
Homemaker, domestic, keeper of order in the home.

(2) *Hephaestus: Masculine Stereotype.*
Craftsman, laborer, wage-earner.

(3) *Dionysius: The Escapist.*
Pleasure-seeker, hedonist, player, epicure, child.

welfare of those dependent upon him or her. Hera is the loyal friend or confidante whose life is structured around warm and reciprocal relationships with peers. Aphrodite subsumes images of self as lover or enchanter/enchantress. The Aphrodite imago personifies passionate love in both its most exalted and its most degraded forms.

Class 2 and 4 imagoes are mixtures of agency and communion. Whereas Class 2 images of self—Apollo, Athene, and Prometheus— suggest powerful and intimate, agentic and communal images, Class 4 imagoes—Hestia, Hephaestus, Dionysius—appear to lack both agency and communion. In personifying agency and communion, the Class 2 imagoes are, in some ways, the most interesting. In these cases, the imago may represent a creative integration of strong needs that, on the surface, may appear to contradict each other. Athene, the imago of peacemaking and teaching, is a powerful force in the environment whose actions are designed to benefit others and promote the merger of independent agents. Apollo, the healer/artist/organizer, likewise channels strong desires to master the environment into arenas of functioning that promote communion.

For each of the 50 interviews from the midlife men and women, my colleagues and I endeavored to derive at least one imago from Table 5.1 for which a good deal of support could be garnered. Given the substantial interpretive effort required, it is not surprising that the reliability in scoring imagoes for two independent coders was only moderate (see McAdams, 1984, pp. 212-214). Deciding between conflicting interpretations by calling in a third independent coder, we were able to find substantial evidence for the presence of at least one imago in 47 of the 50 cases (94 percent). Deeming the one dominant imago "primary" for each case, we determined that 11 cases showed primary imagoes in Class 1 (pure agency: Zeus, Hermes, Ares), 7 cases in Class 2 (agency and communion: Apollo, Athene Prometheus), 12 cases in Class 3 (pure communion: Demeter, Hera, Aphrodite), 17 cases in Class 4 (low agency and low communion: Hestia, Hephaestus, Dionysius), and 3 cases in none. For the men, the distribution of cases across the four imago classes and the unidentified class was 2/6/3/6/3, and for women the distribution was 9/1/9/11/0. In 35 of the 50 cases (70 percent), we found some evidence for a second contrasting image of self, which we termed an anti-imago.

We then related power and intimacy motive scores—as determined by the TAT—to the imago classifications. The power motive (Winter, 1973) is a recurrent preference for experiences of feeling strong and having impact on the environment. The intimacy motive (McAdams, 1980; McAdams & Constantian, 1983) is a recurrent preference for experiences of feeling close to and in communion with other people in the environment. Both motives are conceptualized as relatively stable personality dispositions that function to energize, direct, and select behavior in certain situations. A strong positive relationship was found between power motivation and the prevalence of a primary agentic imago (Class 1 or 2) in one's life story. Likewise, a highly significant relationship was obtained between intimacy motivation and communal imagoes (Class 3 or 2; McAdams, 1984a, 1985a). These findings support the idea, spelled out by Markus (1984) and Martindale (1980), that imagoes give cognitive form and organization to major goals and salient motivational tendencies in human lives.

## Imagoes and Maturity

The theories of clinicians such as Jung and Sullivan suggest that imagoes are often arranged in the self as pairs of opposites and that the integration of these opposites is a hallmark of maturity in self-development. Our data from the 50 men and women at midlife provide a modicum of support for this dialectical proposition. We closely examined the 35 cases in which evidence for two contrasting images of self—a primary imago and anti-imago—could be found in order to determine the extent of integration or synthesis of the two. Marked integration was found in 12 of the 35 cases, though in each case the integration was accomplished in a different way. For instance, one woman integrated a friend imago (Hera) with an image of self as a strong and masterful agent through her role as a psychotherapist. A male professor integrated a teacher/guide imago (Athene) with that of a student/follower in going back to school to get a master's degree in business administration while continuing to teach music. Another woman synthesized an artist (Apollo) imago with that of the "realist"—personifying a conflict in her life that she traced back to her romantic Sicilian father and her pragmatic German mother—by switching from art to a vocation in the business world and adopting a new attitude about her own life as an unfinished piece of art in itself, with respect to which she was now both the artist and the product of the artist's labors, the creator and the created masterpiece (see McAdams, 1985a, pp. 204-210 for a full discussion).

We related the degree of synthesis between two contrasting imagoes in the life story to an independent measure of ego development determined from a sentence-completion test (Loevinger & Wessler, 1978). According to Loevinger, higher stages of ego development indicate that the person has adopted a more complex and less egocentric framework of meaning for understanding the world, embodying internalized ethical standards, tolerance for ambiguity, and an appreciation for both human individuality and interdependence. Thus, the ego is conceived as one's overall framework for making meaning in the world, and higher stages indicate greater ego maturity. Supporting Loevinger's claims about her own measure and the clinicians' argument about integration of imagoes, we found that the 12 subjects for whom substantial imago integration was obtained scored significantly higher in ego development than did their 23 counterparts who evidenced two contrasting imagoes that were not integrated in some way (McAdams, 1985a). Though obtained from a very small sample of predominantly white, middle-class adults, this finding lends some credence to a dialectical conceptualization of imagoes in which personified images of self are arranged as thesis and antithesis awaiting the synthesis of mature selfhood.

## Imagoes and Interpersonal Relationships

Whether agentic, communal, both, or neither in content emphasis, imagoes are inherently social. Forged in the dynamics of one's most significant interpersonal relationships and often embodied in the most influential objects in one's interpersonal world, idealized and personified images of self come to influence one's relationships with others in, I suspect, myriad ways. Nearly all of the theorists reviewed in the first half of this chapter have argued that personified images of self are major influences, for better or for worse, on interpersonal relationships. But what is the precise nature of this influence?

At this point in our inquiry into imagoes, the answer to this question remains unknown. We have yet to undertake an empirical investigation of the direct relation between imagoes and personal relationships such as love, marriage, and friendship. Yet some indirect evidence may provide clues about what to expect. A few studies have looked at linkages between power and intimacy motivation on the one hand and significant interpersonal relationships on the other. Given that a direct relation between these motives and the quality of imagoes has been discovered (McAdams, 1985a) and that imagoes are viewed as giving cognitive form and organization to fundamental motivational tendencies (Markus, 1984; Martindale, 1980), these studies may prove instructive.

McAdams (1984b) has reviewed the literature on motivation and personal relationships. With respect to intimacy motivation, two general findings emerge: (1) intimacy motivation is positively associated with satisfaction in key personal relationships such as marriage and friendship, and (2) people high in intimacy motivation tend to adopt an especially communal orientation toward others in various interpersonal settings. On the first point, McAdams and Vaillant (1982) found that intimacy motivation assessed at age 30 in a cohort of Harvard men was positively associated with marital harmony 17 years later. McAdams (1980) found that heterosexual couples scoring high on Rubin's (1973) "love-scale"—indicating high intensity of love felt toward a partner—were significantly higher in intimacy motivation than a group of comparable undergraduates. McAdams (1985b) reported that midlife adults high in intimacy motivation revealed more extensive and satisfactory friendship networks in their lives than adults low in intimacy motivation. Other studies have indicated that high-intimacy persons adopt a particularly communal orientation in interpersonal relations, engaging in more self-disclosure and listening in the company of close friends (McAdams, Healy, & Krause, 1984), promoting group cameraderie and deemphasizing the self in a friendly psychodrama group (McAdams & Powers, 1981), and engaging in more eye contact, smiling, and laughter in cordial dyadic interviews (McAdams, Jackson, & Kirshnit, 1984).

The picture for power motivation is a bit less clear. Though some studies have indicated that power motivation in *men* is *negatively* associated with satisfaction in important interpersonal relationships such as marriage and love affairs (Stewart & Rubin, 1976; Veroff & Feld, 1970), a recent reanalysis of some of these data suggests that the negative relationships hold only for men whose high power motivation is combined with a very low score on "social responsibility" (Winter, 1984). No consistent findings have been obtained concerning power motivation and relationship satisfaction among women.

McAdams et al. (1984) found that students high in power motivation tended to adopt agentic roles in their interactions with close friends, as evidenced in taking charge of situations, making plans or decisions, offering advice, and helping others when in the company of friends. McAdams (1984b) found that high-power men and women tended to highlight *helping the other* as a crucial theme in significant friendship encounters, whereas high-intimacy persons highlighed *self-disclosure,* or the sharing of secrets. When asked to describe "low points" in a personal friendship history, high-power subjects often pointed to events in which the friend committed a *public transgression* that was embarrassing to the subject, whereas high-intimacy subjects underscored a *violation of trust,* or failure in candor, on the part of one of the friends. Finally, power motivation was positively associated with fearing *conflict* in friendship, whereas intimacy motivation was associated with the fear of *separation.*

Given these findings and my own understanding of imagoes, I have assembled Table 5.2 as a highly speculative and tentative conceptual scheme for understanding the relations between imago types and characteristic orientations to and functions of significant interpersonal relationships. For each of the 12 imago types, I have sketched a corresponding outline of (a) a general orientation toward new relationships in adulthood and (b) the function within the life story of the adult's most significant relationships in the past and present. Therefore, one's primary imago is envisioned as coloring one's present orientation toward new interpersonal opportunities, as in one's general approach to new friendships in adulthood. Furthermore, the imago informs one's interpretation of the meaning of past relationships. It suggests how the most significant relationships from one's past and present fit into the life story—what their function is within the identity configuration.

In general, Class 1 and 3 imagoes suggest agentic and communal emphases in relationships, respectively. Yet, as Table 5.2 shows, there may exist pronounced differences within each of the two imago classes concerning the ways in which agency or communion find their way into characteristic orientations toward new relationships and the life-story functions of significant past and present relationships. Class 2 imagoes, in highlighting both agency and communion, may be associated either with relationships in which the two are blended creatively or with relationships in which the two conflict. Thus, important interpersonal relationships may be more complex, and perhaps more ambivalent, for adults manifesting these images of self than might be the case for adults whose primary imagoes lie in Class 1 or 3. Class 4 imagoes are the most difficult to characterize in terms of relationship orientation and function, because they emphasize neither agency nor communion. I would not be surprised if these imagoes prove the most recalcitrant in studies of interpersonal relationships. Thus, it may be extremely difficult to find consistent and theoretically meaningful linkages between imagoes of self that personify neither agency nor communion on the one hand and the quality of interpersonal relationships on the other.

## CONCLUSION

The concept of the imago promises to serve as an integrative theoretical construct in personality, social, and developmental psych-

TABLE 5.2

Proposed Linkages Between Imago Types and Dimensions
of Interpersonal Relationships

| Imago Type | Orientation to New Relationships[a] | Life-Story Function or Meaning of Most Significant Relationships[b] |
|---|---|---|
| **Class 1** | | |
| Zeus | Controlling Judgmental Distant | Relationships affirm one's own agency; they provide evidence of one's creative powers; relationships enable one to witness the agentic and creative powers of others; significant others are either "creations in one's own image" (self as agentic source for others) *or* creators of one's own image (others as agentic sources for self). |
| Hermes | Enthusiastic Energetic Open | Relationships catalyze change and promote personal growth; they provide opportunities for adventure and exploration; relationships open up new possibilities for the self; significant others either facilitate the self's explorations *or* serve as objects to be explored by the self. |
| Ares | Combative Stiff Wary | Relationships provide opportunities for heroic action on the part of self and others; they mandate that one do one's duty and thereby remain "strong" or "true"; relationships determine victory and defeat; significant others are either co-combatants (allies) *or* adversaries. |
| **Class 3** | | |
| Demeter | Nurturant Altruistic Gentle | Relationships consist of taking care of others or being taken care of by others; they lead to occasional suffering and deprivation, which may be followed by enjoyment and enhancement; significant others are caregivers *or* recipients of care. |
| Hera | Egalitarian Cooperative Warm | Relationships provide opportunities for mutual sharing and intimate self-disclosure; they involve stable bonds forged by loyal partners; relationships emphasize dialogue over affect; significant others are friends, confidants, and communicators. |
| Aphrodite | Charming Affectionate Warm | Relationships are arenas in which passion is displayed; they provide opportunities for erotic union, intense joyful experiences, the pain, pathos, and passion of human love; relationships emphasize affect over dialogue; significant others are lovers who delight and are delighted by the self. |
| **Class 2** | | |
| Apollo | Generative Protective Ambivalent | Relationships are complex in that they affirm both agency and communion; they affirm personal power and interpersonal inter- |

*(continued)*

TABLE 5.2  Continued

| Imago Type | Orientation to New Relationships[a] | Life-Story Function or Meaning of Most Significant Relationships[b] |
|---|---|---|
| | | dependence simultaneously; relationships provide opportunities to heal and be healed, to become "whole" and to enable others to become whole; they provide opportunities for creativity and caring. |
| Athene | Generative Prudent Ambivalent | Relationships are complex in that they affirm both agency and communion; they provide opportunities to teach and learn; relationships call upon abilities to solve conflicts and make peace, to counsel and be counseled; significant others are mentors and protegés. |
| Prometheus | Evangelical Generous Ambivalent | Relationships affirm agency and communion in the face of obstacles, such as oppression; they provide opportunities to support others in the midst of adversity; relationships promote the advancement of ideals, causes, or other "lofty" and abstract ends; significant others may be authority figures against whom one must rebel *or* likeminded rebels who do battle with oppressive forces and figures. |
| *Class 4* | | |
| Hestia | Controlled Ritualized Moderately warm | Relationships function to establish, promote, or maintain security; they help to affirm order and predictability in the world. |
| Hephaestus | Frank Awkward Warm or wary | Relationships function to establish, promote, or maintain security; they help to define one's role as a producer of things and a provider for others. |
| Dionysius | Impulsive Playful Open | Relationships afford diversion and escape; they make available enjoyable experiences, moments of merriment and good cheer among friends; significant others are those with whom one spends leisure time. |

a. Refers to the subject's characteristic manner of approaching new relationships in adulthood.
b. Refers to the function or meaning ascribed by the subject to those relationships in his or her life story that appear to be the most salient, important, or formative.

ology. As idealized and personified images of self, imagoes depict the structure of identity in a way commensurate with contemporary cognitive views emphasizing schemata and prototypes as well as some older psychoanalytic approaches that have focused upon personified components of the personality. Imagoes are carefully crafted identity constituents that bring together under a personified umbrella a myriad of diverse material about the self including consistent roles, interests, wishes, goals, projects, fears, recurrent behavioral scripts, and significant past experiences. Imagoes are often arranged as dialectical pairs in the self, and the integration of the opposing personifications represents an accomplishment of the mature self in adulthood. Furthermore, imagoes are inherently social. They are constructed through significant interpersonal relationships and, in turn, come to structure those relationships.

Imagoes represent the main characters in the life stories we construct as our identities. My study of the life stories of 50 adults resulted in a taxonomy of imago forms that is organized according to the mythology of ancient Greece and the theoretical writings of Bakan (1966). In this chapter, I have elaborated the taxonomy further to include propositions about linkages between particular imago types and the nature of important interpersonal relationships. Much of this remains highly speculative at this point. Further research is needed to determine the usefulness and viability of the imago concept, its amenability to precise measurement, the validity of the imago taxonomy proposed, and the relationships between particular personified images of self and social interaction.

## REFERENCES

Abelson, R. P. (1981). Psychological status of the script concept. *American Psychologist, 36,* 715-729.
Adler, A. (1927). *The practice and theory of individual psychology.* New York: Harcourt, Brace & World.
Angyal, A. (1941). *Foundations for a science of personality.* New York: Viking.
Arlow, J. A. (1982). Problems of the superego concept. In A. J. Solnit, R. S. Eissler, A. Freud, & P. B. Neubauer (Eds.), *The psychoanalytic study of the child* (Vol. 37, pp. 229-244). New Haven, CT: Yale University Press.
Bakan, D. (1966). *The duality of human existence.* Boston: Beacon Press.
Berne, E. (1972). *What do you say after you say hello?* New York: Grove Press.
Bruner, J. S. (1960). Myth and identity. In H. A. Murray (Ed.), *Myth and mythmaking* (pp. 276-287). New York: George Braziller.
Cantor, N., & Mischel, W. (1979). Prototypes in person perception. In L. Berkowitz (Ed.), *Advances in experimental social psychology* (Vol. 12, pp. 3-52). New York: Academic.
Carlson, R. (1981). Studies in script theory: 1. Adult analogs of a childhood nuclear scene. *Journal of Personality and Social Psychology, 40,* 501-510.
Cohen, C. E. (1981). Goals and schemata in person perception: Making sense from the stream of behavior. In N. Cantor & J. F. Kihlstrom (Eds.), *Personality, cognition, and social interaction* (pp. 45-68). Hillsdale, NJ: Lawrence Erlbaum.
Elkind, D. (1981). *Children and adolescents* (3rd ed.). New York: Oxford University Press.

Epstein, S. (1973). The self-concept revisited. Or a theory of a theory. *American Psychologist, 28*, 404-416.

Erikson, E. H. (1959). Identity and the life cycle: Selected papers. *Psychological Issues, 1*, 5-165.

Erikson, E. H. (1963). *Childhood and society* (2nd ed.). New York: Norton.

Fairbairn, W.R.D. (1952). *Psychoanalytic studies of the personality*. London: Routledge & Kegan Paul.

Fowler, J. (1981). *Stages of faith*. New York: Harper & Row.

Freud, S. (1957). Mourning and melancholia. In J. Strachey (Ed.), *The standard edition of the complete psychological works of Sigmund Freud* (Vol. 14). London: Hogarth. (Original work published 1917)

Freud, S. (1955). Beyond the pleasure principle. In J. Strachey (Ed.), *The standard edition* (Vol. 18). London: Hogarth. (Original work published 1920)

Freud, S. (1961). The ego and the id. In J. Strachey (Ed.), *The standard edition* (Vol. 19). London: Hogarth. (Original work published 1923)

Freud, S. (1964). New introductory lectures on psychoanalysis. In J. Strachey (Ed.), *The standard edition* (Vol. 22). London: Hogarth. (Original work published 1933)

Guntrip, H. (1971). *Psychoanalytic theory, therapy, and the self*. New York: Basic Books.

Gutmann, D. L. (1980). The post-parental years: Clinical problems and developmental possibilities. In W. H. Norman & T. J. Scaramella (Eds.), *Mid-life: Developmental and clinical issues* (pp. 38-52). New York: Bruner/Mazel.

Hankiss, A. (1981). Ontologies of the self: On the mythological rearranging of one's life history. In D. Bertaux (Ed.), *Biography and society* (pp. 203-210). Beverly Hills, CA: Sage.

Inhelder, B., & Piaget, J. (1958). *The growth of logical thinking from childhood to adolescence*. New York: Basic Books.

Jacobson, E. (1964). *The self and the object world*. New York: International Universities Press.

James, W. (1963). *Psychology: A briefer course*. Greenwich, CT: Fawcett. (Original work published 1892)

Jung, C. G. (1943). The psychology of the unconscious. In *Collected Works*. Princeton, NJ: Princeton University Press.

Jung, C. G. (1961). *Memories, dreams, reflections*. New York: Random House.

Kelly, G. (1955). *The psychology of personal constructs*. New York: Norton.

Klein, M. (1948). *Contributions to psychoanalysis 1921-1945*. London: Hogarth.

Kuiper, N. A., & Derry, P. A. (1981). The self as cognitive prototype: An application to person perception and depression. In N. Cantor & J. F. Kihlstrom (Eds.), *Personality, cognition, and social interaction* (pp. 214-232). Hillsdale, NJ: Lawrence Erlbaum.

Loevinger, J. (1976). *Ego development*. San Francisco: Jossey-Bass.

Loevinger, J., & Wessler, R. (1978). *Measuring ego development: 1. Construction and use of a sentence completion test*. San Francisco: Jossey-Bass.

Markus, H. (1984). *Possible selves*. Paper presented at the Boston University Symposium for the Interdisciplinary Study of Personality. Boston, MA.

Markus, H., & Sentis, K. (1982). The self in social information processing. In J. Suls (Ed.), *Psychological perspectives on the self* (Vol. 1, pp. 41-70). Hillsdale, NJ: Lawrence Erlbaum.

Martindale, C. (1980). Subselves: The internal representation of situational and personal dispositions. In L. Wheeeler (Ed.), *Review of personality and social psychology* (Vol. 1, pp. 193-218). Beverly Hills, CA: Sage.

McAdams, D. P. (1980). A thematic coding system for the intimacy motive. *Journal of Research in Personality, 14*, 412-432.

McAdams, D. P. (1982). Experiences of intimacy and power: Relationships between social motives and autobiographical memory. *Journal of Personality and Social Psychology, 42*, 292-302.

McAdams, D. P. (1984a). Love, power, and images of the self. In C. Z. Malatesta & C. E. Izard (Eds.), *Emotion in adult development* (pp. 159-174). Beverly Hills, CA: Sage.

McAdams, D. P. (1984b). Human motives and personal relationships. In V. Derlega (Ed.), *Communication, intimacy, and close relationships* (pp. 41-70). New York: Academic.

McAdams, D. P. (1985a). *Power, intimacy, and the life story: Personological inquiries into identity*. Homewood, IL: Dorsey Press.

McAdams, D. P. (1985b). Motivation and friendship. In S. Duck & D. Perlman (Eds.), *Understanding personal relationships: Vol. 1. Sage series in personal relationships.* Beverly Hills, CA: Sage.

McAdams, D. P. (in press). A life-story model of identity. In R. Hogan & W. H. Jones (Eds.), *Perspectives in personality: Theory, measurement, and interpersonal dynamics* (Vol. 2). Greenwich, CT: JAI Press.

McAdams, D. P., & Constantian, C. A. (1983). Intimacy and affiliation motives in daily living: An experience sampling analysis. *Journal of Personality and Social Psychology, 45,* 851-861.

McAdams, D. P., Healy, S., & Krause, S. (1984). Social motives and patterns of friendship. *Journal of Personality and Social Psychology, 47,* 828-838.

McAdams, D. P., Jackson, R. J. & Kirshnit, C. (1984). Looking, laughing, and smiling in dyads as a function of intimacy motivation and reciprocity. *Journal of Personality, 52,* 261-273.

McAdams, D. P., & Powers, J. (1981). Themes of intimacy in behavior and thought. *Journal of Personality and Social Psychology, 40,* 573-587.

McAdams, D. P., & Vaillant, G. E. (1982). Intimacy motivation and psychosocial adjustment: A longitudinal study. *Journal of Personality Assessment, 46,* 586-593.

Murray, H. A. (1938). *Explorations in personality.* New York: Oxford University Press.

Neisser, U. (1976). *Cognition and reality.* San Francisco: Freeman.

Rogers, T. B. (1981). A model of the self as an aspect of the human information processing system. In N. Cantor & J. F. Kihlstrom (Eds.), *Personality, cognition, and social interaction* (pp. 193-214). Hillsdale, NJ: Lawrence Erlbaum.

Rubin, Z. (1973). *Liking and loving.* New York: Holt, Rinehart & Winston.

Steiner, C. M. (1974). *Scripts people live.* New York: Grove.

Stevens, A. (1983). *Archetypes: A natural history of the self.* New York: Quill.

Stewart, A. J., & Rubin, Z. (1976). Power motivation in the dating couple. *Journal of Personality and Social Psychology, 34,* 305-309.

Sullivan, H. S. (1953). *The interpersonal theory of psychiatry.* New York: Norton.

Tomkins, S. S. (1978). Script theory: Differential magnification of affects. In H. E. Howe & R. A. Dienstbler (Eds.), *Nebraska symposium on motivation* (Vol. 26, pp. 201-236). Lincoln: University of Nebraska Press.

Veroff, J., & Feld, S. (1970). *Marriage and work in America.* New York: Van Nostrand Reinhold.

Winter, D. G. (1973). *The power motive.* New York: The Free Press.

Winter, D. G. (1984). *The power motive in women—and men.* Unpublished manuscript. Wesleyan University.

# 6

# Cognitions About the Self

## CONNECTING FEELING STATES
## AND SOCIAL BEHAVIOR

## PETER SALOVEY
## JUDITH RODIN

**Peter Salovey** is a doctoral candidate in clinical psychology at Yale University. His research interests include the effects of mood and emotion on social cognition and social behavior (especially jealousy and envy), the relationship between health cognition and health behavior, and the application of social psychological theory and research to problems in clinical psychology. His dissertation research is based on the work described in this chapter.

**Judith Rodin** is the Philip R. Allen Professor of Psychology and Professor of Psychiatry at Yale University. She was the recipient of an APA Early Career Award in Social Psychology in 1977. Her current work focuses on the mechanisms mediating the role of perceived control in health, aging, eating disorders, and jealousy.

During the past two decades, a huge literature has emerged regarding the effects of mood and emotion on social behavior. Typically, studies in this tradition have involved the laboratory induction of a mood state—joy or sorrow most commonly—and a subsequent opportunity for subjects to engage in some kind of interpersonal behavior, such as helping or sharing (see Rosenhan, Karylowski, Salovey, & Hargis, 1981, for a review). Missing from these various investigations, however, is systematic study of the mediating processes that link these emotional experiences to social behavior. This chapter suggests that this "missing link" between emotional changes and behavioral changes is *the self*; specifically, the differential availability of cognitions about the self as object, including but not limited to self-evaluation, self-attribution, and self-complexity. Moods and emotions

**AUTHORS' NOTE:** We are grateful to Jerome L. Singer, Dennis C. Turk, and Marta E. Moret for their comments on an earlier draft of this chapter, and we are indebted to Jefferson A. Singer for his collaboration in our speculating about self-involvement in the laboratory induction of mood states. We consider Jefferson a co-author of the section entitled "Self-Involving Affect-Induction Procedures." Much of the theorizing in that section derives from lengthy discussions with him, and some of the text appeared in an earlier paper by Salovey and Singer (1983).

are hypothesized to make different aspects of the self more or less salient, and these changes in available cognitions about the self are what mediate the emotion-behavior relationship. The subsequent social behaviors serve to further increase the salience of specific self-cognitions. In this sense, social behaviors feed back to the self in order to prolong or attentuate the emotional experience.

The present chapter is organized in the following way. First, we elaborate a theoretical position regarding the mediating role of the self in the effects of emotion on social behavior. Then we review several self-cognition processes that are affected by moods and emotions, including (a) changes in self-evaluation during emotional experiences, (b) changes in self-attribution induced by emotional states, (c) the interrelationship of self-complexity and mood shift, (d) self-focused attention and the effects of moods on prosocial behavior, and (e) self-involvement in the laboratory induction of moods and emotions.

## THEORETICAL POSITION

Imagine, for a moment, that you are listening to the radio one evening and learn that two of the digits on your Daily Numbers State Lottery Ticket matched the winning solution, and that you will be receiving $1000. The emotion you are likely to experience is joy, and so you run out of the front door of your apartment to tell the world of your good fortune. On your way out, you pass an elderly woman who is struggling with a bag of groceries while fumbling for the keys to her door. Without thinking you say to her, "Here, let me help you with that," and you take the bag from her, bring the groceries into her kitchen and put them on the table. You leave the woman's apartment feeling very happy, and think to yourself, "I certainly am a fine person."

Why, in this instance, did you help her? Many times you have walked past individuals carrying heavy loads, but you cannot recall ever having helped out in this situation before. We might infer that the happiness you are feeling upon winning the lottery may cause you to be more helpful. But why should happiness have led to helpfulness rather than, say, arrogant gloating over your good fortune and contempt for those less lucky and hence more miserable than yourself? We argue that the reason you acted in the way that you did was that the emotion you experienced led to an increase in the accessibility of certain thoughts about yourself such as "good things certainly happen to good people" and "I must be a good person." On seeing the elderly woman, other self-cognitions might come to mind such as, "good guys help others," "I feel good when I help others," or "I'm an altruistic type of person."

Engaging in the helping act, in this example, served also to prolong the positive emotional state by increasing accessibility of other positive thoughts about the self as well.

Let us look at each of the assumptions of this model in more detail. Figure 6.1 depicts the steps involved in the emotion-behavior process. First, an emotion-evoking experience changes the way in which individuals organize information about and evaulate the self. That is, certain aspects of the self become differentially available during an affective experience. Second, these changes in self-cognition serve to promote or inhibit different social behaviors. Third, the social behaviors serve either to maintain positive affects and positive self-cognitions, or to bring negative affects and negative self-cognitions back into equilibrium; that is, return them to their respective states prior to the original emotion-inducing experience. In the present chapter, only the first of these three processes will be examined in detail. However, we shall outline each here.

### Assumption 1: Emotional Mood States Affect Self-Cognitions

The first step in the process by which affective changes impact social behaviors involves emotionally induced transient changes in cognitive structures and processes regarding the self, including (but not limited to) changes in the perceived complexity of the self, the perceived instrumentality of the self, and the amount of positive or negative regard one has for the self, all emanating from the extent to which one is caught up in the eliciting conditions of the mood or emotional state. Emotion- or mood-evoking experiences lead to changes in at least some of these aspects of the self.

The self has been conceptualized within a variety of theoretical frameworks (see Greenwald & Pratkanis, 1984, for a review), and the impact that moods or emotions have on the self could be incorporated into each of these theories. Researchers, according to Greenwald and Pratkanis, have organized the self as either (a) a central structure (Allport, 1961; Combs & Snygg, 1949; Cooley, 1902); (b) a schema (Markus, 1977; Markus & Sentis, 1982; Markus & Smith, 1981); (c) a hierarchical category structure (Rogers, 1981); (d) an unordered (nonhierarchical) collection of features (Smith & Medlin, 1981); (e) a prototype (Kuiper, 1981); (f) an associative network (Bower & Gilligan, 1979); or (g) a multidimensional space (Brecker & Greenwald, 1982). Although the details of these models are beyond the scope of this chapter, each of these structural models could incorporate the notion

TABLE 6.1
Some Self-Involving and Nonself-Involving
Mood Induction Procedures

| |
|---|
| *Self-Involving Inductions* |
| Self-generated imagery (e.g., imagining a recent mood-evoking experience) |
| Success and failure experiences consistent with self-concept |
| Enactive emotional experiences (killing an animal, etc.) |
| Role playing |
| Hypnosis |
| *Nonself-Involving Inductions* |
| Guided imagery |
| Velten mood statements |
| Audiotapes |
| Films |
| Success and failure experiences inconsistent with self-concept |
| General arousal (exercise, etc.) |

that the self—whether schema, network, or something else—might be affected by an induced mood or emotion. Yet, except for Bower's (1981; Bower & Cohen, 1982) conceptualization of emotion as a node within an associative network, little empirical work has been initiated in this area.

Gilligan and Bower (1984) described four ways in which moods and emotions could affect cognitive processing in general: (1) state-dependent recall—superior memory occurs when the recall mood state matches the learning mood state, (2) mood congruity—material agreeing in emotional tone with the subject's mood is learned best, (3) mood intensity—learning is positively correlated with the intensity of a mood, and (4) general cognitive consequences—subjects' thoughts, free associations, fantasies, interpretations, and judgments are thematically congruent with their mood state.

It is the last of these changes that most concerns us here. As was first demonstrated directly by Postman and Brown (1952), affect influences memory most frequently by facilitating the recall of cognitive material congruent with the induced affect. This effect has been found for both positive and negative states (Bower, Montiero, & Gilligan, 1978; Madigan & Bollenbach, 1982; Natale & Hantas, 1982; Snyder & White, 1982; Teasdale & Rezin, 1978; Teasdale & Taylor, 1981; Teasdale, Taylor, & Forgarty, 1980; Wright & Mischel, 1982). Some studies of affect and memory, however, have shown discrepant results for positive versus negative affect. In these studies, positive affect inductions promoted the recall of positively toned cognitions, whereas negative affect inductions failed to lead to parallel effects (Clark & Waddell, 1983; Isen, Shalker, Clark, & Karp, 1978; Nasby & Yando, 1982, Exp. 1; Mischel, Ebbesen, & Zeiss, 1976; Teasdale & Fogarty, 1979). In a recent experiment, Nasby and Yando (1982, Exp. 2) found the mood-congruity effect in encoding for the negative state of anger but not for sadness. We will return to the question of the relative difficulty of finding mood congruency effects in memory during negative affective states as compared with positive ones later in this chapter when we discuss competing "mood repair" processes in negative states. In addition, in the final section, we discuss methodological differences in negative mood induction procedures that characterize some studies in which mood-memory congruency effects were reported versus those in which such results were not obtained.

Bower (1981) has explained the impact of mood on cognitive processes in general in terms of a semantic network model of memory (Anderson & Bower, 1973; Collins & Loftus, 1975):

> The semantic network approach supposes that distinct emotion . . . has a specific node or unit in memory that collects together many other aspects of the emotion that are connected to it by associative pointers. . . . Collected around this emotion node are its associative autonomic reactions, standard role and expressive behaviors . . . and descriptions of standard evocative situations. . . . In addition, each emotion unit is also linked to propositions describing events from one's life during which that emotion was aroused. . . . Activation of an emotion node spreads activation throughout the memory structures to which it is connected, creating subthreshold excitation at those event nodes. Thus, a weak cue that partially describes an event. . . . may combine with activation from an emotion unit to raise the total activation of a relevant memory above a threshold of consciousness. (p. 135)

Mood, particularly positively valenced mood, seems to affect cognitive processing in a systematic way (see Bower and Mayer, 1985, for a recent failure to replicate these findings). The problem is that much less research attention has been focused on how moods affect cognitions about the self. We shall return to the research that has addressed this question shortly; it will form the majority of the present chapter.

### Assumption 2: Changes in Self-Cognitions Will Affect Subsequent Social Behaviors

The notion that thoughts about the self have an impact on one's behavior in interpersonal settings has been investigated by both social and personality psychologists. Attribution theorists in social psychology (e.g., Eiser, 1983; Harvey, Ickes, & Kidd, 1976, 1978, 1981; Jones et al.,

1972) have explored the behavioral consequences of inferring the cause of some external event as either the self or situational factors, and some of this research will be reviewed in a later section of this chapter. The idea that thoughts about oneself account for an individual's behavior is also one of the major theoretical underpinnings of social learning theory and cognitive-behavior therapy. Clinical psychologists working from these perspectives actually focus on individuals' thoughts about themselves revealed during therapy, as these cognitions are believed to have a direct effect on performance in social situations.

The most influential statement of this position is Bandura's self-efficacy theory (Bandura, 1977). Bandura contends that an individual's expectations of personal efficacy in some domain determine whether certain behaviors are, first, initiated and then sustained "in the face of obstacles and aversive experiences" (p. 191). According to Bandura (1982), the incorporation of efficacy expectations into one's self-concept influences choice of activities and environmental setting. People tend to avoid situations they believe will exceed their capabilities but perform activities they judge themselves capable of managing.

Cognitive-behavioral therapies take a more direct approach. According to this school of thought (e.g., Meichenbaum, 1977), cognitions about the self, called "self-statements," largely determine whether behavior is adaptive and functional or maladaptive and anxiety ridden. For example, Schwartz and Gottman (1976) studied high and low assertive individuals and found greater numbers of negative thoughts about the self and fewer positive ones among individuals who had difficulty asserting themselves in a role-playing situation requiring assertive behavior. In a more popular vein, Ellis (e.g., Ellis & Harper, 1961) has identified numerous irrational thoughts about the self that he feels lead to maladaptive behavior patterns (e.g., "I must be loved by everyone," "If I make a mistake, I'm a total failure").

Within social psychology, cognitive consistency theorists of the last decade frequently concerned themselves with determining the conditions under which self-relevant cognitions, such as attitudes or beliefs about the self, might be related to behavior (Abelson et al., 1968; Ajzen & Fishbein, 1977; Bem & Allen, 1974). For example, one's beliefs about one's abilities to size up a situation and quickly determine an appropriate way to behave—that is, one's self-monitoring skills (Snyder, 1974)—directly influence the way in which a person acts in social settings (Berscheid, Graziano, Monson, & Dermer, 1976; Ickes & Barnes, 1977; Lippa, 1976). In addition, individuals may be able to adapt their interpretive strategies to fit situations, processes that Showers and Cantor (1985) refer to as motivated social cognition.

## Assumption 3: Social Behaviors Feed Back to and Affect Mood States and Self-Cognitions

The final assumption in the present model is that social behaviors, when they occur subsequent to an emotionally provocative experience, serve to maintain positive mood states and positive self-cognitions and relieve negative mood states and temper negative self-cognitions. Although this process is relatively straightforward for positive mood states, it may be more complex for negative ones. Negative mood states do, at times, promote the recall of congruent (i.e., negative) cognitions, as Bower and others have demonstrated. We propose, however, that in time these negative cognitions will gradually give way to positive ones, as the individual seeks to terminate the negative mood by recruiting more positive aspects of the self.

Let's take an example in the positive realm first. Tesser's (1980; Tesser & Cambell, 1982, 1984; Tesser & Smith, 1980) model of self-evaluation maintenance argues that people will try to maintain a positive self-regard by engaging in behaviors that help them bask in the reflected glory of successful others when possible or dismiss such performances when they directly compete with one's own goals and actions. According to Tesser, the relevance of the other's performance to one's self-definition determines whether a process of comparison and competition or one of reflection will occur. If the domain of the other person's performance is self-definitionally relevant, comparison results. Reflection occurs when the domain is irrelevant. Given that, according to this theory, we are motivated to maintain (or raise) our self-esteem, we will bask in reflected glory at our friends' self-definitionally non-threatening successes. When relevance is high, however, we maintain self-esteem by engaging in behaviors such as distancing ourselves from the other person, reevaluating the quality of his or her performance, or actually interfering with the other person's behavior. All of these behaviors feed back to our cognitions about ourselves and bolster them.

In a recent study (Salovey & Rodin, 1984), we induced the affective state of envy in individuals by providing them with bogus negative feedback about themselves that was particularly self-relevant, followed by comparison to a similar but successful other person. We found that, subsequently, subjects engaged in a variety of behaviors that served to bolster their threatened self-evaluations: They derogated the rival and expressed diminished interest in befriending him or her. Apparently, individuals can maintain self-esteem by belittling potential rivals, distancing them as objects of possible negative comparison.

Alternatively, Cialdini and his associates (Cialdini, Darby, & Vincent, 1973; Cialdini & Kenrick, 1976; Kenrick, Baumann, & Cialdini, 1979) have argued that negative moods such as sorrow and depression increase helping behavior because by being generous to others, individuals can make themselves feel better. Their theory, called the Negative State Relief Model, holds that people experiencing a negative mood are motivated to terminate it. Because we are socialized to view altruistic acts as personally gratifying, being altruistic is one way people can relieve negative moods. Cialdini et al. (1973) tested this theory by hypothesizing that witnessing or committing a transgression would fail to produce increased helping when an event designed to reduce negative affect was interposed between the transgression and the helping opportunity. As predicted, they found that subjects who caused harm to a confederate were subsequently more helpful except when they received praise or money after the transgression but before the opportunity for altruism.

The idea that a negative mood state should lead to prosocial behavior is not particularly compatible with a spreading activation, associative network model of cognitive processing. In the associative tradition, negative moods should be more closely linked to negative memories and antisocial behaviors. Cialdini et al.'s Negative State Relief Model argues instead for a more functionalist approach by viewing the purpose of such behavior as the elimination of a negative mood state. The reality might be that both associative and mood repair processes occur in response to negative mood states, but in a temporal sequence. That is, initial cognitive (and even behavioral) activity following the induction of a negative mood state might be associative, mood congruent thoughts and behaviors. Given time, and a certain amount of higher-order processing, more functional, negative mood repairing thoughts and behaviors might take over, returning the organism to its initial affective equilibrium (see also Isen, 1984). It is possible that one difference between studies finding negative mood congruent thoughts and behaviors from those reporting opposite effects is the time at which such thoughts and behaviors are elicited. Immediately after negative mood induction, thoughts and behaviors are probably negative and antisocial, respectively. Later, however, they become more positive and prosocial.

So far, we have described three assumptions on which the emotion-social behavior link is based. In the remainder of this chapter, we shall consider the first of these by exploring some of the ways in which moods and emotions influence cognitive structures and processes regarding the self.

## MOOD AND EMOTION AFFECT SELF-EVALUATION

An obvious set of cognitions about the self influenced by moods and emotions are those that represent an individual's regard for himself or herself, that is, the individual's self-evaluation or self-esteem. Mood ratings tend to correlate with self-esteem scales (Wessman & Ricks, 1966), and cognitive theories of depression suggest that lowered self-esteem is one of the causal factors in affective disorders (Beck, 1967). Yet, few studies have actually manipulated mood and then measured changes in self-evaluation. In one such study, Amrhein, Salovey, and Rosenhan (1981) induced joy or sadness in a group of college students using highly evocative audiotapes describing either a Hawaiian vacation or a friend's death from cancer. Interestingly, among males but not among females, the mood induction radically altered self-appraisals. Happy men felt very good about themselves, far better than did happy women. Sad men felt awful about themselves, far worse than did sad women. The effects of these mood inductions seemed especially striking in the area of interpersonal self-evaluation, measured by items such as friendliness, attractiveness, selfishness, trustworthiness, and popularity. In addition, similar findings were noted on items measuring perceived health and self-satisfaction. Amrhein et al. interpreted these results as indicating, at least in men, an attributional vulnerability to taking personal responsibility for the cause of the mood state. The fact that women maintained a relatively stable self-evaluation in the face of mood changes may be due to their greater experience compared with men in dealing with emotion. Thus, when men are overcome by strong emotion, the effects on the self are more powerful simply because they have less skill in handling such emotion (Moore, Underwood, & Rosenhan, 1984).

Mischel, Ebbesen, and Zeiss (1976) induced positive and negative moods through success versus failure feedback on an intelligence test and found that subjects correctly remembered their personal liabilities less than their assets when they expected to succeed than when they expected to fail. Further, those subjects who experienced success remembered significantly more assets than did those who experienced failure. In a similar study (Natale & Hantas, 1982), subjects made to feel sad in a hypnotic mood induction procedure were less likely to recall positive life experiences, had weaker memory strength for positive information about themselves, and were biased toward recalling false negative information in self-descriptions. Subjects who were induced to feel happy were less likely to recall negative events involving themselves and more likely to recall positive events. Additionally, Underwood, Froming, and Moore (1977) induced happiness and found that all subjects subsequently felt more skillful, competent, proficient, and successful than after a sadness induction.

In a more wide-ranging study of the influence of affect on "cognitive social learning person variables" (p. 901), Wright and Mischel (1982) found that positive affect induced by recalling a recent pleasant event led subjects to form higher expectations for future performances, to recall more positive outcomes, and to make more favorable self-appraisals. Conversely, negative affect led to lower expectations about future performance, recall of fewer positive outcomes, and less favorable self-appraisals. Interestingly, the self-appraisal measure in this study was identical to Amrhein et al.'s, yet no gender differences were reported.

Thus, research suggests that experiencing emotion is associated with changes in one's regard for oneself. Although it may be true that individuals make inferences about themselves on the basis of the emotions they see themselves experiencing, it is our hypothesis that the experience of a feeling state causes a focusing of attention on oneself in a relatively "automatic" way, and that changes in available self-cognitions are similarly affected. This issue will be further discussed when we examine the mood/helping behavior literature.

## MOOD AND EMOTION AFFECT SELF-ATTRIBUTION

Another change in self-cognitions that is influenced by moods and emotions is the judging of one's impact on external events. That is, affective states alter perceptions of personal responsibility for successes and failures and the amount of control the individual assumes he or she has over the outcome of events. For example, Alloy and Abramson (1979) compared the abilities of nondepressed and depressed college students to estimate accurately the degree of contingency between a response that they had to make (pushing a button) and an environmental event (the illumination of a lamp). Interestingly, depressed subjects gave relatively accurate estimates of the degree to which they were controlling the external event, whereas nondepressed subjects overestimated their responsibility for this outcome. In general, nondepressed subjects overestimated how much control they had over objectively un-controllable outcomes associated with successes, such as winning money, and underestimated their control over similar events associated with failures, such as losing money (Abramson & Alloy, 1980; Alloy & Abramson, 1980). Apparently, nondepressed individuals labor under a self-serving bias, the "illusion of control" (Langer, 1975) making internal attributions for their successes and external attributions for their failures whereas depression seems to make individuals, according to Alloy and Abramson, "sadder but wiser."

In order to discover, however, whether such changes in the tendency to make self-attributions are due to mood changes rather than some other aspect of depression, affect would have to be induced in subjects followed by tasks similar to those described above that allow subjects to estimate their degree of control over relatively noncontingent outcomes. Alloy, Abramson, and Viscusi (1981) conducted such a study, inducing either elation or depression using the Velten (1968) procedure (reading statements suggesting that the subject feel a particular mood) in samples of depressed and normal college students. Using the same button-pressing and lamp-lighting task described above, Alloy et al. found that naturally depressed students temporarily made elated by the mood induction procedure overestimated the control they thought they had over the uncontrollable external event, whereas nondepressed subjects who were induced to feel saddened accurately judged their personal control over the event. Thus, both groups were influenced by the acute manipulation of affect. Replicating their earlier findings, naturally depressed students exposed to neutral mood inductions accurately judged that they had little responsibility for the external event. Nondepressed subjects in the neutral induction condition, however, overestimated their personal control.

Working within a cognitive model of depression, Alloy, Abramson, and their colleagues have amassed a reasonably large group of studies supporting the findings described above. Interesting findings have also been obtained by other researchers. For example, Hoffman's (1978, cited in Moore et al., 1984) subjects actually attributed increased personal responsibility for success after being made to feel sad, presumably in an attempt to alleviate the sadness. In addition, findings that people act so as to maintain the illusion of control (e.g., Langer, 1975) do not appear to hold for depressed people, who are more likely to attend to and be affected by failure feedback than success feedback (Hammen & Krantz, 1976) and who generally make self-attributions for failures and external attributions for successes (Rizley, 1978).

In sum, one kind of self-relevant cognition that is affected by moods and emotions is the sense of being responsible for external events. Changes in this domain of the self may be closely related to those reviewed earlier in the section on changes in general self-evaluation. Positive moods may raise one's self-regard leading to a biased view of one's control over external events. Negative moods, by diminishing self-evaluation, may eliminate this bias.

## SELF-COMPLEXITY MODERATES MOOD VARIABILITY

One implication of the model proposed in this chapter is that affective states should promote a reduction in self-complexity. That is, when one experiences mood or emotion, one should represent the self more simply, as fewer aspects that are relatively independent from each other. When one is experiencing a particular mood state, it is difficult to call to mind aspects of the self that are inconsistent with the mood state. Rather, a limited set of mood-consistent self-representations is available. Such a change in self-complexity may affect the kinds of social behaviors the individual will subsequently perform.

Changes in self-complexity caused by changes in emotion or mood have yet to be demonstrated. However, Linville (in press) has suggested that the converse is true. That is, the less complex a person's representation of the self, the more extreme are his or her affective states and self-appraisals. In general, cognitive simplicity has been shown to be associated with extreme affective reactions of all kinds, such as stereotyping (Brewer, 1979; Linville, Salovey, & Fischer, in press; Wilder, 1980). It is plausible that changes in mood and self-complexity influence each other in the same way, that is, low self-complexity leading to more extreme affect, and more extreme affect reducing the complexity of one's self-representation.

But what is meant by the complexity of one's self-representation? Depending on one's conceptualization of the self, complexity can be operationalized in a variety of ways, for example, as greater numbers of dimensions in a multidimensional spatial representation (Rosenberg & Sedlak, 1972), greater numbers of features or lower redundancy of features in a feature set representation (Anderson, Kline, & Beasley, 1979), greater numbers of levels in a hierarchical feature tree representation (Sattath & Tversky, 1977), greater numbers of nodes and connections among nodes in an associative network structure (Anderson, 1976), or as a function of the number of aspects that one uses to organize knowledge about the self, and the degree of relatedness of these aspects (Linville, in press).

According to Linville (in press), those lower in self-complexity will experience greater swings in affect and self-appraisal. If an individual can maintain many distinct aspects of the self, the impact of negative events is buffered for that individual because less of the "total self" is affected by them, assuming, though, that many of these aspects of the self are salient or available to the individual. Linville tested this notion by having individuals who were high or low in self-complexity receive bogus feedback of either success or failure on an intelligence test. On both mood and self-evaluation measures, subjects who had low self-complexity (as determined by a role sorting task) felt worse about themselves than subjects higher in self-complexity following failure feedback. Likewise, low complexity subjects felt better and had higher self-appraisals than high complexity subjects following powerful success feedback. In a second study, Linville compared high and low self-complexity subjects for variability on a mood diary completed during a 14-day period. As predicted, low-complexity subjects showed higher variances in their mood ratings during the two-week period than did high complexity subjects.

This research has several implications for our entire three-step model. Individuals with simple self-representations should be particularly likely to show the changes in self-cognitions that we have described, particularly in the attributional and evaluational areas. As Linville points out, once a low-complexity individual is exposed to an event that is affectively negative, negative thoughts and feelings about the self will "spill over" (p. 26) from aspect to aspect causing the mood to persist and coloring many aspects of the self, as such aspects for the low complexity individual are both fewer in number and less independent of each other. We would expect that such individuals would be less likely to use social behavior to ameliorate the depressed mood. With more of the self involved in experiencing the depression, attention may be totally self-absorbed and behavioral opportunities may be ignored. In addition, behavior may simply not be effective in removing the negative mood because so much of the self is wrapped up in it.

### FOCUS OF ATTENTION ON THE SELF
### MEDIATES THE IMPACT OF AFFECT

The notion that the effects of moods and emotions on social behavior are moderated by differential availability of self-relevant cognitions implies that affective experiences cause a focusing of attention on the self, an idea that has received some confirmation (Easterbrook, 1959; Wegner & Giuliano, 1980). Thus, if we examine the effects of moods on social behavior and find that deliberately focusing attention either away from the self or on the self radically alters the consequent social behavior, we have generated some support for our primary premise that changes in self-relevant cognitive activities mediate the relationship between affective states and social behavior. In this section, we shall use the literature on how the effects of moods on helping are mediated by focus of attention to illustrate this point.

In studies by Rosenhan and his associates, joy or sadness was induced using an audiotaped induction procedure, and subjects were instructed to focus on either their own thoughts and feelings or on those of another person. For joy (Rosenhan, Salovey, & Hargis, 1981) subjects listened to a description of the delightful activities that either they or their best friend experienced on a Hawaiian vacation (manipulation checks revealed that subjects in both of these conditions were more joyful than subjects in a neutral control condition). In studies dealing with sadness (Thompson, Cowan, & Rosenhan, 1980), subjects listened to a tape that solemnly described their friend's tragic death from cancer. Subjects were

directed to attend to either the worry, anxiety, and intense pain of their
dying friend or to their own pain and sorrow caused by their friend's
death (these conditions did not differ significantly in the amount of
sadness generated). Both studies included neutral mood control conditions. In each of these experiments, subjects had the opportunity to
help another person (unrelated to the experimenter) following the mood
induction.

Interestingly, joy facilitated helping, but only when attention was
focused on the self. When attention was focused on another, joy actually
depressed helping below the level of the neutral controls. The results for
sadness were the mirror image of those for joy. When attention was
focused on others, sadness promoted helping; whereas when attention
was focused on the self, sadness retarded helping.

In a follow-up study in which only self-focused and other-focused
joy were induced and subjects were given the opportunity to help
someone of higher, same, or lower social status than themselves, self-
focused joy facilitated the helping of higher and same status recipients,
whereas other-focused joy stimulated the helping of lower status
recipients (Salovey & Rosenhan, 1983). Apparently, focusing attention
on the self during a joyful experience may have led to self-cognitions
regarding personal efficacy and competence, whereas when attention
was focused on others during a positive emotional experience, the
central cognitions may have been more empathic in nature, making the
individual more sensitive to those who are less fortunate than oneself
(see Isen, 1970).

Other researchers have examined the mood, focus of attention,
helping question in other ways. In three studies dealing only with
negative affect and helping behavior, Rogers, Miller, Mayer, and Duval
(1982) found that focus of attention mediated the following effect:
Internal attribution of responsibility for a negative mood state increased
willingness to help when the request was made salient, but inhibited it
when the request lacked salience. Apparently, subjects can get so self-
focused during a negative emotional experience that they are unaware of
a subsequent opportunity for helping, unless it is made very salient.

Kidd and Marshall (1982) examined the mediational effects of
attentional focus on the mood/helping relationship in a very direct way.
They hypothesized that both negative and positive feelings would
increase helpfulness. In the case of negative moods, they believed,
helpfulness would be inhibited if the induced affect engendered self-
reflection by associating the bad mood with the person's self-image. To
test this hypothesis, Kidd and Marshall had female subjects read mood-
inducing statements that were negative, neutral, or positive; for negative
mood, they were written in either the first or the third person. Similar to

the Thompson et al. (1980) and Rosenhan et al. (1981) studies, these researchers found that subjects who read the self-focused negative statements were least likely to comply with a helping request, whereas the most helpful were those who read positive statements (which were self-focused) or negative statements that were not self-referencing. Neutral mood subjects helped in intermediate quantities.

All of the studies reviewed in this section suggest that during emotional experiences—and particularly when they are negative—there is a tendency for individuals to focus their attention on themselves, unless the experimenter redirects it elsewhere (see also Dovidio & MacKay, 1983; McMillan, Sanders, & Solomon, 1977). It seems that when individuals have these emotional experiences, they become self-preoccupied. Their attention turns away from external social cues, and shifts inward. There seems to be more of an inclination to search inward for the source of the mood than outward, a tendency that is diffficult to reconcile with a Schachter-Singer (1962) model of emotion. The mood/helping literature provides support for the idea that emotions and moods often cause an inward focusing of attention, presumably on cognitions about the self. Consistently, if natural attentional processes are redirected experimentally, quite different behavioral consequences result.

## SELF-INVOLVING AFFECT-INDUCTION PROCEDURES

One implication of a model of the effects of emotion on social behaviors that posits a significant role for self-relevant cognitive activities between affect and behavior is that laboratory mood-induction procedures involving focusing attention on the self should produce very different kinds of cognitive, psychophysiological, and behavioral consequences than procedures that are less self-involving. Salovey and Singer (1983) have proposed that in laboratory affect induction procedures, self-involving processes are those that engage the subject in vivid imagery of previous or potential emotional experiences. Nonselfinvolving induction procedures are those that fail to elicit vivid, selfengaging imagery. Examples of each of these types of procedures can be found in Table 6.1.

Based on high versus low self-involvement produced by the way in which affect was elicited, two different patterns of effects were proposed. The first pattern, which they called "emotion," is induced by techniques that promote highly self-involving imagery, and consists of differential patterns of physiology, facial expression, and cognitive activity in addition to an identifiable and discrete subjective experience. The second pattern, which they called "mood," is induced by nonself-

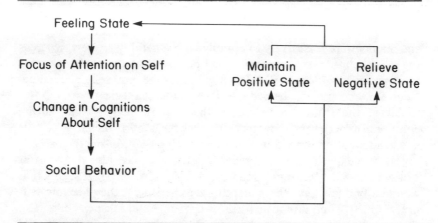

Figure 6.1  **Feeling states are linked to social behaviors through cognitions about the self.**

involving procedures that fail to invoke vivid, differential images. A nonspecific arousal results, prompting a search for internal and external cues and appropriate appraisal. Subjects do not rely on physiological differentiation for aid in identifying their emotional states, but rather attend to the transient demands of the moment.

Historically, in psychological research on affect, the first position ("emotion") is the characteristic view of affect of personality psychologists (e.g., Izard, 1972, 1977; Singer, 1974; Tomkins, 1962, 1963, 1979, 1981) and psychophysiologists (e.g., Schwartz, 1982). On the other hand, social psychologists usually operate within the second alternative (e.g., Clark & Isen, 1982; Schachter & Singer, 1962). With the increased attention being given to the integration of personality processes, cognitive activities, and social behaviors (e.g., Bower, 1981; Cantor & Kihlstrom, 1981; Isen, 1984; Kihlstrom, 1981; Showers & Cantor, 1985; Zajonc, 1980), affect is finally being studied more systematically, integrating psychophysiological, cognitive, and behavioral dependent variables. Yet, this integration has led to an invigorating and, at times, acrimonious debate regarding the fundamental nature of affect. In general, personality psychologists have rejected undifferentiated arousal models as physiologically primitive and phenomenologically uncompelling. Social psychologists, however, have generally found theories involving psychophysiologically differentiated emotions to be vague, unoperationalizable, and too biologically determined.

Although Schachter's "undifferentiated arousal" model of affect is not an adequate explanation for all emotional experiences, neither are all

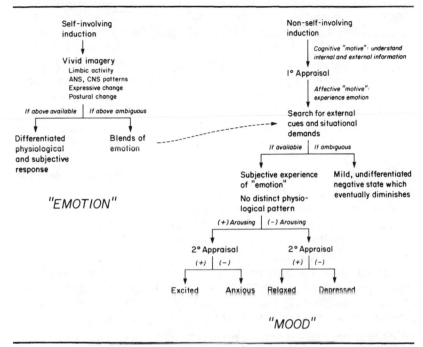

Figure 6.2  Self-involvement distinguishes emotions from moods. Adapted from "Self-involving imagery and the experience of affect: An integration of findings from the facial feedback, memory, and helping literatures" by P. Salovey and J. A. Singer, 1983. Unpublished manuscript, Yale University.

affective processes characterized by distinct physiological patterning. Appraisal of undifferentiated arousal may characterize mood states, whereas the generation of distinct physiological patterns may characterize an emotional experience. Emotions tend to be intense but transient; moods are often longer lasting but less powerful. Often, emotions tend to diminish and leave a moodlike residue as their final stage. As Figure 6.2 illustrates, affect may involve both a display (or communicative) component and an imagery component. These two components are thought to be less associated in mood states but are typically quite correlated in emotions.

During an emotional experience, the imaginal processing associated with that emotion requires distinct cardiovascular and limbic system feedback in order to invoke the requisite feeling. Such changes are detected by subjective report, as well as changes in heart rate, blood pressure, EEG, and facial expression. If all of the components diagrammed in Figure 6.2 are present, enough internal information is obtained to achieve a specific emotional reaction. This state should be manifested by distinct patterns in the aforementioned variables. However, if some of these components are missing or ambiguous, there will be a search by the subject to recognize his or her emotional state. In other words, a lack of physiological differentiation or discrete imagery will lead the individual to rely on external cues and self-perception to determine his or her feeling state. If the cues are not present or are ambiguous, a mildly negative yet undifferentiated mood state will be experienced. If the individual's physiological state is excitatory, and positively toned cues *are* available, the mood state will be excitement, but if negative cues are available, the mood state will be anxiety. If the physiological state is inhibitory, the presence of positive cues will result in relaxation; negatively toned cues will promote depression.

The implication of this differentiation of two kinds of affective processes (for which the names "emotion" and "mood" may prove not to be ideal) is that the kinds of self-relevant cognitions that we have been discussing should be easily available to the individual experiencing the fully integrated emotional experience. For mood states, attention must be more actively focused on the self for an individual to become aware of changes in self-cognitions. When mood states are accompanied by specific instructions to focus attention on the self, a greater awareness of the differential availability of aspects of the self results.

In fact, studies that use self-involving affect inductions often report results incompatible with those obtained from inductions that are not self-involving. For example, compare the Amrhein et al. (1981) study of self-evaluation changes after mood induction with that of Wright and Mischel (1982). Both studies used the same measure of self-evaluation, but changes after mood induction were found only on some of the items and only by male subjects in the Amrhein et al. study, yet changes were noted on nearly all items and by all subjects in the Wright and Mischel study. The only major difference between these two experiments was that Wright and Mischel used a more self-involving affect induction procedure (self-generated imagery as opposed to the guided imagery manipulation used by Amrhein et al.).

Similarly, consider the mood and memory studies briefly reviewed earlier. Some showed mood congruency effects in recall for both positive and negative moods and others only for positive moods, with no effect for negative moods. One feature that characterizes these latter experiments is their reliance on nonself-involving mood induction procedures. For example, Clark and Waddell (1983) used guided imagery, Isen et al. (1978) used success or failure on a Star Trek video game, Mischel et al. (1976) employed false feedback on a personality test, and Teasdale and Fogarty (1979) used the Velten Mood Statements.

Although threat of shock or false personality feedback may seem self-involving, the subject's experience in these inductions is as likely to be one of uncertainty or confusion as it is to be a specific emotional state such as sadness. That is, subjects whose self-images are abruptly challenged by false feedback are as likely to feel defensive and questioning as they are to feel depressed. Similarly, if subjects experience nonself-involving general anxiety rather than a differentiated negative emotion, they do not show the expected mood congruency effects in recall (Macht, Spear, & Levis, 1977).

On the other hand, studies reporting mood congruency effects in memory for both positive and negative feeling states often use more self-involving affect induction procedures (resulting in the affective process called "emotion," above). For example, Bower et al. (1978) used hypnosis to induce positive or negative feeling states (see also Bower, 1981), Natale and Hantas (1982) used the Velten (1968) statements but in a hypnotic context, and Wright and Mischel (1982), described earlier, had subjects generate their own affect-invoking imagery. Future research must validate this argument, however, as exceptions to this general trend can be located (e.g., Madigan & Bollenbach, 1982; Snyder & White, 1981; Teasdale & Taylor 1981; Teasdale et al., 1980).

## SUMMARY AND INTEGRATION

This chapter opened with a description of a three-step model to account for the processes by which cognition about the self mediates the relationship between affective experiences and social behaviors. These three steps can be summarized as follows: (1) moods and emotions affect self-relevant cognitive processes, (2) changes in these self-cognitions affect subsequent social behaviors, and (3) the cognitions and affects engendered by these social behaviors feed back to the self and can prolong positive states or relieve negative states. Evidence for each of these assumptions was briefly presented, but the remainder of the chapter dealt primarily with the first proposition.

This first premise, that moods and emotions affect self-relevant cognitive processes, was elaborated by drawing on research in disparate areas that supports it. Thus, self-relevant cognitive processes that are or might be influenced by affect were discussed, including (a) the impact of emotional states on self-evaluation, (b) the effects that moods and emotions have on the tendency to make internal (self) attributions for external events, (c) the association between complexity in one's self-representation and vulnerability to mood changes, (d) the fact that shifts in focus of attention from the self to others dramatically alter the helping behavior that follows a mood induction, and (e) the ways in which self-involving affect induction procedures differ from those that involve the self to a lesser extent. The third area, the association between complexity in self-representation and vulnerability to mood changes, really does not yet provide evidence for changes in self-cognition following the experience of affect. The data on how complexity affects mood shift suggest that there is reason to believe the converse might be true. Such a demonstration, however, awaits further research.

These five areas of research do not address the question of *how* affect changes self-relevant cognitive processes directly. That too will be the aim of future work. However, the first two research areas (the influence of affect on self-evaluation and self-attributions) provide firm evidence for changes in the content of self-cognitions during affective experiences. The third area, self-complexity and mood variability, suggests that changes in structural characteristics of the self might be linked to emotional changes as well. The fourth research area, focus of attention, provides evidence for the importance of cognitions about the self in mediating the affect/behavior relationship by noting the changes in behavior that result from a failure to attend to these self-cognitions. This is an issue also addressed by the fifth area—which is admittedly more speculative—examining the role of self-involvement in the laboratory induction of feeling states.

Separately, these five lines of research do not prove the major thesis of this chapter. But, as we progressed from one area to the next, we increased the scope of the self's involvement in feeling states, moving from changes in the content of the self, to changes in the structure of the self, to, finally, a point where feeling states and self-cognitions were mutually interdependent. Taken together, these areas of study provide strong evidence for the importance of considering changes in self-relevant cognitive processes and structures as the key to understanding the link between affect and subsequent social behavior.

## REFERENCES

Abelson, R. P., Aronson, E., McGuire, W. J., Newcomb, T. M., Rosenberg, M. J., & Tannenbaum, P. H. (1968). *Theories of cognitive consistency: A sourcebook.* Chicago: Rand McNally.

Abramson, L. Y., & Alloy, L. B. (1980). Judgment of contingency: Errors and their implications. In A. Baum & J. E. Singer (Eds.), *Advances in environmental psychology* (Vol. 2). Hillsdale, NJ: Lawrence Erlbaum.

Ajzen, I., & Fishbein, M. (1977). Attitude-behavior relations: A theoretical analysis and review of empirical research. *Psychological Bulletin, 84*, 888-918.

Alloy, L. B., & Abramson, L. Y. (1979). Judgment of contingency in depressed and nondepressed students: Sadder but wiser? *Journal of Experimental Psychology: General, 108*, 441-485.

Alloy, L. B., & Abramson, L. Y. (1980). The cognitive component of human helplessness and depression: A critical analysis. In J. Garber & M.E.P. Seligman (Eds.), *Human helplessness: Theory and application.* New York: Academic.

Alloy, L. B., Abramson, L. Y., & Viscusi, D. (1981). Induced mood and the illusion of control. *Journal of Personality and Social Psychology, 41,* 1129-1140.

Allport, G. W. (1961). *Pattern and growth in personality.* New York: Holt, Rinehart, & Winston.

Amrhein, J., Salovey, P., & Rosenhan, D. L. (1981). *Joy and sadness generate attributional vulnerability in men.* Unpublished manuscript, Stanford University.

Anderson, J. R. (1976). *Language, memory, and thought.* Hillsdale, NJ: Lawrence Erlbaum.

Anderson, J. R., & Bower, G. H. (1973). *Human associative memory.* Hillsdale, NJ: Lawrence Erlbaum.

Anderson, J. R., Kline, P. J., & Beasley, C. M. (1979). A general learning theory and its application to schema abstraction. In G. Bower (Ed.), *The psychology of learning and motivation* (Vol. 13). New York: Academic.

Bandura, A. (1977). Self-efficacy: Toward a unifying theory of behavioral change. *Psychological Review, 84,* 191-215.

Bandura, A. (1982). The self and mechanisms of agency. In J. Suls (Ed.), *Social psychological perspectives on the self* (Vol. 1). Hillsdale, NJ: Lawrence Erlbaum.

Beck, A. T. (1967). *Depression: Clinical, experimental, and theoretical aspects.* New York: Harper & Row.

Bem, D. J., & Allen, A. (1974). On predicting some of the people some of the time: The search for cross-situational consistencies in behavior. *Psychological Review, 81,* 506-520.

Berscheid, E., Graziano, W., Monson, T., & Dermer, M. (1976). Outcome dependency: Attention, attribution, and attraction. *Journal of Personality and Social Psychology, 34,* 978-989.

Bower, G. H. (1981). Mood and memory. *American Psychologist, 36,* 129-148.

Bower, G. H., & Cohen, P. R. (1982). Emotional influences in memory and thinking: Data and theory. In M. S. Clark & S. T. Fiske (Eds.), *Affect and cognition.* Hillsdale, NJ: Lawrence Erlbaum.

Bower, G. H., & Gilligan, S. G. (1979). Remembering information related to one's self. *Journal of Research in Personality, 13,* 420-461.

Bower, G. H., & Mayer, J. D. (1985). Failure to replicate mood-dependent retrieval. *Bulletin of the Psychonomic Society, 23,* 39-42.

Bower, G. H., Montiero, K. P., & Gilligan, S. G. (1978). Emotional mood as a context for learning and recall. *Journal of Verbal Learning and Verbal Behavior, 17,* 573-585.

Breckler, S. J., & Greenwald, A. G. (1982). *Charting coordinates for the self-concept in multi-dimensional trait space.* Presented at the annual meeting of the American Psychological Association, Washington, DC.

Brewer, M. B. (1979). Ingroup bias in the minimal intergroup situation: A cognitive-motivational analysis. *Psychological Bulletin, 86,* 307-324.

Cantor, N., & Kihlstrom, J. F. (1981) *Personality, cognition, and social interaction.* Hillsdale, NJ: Lawrence Erlbaum.

Cialdini, R. B., Darby, B. L., & Vincent, J. E. (1973). Transgression and altruism: A case for hedonism. *Journal of Experimental Social Psychology, 9,* 502-516.

Cialdini, R. B., & Kenrick, D. T. (1976). Altruism as hedonism: A social development perspective on the relationship of negative mood state and helping. *Journal of Personality and Social Psychology, 34,* 907-914.

Clark, M. S., & Isen, A. M. (1982). Toward understanding the relationship between feeling states and social behavior. In A. Hastorf & A. M. Isen (Eds.), *Cognitive social psychology.* New York: Elsevier North-Holland.

Clark, M. S., & Waddell, B. A. (1983). Effects of moods on thoughts about helping, attraction, and information acquisition. *Social Psychology Quarterly, 46,* 31-35.

Collins, A. M., & Loftus, E. F. (1975). A spreading-activation theory of semantic processing. *Psychological Review, 82,* 407-428.

Combs, A. W., & Snygg, D. (1949). *Individual behavior: A perceptual approach to behavior.* New York: Harper Brothers.

Cooley, C. H. (1902). *Human nature and the social order.* New York: Scribners.

Dovidio, J. F., & MacKay, K. S. (1983). *Helping behavior, attention, and mood.* Presented at the annual convention of the American Psychological Association, Anaheim, CA.

Easterbrook, J. A. (1959). The effects of emotion on cue utilization and the organization of behavior. *Psychological Review, 66,* 183-200.

Eiser, J. R. (1983). From attributions to behavior. In M. Hewstone (Ed.), *Attribution theory: Social and functional extensions.* Oxford: Basil Blackwell.

Ellis, A., & Harper, R. A. (1961). *A guide to rational living.* Englewood Cliffs, NJ: Prentice-Hall.

Gilligan, S. G., & Bower, G. H. (1984). Cognitive consequences of emotional arousal. In C. Izard, J. Kagen, & R. Zajonc (Eds.), *Emotions, cognitions, and behavior.* New York: Cambridge University Press.

Greenwald, A. G., & Pratkanis, A. R. (1984). The self. In R. S. Wyer & T. K. Srull (Eds.), *Handbook of social cognition* (Vol. 3). Hillsdale, NJ: Lawrence Erlbaum.

Hammen, C. L., & Krantz, S. (1976). Effects of success and failure on depressive cognitions. *Journal of Abnormal Psychology, 85,* 577-586.

Harvey, J. H., Ickes, W. J., & Kidd, R. F. (1976). *New directions in attribution research* (Vol. 1). Hillsdale, NJ: Lawrence Erlbaum.

Harvey, J. H., Ickes, W. J., & Kidd, R. F. (1978). *New directions in attribution research* (Vol. 2). Hillsdale, NJ: Lawrence Erlbaum.

Harvey, J. H., Ickes, W. J., & Kidd, R. F. (1981). *New directions in attribution research* (Vol. 3). Hillsdale, NJ: Lawrence Erlbaum.

Ickes, W. J., & Barnes, R. D. (1977). The role of sex and self-monitoring in unstructured dyadic interactions. *Journal of Personality and Social Psychology, 35,* 315-330.

Isen, A. M. (1970). Success, failure, attention, and reaction to others: The warm glow of success. *Journal of Personality and Social Psychology, 15,* 294-301.

Isen, A. M. (1984). Toward understanding the role of affect in cognition. In R. S. Wyer & T. K. Srull (Eds.), *Handbook of social cognition* (Vol. 3). Hillsdale, NJ: Lawrence Erlbaum.

Isen, A. M., Shalker, T. E., Clark, M., & Karp, L. (1978). Affect, accessibility of material in memory, and behavior: A cognitive loop? *Journal of Personality and Social Psychology, 36,* 385-393.

Izard, C. E. (1972). *The face of emotions.* New York: Appleton-Century-Crofts.

Izard, C. E. (1977). *Human emotion.* New York: Plenum.

Jones, E. E., Kanouse, D. E., Kelley, H. H., Nisbett, R. E., Valins, S., & Weiner, B. (1972). *Attribution: Perceiving the causes of behavior.* Morristown, NJ: General Learning Press.

Kenrick, D. T., Baumann, D. J., & Cialdini, R. B. (1979). A step in the socialization of altruism as hedonism: Effect of negative mood on children's generosity under public and private conditions. *Journal of Personality and Social Psychology, 37,* 747-755.

Kidd, R. F., & Marshall, L. (1982). Self-reflection, mood, and helpful behavior. *Journal of Research in Personality, 16,* 319-334.

Kihlstrom, J. F. (1981). On personality and memory. In N. Cantor & J. F. Kilhstrom (Eds.), *Personality, cognition, and social interaction.* Hillsdale, NJ: Erlbaum.

Kuiper, N. A. (1981). Convergent evidence for the self as a prototype: The "inverted-U RT effect" for self and other judgments. *Personality and Social Psychology Bulletin, 7,* 438-443.

Langer, E. J. (1975). The illusion of control. *Journal of Personality and Social Psychology, 32,* 311-328.

Linville, P. W. (1982). The complexity-extremity effect and age-based stereotyping. *Journal of Personality and Social Psychology, 42,* 193-211.

Linville, P. W. (in press). Self-complexity and affective extremity: Don't put all of your eggs in one cognitive basket. *Social Cognition.*

Linville, P. W., Salovey, P., & Fischer, G. (in press). Variance and covariance in social categorization: Familiarity breeds differentiation. In S. Gaertner & J. Dovidio (Eds.), *Contemporary racial attitudes: Motivational and cognitive approaches.* New York: Academic.

Lippa, R. (1976). Expressive control and the leakage of dispositional introversion-extroversion during role-playing teaching. *Journal of Personality, 44,* 541-559.

Macht, M. L., Spear, N. E., & Levis, D. J. (1977). State-dependent retention in humans induced by alternatives in affective state. *Bulletin of the Psychonomic Society, 10,* 415-418.

Madigan, R. J., & Bollenbach, A. K. (1982). Effects of induced mood on retrieval of personal episodic and semantic memories. *Psychological Reports, 50,* 147-157.

Markus, H. (1977). Self-schemata and processing information about the self. *Journal of Personality and Social Psychology, 35,* 63-78.

Markus, H., & Sentis, K. (1982). The self in information processing. In J. Suls (Ed.), *Psychological perspectives on the self* (Vol. 1). Hillsdale, NJ: Lawrence Erlbaum.

Markus, H., & Smith, J. (1981). The influence of self-schema on the perception of others. In N. Cantor & J. Kihlstrom (Eds.), *Personality, Cognition, and Social Interaction*. Hillsdale, NJ: Lawrence Erlbaum.

McMillan, D. S., Sanders, D. Y., & Solomon, G. S. (1977). Self-esteem, attentiveness, and helping behavior. *Personality and Social Psychology Bulletin, 3*, 257-262.

Meichenbaum, D. (1977). *Cognitive-behavior modification: An integrative approach*. New York: Plenum.

Mischel, W., Ebbesen, E. E., & Zeiss, A. (1976). Determinants of selective memory about the self. *Journal of Consulting and Clinical Psychology, 44*, 92-103.

Moore, B., Underwood, B., & Rosenhan, D. L. (1984). Emotion, self and others. In C. Izard, J. Kagan, & R. Zajonc (Eds.), *Emotions, cognitions, and behavior*. New York: Cambridge University Press.

Nasby, W., & Yando, R. (1982). Selective encoding and retrieval of affectively-valent information: Two cognitive consequences of mood. *Journal of Personality and Social Psychology, 43*, 1244-1253.

Natale, M., & Hantas, M. (1982). Effect of temporary mood states on selective memory about the self. *Journal of Personality and Social Psychology, 42*, 927-934.

Postman, L., & Brown, D. R. (1952). The perceptual consequences of success and failure. *Journal of Abnormal and Social Psychology, 47*, 213-221.

Rizley, R. (1978). Depression and distortion in the attribution of causality. *Journal of Abnormal Psychology, 87*, 32-48.

Rogers, T. B. (1981). A model of the self as an aspect of the human information processing system. In N. Cantor & J. Kihlstrom (Eds.), *Personality, cognition, and social interaction*. Hillsdale, NJ: Lawrence Erlbaum.

Rogers, M., Miller, N., Mayer, F. S., & Duval, S. (1982). Personal responsibility and salience of the request for help: Determinants of the relation between negative affect and helping behavior. *Journal of Personality and Social Psychology, 43*, 956-970.

Rosenberg, S., & Sedlak, A. (1972). A structural representation of implicit personality theory. In L. Berkowitz (Ed.), *Advances in experimental social psychology* (Vol. 6). New York: Academic.

Rosenhan, D. L., Karylowski, J., Salovey, P., & Hargis, K. (1981). Affect and altruism. In J. P. Rushton & R. M. Sorrentino (Eds.), *Altruism and helping behavior*. Hillsdale, NJ: Lawrence Erlbaum.

Rosenhan, D. L., Salovey, P., & Hargis, K. (1981). The joys of helping: Focus of attention mediates the impact of positive affect on altruism. *Journal of Personality and Social Psychology, 40*, 899-905.

Salovey, P., & Rodin, J. (1984). Some antecedents and consequences of social-comparison jealousy. *Journal of Personality and Social Psychology, 47*, 780-792.

Salovey, P., & Rosenhan, D. L. (1983). *Effects of joy, attention, and recipient's status on helpfulness*. Presented at the annual meeting of the American Psychological Association, Anaheim, CA.

Salovey, P., & Singer, J. A. (1983). *Self-involving imagery and the experience of affect: An integration of findings from the facial feedback, memory, and helping literatures*. Unpublished manuscript, Yale University.

Sattath, S., & Tversky, A. (1977). Additive similarity trees. *Psychometrika, 42*, 319-345.

Schachter, S., & Singer, J. E. (1962). Cognitive, social and physiological determinants of emotional state. *Psychological Review, 62*, 379-399.

Schwartz, G. (1982). Physiological patterning and emotion: Implications for the self-regulation of emotion. In K. R. Blankstein & J. Polivy (Eds.), *Self-control and self-modification of emotional behavior*. New York: Plenum.

Schwartz, R. M., & Gottman, J. M. (1976). Toward a task analysis of assertive behavior. *Journal of Consulting and Clinical Psychology, 44*, 910-920.

Showers, C., & Cantor N. (1985). Social cognition: A look at motivated strategies. In M. R. Rosenzweig & L. W. Porter (Eds.), *Annual review of psychology* (Vol. 36). Palo Alto, CA: Annual Reviews.

Singer, J. L. (1974). *Imagery and daydream methods in psychotherapy and behavior modification*. New York: Academic Press.

Smith, E. E., & Medin, D. L. (1981). *Categories and concepts*. Cambridge: Harvard University Press.

Snyder, M. (1974). Self-monitoring of expressive behavior. *Journal of Personality and Social Psychology, 30*, 526-537.

Snyder, M., & White, P. (1982). Moods and memories: Elation, depression, and the remembering of events in one's life. *Journal of Personality, 50*, 149-167.

Teasdale, J. D., & Fogarty, S. J. (1979). Differential effects of induced mood on retrieval of pleasant and unpleasant events from episodic memory. *Journal of Abnormal Psychology, 88*, 248-257.

Teasdale, J. D., & Rezin, V. (1978). The effects of reducing frequency of negative thoughts on the mood of depressed patients—tests of a cognitive model of depression. *British Journal of Social and Clinical Psychology, 17*, 65-74.

Teasdale, J. D., & Taylor, R. (1981). Induced mood and accessibility of memories: An effect of mood state or of induction procedure? *British Journal of Clinical Psychology, 20*, 39-48.

Teasdale, J. D., Taylor, R., & Forgarty, S. J. (1980). Effects of induced elation-depression on the accessibility of memories of happy and unhappy experiences. *Behavior Research and Therapy. 18*, 339-346.

Tesser, A. (1980). Self-esteem maintenance in family dynamics. Journal of *Personality and Social Psychology, 39*, 77-91.

Tesser, A., & Cambell, J. (1982). Self-evaluation maintenance and the perception of friends and strangers. *Journal of Personality, 50*, 261-279.

Tesser, A., & Cambell, J. (1984). Self-definition and self-evaluation maintenance. In J. Suls & A. Greenwald (Eds.), *Social psychological perspectives on the self* (Vol. 2). Hillsdale, NJ: Lawrence Erlbaum.

Tesser, A., & Smith, J. (1980). Some effects of task relevance and friendship on helping: You don't always help the one you like. *Journal of Experimental Social Psychology, 16*, 582-590.

Thompson, W. C., Cowan, C. L., & Rosenhan, D. L. (1980). Focus of attention mediates the impact of negative affect on altruism. *Journal of Personality and Social Psychology, 38*, 291-300.

Tomkins, S. S. (1962). *Affect, imagery, and consciousness, Vol. 1: The positive affects.* New York: Springer.

Tomkins, S. S. (1963). *Affect, imagery, and consciousness, Vol. 2: The negative affects.* New York: Springer.

Tomkins, S. S. (1979). Script theory: Differential magnification of affects. In H. E. Howe & R. A. Dienstbier (Eds.), *Nebraska Symposium on Motivation, 1978* (Vol. 26). Lincoln: University of Nebraska Press.

Tomkins, S. S. (1981). The quest for primary motives: Biography and autobiography of an idea. *Journal of Personality and Social Psychology, 41*, 306-329.

Underwood, B., Froming, W. J., & Moore, B. S. (1977). Mood, attention and altruism: A search for mediating variables. *Developmental Psychology, 13*, 541-542.

Velten, E. A. (1968). A laboratory task for induction of mood states. *Behavior Research and Therapy, 6*, 473-482.

Wegner, D. M., & Giuliano, T. (1980). Arousal-induced attention to self. *Journal of Personality and Social Psychology, 38*, 719-726.

Wessman, A. E., & Ricks, D. F. (1966). *Mood and personality.* New York: Holt, Rinehart & Winston.

Wilder, D. A. (1980). Perceiving persons as a group: Categorization and intergroup relations. In D. L. Hamilton (Ed.), *Cognitive processes in stereotyping and intergroup behavior.* Hillsdale, NJ: Lawrence Erlbaum.

Wright, J., & Mischel, W. (1982). Influence of affect on cognitive social learning person variables. *Journal of Personality and Social Psychology, 43*, 901-914.

Zajonc, R. B. (1980). Feeling and thinking: Preferences need no inferences. *American Psychologist, 35*, 151-175.

# 7

# Limitations of Self-Knowledge

## MORE ON TELLING MORE THAN WE CAN KNOW

TIMOTHY D. WILSON
JULIE I. STONE

**Timothy D. Wilson** is currently Associate Professor of Psychology at the University of Virginia. His research interests include causal judgment, introspection, and theory-based judgments of affect.

**Julie I. Stone** is a Project Director at ARBOR Inc., a Philadelphia market research firm. She received her Ph.D. from the University of Virginia in 1984. Her dissertation was concerned with some of the factors (besides accuracy) that affect eyewitness confidence. Her other research interests include social cognition, nonverbal communication, and consumer behavior.

In 1977, Nisbett and Wilson presented what proved to be a controversial argument about how people determine the causes of their evaluations, judgments, decisions, and behavior. They argued that access to higher-order mental processes is poor, which limits people's ability to know the causes of their responses. When asked questions such as, "Why did you like the movie?" or "Why did you buy a Pontiac?" introspection may be of little help. Unable to examine the workings of their own minds, people may rely on a priori theories about causality. Given that these theories are generally shared by members of the same culture, actors' causal reports are no more accurate than those of observers who possess the same theories.

The Nisbett and Wilson (1977) position has been challenged on both theoretical and methodological grounds (Adair & Spinner, 1981; Birnbaum & Stegner, 1981; Ericsson & Simon, 1980, 1984; Kellogg, 1982; Kraut & Lewis, 1982; Lieberman, 1979; McClure, 1983; Rich, 1979; Sabini & Silver, 1981; Smith & Miller, 1978; Weitz & Wright, 1979; White, 1980; Wright & Rip, 1981). No attempt will be made here

**AUTHORS' NOTE:** The writing of this chapter was supported by National Science Foundation grants BNS-7921155 and BNS-8316189. Bella DePaulo and Dan Lassiter provided valuable comments on an earlier draft.

to address all of these criticisms, as most of them have been discussed elsewhere (Nisbett & Ross, 1980; Weiss & Brown, 1977; Wetzel, Wilson, & Kort, 1981; Wilson, 1985; Wilson, Laser, & Stone, 1982; Wilson & Nisbett, 1978). Our focus will be on the two questions that are most central to the Nisbett and Wilson (1977) position: (1) Are actors' causal reports generally more accurate than observers' reports? (2) To what extent do people use privileged information versus public theories when making causal reports?

Nisbett and Wilson's (1977) answer to the first question was clearly stated: Actors' causal reports are not generally more accurate than observers' reports. Their statement of why this is the case was not, perhaps, as clear as it might have been. At one point they implied that actors and observers use the same information when making causal explanations, namely shared theories:

> It seems likely [that] . . . ordinary people in their daily lives do not even attempt to interrogate their memories about their cognitive processes when they are asked questions about them. Rather, they may resort . . . to a pool of culturally supplied explanations for behavior. (Nisbett & Wilson, 1977, p. 249)

At a later point, however, they stated that people do have access to a great deal of private data that is sometimes used in self-attribution. These data include knowledge of one's past history, goals for the future, one's current focus of attention, and the unique meaning attached to stimuli (see Jones & Nisbett, 1972; Nisbett & Ross, 1980). This information constitutes mental *contents,* they argued, not mental processes, leaving intact the argument that access to process is limited.

The distinction between access to mental processes and access to mental contents was, perhaps, not a wise one, as pointed out by several critics (e.g., Ericsson & Simon, 1980). It is difficult to define the boundary between process and content, weakening the argument that people have access to one but not the other. Our purpose here is to clarify this issue, and to assess the current standing of Nisbett and Wilson's position. We will argue the following:

(1) Nisbett and Wilson's (1977) conclusion that actors' causal reports are generally no more accurate than observers' causal reports has been supported by subsequent research.

(2) Actors and observers do, however, use different information when making causal reports. Actors use both shared theories and privileged information. Recent evidence suggests, however, that this privileged information can both enhance and impair the accuracy of actors' causal reports.

Evidence for these conclusions will be presented, as will a discussion of the contributions to accuracy of specific types of privileged information.

### RELATIVE ACCURACY OF ACTORS VERSUS OBSERVERS

All known research addressing the accuracy of actors' versus observers' causal reports, conducted since the Nisbett and Wilson (1977) studies, can be briefly summarized as follows:

(1) Actors in a study by Nisbett and Bellows (1977) rated an applicant for a counseling job, then assessed how various attributes of the applicant (e.g., her appearance, her academic record) influenced their ratings. Observers—strangers to the actors—rated what effect the attributes would have on their own ratings of an applicant for a counseling job.

(2) Actors in studies by Weiss and Brown (1977) and Wilson, Laser, and Stone (1982) filled out questionnaires every day for several weeks concerning their mood and possible predictors of their mood (e.g., amount of sleep received the night before, the weather). After completing the questionnaires, actors assessed the relationship between their mood and the predictor variables. Observer subjects—strangers to the actors—judged how mood was related to the predictor variables for the average student.

(3) High school students in two studies by Wright and Rip (1981) read descriptions of different colleges and rank ordered them according to how much they wanted to apply to each one. These actors then rated the desirability of each attribute of the colleges; for example, the desirability of a college being close to home and the desirability of it being far from home. These desirability ratings were viewed as causal assessments by actors of the effects of the colleges' attributes on their rankings. Observer subjects (family members in Study 1, strangers in Study 2) rated how desirable each attribute of the colleges was for a specific actor.

(4) Actors in a study by Kraut and Lewis (1982) viewed a videotape of U.S. Customs agents interrogating several travelers, and rated how friendly, deceptive, and intelligent they thought each traveler was. The actors then assessed how much each of several characteristics of the travelers, such as their age and sex, had influenced their ratings. Observer subjects rated how much each characteristic of the travelers would have affected their evaluations had they been in the study.

In each study some measure of the actual effects of the stimuli on actors' evaluations was computed, and compared to both actors' and observers' causal reports about the stimulus effects. Kraut and Lewis (1982), for example, measured actual effects by correlating the stimulus characteristics (e.g., the age of the travelers) with the actors' evaluations of the travelers, on a within-subject basis. Accuracy of causal reports was measured by correlating these *actual* weights with both actors' and observers' *subjective* weights; that is, their reports about how the travelers' attributes influenced their ratings. Because it was a within-subject design, each actor had an accuracy correlation (between actual and reported effects of the travelers' attributes) and a correlation between his or her actual effect and the reported effects of a randomly-paired observer.[1] According to Nisbett and Wilson (1977), the correlations between actual stimulus effects and actors' causal reports should be no higher than the correlations between actual stimulus effects and observers' causal reports.

Table 7.1 lists the actor and observer accuracy correlations for each study. Averaging across studies, actors achieved an accuracy score of .33, indicating modest but significant accuracy.[2] Observers achieved an almost identical score of .32. This is an impressive finding, because in four of the six studies—all but Wright and Rip's (1981) two experiments—the observers had no knowledge of the actors' past histories, thoughts, or idiosyncracies.

## INFORMATION USED BY
## ACTORS VERSUS OBSERVERS

The accuracy correlations in Table 7.1 do not reveal the *way* in which actors and observers make attributions. Even though they failed to outdo observers in accuracy, actors may have arrived at their judgments via a different route. In this section, the ways people make causal judgments and the type of information they use are considered.

There has been some confusion in the literature about precisely what sorts of information actors might use when making causal reports. References have been made to shared theories, "founts of privileged knowledge," mental contents, mental processes, memories, and observations of behavior, with no clear indication of how these various types of information differ or precisely which are private and which public.

Actors can be said to have at their disposal two types of causal theories, defined as stored expectations or hypotheses about cause and effect relationships, and two types of "data," defined as information about the specific response in question. Some theories are shared by members of the same culture, and thus are public. It is important to note that the term "shared theory" is not meant to refer only to explicit,

TABLE 7.1
Correlations with Actual Effects of Stimuli

|  | Correlations | |
| --- | --- | --- |
|  | *Actual Effects X Actor Reports* | *Actual Effects X Observer Reports* |
| Kraut & Lewis (1982)[a] | .42 | .35 |
| Nisbett & Bellows (1977)[b] | .39 | .45 |
| Wilson, Laser, & Stone (1982)[a] | .42 | .45 |
| Wright & Rip (1981), Study 1[a] | .38 | .32 |
| Wright & Rip (1981), Study 2[c] | .58 | .40 |
| Weiss & Brown (1977)[d] | −.31 | −.09 |
| Means (r → z → r) | .33 | .32 |

a. Average within-subject correlations.
b. Because the Nisbett and Bellows study utilized a between-subjects design, within-subject correlations could not be computed. The correlations reported here are between the mean actual effects of the stimuli, the mean actor reports, and the mean observer reports, where n = five stimulus characteristics. These correlations were then averaged across the four types of judgments subjects made.
c. Average within-subject correlations, based on actors for whom observer data were available.
d. Weiss and Brown did not report the average within-subject correlations. From the data they reported, the closest approximation to accuracy correlations that could be computed were the rank-order correlations between the mean actual effects of stimuli, mean actor reports, and mean observer reports.

culturally supplied axioms about cause and effect. Members of the same culture may generate similar causal explanations about the effects of novel stimuli on novel responses, by virtue of the fact that they share similar connotative networks. Thus, even if people do not have a ready-made cultural axiom to explain an effect, they may still agree on the most plausible explanation (Nisbett & Wilson, 1977).

Actors also have idiosyncratic theories; that is, expectations about cause and effect relationships that are peculiar to themselves (e.g., "I'm unlike most people—drinking coffee makes me sleepy"). These theories may be learned from others (e.g., a mother teaching her child that eating honey prevents the common cold) or learned from experience ("Every time I drink coffee I seem to get drowsy"). By definition, they are not generally shared by members of the same culture.

Actors have access to two types of data that are usually unavailable to observers. The first consists of knowledge of the "working of one's own mind," obtained via introspection. This may consist of memories of prior thoughts and feelings or concurrent observations of one's reactions to a stimulus (Ericsson & Simon, 1980). Second, actors can observe the covariation between their responses and antecedent stimulus conditions (Bem, 1972; Kelley, 1967). Independent of people's shared or idiosyncratic theories, or of their thoughts and memories (introspective data), they might observe how the presence of a stimulus attribute (e.g., brown hair) covaries with a response (liking), and infer a causal relationship accordingly.

It is usually the case that idiosyncratic theories, introspective data, and observations of covariation are privileged, whereas shared theories are not. In principle, each of the other types of information could be available to observers if they were to observe an actor's behavior as often as the actor, or if actors were to communicate to observers what their thoughts and idiosyncratic theories were (Andersen, 1984). In practice, however, actors almost always have more access to this information than do observers. For purposes of the present discussion, then, introspective data, observations of behavior, and idiosyncratic theories will be referred to as privileged information.

Given that actors have much more information about what might be causing their responses, the question arises as to why actors are no more accurate, on average, than observers in self-attribution. Following are at least three reasons this result could occur:

*(1) Actors and observers use only shared theories.* Perhaps actors do not have access to privileged information, and thus are forced to rely only on shared theories. As discussed elsewhere, people's access to their own mental states does appear to be limited (Wilson, 1985). Surely, however, actors have at their disposal at least some mental processes and internal states. Alternatively, actors might have access to a good deal of privileged information but choose not to use it. Perhaps shared theories are often very persuasive, and thus overshadow idiosyncractic theories and private data. People often revel in reciting unique "insights" about the causes of their own responses, however, accentuating rather than ignoring privileged information.

There is now empirical evidence supporting the view that actors do indeed use privileged information when making causal reports. A reanalysis of data reported by Wilson et al. (1982) suggests that observers use shared theories, whereas actors, at least in part, use privileged information. In this study there were 22 observer subjects, each of whom estimated the relationships between several predictor variables (e.g., the weather, day of the week) and the average student's mood. The average intercorrelation of the observers' estimates was .78, suggesting that they were using a shared body of knowledge to generate their reports.

If actors were in the same epistemological position as observers, relying primarily on shared theories, the amount of interactor agreement about the relationship of the predictor variables to their mood should have been as high as the interobserver agreement. However, the average intercorrelation among actors' reports was only .33, suggesting that actors were not operating from as common a base as observers. It is not clear from this result *what sort* of privileged information actors were using—idiosyncratic theories, introspections of mental processes, or observations of covariation—but it does suggest that they relied on some sort of individuating data.

*(2) Observers recall previous exposures to the stimulus, remembering how they were affected.* Observers might recall times when they were in similar situations to the actor, remembering what they were thinking and feeling at the time: "When I gave Bob flowers, my intention was to make up for the fact that I had been very busy and not paying attention to him. Perhaps this is why Mary gave John flowers." Thus, instead of calling upon theories of any sort, observers might remember exactly how they were affected by the stimuli in the past. Alternatively, observers might use their own idiosyncratic causal theories, rather than theories shared by everyone. Because they live in the same culture as the actors, observers' idiosyncratic theories and past experiences are likely to overlap with at least some of the actors' idiosyncratic theories and past experiences, explaining the commonality in actors' and observers' causal reports.

We do not doubt that observers sometimes rely on their idiosyncratic theories and past experiences. In the present studies, however, this does not appear to have occurred. First, if observers were introspecting about their own past experiences or using idiosyncratic theories, there should have been some divergence in their causal reports, as it is unlikely that these experiences and theories would be the same for everyone (e.g., concerning flower-giving or mood changes). Yet, in the Wilson et al. (1982) study there was a very high level of agreement among observers about the predictors of mood. Second, some studies have found that actors and observers make very similar reports, but in an inaccurate direction (e.g., Weiss & Brown, 1977). This suggests that observers were not making *accurate* introspections about what influenced them in similar situations in the past. Both actors and observers must have been following some rule that led to the same incorrect causal attributions.

*(3) Actors use both public and private information; observers use public information.* According to this interpretation actors use both shared theories and private information, whereas observers—due to their lack of access to the actors' private information—use public theories.

In one sense this view states the obvious, namely that actors and observers make use of whatever information is available. What is puzzling, however, is why actors are no more accurate than observers, when they have so much more information. The key to this argument, as noted by Nisbett and Wilson (1977) and Nisbett and Ross (1980), is that actors' privileged information can both help and hinder accuracy. Obviously, actors' privileged information often gives them a big advantage over observers. Actors know to which stimuli they were attending, what their intentions were, at least in part what their thoughts and feelings were, and how they responded in the past. Sometimes, however, this extra information misleads actors, causing them to be *less* accurate than observers, as when people call upon explanations that are very salient and available in memory but are nevertheless incorrect. For example, medical students studying insulin disorders might attribute their dizziness to diabetes, because features of this disease are highly available in memory. Observers who do not share the actors' knowledge about diabetes are likely to use a more common explanation, such as having stood up too quickly. If the latter explanation happens to be correct, actors' causal reports will be less accurate than those of observers.

Nisbett and Wilson's (1977) and Nisbett and Ross's (1980) discussions of the costs and benefits of using privileged information were speculative, with no supporting evidence. Evidence is now available that supports these arguments. First, there is the fact that actors do seem to use private information, as seen by the low interactor agreement in the Wilson et al. (1982) study, yet they are not more accurate, on the average, than observers (see Table 7.1). This suggests that privileged information does not uniformly improve accuracy.

More specific evidence comes from the computation of partial correlations in the Kraut and Lewis (1982) and Wilson et al. (1982) studies. Kraut and Lewis calculated the average partial correlation between actual stimulus effects and actors' reports about stimulus effects, controlling for observers' causal reports. Partialling out the observer judgments controls for the actors' use of shared theories. That is, if actors' self-reports are significantly related to the actual stimulus effects, even after statistically controlling the accuracy of observer subjects, we could conclude that actors can achieve accuracy beyond that obtained by the use of shared theories. Kraut and Lewis found this to be the case. The mean correlation between actual stimulus effects and actors' reports—partialing out the reports made by a randomly paired observer—was .31, which was significantly greater than zero. A reanalysis of Wilson et al.'s (1982) data also found this partial correlation to be significant, mean r = .26.

According to Kraut and Lewis (1982), this finding indicates that actors use some private information, which makes them more accurate than observers. Although agreeing that actors' private information accounts for some accuracy that public theories do not, we disagree with the conclusion that this privileged information will make actors *generally* more accurate than observers. It may enable actors to correctly isolate some stimulus effects unaccounted for by cultural theories about causality. As argued earlier, however, privileged information may have its costs as well. This can be demonstrated by a different partial correlation, namely that between actual stimulus effects and observers' reports, controlling for actors' reports. If this partial r were significantly positive, it would suggest that actors sacrifice some accuracy by *not* relying solely on shared theories. Stated differently, shared theories can explain some of the variance of the actual impact of stimuli that actors do not explain. In support of this conclusion, the mean correlations between actual effects and observer reports, controlling for actors' reports, were .15 and .32 in the Kraut and Lewis (1980) and Wilson et al. (1982) studies, respectively. Both of these correlations were significantly greater than zero.[3]

Figure 7.1 displays these significant partial correlations pictorially. The overlap between actors' and observers' causal reports represents the extent to which actors rely on shared theories. The fact that this overlap is not complete suggests that actors use privileged information as well as shared theories. Some of the actors' accuracy comes from using shared theories (area B in Figure 7.1), some from their privileged data (area A in Figure 7.1). Area A reflects the positive actual × actor · observer correlations found by Kraut and Lewis (1982) and Wilson et al. (1982).

The extent to which shared theories are accurate is represented by the sum of areas B and C. Area C reflects the accuracy actors lose by favoring privileged information at the expense of shared theories, as indicated by the positive actual × observer · actor correlations reported above. Thus, both actors and observers can obtain some accuracy that is unique. Their sum total of accuracy, however (e.g., A + B versus B + C) is about equal, as seen in the correlations averaged across studies in Table 7.1.

An important caveat should be mentioned concerning observers' reliance on shared theories. In the studies reviewed here, observers were deliberately not given individuating information about the actors, and this omission may have increased their use of shared theories. The point of the studies was to assess actors' use of privileged information versus shared theories; observers with no access to the privileged information (the actors' thoughts and behavior) were thus necessary as controls. In everyday life, of course, observers often know a good deal about actors when making causal attributions. Knowledge about the actor's past behavior, idiosyncracies, and personality may reduce a reliance on

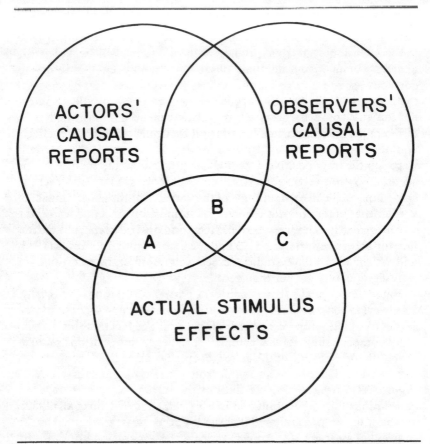

Figure 7.1 The contribution of shared theories and idiosyncratic information to accuracy in self-attribution.

shared theories, and affect the amount of overlap between actors' and observers' causal reports.

Nor do we mean to suggest that areas A, B, and C in Figure 7.1 will be equal in all situations. In some situations, as noted by Nisbett and Wilson (1977), actors' private data will produce reports more accurate than observer reports (i.e., area A will exceed area C). In others, the actors' private data will be misleading, and area C will exceed area A. The evidence available to date, as reviewed in Table 7.1, suggests that averaging across situations, tasks, and types of evaluations, actor and observer accuracy is about equal.

It should be noted that our argument departs significantly from the original Nisbett and Wilson position in stating that actors rely on privileged information when making causal reports. However, our position reaches the same *conclusion* as Nisbett and Wilson: Whatever the extent of privileged information, it does not lead actors to be generally more accurate than observers in judging the causes of their responses.[4]

### CONTRIBUTIONS TO ACCURACY OF SPECIFIC TYPES OF PRIVILEGED INFORMATION

The evidence reviewed so far suggests that actors do use privileged information, which can enhance or impair accuracy. The lack of interactor agreement and the partial correlations discussed earlier, however, do not specify the type of private information actors use. It is possible, for example, that actors rely very much on idiosyncratic theories but little on observations of covariation, or that introspections on one's thoughts while deciding how to respond are used more than memories of past mental processes. Independent of which type of information actors do use, it is interesting to consider which types they *should* use—that is, which contribute more to accuracy. For example, would actors make more accurate reports using observations of covariation than they would using idiosyncratic theories? (In other words, what sort of information is characterized by Area A in Figure 7.1?)

There is very little research on these questions. Ericsson and Simon (1980) argued that actors will be more accurate when making concurrent reports of thought processes than when making retrospective reports of past thoughts, but few studies have directly compared the two types of reports in situations where there is an independent means of assessing accuracy. Andersen (1984) found that observers who listened to actors describe their thoughts and feelings made more accurate assessments of the actors' personality then did observers who listened to actors describe their behavior (with accuracy defined as the extent to which observers' ratings corresponded with both actors' ratings and ratings made by close friends of the actors). Further, actors reported that their thoughts and feelings were better indicators than their behavior of the kind of people they were (Andersen & Ross, 1984). There is no direct evidence, however, that actors usually do make more accurate reports about the causes of their responses by using thoughts and feelings rather than observations of behavior.

Thus, answers to the question of which types of privileged information are preferred and which contribute to accuracy are not clear at this time. One type of private information, observations of covariation, has received a fair amount of attention, and thus it is possible to reach some conclusions about its usefulness. As argued by Bem (1972) and Kelley (1967), people sometimes infer causality by making covariation judgments; that is, by observing over time the relationship between the presence and absence of a stimulus and the presence and absence of their response. Nisbett and Wilson (1977) acknowledged that this process sometimes occurs, and that observations of covariation would give actors an advantage over observers (at least over observers who had not had an opportunity to observe the actor's responses over time). Following Chapman and Chapman (1967, 1969), however, they argued that covariation assessment is often beyond the computational powers of the lay psychologist, and rarely forms the basis of causal judgment.

Recent research has supported the idea that covariation detection is difficult, and can be accomplished only under severely restricted conditions, such as when (a) people do not possess a strong theory that contradicts the actual relationship in the data, (b) there is an opportunity to observe many occurrences of the events in a short period of time, (c) the time interval between the occurrence of the two events is extremely short, and (d) the events are very salient and presented in an easily codable form (Crocker, 1981; Jennings, Amabile, & Ross, 1982; Nisbett & Ross, 1980).

Five of the six studies in Table 7.1 used within-subject designs (all except Nisbett and Bellows), allowing actors the opportunity to observe the covariation of their responses over time under different stimulus conditions. These five studies differed, however, in the ease with which actors could adopt a successful covariation assessment strategy. Two of the studies met most of the criteria necessary for people to detect covariation, e.g., the data were presented in summated form sequentially in a short period of time, and the number of stimuli that could influence people's responses was severely restricted (Wright & Rip, 1981, Studies 1 and 2). Two others used tasks that made covariation assessment much more difficult, as subjects' responses occurred over several weeks, and the number of possible influences on their responses was very large (Weiss & Brown, 1977; Wilson et al., 1982). The fifth study fell between the others in ease of covariation assessment (Kraut & Lewis, 1982). It was performed in a relatively short period of time in the laboratory, making covariation detection easier than in the Weiss and Brown (1977) and Wilson et al. (1982) studies, but the stimuli were not in summated, coded form and were more numerous than in the Wright and Rip (1982) studies.

Table 7.2 lists the actor and observer accuracy correlations according to this rough classification of ease of covariation assessment. It can be seen that actors were superior to observers in causal judgment when

TABLE 7.2
Accuracy Correlations by Difficulty of Covariation Assessment

| Correlation of Actual Effects with: | Difficulty of Covariation Assessment | | |
|---|---|---|---|
| | Low[a] | Medium[b] | High[c] |
| Actor reports | .49 | .42 | .06 |
| Observer reports | .36 | .35 | .19 |
| Actor-observer | +.13 | +.07 | −.13 |

a. Wright & Rip (1981), Studies 1 and 2.
b. Kraut & Lewis (1982).
c. Weiss & Brown (1977); Wilson et al. (1982).

covariation assessment was relatively easy, but this superiority was lost when covariation assessment was more difficult.

The classification scheme in Table 7.2 is rough, and admittedly post hoc. More convincing evidence about the role of covariation detection in causal judgment comes from a demonstration study of ours that manipulated the ease with which a covariation strategy could be adopted. Subjects were presented with seven pieces of information about several target students, such as their sex, grade point average, and whether they were described by friends as listeners or talkers in social interactions. Subjects rated how much they liked each target student and how flexible in solving problems each student was. The seven pieces of information were manipulated orthogonally so that the actual effect of each piece of information (alone and in interaction with the other information) on subjects' judgments could be assessed.[5] Because a within-subject design was used, the actual impact of the information was computed for each subject. Subjects then rated how much they thought each piece of information, alone and in combination with the other factors, had influenced their ratings. The estimates of actual effects were correlated with subjects' causal reports to form accuracy correlations. Observer subjects—strangers to the actual participants—estimated the effects of the stimuli on the average student.

Our reasoning was that part of this task—estimating the main effects of the seven pieces of information—should be relatively easy for subjects if they used a covariation assessment strategy. The amount of information they received about the target students was limited, the time interval between receiving the information and making their judgments was short, and the information was presented in an already coded form (e.g., subjects did not have to do additional processing to determine who was a talker and who was a listener, because this information was "coded" for them). Therefore, we predicted that subjects would make accurate reports about the main effects of the seven pieces of information on their liking and flexibility ratings, reports that would be more accurate than those made by observer subjects, who did not know how the actors' responses covaried with the stimulus information. (Actors could also achieve more accuracy than observers by using idiosyncratic theories that happened to be correct. It seems unlikely, however, that people would possess theories about such a seldom-made judgment as how flexible someone is, and more likely that subjects attempted to recall the covariation between their responses and the stimulus information.)

In contrast, it was much more difficult for subjects to observe the covariation between their ratings and the *interactions* between the seven pieces of information, such as the joint effect of the target people's sex and talkativeness. There were more interactions than main effects to attend to, plus it is likely that subjects did not focus their attention as much on the joint effect of two factors as they did on the main effects.

As predicted, subjects made very accurate judgments about the main effects of the seven pieces of information on both their liking and flexibility judgments (we averaged across these two ratings, because they produced very similar results). The average correlation between the actual and reported effects of the seven main effects was .75. In contrast, the average correlation between observers' judgments and the actual effects was only .28. The difference between these two mean correlations is highly significant, $t(44) = 10.03$, $p < .0001$. When the subjects' task was more difficult—estimating the joint effect of the seven pieces of information (i.e., the two-way interactions)—accuracy was much lower (mean $r = .15$) and did not significantly exceed the observers' mean r of .10.[6]

People may use a covariation assessment strategy successfully in the confines of the laboratory, when the task is simple. Our subjects appear to have used this strategy when estimating the main effects, giving them an advantage over observers who were unable to see the covariation between the actors' responses and the stimulus characteristics. The actor's advantage is likely to be lost in everyday life, however, where covariation assessment is much more difficult. In our study, actors' superiority over observers was lost when the task was made only slightly more difficult, judging 15 two-way interactions versus seven main effects. Compare this task to everyday life, where stimulus characteristics are not manipulated orthogonally, people do not observe several pairings between their responses and stimulus conditions in a short period of time, stimulus characteristics are not always salient and in summated form, and the number of possible influences on responses is often very large.

Of the different sorts of privileged information available to actors, then, observations of covariation may not contribute very often to accuracy, given the complexity of the social world and people's limited computational capabilities. The contributions to accuracy of other types of privileged information, such as idiosyncratic theories and introspections on thoughts and feelings, is an open question. Two points can now be made, however, with much greater certainty than at the time of Nisbett and Wilson's review: Actors are more knowledgeable than observers, having at their disposal a wealth of privileged information. Even so, actors' causal reports seem to be no more accurate, on average, than inferences made by observer subjects.

Of the many implications of this conclusion for psychological theory and research, one is particularly relevant to the area of personality and social behavior. Questionnaire and interview measures of people's impressions about the causes of their responses should be interpreted with caution. These impressions may well be based (at least in part) on information available only to the respondent. The fact that privileged information is used, however, does not guarantee the accuracy of causal reports.

## NOTES

1. Several different methods of pairing observers with actors have been used, including random matching (Kraut & Lewis, 1982; Wright & Rip, 1981, Study 2), comparing each observer's reports with the stimulus effects of every actor (Wilson et al., 1982), and yoking each actor to an observer within the same family (Wright & Rip, 1981, Study 1).

2. All of the mean accuracy correlations from the studies that used within-subject designs were significant, except for those found by Weiss and Brown. Combining p-levels across studies results in a highly significant p-level for both actor and observer correlations.

3. The actual $\times$ observer $\cdot$ actor correlation from the Kraut and Lewis (1982) study is approximate, accurate within 10 percent (R. E. Kraut, personal communication, February 23, 1982).

4. The argument that actors' causal reports tend to be no more accurate than observers' reports seems, on the face of it, to conflict with Jones and Nisbett's (1972) conclusion that actors are more prone to make situational attributions than observers, and hence are more accurate (Jones, 1976). The question of the accuracy of actors' versus observers' reports can only be answered, however, when there is a means of assessing what is actually influencing actors' responses, as was done in the six studies summarized in Table 7.1. Unfortunately, it is much easier to manipulate and assess the effects of situational factors than it is to manipulate and assess the effects of dispositional factors, and indeed, all of the studies in Table 7.1 compared actors' and observers' reports only about different situational effects. Perhaps if situational and dispositional factors were somehow manipulated simultaneously, actors would prove to be more accurate than observers. There is considerable debate, however, over whether situational or dispositional explanations of behavior are more accurate (see, for example, Epstein, 1983; Harvey, Town, & Yarkin, 1981; Mischel & Peake, 1982; Monson & Snyder, 1977). Giving actors and observers both situational and dispositional factors to choose from would probably reduce the overlap of their responses, but whether it would always make actors more accurate is unclear.

5. A quarter-fractional design was used, such that the seven main effects and 15 of the possible 21 two-way interactions could be estimated (Cochran & Cox, 1957). An extensive pretest of the remaining six two-way interactions indicated that they had negligible effects.

6. Possible artifactual reasons for the lower accuracy correlations for the interactions, such as the possibility that there was a restriction in range of the actual effects of the interactions, were tested and ruled out.

## REFERENCES

Adair, J. G., & Spinner, B. (1981). Subjects' access to cognitive processes: Demand characteristics and verbal report. *Journal for the Theory of Social Behaviour, 11*, 31-52.

Andersen, S. M. (1984). Self-knowledge and social influence: II. The diagnosticity of cognitive/affective and behavioral data. *Journal of Personality and Social Psychology, 46*, 294-307.

Andersen, S. M., & Ross, L. (1984). Self-knowledge and social inference: I. Perceptions of cognitive/affective and behavioral data. *Journal of Personality and Social Psychology, 46*, 280-293.

Bem, D. J. (1972). Self-perception theory. In L. Berkowitz (Ed.), *Advances in experimental social psychology* (Vol. 6, pp. 1-62). New York: Academic.

Birnbaum, N. H., & Stegner, S. E. (1981). Measuring the importance of cues in judgment for individuals: Subjective theories of I.Q. as a function of heredity and environment. *Journal of Experimental Social Psychology, 17*, 159-182.

Chapman, L. J., & Chapman J. P. (1967). Genesis of popular but erroneous diagnostic observations. *Journal of Abnormal Psychology, 72*, 193-204.

Chapman, L. J., & Chapman, J. P. (1969). Illusory correlation as an obstacle to the use of valid psychodiagnostic signs. *Journal of Abnormal Psychology, 74*, 271-280.

Cochran, W. G., & Cox, G. M. (1957). *Experimental designs* (2nd ed.). New York: John Wiley.

Crocker, J. (1981). Judgment of covariation by social perceivers. *Psychological Bulletin, 90*, 272-292.

Epstein, S. (1983). The stability of confusion: A reply to Mischel and Peake. *Psychological Review, 90*, 179-184.

Ericsson, K. A., & Simon, H. A. (1980). Verbal reports as data. *Psychological Review, 87*, 215-251.

Ericsson, K. A., & Simon, H. A. (1984). *Protocol analysis: Verbal reports as data*. Cambridge, MA: MIT Press.

Harvey, J. H., Town, J. P., & Yarkin, K. L. (1981). How fundamental is "The Fundamental Attribution Error"? *Journal of Personality and Social Psychology, 40*, 346-349.

Jennings, D., Amabile, T. M., & Ross, L. (1982). Informal covariation assessment: Data-based vs. theory-based judgments. In A. Tversky, D. Kahneman, & P. Slovic (Eds.), *Judgment under uncertainty: Heuristics and biases* (pp. 211-238). New York: Cambridge University Press.

Jones, E. E. (1976). How do people perceive the causes of behavior? *American Scientist, 64*, 300-305.

Jones, E. E., & Nisbett, R. E. (1972). The actor and the observer: Divergent perceptions of the causes of behavior. In E. E. Jones, D. E. Kanouse, H. H. Kelley, R. E. Nisbett, S. Valins, & B. Weiner (Eds.), *Attribution: Perceiving the causes of behavior* (pp. 79-94). Morristown, NJ: General Learning.

Kelley, H. H. (1967). Attribution theory in social psychology. In D. Levine (Ed.), *Nebraska symposium on motivation* (Vol. 15, pp. 192-240). Lincoln: University of Nebraska Press.

Kellogg, R. T. (1982). When can we introspect accurately about mental processes? *Memory and Cognition, 10*, 141-144.

Kraut, R. E., & Lewis, S. H. (1982). Person perception and self-awareness: Knowledge of influences on one's own judgments. *Journal of Personality and Social Psychology, 42*, 448-460.

Lieberman, D. A. (1979). Behaviorism and the mind: A (limited) call for a return to introspection. *American Psychologist, 34*, 319-333.

McClure, J. (1983). Telling more than they can know: The positivist account of verbal reports and mental processes. *Journal for the Theory of Social Behavior, 13*, 111-127.

Mischel, W., & Peake, P. K. (1982). Beyond deja vu in search for cross-situational consistency. *Psychological Review, 89*, 730-755.

Monson, T. C., & Snyder, M. (1977). Actors, observers, and the attribution process. *Journal of Experimental Social Psychology, 13*, 89-111.

Nisbett, R. E., & Bellows, N. (1977). Verbal reports about causal influences on social judgments: Private access versus public theories. *Journal of Personality and Social Psychology, 35*, 613-624.

Nisbett, R. E., Ross, L. (1980). *Human inference: Strategies and shortcomings.* Englewood Cliffs, NJ: Prentice-Hall.

Nisbett, R. E., & Wilson, T. D. (1977). Telling more than we can know: Verbal reports on mental processes. *Psychological Review, 84*, 231-259.

Rich, M. C. (1979). Verbal reports on mental processes: Issues of accuracy and awareness. *Journal for the Theory of Social Behaviour, 9*, 29-37.

Sabini, J., & Silver, M. (1981). Introspection and causal accounts. *Journal of Personality and Social Psychology, 40*, 171-179.

Smith, E. R., & Miller, F. D. (1978). Limits on perception of cognitive processes: A reply to Nisbett and Wilson. *Psychological Review, 85*, 355-362.

Weiss, J., & Brown, P. (1977). *Self-insight error in the explanation of mood.* Unpublished manuscript, Harvard University.

Weitz, B., & Wright, P. (1979). Retrospective self-insight on factors considered in product evaluation. *Journal of Consumer Research, 6*, 280-294.

Wetzel, C. G., Wilson, T. D., & Kort, J. (1981). The halo effect revisited: Forewarned is not forearmed. *Journal of Experimental Social Psychology, 71*, 427-439.

White, P. (1980). Limitations on verbal reports of internal events: A refutation of Nisbett and Wilson and Bem. *Psychological Review, 87*, 105-112.

Wilson, T. D. (1985). Strangers to ourselves: The origins and accuracy of beliefs about one's own mental states. In J. H. Harvey and G. Weary (Eds.), *Attribution in contemporary psychology* (pp. 9-36). New York: Academic.

Wilson, T. D., Laser, P., & Stone, J. (1982). Judging the predictors of one's own mood: Accuracy and the use of shared theories. *Journal of Experimental Social Psychology, 18*, 537-556.

Wilson, T. D., & Nisbett, R. E. (1978). The accuracy of verbal reports about the effects of stimuli on evaluations and behavior. *Social Psychology, 41*, 118-131.

Wright, P., & Rip, P. D. (1981). Retrospective reports on the causes of decisions. *Journal of Personality and Social Psychology, 40*, 601-614.

# 8

# Personality and Person Perception

## VICTOR BATTISTICH, AVI ASSOR,
## LAWRENCE A. MESSÉ, and JOEL ARONOFF

**Victor Battistich** is Senior Research Associate at the Developmental Studies Center in San Ramon, California. His major areas of interest are personality influences on social cognition and social behavior.

**Avi Assor** is Lecturer in Educational Psychology at Ben Gurion University in Israel. His research interests center upon the influences of personality variables on defensive cognitive processes.

**Lawrence A. Messé** is Professor of Psychology at Michigan State University. His research has focused primarily upon the role that personal factors, such as norms and motives, play in interpersonal behavior.

**Joel Aronoff** is Professor of Psychology at Michigan State University. The author (with John Wilson) of the recent *Personality in the Social Process* (Erlbaum, 1985), his research interests focus on personality influences on group functioning.

$M$uch of the early work on personality processes in person perception was stimulated by an intriguing program of research begun in the 1940s. These studies, collectively known as the "new look in perception," were designed to demonstrate that a complex set of psychological mechanisms, identified by psychodynamic theorists as having special impact on a myriad of perceptual and cognitive activities, was amenable to careful experimental study. For example, a classic set of studies examined the proposition that perceivers' values are associated with increased sensitivity to environmental stimuli related to those values (e.g., Postman, Bruner, & McGinnies, 1948). In general, such studies were designed to demonstrate that differences in the salience of stimuli with particular meanings could be directly related to personality variables.

**AUTHORS' NOTE:** We wish to thank Ranald Hansen for his incisive comments on an earlier draft of this chapter.

These early studies instigated a massive amount of research on person perception processes during the next two decades. Unfortunately, comprehensive reviews of this body of work (e.g., Schneider, 1973; Shrauger & Altrocchi, 1964; Tagiuri, 1969; Warr & Knapper, 1968) conclude that although *cognitive* processes have been shown to have a pervasive influence on person perception (see, for example, the research on expectancy and schema effects noted below), it has proven much more difficult to demonstrate reliable effects of personality variables. Reviewers have repeatedly noted that inconsistent and complex patterns of results hamper conceptual progress in this area.

From the vantage point of contemporary work on the interaction of personality and situational variables (e.g., Endler & Magnusson, 1976), the generally disappointing findings from empirical tests of the new look perspective appear to be due in large part to specifiable methodological and conceptual problems. These problems involve (1) the nature of the personality variables examined, (2) the type of social context employed in the research (including both the characteristics of the stimulus person and the experimental situation), (3) the sequence of information-processing stages through which the social context is examined, and (4) the nature of the "perceptual" processes that should be affected by the interaction of personality and situational variables. We briefly review each of these aspects of the person perception process and suggest ways in which contemporary interactionist perspectives (Aronoff & Wilson, 1985) may allow us to study personality effects on person perception more successfully.

We maintain that personality influences on person perception are largely dependent on the circumstances in which these processes occur. In order to provide a framework for considering how personality affects these basic perceptual mechanisms, we consider four major issues. We begin with a brief description of the kinds of personality factors that theoretically should have the most impact on person perception processes, then move to a brief discussion of the most salient aspects of social experience that must be considered when identifying the social context, as well as the information-processing stages through which the social context is typically examined. We conclude with a general review of the range of "perceptual" variables that might be affected by the interaction of these classes of variables. Using this framework, we argue that personality influences on person perception can best be understood from a "person × situation interaction" perspective—that personality will affect perception when the observer construes features of the stimulus targets as having implications for his or her own welfare (i.e., when the target is understood to be hedonically relevant to the observer). However, we suggest that personality will have little effect on the processing of person information when the setting does not engage the particular personality variables under consideration. Finally, we review in detail some work (both early and recent) on the effects of social motives on person perception, in order to suggest that the approach taken in this chapter is promising.

## COMPONENTS OF THE PERSON PERCEPTION PROCESS

### Personality Variables

As noted in the reviews cited above, many of the personality factors examined in past research have tended to be conceptually amorphous and largely unrelated to the type of psychological functioning with which they were expected to be empirically associated. For example, many researchers (see Schneider, 1973) have attempted to relate perceivers' personality characteristics to differences in the salience of particular trait dimensions used to describe a group of stimulus persons. The general failure of these studies to yield strong relationships appears to have been due to a mismatch between the personality variables examined and the stimulus information presented, on the one hand, or the nature of the actual judgments that were made, on the other. Frequently, the personality variables studied seem related more to intelligence and general cognitive functioning than to social behavior.

We use the term "personality" to refer to the relatively stable structure of internal psychological processes that emerges through transactions with the social environment and guides additional transactions in ways that affect a person's thoughts, feelings, and actions. Of the many kinds of personality variables that might be chosen for study, interpersonal motives and cognitive controls seem especially relevant to person perception processes. Motives are psychological factors that impell the individual toward reinforcing aspects of the environment, and hence provide both direction to behavior and bases for the evaluation of social experiences (Aronoff & Wilson, 1985). By inter-personal motives, we mean motives whose gratification is dependent on social processes, particularly interaction with other people. With respect to person perception processes, interpersonal motives determine the characteristics perceivers will seek or avoid in other people, and influence the emotions they experience in social encounters.

A second set of personality variables that are potentially important to person perception involves the cognitive controls, or styles of cognitive operations, characteristically used for processing information (e.g.,

Gardner, Jackson, & Messick, 1960). These variables appear to have a special influence on such aspects of information processing as search persistence and flexibility, and on such outcomes as the level of differentiation in perceivers' impressions—phenomena that, we argue below, should be included within the conceptual framework of person perception processes. At least initially, interpersonal motives are likely to affect the particular aspects of a social environment to which perceivers attend, whereas cognitive controls are likely to determine how such information will be processed. Of particular importance, cognitive controls appear to be involved in defensive operations and other distortions in person perception.

## Characteristics of the Social Context

Psychological processes in which personality variables are heavily involved can be expected to evoke affect. However—in contrast to natural social cognition—in much of the early work on personality and person perception the "person" who was to be "perceived," and, so, "experienced," was presented to the perceiver only in the form of trait adjectives or brief written descriptions of behavior. Similarly, the social situation was also presented to the subject in a limited manner—or else not specified at all. These rather schematic stimulus materials seriously constrain person perception processes. In contrast to psychological events in which perceivers directly observe the complex behavior of a complex stimulus person within a complex social situation, the presentation to a "perceiver" of trait descriptions frequently preempts much of the selection and encoding processes that characterize the ways in which individuals naturally examine their perceptual field (Warr & Knapper, 1968). Thus, the procedures used in much of the early work in person perception confronted subjects with such limited amounts of social information that personality factors could influence information processing only through extended inference processes (i.e., perceived trait interrelations and inferences about nonobserved characteristics).

Recent advances in videotape technology have made it possible to construct "ecologically valid," and yet standardized, vignettes to be used as stimulus materials in person perception research (e.g., Battistich & Aronoff, in press). Such stimulus materials retain considerable experimental rigor while confronting perceivers with a situation that approaches the complexity of naturally occurring social encounters.

A related problem concerns the nature of the relationship between the social situation and the perceiver. Typically, perceivers have been asked to form impressions of hypothetical stimulus persons. Under such "simulation design" conditions (Fontaine, 1975), there is little, if any, involvement between perceiver and stimulus person, and hence no reason (beyond the experimenter's request) for the perceiver to process the stimulus information. Yet, some degree of involvement between perceiver and stimulus person seems essential in order to engage a personality variable in the person perception process. Only when the perceiver and stimulus person are involved in some kind of relationship does the stimulus person become a real source of potential rewards and punishments for the perceiver, and only then is there appreciable motivation to acquire information about the stimulus person's characteristics (Berscheid, Graziano, Monson, & Dermer, 1976). In fact, a central tenet of attribution theory (Heider, 1944) is that individuals collect and process information about others for the purpose of controlling their own hedonic outcomes. When the characteristics of the stimulus person are not "hedonically relevant" (Chaiken & Cooper, 1973) to the perceiver, there is likely to be little interest or involvement in person perception processes. Without such involvement, perceivers' impressions may be determined primarily by logical considerations, such as the connotative similarity among trait adjectives and/or the desire to maintain consistency in one's descriptions of others (e.g., Koltuv, 1962).

## Information-Processing Stages
## in Person Perception

Contemporary approaches to information processing suggest a potentially fruitful way to expand the conceptual and methodological framework for understanding personality effects on person perception processes as they occur in naturalistic settings. Not only could these perspectives provide more valid methodological tools, but they could allow us to apply a wider corpus of empirical results than is currently incorporated into the study of personality and person perception. A broad-based information-processing approach is useful because, although we sometimes acquire information about others through such means as reading a description of a person's attributes and behaviors, most often we learn about other people through direct observation over a period of time within a complex social situation in which we take part. Thus, when perceiving persons, a broad range of social information-processing procedures are typically employed to select, encode, and elaborate information; in other words, a sequence of information-processing stages underlies the construction of a social cognition (e.g., Aronoff & Wilson, 1985).

## Selection

Typically, the first stage of processing is described as involving the selection of information or "cues." Because of the informational richness of any social situation, the perceiver must attend to certain stimulus elements while ignoring others. When the perceiver has no preexisting expectations about how the stimulus person will behave (e.g., Berman, Read, & Kenny, 1983) or is not observing the stimulus person for a specific purpose (e.g., Jones & Thibaut, 1958), the particular cues to which he or she initially attends are probably determined by factors such as novelty (Berlyne, 1960; McArthur & Post, 1977) that affect attentional processes in general. In most cases, however, the perceiver begins an observation "primed" with certain expectations about the stimulus person, and these predetermine to some extent the cues to which he or she will attend. Moreover, even when the initial selection is exclusively determined by the stimulus person's behavior (e.g., the stimulus person engages in an unexpected action), as the observation continues the perceiver develops expectations about the stimulus person's characteristics, and subsequently more actively engages in a preferential search for particular types of information (e.g., Snyder & Swann, 1978).

Furthermore, perceivers may differ not only in the particular cues they select but also in the degree of flexibility and persistence with which they search for information in that social context (Aronoff & Wilson, 1985). By flexibility, we refer to the perceiver's openness to information that is inconsistent with expectations; persistence refers to the amount of confirmatory information sought before forming a judgment about the stimulus person.

## Encoding

Once the perceiver has selected certain attributes of the stimulus person for further processing, he or she encodes (or interprets) these attributes. Information processing during this stage involves inferential and attributional processes in which the perceiver categorizes the observed actions of the stimulus person into discrete behavioral events (Newtson, 1976) and attributes the observed behavior to characteristics of the stimulus person or the situation (Jeffrey & Mischel, 1979; Jones & Nisbett, 1971).

## Elaboration

Finally, the perceiver elaborates the observed stimulus information by inferring additional characteristics of the stimulus person that seem likely given his or her observed characteristics. These "extended inference" processes (Shrauger & Altrocchi, 1964) are typically seen as being determined by the perceiver's "implicit personality theory" (Bruner & Tagiuri, 1954; Schneider, 1973). Having observed that a person is physically attractive, for example, a perceiver may also infer that he or she is kind, intelligent, friendly, and helpful (e.g., Dion, Berscheid, & Walster, 1972).

### The Person Perception Variable

The vast majority of these studies have assessed impression in terms of perceivers' ratings on preselected trait adjective scales. There is considerable evidence that this restricted range of dependent variables, although extremely convenient, may not be scientifically adequate. For example, it is known that perceivers' ratings differ greatly as a function of the personal relevance of the trait adjectives presented to them. Thus, Koltuv (1962) found that the intercorrelations among perceivers' trait ratings were much greater for personally relevant than for nonrelevant traits. Perceivers have also been shown to make more extreme ratings of others on self-generated traits (e.g., Landfield, 1968), and to preferentially select traits that are represented in their "personal construct system" (Kelly, 1955) or are relevant for self-evaluation (e.g., Shrauger & Patterson, 1974). Finally, recent research on "self-schemata" (e.g., Rogers, Kuiper, & Kirker, 1977) indicates that information that is relevant for self-evaluation is more readily perceived, encoded, and retrieved from memory than is information that is unrelated to the self. Collectively, these findings indicate that caution needs to be exercised when using preselected trait adjectives to examine personality influences on person descriptions.

Aside from relying too heavily on trait ratings, previous research has tended to be concerned almost exclusively with the *content* of person descriptions. Relatively little attention has been devoted to personality influences on the *structure* (e.g., complexity) or *evaluative aspects* of impressions (Higgins, Kuiper, & Olson, 1981), or to aspects of the selection process other than salience (e.g., search persistence and search flexibility). We believe it will prove useful to ground the choice and analysis of dependent variables more firmly in a broader information-processing perspective. In such a perspective, the components of person perception can be seen to be identical with components of social cognition studied recently by social psychologists.

### Impressions

The major cognitive outcome of person perception is an impression of the stimulus person in the form of a configuration of his or her characteristics. Although much of the previous research on person perception quite properly was concerned with the content of person descriptions (as well as the salience, or relative weight, of particular trait dimensions), it may prove useful to broaden the investigation of such contents to include features of their structure as well. Thus, a second aspect of person impressions that may prove worthy of study in the future is the complexity, or the level of differentiation and integration, present in the configuration of characteristics (e.g., Crockett, 1965).

## Evaluation

Evaluation of a stimulus person is a significant component of perceivers' trait ratings of that person (e.g., Rosenberg, Nelson, & Vivekananthan, 1968). Operationally, evaluative reactions to a stimulus person may be assessed in terms of the social desirability of traits attributed to him or her, or from overall judgments of the person's value, goodness, and so on. Also, although conceptually distinct (e.g., Crano & Messé, 1982), evaluation and interpersonal attraction often have been theoretically and empirically linked. Thus, person perception studies frequently have measured how much the perceiver likes the stimulus person or would enjoy interacting with him or her. Although there is now a large body of research on general evaluations and interpersonal attraction per se (e.g., Byrne, 1971), there has been relatively little research on the influence of personality on these evaluative outcomes of person perception processes (Aronoff & Wilson, 1985). In fact, the role of affect in social cognition has yet to be explored in depth (Higgins, Kuiper, & Olson, 1981).

## Person Memory

It seems clear that memory processes are an essential element of person perception (e.g., Hastie et al., 1980). During the course of an extended interpersonal event, perceivers must store their observations of the stimulus person and later recall them in order to produce an impression. Over time, perceivers also develop certain generalized expectations about the relationships among behaviors and the ways in which behavior is associated with environmental circumstances. These generalized "schemata" (Taylor & Crocker, 1981) or "scripts" (Schank & Abelson, 1977), once established, exert a considerable influence on subsequent social information processing. For example, perceivers appear to have expectations about the causes of behavior within particular types of situations (e.g., Snyder, 1978) and, as a result of these schemata, tend to ignore sources of information not considered to have causal implications in a particular situation (e.g., Ajzen, 1977). There is also considerable evidence that perceivers more easily recognize and recall stimulus information that is consistent with their preexisting schemata than schema-irrelevant or schema-inconsistent information (e.g., Cantor & Mischel, 1970).

In summary, it appears that a number of conceptual and methodological problems can account for the generally disappointing findings of early investigations of personality influences on person perception. Consistent with the conclusions of most other reviewers of this literature, we have argued that researchers must adopt a more complex conceptualization of person perception processes. Moreover, research strategies must reflect more accurately the complexity of the phenomena being investigated, if strong and consistent relationships between personality and person perception are to be demonstrated. Careful attention needs to be paid to the hedonic relevance of the stimulus person and situation for specific aspects of the perceiver's personality. In short, we need to adopt an interactive model of personality influences on person perception, and focus our attention on how particular personality variables influence particular aspects of impressions of particular kinds of stimulus persons under particular circumstances.

## SOME EMPIRICAL FINDINGS CONCERNING PERSONALITY AND PERSON PERCEPTION

We propose that features of the social context (components of the physical or human environment) provide clues about the relevance of a target person for the observer's welfare, and these clues mediate the effects, if any, that personality factors will have on person perception. When the context is such that the observer construes the target as having little, if any, impact on the observers' outcomes (i.e., motive satisfaction/frustration; support/disconfirmation of value systems; etc.) personality effects will be minimal. In contrast, when features of the context cause an observer to believe that the target will influence the observer's outcomes, the situation should promote attempts at accurate person perception (i.e., heightened sensitivity, processing person information at a more molecular level, etc.). Or, when contextual features warn the observer that the stimulus person may be a source of negative outcomes over which the observer has little control, the relevant personality factors should cause biased, inaccurate, defensive perceptual processing.

In the following discussion, we review a portion of existing work that bears on the utility of this person $\times$ situation interactionist perspective, concentrating on some recent studies of the impact of interpersonal motives on defensive processing of person information. We begin by describing the general effects of interpersonal motives and cognitive controls on person perception processes and then discuss how situational factors can mediate these personality influences. In keeping with our position that person perception processes should be understood more broadly within an information-processing perspective, we organize our discussion around the stages of social information processing summarized above.

## Selection Processes

Given that the perceiver's interpersonal motives define the types of outcomes he or she seeks from social relationships, they also should be related to the type of information the perceiver finds particularly salient when observing others. Several studies indicate that motives influence perceivers' sensitivity to particular characteristics of others (Carlson, 1961). For example, people with a strong need for affiliation are generally more attentive to the characteristics of other people than are low need-affiliation perceivers (e.g., Taylor & Oberlander, 1969), and the need for approval is positively correlated with the recall of others' statements that are consistent with personal attitudes and negatively correlated with the recall of attitude-inconsistent information (Johnson & Gormly, 1976). The results of the few studies that have investigated the role of other personality variables (e.g., dominance and authoritarianism) on selection processes have been mixed, however (Aronoff & Wilson, 1985).

There has been even less research on the relationships between personality and search flexibility or persistence. The major exceptions are studies that have investigated the influence of authoritarianism and dogmatism on these selection processes. For example, in an impression formation task, Robbins (1975) found that dogmatic subjects requested less information than nondogmatic subjects, and Taylor and Dunnette (1974) found that dogmatic subjects reached a decision about hiring a hypothetical employee much faster that did nondogmatic subjects. Such findings are consistent with the cognitive rigidity and intolerance of ambiguity said to characterize the authoritarian and dogmatic personalities (Adorno, Frenkel-Brunswik, Levinson, & Sanford, 1950; Rokeach, 1960).

## Encoding Processes

As noted earlier, there has been little research on the types of cues perceivers use when making particular judgments about a stimulus person and no research of which we are aware that deals with personality influences. Studies of the influence of expectations and schemata on person memory, however, suggest ways in which personality could influence encoding processes. Typically, this research has examined perceivers' differential recall of specific behaviors of a stimulus person that were either consistent or inconsistent with preexisting expectations or schemata. Memory bias in favor of schema-consistent stimulus information seems to be a robust phenomenon (e.g., Cantor & Mischel, 1977). Interestingly, similar biases in recall for stimulus information that is consistent with expectations have been found when subjects are given an interpretive schema after having been exposed to the stimulus information (Snyder & Uranowitz, 1978), suggesting that the bias operates when information is recalled, as well as when it is selected.

Although the mechanisms underlying these biases are unclear (Ebbeson, 1980), it is apparent that characteristics attributed to the stimulus person in perceivers' impressions tend to be consistent with preexisting schemata. If we assume that interpersonal motives affect and are represented in perceivers' self-schemata (Rogers et al., 1977), then it is plausible that motives would influence encoding through schematic processes. Thus, for example, perceivers would more readily perceive and encode information relevant to their interpersonal motives than nonrelevant stimulus information, as has been found for other elements of self-schemata (Riggs & Cantor, 1984).

Although we expect interpersonal motives generally to have greater effects on selection and encoding processes, it is important to note that under certain circumstances perceivers' cognitive characteristics may also influence these processes. Specifically, when information about a stimulus person is threatening to perceivers, defensive cognitive operations may be invoked to reduce anxiety. For example, perceivers' flexibility in searching for information may be reduced so that threatening cues are avoided, or perceivers may attribute threatening cues to aspects of the situation rather than to dispositional qualities of the target. Other defensive operations might be reflected in elaboration processes, as we discuss below.

## Elaboration Processes

We expect perceivers' cognitive controls to have the greatest impact on elaborative processes such as conceptual differentiation, the flexibility and persistence of processing, and extended inferences. Research on the relationships between personality and conceptual differentiation or cognitive complexity has yielded mixed results (Shrauger & Altrocchi, 1964). Perhaps the most extensive body of research in this area has focused on the personality variables of authoritarianism and dogmatism. Several studies (e.g., Foulkes & Foulkes, 1965) have found that authoritarian or dogmatic subjects form less differentiated person impressions and are less tolerant of inconsistent information. Overall, however, the findings regarding authoritarian and cognitive rigidity have been mixed (see Goldstein & Blackman, 1978). Of special interest to the present chapter is a study by White, Alter, and Rardin (1965), which found that authoritarian subjects used fewer and broader categories than nonauthoritarians only for stimulus information of personal relevance. These findings underscore the necessity of considering the relevance of stimulus conditions for the personality variables under investigation.

Although there is little directly relevant information available for review, we would expect the effects of cognitive controls on the complexity of impressions to be greatest when the stimulus information is threatening to the perceiver. This reasoning is based on evidence that high levels of anxiety, in general, result in a narrowing of attention and the encoding of fewer categories of the stimulus field (Mueller, 1980). When a perceiver expects, or actually incurs, negative hedonic outcomes from his or her relationship with a stimulus person, then the perceiver should become negatively aroused—which should then lead to a less differentiated impression of the stimulus person.

There has been considerably more research on personality and extended inference processes. From the findings cited earlier, which indicate that personality-relevant characteristics are preferentially used for describing others and that perceivers show stronger interrelationships among ratings of personally relevant than among ratings of nonrelevant trait dimensions (e.g., Koltuv, 1962), we would generally expect perceivers' inferences to be stronger and more consistent for motive-relevant than motive-irrelevant attributes. For example, perceivers might attempt to deal with threatening information by denigrating the social competence of the stimulus person or otherwise negatively biasing their inferences about nonobserved characteristics (Assor, Aronoff, & Messé, 1981). With respect to cognitive controls, once again we would expect the influence of personality to be greatest under anxiety-arousing conditions.

It is with respect to affective responses to stimulus information that we would expect to see the interaction of motivational and cognitive processes most clearly. When stimulus characteristics are theatening to the perceiver, various cognitive operations should be employed to reduce anxiety. Generally speaking, perceivers should like and positively evaluate stimulus persons whose characteristics are expected to facilitate need satisfaction and, conversely, dislike and negatively evaluate stimulus persons whose characteristics are incongruent with satisfaction of interpersonal motives. For example, Hewitt and Goldman (1974) reported that perceivers with a strong need for approval (and low esteem) formed more positive impressions of a stimulus person who evaluated them positively, as compared with a stimulus person who evaluated them negatively. Individuals with the opposite characteristics showed no difference in response to a positive and a negative evaluator.

It is important to note that situational factors should play a major role in determining whether or not personality-related differences in evaluation will be observed and, if so, in determining the direction of such differences. It is implicit in the above hypothesis that differential evaluation will occur only if stimulus persons have characteristics with different hedonic implications for perceivers' motives. For example, Jones and Daugherty (1959) found that the more Machiavellian a perceiver, the more negative his or her impressions were when expecting to compete with a politically oriented stimulus person. In contrast, Machiavellianism was not significantly correlated with evaluation when a cooperative interaction was expected or when no interaction was expected; moreover, Machiavellianism was not significantly correlated with evaluation of an aesthetically oriented stimulus person under any conditions (aesthetic orientation presumably being generally irrelevant to a Machiavellian's goals). Thus, when the stimulus person's characteristics were not hedonically relevant, there were no personality differences in evaluation. However, when the characteristics of the social context (both the stimulus person and the situation) were hedonically relevant and quite negatively arousing, Machiavellians formed more negative impressions of a stimulus person than did non-Machiavellians.

Finally, under negatively arousing conditions, the perceiver might engage in defensive operations reflected in his or her extended inferences and evaluations of the stimulus person. For example, perceivers could attempt to reduce the anxiety of an anticipated interaction with a highly theatening stimulus person by denigrating his or her social competence or desirability. Alternatively, the perceiver could attempt to deny the threatening information by distorting his or her inferences and attributions. Either of these processes would be effective in reducing anxiety; which alternative is used might depend upon situational factors, such as the amount of ambiguity or inconsistency in the stimulus information or the degree of anxiety aroused in the perceiver by that situation. Generally speaking, we would expect that when the stimulus person's characteristics are strongly and clearly threatening to the perceiver, defensive processes would involve biases in nonobserved characteristics. On the other hand, when there is some ambiguity or inconsistency in degree of threat or in the observed characteristics of the stimulus person, defensive processes would involve direct distortion of observed characteristics. For example, when confronted with a clearly assertive and competent stimulus person, dominant perceivers might try to reduce

their anxiety by altering their inferences regarding nonobserved characteristics, such as the person's interpersonal warmth or sensitivity (Assor,
Aronoff, & Messé, 1981). On the other hand, if there is some ambiguity
about the stimulus person's threatening characteristics, the perceiver
might try to reduce anxiety by directly distorting the observed
characteristics in a "wish-fulfilling" (i.e., less threatening) direction (e.g.,
Darley & Berscheid, 1967).

*Outcome Dependency*

When hypotheses concerning person perception are predicated upon
an affective response in the observer, we stress the need for significant
degrees of involvement between the observer and the observed. In the
absence of any involvement between perceiver and stimulus person
there should be very weak, if any, personality effects. When the stimulus
person is not a source of hedonic outcomes for the perceiver, person
perception processes should be determined primarily by generally
salient features of the stimulus context, such as the unusualness or
extremity of the target's behaviors (e.g., McArthur & Post, 1977). Most
previous research on social cognition has examined social contexts that
fall into this category.

Even when the perceiver is outcome-dependent on the stimulus
person, we would expect weak personality influences when the attributes
of the stimulus person are not relevant to the personality variables under
investigation. Under these circumstances, the environment is essentially
neutral with respect to motive-relevant outcomes. It is worth noting,
however, that outcome dependency per se is associated with greater
attention to and processing of stimulus information (e.g., Berscheid et
al., 1976) and with a general bias toward describing the stimulus person
in socially desirable, nonthreatening terms (e.g., Darley & Berscheid,
1967). However, these aspects of person perception should not be
differentially influenced by personality under such conditions.

In contrast, we would expect strong personality effects when the
perceiver is outcome-dependent on the stimulus person and the stimulus
person's characteristics are relevant to gratification or frustration of the
perceiver's motives. In particular, the perceiver should concentrate on
the motive-relevant characteristics of the stimulus person in forming his
or her impression. If the stimulus person's observed characteristics are
hedonically gratifying, the perceiver would experience a positive
emotional response that should be reflected in the evaluative outcomes
of person perception. For example, the perceiver should like the
stimulus person, expect their relationship to be pleasant and gratifying,
and form a positive impression of the stimulus person with respect to
nonobserved characteristics. Depending on the ambiguity of the

stimulus person's motive-relevant characteristics, we would also expect certain biases or distortions in the perceiver's impressions. In general, these distortions would be in a favorable direction, such that the stimulus person would be seen as more rewarding than objectively justified given the available information.

When the perceiver is outcome-dependent on a stimulus person whose characteristics are hedonically threatening to motive gratification, we would expect the perceiver to experience a negative emotional reaction (e.g., anxiety). This reaction, in turn, should lead the perceiver to engage in various operations to reduce the level of discomfort. Once again, however, the precise nature of these operations probably depends on the amount of ambiguity in the observed stimulus characteristics. When the motive-relevant characteristics of the stimulus person are clear, we would not expect distortion in impressions of these stimulus attributes. Rather, under these conditions, the perceiver is likely to denigrate the stimulus person by forming a negative impression of other attributes, ones that are either observed but ambiguous or not observed at all. In addition, the perceiver should dislike the stimulus person and have negative expectations about the outcomes of their encounters and long-term relationship. In contrast, when the stimulus person's motive-relevant characteristics are threatening but ambiguous, we would expect distortions in impressions of these attributes as well as of other, nonobserved characteristics. If there is ambiguity concerning the stimulus person's threatening characteristics, the easiest way to reduce anxiety is to deny or distort the threatening information such that the stimulus person is perceived as more or less favorable than is objectively warranted.

## INTERACTIONAL STUDIES OF PERSON PERCEPTION

We have completed three studies designed to explore a set of predictions derived from the interactional approach to person perception processes outlined above. Although these studies only begin to examine the many aspects of the impression formation process summarized here, we believe they provide considerable support for the utility of the interactional approach.

Although each of the three studies focuses on somewhat different aspects of the person perception process, they have several important features in common. First, all of them examine the influence of the same two motives, dominance and dependency, on person perception; and the motives are assessed with the same instruments—the Dominance scale of the California Psychological Inventory (Gough, 1969) and the Succorance scale of Edward's Personal Preference Schedule (Edwards,

1959). Second, all three used highly realistic videotapes of social encounters as stimulus materials. Third, all took steps to ensure that perceivers were involved in a social situation.

## Experiment 1

The first study (Assor, Aronoff, & Messé, 1981) tested the hypothesis that perceivers' motivation interacts with the attributes of a stimulus person to affect evaluations of that person. Undergraduates completed the personality measures described above, and then watched a short videotape of two capable and pleasant students performing a number of tasks together. In order for attributes of the stimulus persons to have different impacts on dominant and dependent perceivers, one of the two actors was described as being of relatively high status, whereas the other was described as being of relatively low status (these descriptions were, of course, systematically varied). After viewing the videotape, subjects rated each actor on bipolar evaluative scales (e.g., cold-warm, likeable-unlikeable) and on similar scales assessing perceived competence (e.g., competent-incompetent, weak-strong). We reasoned that the high-status person would be threatening to dominant perceivers, but would provide a potential source of gratification to dependent perceivers. Conversely, we reasoned that the low-status person would be gratifying to dominant perceivers, but would be threatening to dependent perceivers. It was predicted, then, that in this situation where behavior of both stimulus persons was clearly competent with respect to the task, dominant perceivers would form more favorable impressions of the low-status than of the high-status person, and dependent perceivers would form more favorable impressions of the high-status than of the low-status person. As shown in Figure 8.1, these predictions were confirmed.

The findings of this first study provide support for the hypothesis that personality variables interact with situational factors (in this case, the attributes of the stimulus person) to affect person perception processes. In addition the differences in evaluative ratings provide evidence of motive-related distortions in a manner consistent with hedonic gratification: Each group of perceivers distorted their impressions in a positive direction for the stimulus person with gratifying characteristics and in a negative direction for the stimulus person with threatening characteristics.

## Experiment 2

Although the findings of Assor et al. (1981) provide some evidence of defensive processes in person perception, they do not demonstrate that

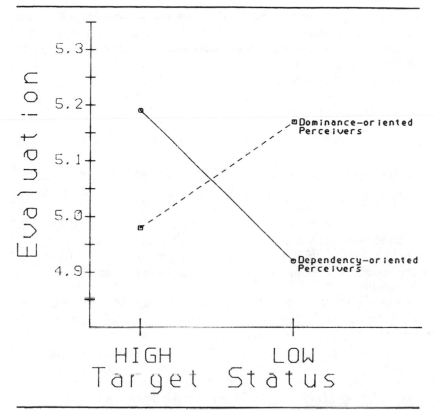

**Figure 8.1** Impressions of high- and low-status targets by dominance- and dependency oriented · perceivers. Adapted from "Attribute relevance as a
moderator of the effects of motivation on impression formation" by
A. Assor et al., 1981, *Journal of Personality and Social Psychology, 41,*
p. 790. Adapted by permission.

emotional arousal and its reduction mediate such distortions. The
second study (Assor, Aronoff, & Messé, in press) used psychophysiological techniques to assess subjects' autonomic arousal
during various stages of person perception to demonstrate that (a)
dominant and dependent perceivers are differentially aroused by
particular characteristics of a stimulus person; and (b) defensive
cognitive operation are associated with lower levels of arousal.

As in the first experiment, dominant and dependent perceivers
observed two confederates interacting via videotape. In this study,
hedonic relevance was achieved by leading the perceivers to expect that
they would later be interacting with one of the two confederates. In
addition, the two confederates behaved very differently on the videotape;

one acted in a dominant and competent manner, whereas the other acted in a passive and submissive manner. In this study, then, relevant attributes of the stimulus person were manipulated directly through observed behavior. We reasoned that dominant perceivers would be threatened by expecting to interact later with an assertive, competent individual, but would feel quite comfortable with the prospect of interacting with a submissive individual. In contrast, dependent perceivers would find the prospect of working with the submissive individual threatening, but would feel positive about interacting with the dominant and competent individual.

Male perceivers were told that they were participating in a study of the "nature of generations" in a social group. They were seated in a comfortable chair and asked to watch, ostensibly via closed-circuit TV, two members of the present generation of a group in which they would soon replace one of the members. They were told that were to observe the two persons carefully, because later they would be asked to evaluate the person with whom they would be working in the next generation of the group.

Subjects then watched the videotaped interaction between the two confederates. Half of the subjects expected to evaluate and later interact with the dominant and competent stimulus person, and the remainder expected to judge and interact with the submissive and incompetent stimulus person. After reviewing the videotape, subjects evaluated their future work partner by responding out loud to a series of semantic differential scales that were displayed on the television screen.

In order to test the first hypothesis—that dominant perceivers would be more aroused by the dominant and competent than by the submissive and incompetent stimulus person, whereas dependent perceivers would show an opposite pattern of arousal for the two stimulus persons— perceivers' phasic electrodermal activity was monitored for several standard time periods during the experiment. The results strongly confirmed the hypothesis. Dominant perceivers showed higher levels of autonomic arousal when they expected to interact with the dominant and competent stimulus person than when they expected to interact with the submissive person. In contrast, dependent perceivers showed higher levels of autonomic arousal when they expected to interact with the submissive person than when they expected to interact with the dominant stimulus person. In addition, the second hypothesis was strongly confirmed during the evaluation phase of the experiment for the dominant (although not the dependent) perceivers. Indicating support for our hypotheses on defensive construction of the impression, for the dominant group there was a sizable inverse relationship between evaluation and arousal level.

## Experiment 3

Whereas the first two studies focused on evaluative aspects of impressions and defensive reconstruction, the third study attempted to provide a more general test of interactional effects of personality and context. As in the earlier studies, dominant and dependent perceivers observed a videotaped interaction between two confederates, under the expectation that they would later interact with one of the two stimulus persons. In this third study (Battistich & Aronoff, in press), however, the nature of the interaction situation was manipulated, as well as the observed behaviors of the stimulus person. Moreover, whereas the earlier studies focused on elaborative person perception processes, this study was concerned with attentional processes (as measured by the salience of motive-related aspects of impressions) and perceivers' expectancies about the outcomes of their forthcoming interaction with the stimulus person.

Dominant and dependent male perceivers were told that they were participating in a study of "how well people with different social orientations work together." Perceivers viewed a videotape of two confederates engaged in a "get acquainted" discussion, under the expectation that they would later be either cooperating with or competing against one of these two stimulus persons. The behavior of the "nontarget" interactant was always moderately assertive and affiliative. In contrast, the behavior of the target interactant in the videotape was manipulated in terms of his assertive and affiliative behaviors, resulting in four distinct stimulus characters: assertive and affiliative, assertive and disaffiliative, submissive and affiliative, and submissive and disaffiliative. Thus, each perceiver expected to be interacting with one of the four stimulus characters under either cooperative or competitive conditions.

With respect to salience of stimulus behaviors, it was predicted that, compared to dependent perceivers, dominant perceivers would focus more on assertive characteristics in their target descriptions, whereas dependent perceivers would focus more than dominant perceivers on affiliative characteristics of the stimulus person. In order to test this hypothesis, perceivers' free-response descriptions were scored for the relative frequency of assertive and affiliative target characteristics. The results of this experiment supported the hypothesis quite strongly. Dominant perceivers focused significantly more than dependent perceivers on assertiveness-related characteristics, and dependent perceivers focused more than dominant perceivers on affiliativeness-related behaviors.

Following the principle of complementarity, it was also predicted that dominant perceivers would like submissive persons more than assertive persons, whereas dependent perceivers would like assertive persons more than submissive persons. This hypothesis was generally supported by the results of the experiment. Dominant perceivers liked the submissive stimulus person more than the assertive stimulus person regardless of the stimulus person's level of affiliativeness. Contrary to the hypothesis, however, dependent perceivers liked the assertive person more than the submissive person only when the stimulus person was also disaffiliative.

Finally, this study extended our previous work by examining the effects of interactional goals on person perception. We expected that perceivers would have positive expectations about their interaction with the stimulus person when the goals of the interaction were congruent with expression of the perceivers' motives. Thus, dominant perceivers should expect more favorable outcomes from competitive than cooperative interactions, whereas dependent perceivers should prefer cooperation to competition. The findings confirmed this hypothesis, as the interaction between perceiver motivation and interactional goals for expected pleasantness, shown in Figure 8.2, illustrates. The pattern of results depicted in Figure 8.2 (as well as in Figure 8.1) indicates the kind of person $\times$ situation interaction that we have found repeatedly in our work and that we believe characterizes the underlying bases of many person perception processes in the real world.

### DIRECTIONS FOR FUTURE RESEARCH

The findings of these three studies have implications that go beyond the specific phenomena they investigated. Taken together, they provide compelling evidence in support of the assumption—which was first explicitly stated over 40 years ago—that the personality characteristics of perceivers influence their social cognitions. Of even greater importance, the results show the advantages of basing person perception research on an interactionist framework. This framework, which emphasizes the need to select carefully the personality and situational variables that are hedonically relevant to each other, provides important theoretical guidance for the study of personality influences on the person perception process. Equally important, this perspective provides guidance as to the most appropriate methodological approaches to use in examining substantive hypotheses. Of course, much additional work remains to be done before a precise, comprehensive model of the links between personality factors, contextual features, and person perception can evolve. Still, the work summarized here indicates that the interactionist perspective is a promising path to take in the study of a more inclusive set of variables.

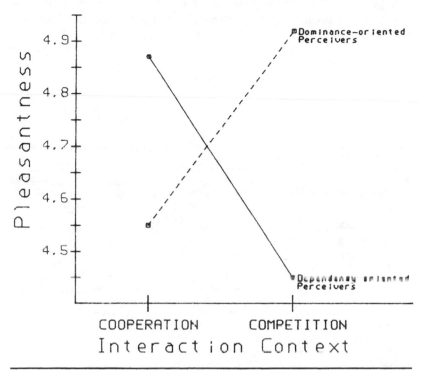

Figure 8.2 Dominance- and dependency oriented perceivers' expectations about a cooperative or competitive social encounter. From "Perceiver, target, and situational influences on social cognition: An interactional analysis" by V. A. Battistich and J. Aronoff, in press, *Journal of Personality and Social Psychology*. Reprinted by permission.

More broadly, the study of social cognition is an important part of social psychology because cognitive elements are generally thought to be a major determinant of complex interpersonal behavior. Thus, as personality variables appear to contribute to the social perception process, it seems necessary to explore the ways in which personality factors *mediate* the relationship between person perception and interpersonal behavior. Research on a number of specific phenomena— physical appearance, group process, mothers' impressions of their babies, general inclinations to perceive others negatively—has amply demonstrated that the behaviors expressed in a variety of social contexts can be influenced profoundly by the interactants' perceptions of each other (e.g., Broussard, 1978; Messé, Stollak, Larson & Michaels, 1979; Nover, Shore, Timberlake, & Greenspan, 1984; Snyder, Tanke, & Berscheid, 1977). We think that what remains to be explored is the specific manner in which personality variables influence significant interpersonal actions, through their effects on the social perception process.

## REFERENCES

Adorno, T. W., Frenkel-Brunswik, E., Levinson, D. J., & Sanford, R. N. (1950). *The authoritarian personality*. New York: Harper.

Ajzen, I. (1977). Intuitive theories of events and the effects of base-rate information on prediction. *Journal of Personality and Social Psychology, 35,* 303-314.

Aronoff, J., & Wilson, J. P. (1985). *Personality in the social process*. Hillsdale, NJ: Lawrence Erlbaum.

Assor, A., Aronoff, J., & Messé, L. A. (1981). Attribute relevance as a moderator of the effects of motivation on impression formation. *Journal of Personality and Social Psychology, 41,* 789-796.

Assor, A., Aronoff, J., & Messé, L. A. (in press). An experimental test of defensive processes in impression formation. *Journal of Personality and Social Psychology.*

Battistich, V. A., & Aronoff, J. (in press). Perceiver, target, and situational influences on social cognition: An interactional analysis. *Journal Personality and Social Psychology.*

Berlyne, D. (1960). *Conflict, arousal, and curiosity*. New York: McGraw-Hill.

Berman, J. S., Read, S. J., & Kenny, D. A. (1983). Processing inconsistent social information. *Journal of Personality and Social Psychology, 45,* 1211-1224.

Berscheid, E., Graziano, W., Monson, T., & Dermer, M. (1976). Outcome dependency: Attention, attribution, and attraction. *Journal of Personality and Social Psychology, 34,* 978-989.

Broussard, E. R. (1978). Psychological disorders in children: Early assessment of infants at risk. *Continuing Education.* February, 44-57.

Bruner, J. S., & Tagiuri, R. (1954). The perception of people. In G. Lindzey (Ed.), *Handbook of social psychology* (Vol. 2). Cambridge, MA: Addison-Wesley.

Byrne, D. (1971). *The attraction paradigm*. New York: Academic.

Cantor, N., & Mischel, W. (1977). Traits as prototypes: Effects on recognition memory. *Journal of Personality and Social Psychology, 35,* 38-48.

Carlson, E. R. (1961). Motivation and set in acquiring information about persons. *Journal of Personality, 29,* 285-293.

Chaiken, A. L., & Cooper, J. (1973). Evaluation as a function of correspondence and hedonic relevance. *Journal of Experimental Social Psychology, 9,* 257-264.

Crano, W. D., & Messé, L. A. (1982). *Social Psychology*. Homewood, IL: Dorsey.

Crockett, W. H. (1965). Cognitive complexity and impression formation. In B. A. Maher (Ed.), *Progress in experimental personality research* (Vol. 2). New York: Academic.

Darley, J., & Berscheid, E. (1967). Increased liking as a result of the anticipation of personal contact. *Human Relations, 20,* 29-40.

Dion, K. K., Berscheid, E., & Walster, E. (1972). "What is beautiful is good." *Journal of Personality and Social Psychology, 24,* 285-290.

Ebbesen, E. B. (1980). Cognitive processes in understanding ongoing behavior. In R. Hastie, T. M. Ostrom, E. B. Ebbesen, R. S. Wyer, D. L. Hamilton, & D. E. Carlston (Eds.), *Person memory: The cognitive basis of social perception*. Hillsdale, NJ: Lawrence Erlbaum.

Edwards, A. L. (1959). Social desirability and the description of others. *Journal of Abnormal and Social Psychology, 59,* 434-436.

Endler, N. S., & Magnusson, D. (Eds.). (1976). *Interactional psychology and personality*. Washington, DC: Hemisphere.

Fontaine, G. (1975). Causal attribution in simulated versus real situations: When are people logical, when are they not? *Journal of Personality and Social Psychology, 32,* 1021-1029.

Foulkes, D., & Foulkes, S. H. (1965). Self-concept, dogmatism, and tolerance of trait inconsistency. *Journal of Personality and Social Psychology, 2,* 104-111.

Gardner, R. W., Jackson, D. N., & Messick S. J. (1960). Personality organization in cognitive controls and intellectual abilities. *Psychological Issues, 2* (4, Whole No. 8).

Goldstein, K. M., & Blackman, S. (1978). *Cognitive style.* New York: John Wiley.

Gough, H. G. (1969). (Rev. Ed.). *The CPI Manual,* Palo Alto, CA: Consulting Psychologists' Press.

Hastie, R., Ostrom, T. M., Ebbesen, E. B., Wyer, R. S., Hamilton, D. L., & Carlston, D. E. (Eds.). (1980). *Person memory: The cognitive basis of social perception.* Hillsdale, NJ: Lawrence Erlbaum.

Heider, F. (1944). Social perception and phenomenal causality. *Psychological Review, 51,* 358-374.

Hewitt, J., & Goldman, M. (1974). Self-esteem, need for approval, and reactions to personal evaluations. *Journal of Experimental Social Psychology, 10,* 201-210.

Higgins, E. T., Kuiper, N. A., & Olson, J. M. (1981). Social cognition: A need to get personal. In E. T. Higgins, C. P. Herman, & M. P. Zanna (Eds.), *Social cognition: The Ontario Symposium* (Vol. 1). Hillsdale, NJ: Lawrence Erlbaum.

Jeffery, K. M., & Mischel, W. (1979). Effects of purpose on the organization and recall of information in person perception. *Journal of Personality, 47,* 397-419.

Johnson, C. D., & Gormly, A. V. (1975). Personality, attraction, and social ambiguity. *Journal of Social Psychology, 97,* 227-232.

Jones, E. E., & Daugherty, B. N. (1959). Political orientation and the perceptual effects of an anticipated interaction. *Journal of Abnormal and Social Psychology, 59,* 340-349.

Jones, E. E., & Nisbett, R. E. (1971). *The actor and the observer: Divergent perspectives on the cause of behavior.* Morristown, NJ: General Learning Press.

Jones, E. E., & Thibaut, J. W. (1958). Interaction goals as bases of inference in interpersonal perception. In R. Tagiuri & L. Petrullo (Eds.), *Person perception and interpersonal behavior.* Stanford, CA: Stanford University Press.

Kelly, G. A. (1955). *The psychology of personal constructs* (Vols. 1 & 2). New York: Norton.

Koltuv, B. B. (1962). Some characteristics of intrajudge trait intercorrelations. *Psychological Monographs, 76* (Whole No. 552), 1-33.

Landfield, A. W. (1968). The extremity rating revisited within the context of personal construct theory. *British Journal of Social and Clinical Psychology, 7,* 135-139.

McArthur, L. Z., & Post, D. D. (1977). Figural emphasis and person perception. *Journal of Experimental Social Psychology, 13,* 520-535.

Messé, L. A., Stollak, G. E., Larson, R. W., & Michaels, G. Y. (1979). Interpersonal consequences of person perception processes in two social contexts. *Journal of Personality and Social Psychology, 37,* 369-379.

Mueller, J. H. (1980). Test anxiety and the encoding and retrieval of information. In I. G. Sarason (Ed.), *Test anxiety: Theory, research and applications.* Hillsdale, NJ: Lawrence Erlbaum.

Murray, H. A. (1938). *Explorations in personality.* New York: John Wiley.

Newtson, D. (1976). Foundations of attribution: The perception of ongoing behavior. In J. H. Harvey, W. J. Ickes, & R. F. Kidd (Eds.). *New directions in attribution research* (Vol. 1). Hillsdale, NJ: Lawrence Erlbaum.

Nover, A., Shore, M. F., Timberlake, E. M., & Greenspan, S. I. (1984). The relationship of maternal perception and maternal behavior: A study of normal mothers and their infants. *American Journal of Orthopsychiatry, 54,* 210-223.

Postman, L., Bruner, J. S., & McGinnies, E. (1948). Personal values as selective factors in perception. *Journal of Abnormal and Social Psychology, 43,* 142-154.

Riggs, J. M., & Cantor, N. (1984). Getting acquainted: The role of the self-concept and preconceptions. *Personality and Social Psychology Bulletin, 10,* 432-445.

Robbins, G. E. (1975). Dogmatism and information gathering in personality impression formation. *Journal of Research in Personality, 9,* 74-84.

Rogers, T. B., Kuiper, N. A., & Kirker, W. S. (1977). Self-reference and the encoding of personal information. *Journal of Personality and Social Psychology, 35,* 677-688.

Rokeach, M. (1960). *The open and closed mind.* New York: Basic Books.

Rosenberg, S., Nelson, C., & Vivekananthan, P. S. (1968). A multidimensional approach to the structure of personality impressions. *Journal of Personality and Social Psychology, 9,* 283-294.

Schank, R., & Abelson, R. (1977). *Scripts, plans, goals, and understanding: An inquiry into human knowledge structures.* Hillsdale, NJ: Lawrence Erlbaum.

Schneider, D. J. (1973). Implicit personality theory: A review. *Psychological Bulletin, 79,* 294-309.

Shrauger, S., & Altrocchi, J. (1964). The personality of the perceiver as a factor in person perception. *Psychological Bulletin, 62,* 289-308.

Shrauger, J. S., & Patterson, M. B. (1974). Self-evaluation and the selection of dimensions for evaluating others. *Journal of Personality, 42,* 569-585.

Snyder, M. (1976). Social perception and social causation. In J. H. Harvey, W. J. Ickes, & R. F. Kidd (Eds.), *New directions in attribution research,* (Vol. 1). Hillsdale, NJ: Lawrence Erlbaum.

Snyder, M., & Swann, W. B. (1978). Hypothesis-testing in social interaction. *Journal of Personality and Social Psychology, 36,* 1202-1212.

Snyder, M., Tanke, E. E., & Berscheid, E. (1977). Social perception and interpersonal behavior. *Journal of Personality and Social Psychology, 35,* 656-666.

Snyder, M., & Uranowitz, S. W. (1978). Reconstructing the past: Some cognitive consequences of person perception. *Journal of Personality and Social Psychology, 36,* 941-950.

Tagiuri, R. (1969) Person perception. In G. Lindzey & E. Aronson (Eds.), *Handbook of social psychology,* (2nd. Ed.) (Vol. 3). Reading, MA: Addison-Wesley.

Taylor, S. E., & Crocker, J. (1981). Schematic bases of social information processing. In E. T. Higgins, C. P. Herman, & M. P. Zanna (Eds.), *Social cognition: the Ontario Symposium,* (Vol. 1). Hillsdale, NJ: Lawrence Erlbaum.

Taylor, D. A., & Oberlander, L. (1969). Person perception and self-disclosure: Motivational mechanisms in interpersonal processes. *Journal of Experimental Research in Personality, 4,* 14-28.

Taylor, R. N., & Dunnette, M. D. (1974). Influence of dogmatism, risk-taking propensity, and intelligence on decision-making strategies for a sample of industrial managers. *Journal of Applied Psychology, 59,* 420-423.

Warr, P. B., & Knapper, C. (1968). *The perception of people and events.* London: John Wiley.

Warr, P. B., & Sims, A. (1965). A study of cojudgment processes. *Journal of Personality, 33,* 598-604.

White, B. J., Alter, R. D., & Rardin, M. (1965). Authoritarianism, dogmatism, and usage of conceptual categories. *Journal of Personality and Social Psychology, 2,* 293-295.

# 9

# Personality, Gender, and the
# Phenomenology of Romantic Love

KAREN K. DION
KENNETH L. DION

**Karen K. Dion** is Professor of Psychology at the University of Toronto. In addition to her collaborative research with Kenneth Dion on romantic love, her research has focused on the social psychological effects and correlates of physical attractiveness. Her most recent research interests concern socialization in adulthood and adult development.

**Kenneth L. Dion** is Professor of Psychology at the University of Toronto and a Fellow of the Canadian Psychological Association. He is a former Associate Editor of the *Journal of Experimental Social Psychology.* His research interests have focused on small groups, prejudice and intergroup relations, as well as romantic love and interpersonal attraction. A phenomenological approach has characterized some of his research in these areas, including his collaborative work with Karen Dion on correlates of romantic love.

On Friday, August 30, 1974, the following letter appeared in Dr. Joyce Brothers's column in the *Detroit Free Press:*

> Dear Dr. Brothers: Do you think it's effeminate for a 19-year-old guy to fall in love so hard it's like the whole world's turned around? I think I'm really crazy because this has happened several times now and love just seems to hit me on the head from nowhere. . . . My father says this is the way girls fall in love and that it doesn't happen this way with guys—at least it's not supposed to. I can't change how I am in this way but it kind of worries me.—P. T.

Some answers to P. T.'s questions are provided by studies we and others have conducted into the connections between personality, gender, and the phenomenon of heterosexual romantic love. This research is the focus of the present chapter. Essentially, we shall argue that certain persons, well illustrated by P. T.'s case, fall in love much more easily and readily than others. An individual's personality, along with his or her gender, we believe, helps to predict the proneness to fall in love. Equally

**AUTHORS' NOTE:** Thanks are due to Phillip Shaver, Cindy Hazan, Harry Reis, and William Ickes for their detailed and thoughtful comments on a prior version of this chapter. Preparation of this chapter was facilitated by an SSHRC Leave Fellowship to the second author.

important, we propose that romantic love is not a uniform experience. On the contrary, in reporting what love feels like to them (i.e., its phenomenology), people describe very different experiences. In this regard too, personality and gender are important because they are systematically associated with subjectively different experiences or "phenomenologies" of romantic love.

## A PHENOMENOLOGICAL
## APPROACH TO ROMANTIC LOVE

We refer to our approach as *phenomenological* because we focus on individuals' descriptions of their personal experiences of romantic love. A *strict* phenomenological approach (MacLeod, 1947) also dictates that the investigator not impose his or her categories upon the respondents' descriptions of their inner experience. However, because of the difficulties of open-ended measurement procedures, we have chosen to rely instead on more conventional methods. Specifically, we have asked individuals to respond to a questionnaire that contains items pertaining to several different aspects of romantic love. In the initial version of this questionnaire, respondents were asked whether or not they had ever been in love and if so, how many times, how intensely, and for how long. Individuals' subjective reactions to love were assessed with several classes of measures. Specifically, respondents indicated the extent to which they experienced symptoms commonly believed to be associated with romantic love. In addition, we asked them to describe the qualitative features of their heterosexual love experiences in terms of a series of bipolar dimensions. (Examples of specific items will be cited in subsequent sections of this chapter.) Finally, the questionnaire contained Likert-type items that measured attitudes toward romantic love.[1] In this research, each class of measures reflecting subjective reactions to love was factor analyzed, with the items having sufficient loadings on each factor summed together to yield indices for each respondent. After our initial study, the Romantic Love Questionnaire was expanded to include an item concerning the incidence and frequency of unrequited love. This expanded version also measured attitudes toward one's partner, using Rubin's (1970) 13-item love and liking scales and a 4-item trust scale that we designed (Dion & Dion, 1975; Dion & Dion, 1976). In the most recent version of our questionnaire, we also included 4 items from Pam, Plutchik, and Conte's (1975) subscale assessing physical attraction toward one's partner.

In our approach to the study of love, dimensions of personality are conceptualized as systems of interrelated needs and beliefs about self and others that provide frameworks for individuals' interpretations of their experiences in close relationships. The subjective experience of love should therefore be qualitatively different for individuals who vary in key personality dimensions. Based on the available literature concerning particular personality dimensions and on the basis of relevant theoretical viewpoints concerning personality and love, in each study specific hypotheses have been formulated concerning an individual's predicted love experiences.

## Locus of Control:
## A Correlate of Romantic Love

In our first study (Dion & Dion, 1973), we examined the relation between the personality dimension of locus of control and individuals' reported experiences of love. As conceptualized by Rotter (1966), the locus of control dimension consists of opposing orientations (internal versus external control) that reflect different generalized expectancies regarding one's personal efficacy. Individuals with an internal orientation typically regard events that affect them as being largely under their own control. In contrast, persons characterized by an external orientation are likely to view the events affecting them as outside their personal control, attributing causality instead to powerful external forces (e.g., fate or luck).

Romantic love in Western culture has often been depicted as a mysterious *external* force that overwhelms "fated" persons in an experience surpassing ordinary pleasures (Schon, 1963). Considering the cultural stereotype of romantic love, we predicted that compared to externals, internals should be less likely to report that they had ever experienced love because of their proclivity for interpreting events as being under their personal control. Furthermore, we expected that among those who had been in love, internals would be less likely than externals to describe their experience of love in traditionally stereotypic terms as a mysterious, volatile, and idealized experience.

We also reasoned that the accounts of their love experiences might differ because of the respective orientations of internals and externals to interpersonal influence. There is evidence to suggest that internals dislike being influenced by others and are oriented instead toward controlling others (Phares, 1965, 1976). Such an orientation should endow the heterosexual relationships of internally-controlled persons with a rational, calculated quality and also detract from an idealistic attitude toward romantic love. From both of the preceding perspectives, then, one would expect internally controlled people to be less likely than externals to "fall in love" or to experience romantic attraction as mysterious, volatile, and idealized.

To test these hypotheses, 243 undergraduates at the Minneapolis campus of the University of Minnesota completed both Rotter's (1966) I-E Scale measuring locus of control and the Romantic Love Questionnaire described above. Rotter's I-E Scale contains 23 forced-choice items. On each item, respondents choose between a statement endorsing the inevitability of events (externality) and another one reflecting a belief in the perceived controllability of events (internality). Thus, the items concern the person's "*belief* about the nature of the world" rather than their "preference" for internal or external control (Rotter, 1966, p. 10). The I-E Scale is said to gauge *generalized expectancies* concerning perceived locus of control because the item content taps a variety of different domains (e.g., politics, scholastic achievement, vocational success, leadership).

Another aspect of the our general research procedure deserves emphasis. When several self-report measures are administered to respondents in a single session, personal and situational response sets and perceived demand characteristics can artifactually heighten any correlation that may be obtained between them. To minimize this problem, we have, whenever possible, administered the personality measure(s) and the Romantic Love Questionnaire to small groups of respondents in separate laboratory sessions under different rationales and with different experimenters. In the locus of control study, for example, this procedure was followed for a large proportion of the sample, with the remainder completing both measures in the same session due to time pressures at the end of the academic year.

Personality differences in locus of control were indeed related to reporting that one had or had not experienced romantic love. As predicted, internals were proportionally less likely than externals to report ever having experienced romantic love. Among respondents who had experienced romantic love, internals did not, however, differ from externals in the frequency of their reported experiences. Second, among those respondents who indicated having been in love, the reported qualities of their love experiences differed as well. Factor analysis of the adjective ratings of romantic love yielded five factors. For example, the "volatile love" index was defined by the items unpredictable, tense, short, changing, and mysterious. The "rational love" index consisted of the items sophisticated, predictable, deliberate, logical, systematic, controllable, and rational.[2] As predicted, on these indices, internals described their subjective experience of romantic love as more rational and tended to describe love as less volatile than did externals. Finally, on the attitude items, internals tended to disagree more with an idealistic view of love than did externals. In general, then, this pattern of findings supported our hypotheses that individuals differing on the personality dimension of internal versus external control were likely to report qualitatively different experiences of love.

Subsequent to our study, other researchers have explored the relation between personality differences in locus of control and attitudes toward romantic love. For example, Elkins (1978) administered a scale assessing attitudes toward love (Hinkle & Sporakowski, 1975), Rotter's (1966) locus of control scale, and a measure of "irrational beliefs" to a sample of 145 undergraduates at a "large Southwestern university" in the United States. Although unrelated to the number of irrational beliefs endorsed, locus of control scores did correlate significantly with romanticism. Specifically, the more strongly pronounced the respondents' external orientation, the stronger the romanticism in their attitudes toward love.

Similarly, with three separate samples of undergraduates at a small college in New Jersey, Lester, Edge, Kawich, and Lee (1983) investigated the relation between romanticism in attitudes toward love using Knox and Sporakowski's (1968) measure, on the one hand, and scores on Levenson's (1974) locus of control scale (N = 51), Maslow's (1945) Security-Insecurity Inventory (N = 75), and a measure of beliefs about fidelity in dating behavior (N = 84), on the other hand. Although it was uncorrelated with insecurity scores, romanticism in attitudes toward love tended to be positively associated with stronger beliefs in perceived control by others and was positively related to perceived control by chance as well as a stronger belief in the desirability of fidelity in dating behavior.

Finally, Munro and Adams (1978) administered Valecha and Ostrom's (1974) abbreviated measure of internal-external control along with several different attitudinal measures of love to 326 Canadian women and men in their homes. These respondents were recruited by phone or on the street in Calgary, Alberta, and were differentiated into separate college-educated and high school-educated samples, as well as different phases of family life (single; married, no children; married, children at home; married, children left home). The different measures of love included Rubin's (1970) Love scale, the Knox Love Attitude Inventory (Knox, 1970), and a Love Attitude Scale designed by Munro and Adams consisting of three subscales ("romantic idealism," "romantic power," and "conjugal love").

In the college-educated sample, internals tended to exhibit less romantic attitudes toward love on Knox's measure than externals. For the high school-educated sample, internals were more "rational" in their attitudes toward love compared to externals on the Munro and Adams conjugal love subscale. Among high school-aged students, externals scored higher than internals on Munro and Adams's romantic idealism subscale and on Rubin's (1970) attitudinal measure of love for one's partner. Consistent with our earlier research, Munro and Adams (1978, p. 214) concluded that "the findings are consistent with the assumption that externals are more likely than internals to be swayed by a cultural stereotype into believing that love is an intense, mysterious, and idealized experience." Munro and Adams's conclusion is especially applicable to their high school student sample.

To summarize several studies of North American samples, the evidence suggests that personality differences in locus of control relate to romantic attraction and attitudes toward romantic love. Dion and Dion (1973) predicted and found that externals were more likely to report having experienced romantic love than internals. Among those respondents who had been in love, the love experiences of externals were more in keeping with the cultural stereotype of romantic love that portrays it as mysterious and volatile. Moreover, using various locus of control scales, we and others also have found that externals are more idealistic about love and prone to greater romanticism than are internals.

## Dimensions of Self-Concept and Romantic Love

### Self-Esteem

Several important personality dimensions relating to the self-concept have also been explored as correlates of romantic love. For example, we have investigated the relation between self-esteem and the phenomenology of romantic love (Dion & Dion, 1975). We focused on this dimension because the relationship between self-esteem and romantic love is a theoretically contentious issue. Self-actualization theorists (e.g., Fromm, 1939; Rogers, 1959; Maslow, 1970) have proposed that genuinely self-accepting persons (i.e., those characterized by high self-esteem and low defensiveness) are more capable than other people of giving and receiving love. Thus, these individuals should respond more favorably to the experience of love and to an accepting partner. However, some self-esteem theories (Walster, 1965; Jones, 1973) yield the opposite prediction. According to these perspectives, individuals with low self-esteem possess strong needs for affection and self-enhancement. If so, it is those lacking in self-esteem who should respond more favorably to a romantic partner and find the experience of love more rewarding.

We tested these competing hypotheses by obtaining two types of self-esteem measures from 156 undergraduates at the University of

Toronto: an updated version of a standard self-esteem measure in which respondents rated their perceived self, self-esteem, and ideal self on a series of adjectives (Bills, Vance, & McLean, 1951) as well as two items from Ziller's Self-Social Symbols Tasks (Ziller & Grossman, 1967; Ziller, Hagey, Smith, & Long, 1969) designed to measure social self-esteem. For example, one of the latter items presents the respondent with a horizontal series of ten circles and asks that they be labeled with letters representing self and several specified significant others (e.g., father, spouse or dating partner, friend). On the assumption that leftward placement reflects greater perceived importance, more leftward placement of the symbol for self relative to the social symbols yields higher self-esteem scores. Ziller (1973) has termed this and similar items as reflecting *social self-esteem* because the respondent locates the self in the context of significant others. Ziller and his colleagues have also claimed that their index of social self-esteem is less susceptible to social desirability biases than traditional self-rating measures of self-esteem (Ziller et al., 1969; Ziller, 1973).

Crowne and Marlowe's (1964) Social Desirability Scale was also included along with the self-esteem measures in the first testing session as a check for any such confounding between measures of self-esteem and social desirability. Although originally intended to index one's need for approval, Crowne and Marlowe (1964) and others (e.g., Ford & Hersen, 1967) have shown that scores on the Social Desirability Scale also reflect differences in chronic defensiveness. As anticipated, different components of the standard self-esteem measure were positively correlated with social desirability scores from the Marlowe-Crowne scale. In contrast, Ziller's social self-esteem index correlated positively with several components of the standard self-esteem measure but *not* with defensiveness. Thus, by defining self-esteem in terms of the social self-esteem measure, we could minimize social desirability biases and treat self-esteem and defensiveness as independent factors in analyses of variance on the dependent measures. Thus far, we have discussed the measures that respondents completed during their first testing session. In their second session several weeks later, participants completed the Romantic Love Questionnaire. In addition, they appraised their respective romantic partners using the same adjectives that were used in the updated Bills et al., questionnaire measure of self-esteem.

An interesting pattern of findings emerged in this study. There was no association between social self-esteem or defensiveness, on the one hand, and respondents' reports of whether or not they had ever experienced romantic love, on the other hand. In this sample, however, very few respondents (N = 20) reported never having been in love. Among those who had experienced romantic love, individuals high in social self-esteem and low in defensiveness reported more *frequent* experiences of love than any of their counterparts, a finding that is consistent with a self-actualization perspective. In other respects, however, the findings accorded better with predictions from self-esteem theories. Main effects for social self-esteem occurred on several measures. Compared to those with high social self-esteem, individuals with low social self-esteem described their love experiences as being more intense and less "rational" (a factor defined by the items controllable, understandable, predictable, and superficial). Moreover, persons with low social self-esteem expressed stronger attitudes of love, liking, and trust toward their partners and evaluated their partner's personal attributes more favorably than did those with high social self-esteem.

## Defensiveness

The personality dimension of defensiveness is relevant in its own right to the phenomenology of love. In particular, highly defensive persons reported falling in love less frequently than less defensive individuals. As well, those high in defensiveness differed from those low in defensiveness on their ratings of the subjective experience of love. Compared to less defensive persons, more defensive individuals described their experience of love as more "rewarding" and "steadier" but also as more "circumspect" or guarded. Also, more defensive people showed a tendency to describe their love experiences as less "straightforward" than did less defensive individuals.[3] When indicating their general beliefs about romantic love, persons high in defensiveness also agreed more strongly with a cynical view when compared to less defensive individuals.

Considered together, these findings suggest an ambivalent reaction to intimate heterosexual relationships on the part of defensive individuals. Defensive persons are known to be primarily concerned with protecting a vulnerable self-image from threats (Crowne & Marlowe, 1964). In trying to minimize their vulnerability, persons characterized by high defensiveness may be less likely to become involved in interpersonal relationships that press for extensive self-disclosure. Furthermore, more defensive people may respond less favorably than less defensive individuals to others who show more intimate self-disclosure.

We tested some of this reasoning in a study (Dion & Dion, 1978) in which undergraduate women varying in defensiveness anticipated that they would take part in a conversation with another person on sets of preselected topics that varied in intimacy of disclosure. The college women were presented with the topic choices of four different prospective partners who differed in the intimacy level of the topics they had allegedly selected (high versus low) and in whether they were female or male. The respondent's task was to choose topics from a different list that she would be willing to discuss with each of the prospective conversants and to indicate her expected liking of each individual. We hypothesized that compared to those low in defensiveness, highly defensive women would be less likely to reciprocate intimacy of self-disclosure or to respond favorably to high disclosers, especially those of the opposite sex.

Consistent with these expectations, highly defensive women indicated less expected liking for high self-disclosing stimulus persons than for low self-disclosers and also liked males less than females. These findings suggested that the more defensive women felt uncomfortable when confronted with a more personal, revealing level of disclosure from another individual. Considered together with the finding that highly defensive women expected to like male peers less than female peers, the pattern of results suggested that responding to intimacy in opposite-sex encounters might be problematic for these women. Further research is needed to examine the relation between defensiveness in women as well as men and their reactions to their partner's disclosure of personal information in heterosexual relationships, especially in view of some evidence that extent of self-disclosure between partners is positively related to the development of personal closeness and romantic love (Rubin, 1974).

## Self-Actualization

Another way to explore the relation of self-actualization and romantic love is to employ Shostrom's (1964, 1974) Personal Orientation Inventory (POI) to assess personality differences in self-actualization (Dion & Dion, 1976). Shostrom devised the POI on a rational basis from the writings of Maslow, May, Perls, and Rogers, and from Riesman's concept of the inner-directed person, as well as in consultation with Maslow. In creating the POI, Shostrom set out to devise a measure that would reflect an individual's positive mental health and the degree to which one is fulfilling his or her potential.

The POI consists of 150 items in which respondents choose between two statements expressing opposing points of view (e.g., "People should always control their anger" versus "People should express honestly felt anger"). Two major scales underlie the POI.[4] The I or "inner support" scale accounts for 127 of the 150 items of the POI and indexes the respondent's inner-directedness and autonomy from external pressures. The Tc or "time competence" scale accounts for the remaining 23 items and reflects the extent to which the respondent is focused on the present rather than dwelling in the past or the future. Comparing different procedures for combining scores from these two scales into an overall index of self-actualization, Damm (1969) suggested summing the raw scores from the I and Tc scales—the procedure followed in the two studies of self-actualization and romantic love discussed below.

There is considerable evidence to support the construct validity of the POI as a personality measure of self-actualization. For example, persons judged by clinical psychologists to be self-actualized have obtained higher scores on the I and Tc scales of the POI than others deemed to be nonself-actualized or normal (Shostrom, 1964). Further, hospitalized psychiatric patients (Fox, Knapp, & Michael, 1968) and college students scoring high on the Neuroticism scale of the Eysenck Personality Inventory (Knapp, 1965), respectively, have scored lower on the major POI scales than comparison groups. On the other hand, experiences conducive to better mental health, such as sensitivity training and psychotherapy, have been associated with higher scores on POI scales. The POI is also relatively immune to attempts by college students to "fake good," unless they are given explicit information about its underlying rationale and "concept training" in improving their scores (e.g., Warehime, Routh, & Foulds, 1974). Although Shostrom has since suggested another instrument as a refinement and extension of the POI, evidence to date still points to the POI as the best available measure of self-actualization (Hattie, Hancock, & Brereton, 1984).

How do POI scores relate to the other correlates of romantic love discussed in this chapter? As regards internal-external control, Wall (1970) reported no correlations between the I and Tc scales of the POI and college students' scores on Rotter's I-E Scale, whereas Warehime and Foulds (1971) found a negative correlation between the I scale from the POI and externality for females but not males. In the case of defensiveness, several studies (Warehime & Foulds, 1973; Warehime et al., 1974) have found that in the absence of specific information about the POI, high-scorers on the Marlowe-Crowne Social Desirability Scale have obtained lower scores on the POI. Even with information and training on the concept of self-actualization, high versus low scorers on the Marlowe-Crowne Scale do not respond differently on the POI (Warehime et al., 1974). Sex differences on the Tc scale (and several subscales) of the POI were found in the sample used for norming the POI, but the mean scale differences between the sexes were consistently small (Shostrom, 1974; Tosi & Lindamood, 1975). Finally, although we know of no studies relating them, measures of self-esteem and self-actualization should correlate highly and positively with one another because the two constructs have much in common and also because the POI includes self-acceptance and self-regard as two subscales.

Having shown that the POI is useful as an index of self-actualization, let us discuss two studies that have used it in exploring the relation of self-actualization to romantic love. Dietch (1978) used the POI in a study designed to test some aspects of Maslow's earlier theorizing concerning self-actualization and romantic love. Maslow (1968, 1970), for example, suggested that there are two different types of love, which differ in their motivational basis. One type, which he referred to as "D love" (deficiency love), reflected the individual's attempt to satisfy unfulfilled needs and was assumed to have a possessive, selfish quality. A second type, labeled "B love," was presumably based not on need satisfaction but rather on "love for the being of the other" (Maslow, 1970, p. 199)—loving the partner for her or his individual qualities. B or "being" love was assumed to reflect an absence of self-protective, defensive behavior and a willingness to reveal oneself, including one's faults, to a partner. Maslow proposed that self-actualized people would be more prone than the less self-actualized to experience B love.

Following Maslow's line of thought, Dietch (1978) hypothesized that being in love, or having been in love, would be related to greater self-actualization. Moreover, the love experiences of more self-actualized individuals were expected to be characterized by a greater degree of B-love, as previously conceptualized by Maslow. Finally, among those whose romantic relationships had terminated, Dietch predicted that the more self-actualized persons would be less resentful of their partners. To test these ideas Dietch (1978) devised a 16-item scale to assess B-love and administered it to 126 university undergraduates, along with the POI and a questionnaire requesting information about the respondents' love relationships in the three preceding years, including their length, current status, and resentment over terminated relationships.

The results supported the hypotheses of a positive relation between self-actualization and love. For example, Dietch found that those who indicated having been "really in love" (presumably, as opposed to being merely infatuated) at least once in the last three years had higher self-actualization scores (i.e., the simple, unweighted sum of I and Tc scale scores from the POI) than those who had not. Second, among those who had been in love at least once in the past three years, self-actualization scores were positively correlated with scores on the B-love scale. Finally, among those who had terminated a love relationship, persons high in self-actualization were less resentful of their partners than those scoring low in self-actualization.

We also explored the relation of self-actualization to romantic love (Dion & Dion, 1985). Our investigation was a *panel study* in which University of Toronto undergraduates completed the POI, Wessman and Ricks's (1966) Inventory of Affect Scales, and our Romantic Love Questionnaire in randomized orders on two different occasions separated by several months. Thus, there are two important differences between Dietch's study and ours. First, by having measured self-actualization and romantic love on two occasions, we can test the different causal sequences that underlie any obtained positive correlations between these variables (see Cook & Campbell, 1979) that Dietch was unable to explore: (1) self-actualization predisposes individuals to experience romantic love, (2) experiencing romantic love enhances one's level of self-actualization, and (3) self-actualization and romantic love have a reciprocal causal relation.

A second important difference between Dietch's study and our own concerns the measurement of romantic love. Although Dietch's attempt to devise his own scale of B-love based on Maslow's writings is laudable, the scale's psychometric properties and its validity as a measure of love are unknown. Instead, we relied on Rubin's (1970) scale of romantic love, for which there is some validational evidence (see Rubin, 1970; Dion & Dion, 1976), and the Love Scale from Wessman and Ricks's Inventory of Affect Scales, for which there is normative information.

These latter two scales illustrate, we believe, a key distinction in attempting to measure one's experience of love that is not yet reflected in the current literature on the subject. Rubin (1970) has conceptualized and measured romantic love as an *interpersonal attitude*. A respondent completing Rubin's love scale is asked to indicate the extent to which he or she has certain reactions or feelings with regard to his or her romantic partner on a 13-item attitude scale. Here are two sample items: "I would do almost anything for _____" and "I feel responsible for_____'s well-being." Recent research by Steck, Levitan, McLane, and Kelley (1982) has suggested that three different dimensions underlie the various items of Rubin's love scale: caring, need, and trust. Thus, based on Steck et al.'s (1982) research, the investigator can derive scores for the dimensions of caring, need, and trust by summing across separate clusters of the items constituting Rubin's original love scale. Whether one sums across all of its 13 items to generate a single, overall "love" score for a respondent or sums subsets of these items to yield scores for caring, need, and trust, respectively, the Rubin Love Scale is assessing a set of reported feelings, cognitions, and behaviors toward a particular person as a reflection of one's love for that individual.

In contrast to love as an attitude toward one's romantic or sexual partner, one can also conceptualize the extent of love as a subjective state experienced by the lover, including an explicit sexual component, which can vary in intensity, personal satisfaction, and feeling of relatedness with the partner. The latter is the approach reflected in the Love and Sex Scale from Wessman and Ricks's Inventory. On their Love and Sex Scale, the respondent is asked to indicate "the extent to which you feel loving and tender, or sexually frustrated and unloving" on a 10-point scale with each point clearly defined. At one end of the scale (a rating of 1) is the alternative "Hopeless, cold, unloved, and unloving." A rating of 5 is associated with the description: "Not much feeling of mutual understanding. Some lack of interest. Slightly frustrated." Perhaps appropriately, a rating of 10 is reserved for those who "feel the rapture of full, joyous, and complete love."

Although analyses of the causal patterns have not been completed at the time of this writing, we can report the results concerning self-actualization and romantic love from the data for the first of the two testing sessions. For these latter analyses, respondents' scores on the Tc and I scales of the POI were summed together, and the resulting self-actualization scores were split at the median for each sex in order to categorize individuals as being high or low in self-actualization. (Analysis of the self-actualization scores showed no sex differences.) Then, with self-actualization and sex of respondent as independent variables, analyses of variance were performed on the aforementioned love measures as well as other indices derived from the Romantic Love Questionnaire.

The results of these analyses show the importance of distinguishing between love as an interpersonal attitude toward one's romantic or sexual partner and as an emotional experience generating a sense of subjective satisfaction. Main effects for self-actualization were found on overall love scores from the Rubin Love Scale and also on the caring and need components of this scale. Specifically, those high in self-actualization tended to have *lower* overall love scores on the Rubin Scale and also scored *lower* in caring and need for their partner than those low in self-actualization. In contrast, Wessman and Ricks's Love and Sex Scale focusing on love as an emotional experience yielded a positive (main effect) relation between self-actualization and romantic love: Individuals high in self-actualization reported a richer, more satisfying love experience, when describing a present or previous relationship with a member of the opposite sex, than did persons low in self-actualization.

On other measures from the Romantic Love Questionnaire, highly self-actualized individuals described their subjective experience of love as being less circumspect or guarded and also tended to rate their love experiences, on average, as being more intense than less self-actualized persons. However, high self-actualized persons tended to espouse less idealism and more pragmatism in their attitude toward love than those less self-actualized.

These findings partly support self-actualization theory. Most notably, our finding on Wessman and Ricks's measure, which concerns the experience of love, accords nicely with Maslow's (1970) description of self-actualizing people. His account suggests that for these individuals, the experience of love is very personally satisfying as illustrated by the following comment: "It is quite characteristic of self-actualizing people that they can enjoy themselves in love and sex" (Maslow, 1970, p. 194). Our finding that self-actualized persons describe their love experiences as less guarded would also be predicted by self-actualization theory. Maslow cited the "dropping of defenses" as an important feature of the love relationships of those who were self-actualizing.

The findings on the caring and need components of the Rubin Love Scale are only partly consistent with self-actualization theory. From this theoretical perspective, the highly self-actualized individuals should show less need and more caring for their partner than persons low in self-actualization. According to Maslow, the love relationships of self-actualized persons presumably have a less possessive quality reflecting need or dependency. On the other hand, Maslow (1970, pp. 192-194) also suggested that self-actualized individuals would have love relationships characterized by caring and empathy for one another. As previously noted, we found that highly self-actualized individuals expressed less need and less caring for their partners compared to those low in self-actualization. As discussed below, self-esteem theories seem better able to account for these findings. One point about self-actualizing persons may, however, be pertinent. Maslow (1970, p. 199) suggested that self-actualized individuals' enjoyment of their love relationships coexists with some detachment about them, as shown by the following comment: "One has the definite feeling that they enjoy each other tremendously but would take philosophically a long separation or death." Such a sense of detachment may explain both the lesser need and lesser caring exhibited by the more self-actualized persons in our sample.

In summary, research exploring dimensions of the self as correlates of romantic love has been aimed largely at testing the competing predictions of self-actualization theory and self-esteem theories. According to self-actualization theory, genuinely self-accepting or "self-actualized" individuals should be more capable of loving and experiencing satisfying interpersonal relations than others. On the other hand, advocates of self-esteem theories have proposed that persons low in self-esteem should be the ones who are more responsive to romantic love and more appreciative of their partner. Genuine self-acceptance or self-actualization has been operationalized by two alternative procedures: (1) using measures of self-esteem and defensiveness together and taking the combination of high self-esteem and low defensiveness as a reflection of genuine self-acceptance and self-actualization (Dion & Dion, 1975), and

(2) employing Shostrom's Personal Orientation Inventory (POI) to measure personality differences in self-actualization (Dietch, 1978; Dion & Dion, 1985). (Although these two procedures have not been compared directly, we believe that they are equivalent, alternative ways of approaching the same construct.

The three studies to date yield some support for self-actualization theory. For example, genuinely self-accepting persons reported more frequent experiences of romantic love as well as unrequited love than others, suggesting that they are more open to the experience of love (Dion & Dion, 1975). In Dietch's (1978) investigation, respondents' degree of self-actualization as indexed by POI scores correlated positively with reports of having been "really in love" and with scores on a B-love scale. Using the same measure of self-actualization, Dion and Dion (1985) found that highly self-actualized individuals described their love experiences as being more fulfilling and less guarded than those less self-actualized.

On the other hand, the evidence from these studies also partially supports the predictions of self-esteem theories. For example, we found that low self-esteem individuals described more intense love experiences, rated their partners more positively, and expressed stronger attitudes of love, liking, and trust than those higher in self-esteem (Dion & Dion, 1975). Complementing these findings, individuals low in self-actualization similarly indicated a stronger interpersonal attitude of love for their partner—especially caring and need—than those high in self-actualization (Dion & Dion, 1985).

We conclude from this pattern of findings that *both* self-actualization and self-esteem theories are needed to understand how key dimensions of the self-concept relate to the experience of love. In particular, individuals high in genuine self-acceptance or self-actualization seem more open to the *experience* of love and find greater personal fulfillment from the *experience* of loving another. On the other hand, perhaps because of a greater need or appreciation for interpersonal affection, persons lower in self-esteem or self-actualization clearly are fonder of their partners and esteem them more highly.

Finally, a distinction that may prove important in future research is that between love as an interpersonal attitude toward one's partner versus love as an experience with a sexual component and feelings of subjective satisfaction with the relationship. Both types of measures may be needed to understand love properly. In our self-actualization study (Dion & Dion, 1985), Rubin's (1970) measure of love as an interpersonal attitude was uncorrelated with the Wessman and Ricks's Love and Sex Scale assessing the experience of love. In retrospect, it is perhaps not surprising that there are aspects of love not reflected by a measure of love—such as Rubin's—that focuses solely on esteem and affection for one's partner, without considering the lover's own satisfaction with the relationship.

## Gender Differences in Love

We now turn to the issue of differences between women and men in the phenomenology of love. The quotation at the beginning of the chapter nicely illustrates the traditional cultural stereotype of romantic love prevalent in North America. According to this stereotype, women are supposed to be more likely to be "swept away" by heterosexual love and to be more "romantic" than men. P. T. expresses concern because his personal experiences of romantic love are similar to what is supposedly a typical female experience. As the research discussed in this section will illustrate, however, the gender differences in romantic love that have been observed by psychologists and sociologists often run counter to the cultural stereotype.

### Attitude Toward Love:
### A Functionalist Perspective

We have explored gender differences in beliefs about love in two studies with college undergraduates. Our initial study (Dion & Dion, 1973) yielded an intriguing pattern of findings on the attitudinal orientations toward love that were definitely *not* consistent with the traditional stereotypic view that women are the more "romantic" sex. From analyzing items concerning attitude toward love, we found instead that among the University of Minnesota students, the college women were *less* idealistic and also *less* cynical about heterosexual, romantic love but *more* pragmatically oriented toward it than the college men.

We interpreted these gender differences in attitude toward love in terms of a functionalist perspective on romantic love based in the sociological literature. Advocates of this viewpoint focus on the role that romantic love plays in enabling individuals to adapt to society and on how romantic love helps to maintain social institutions such as marriage. This theoretical perspective on romantic love began with Beigel's (1951) speculative paper on the origin and nature of romantic love, was later reflected by Hobart (1958) and Kephart (1967) in their interpretations of early findings of gender differences in attitude toward love, and has been most systematically elaborated in the writing and research of Rosenblatt and his associates on cross-cultural patterns of romantic love (Rosenblatt, 1974).

Working from this viewpoint, Rosenblatt has suggested that romantic love is one of several types of bonds for consolidating men and women in marriage. Essentially, romantic love is regarded as a functional substitute operating when other types of bonds between women and men (e.g., economic interdependence) are weak or absent in a given society. Also, romantic love can sustain marital relationships against countervailing role pressures. For one example, Rosenblatt assessed the importance of love to marriage as a function of marital residence across a number of societies for which adequate information was available in the Human Relations Area Files. Two interpretations were offered to explain the finding that romantic love was more important as a basis for marriage in societies with non-neolocal residence (i.e., residence with the partner's kin group): (1) In such societies, romantic love may be necessary to protect the marital relationship from the pressures of intrusion from kinsmen. (2) Because economic interdependence and security would usually be provided by co-resident kinsmen rather than by one's spouse in these societies, romantic love might be needed as a substitute bond to keep couples together.

This line of reasoning was extended in a subsequent study by Coppinger and Rosenblatt (1968), which revealed that romantic love has greater importance to marriage in societies where men and women contribute differentially in food-production or gathering. Here too, it was suggested that where members of one sex primarily provide for economic subsistence, mutual economic dependence is precluded for binding the two members of a married couple together; hence some other bond, such as romantic love, is necessary to serve this purpose.

Rosenblatt (1974) has also applied this reasoning to contemporary North American society by suggesting that the emphasis on romantic love in our culture reflects the relative absence of economic reasons for marrying. Of particular relevance to our findings, Rosenblatt (1974, p. 82) proposed that "individual differences in the importance of romantic love in the United States would be related to the existence of other bonds holding a couple together, including their mutual economic dependence, pressures from relatives, and ties to children."

Following this line of thought, we argued (Dion & Dion, 1973) that in North American society, those who contribute less to economic subsistence have the most to gain by romantic love being linked to marriage. Because many women traditionally have contributed less to economic subsistence of the nuclear family in this society, they should perhaps be more prone to value romantic love in pragmatic terms, as a basis for marriage, rather than for idealistic reasons. After all, women following traditional gender-role patterns in our society in effect determine their standard of living by choosing a husband. In contrast, because men traditionally have been socialized to be economically self-sufficient, they have not had to be as concerned with this issue.

Phrased in these terms, the attitudinal differences we found between women and men in college become more understandable. From the functionalist interpretation, one would expect women to be more pragmatically concerned about romantic love and also less idealistic about it than men. Similarly, from this perspective, women cannot afford to be cynical about the importance of romantic love to marriage, if romantic love functions as an inducement for men to marry them. Complementing the latter findings, we found further evidence for the functionalist interpretation in a subsequent study (Dion & Dion, 1975): Compared to their male counterparts, female undergraduates at the University of Toronto (Canada) were more reluctant to dissociate love from the institution of marriage.

Other researchers have also found similar gender differences in college students' beliefs about love that fit well with the functionalist viewpoint we have proposed. Hobart (1958) found that college men scored consistently higher on a Romanticism Scale than college women across different categories of courtship stage and separation status. Using the same scale a decade later, Rubin (1969) likewise found that male undergraduates were more likely to agree with "romantic" attitude items (e.g., "A person should marry whomever he loves regardless of social position") and to disagree more than female undergraduates with "nonromantic" statements (e.g., "Economic security should be carefully considered before selecting a marriage partner"). In another study of college students' beliefs about love (Knox & Sporakowsky, 1968), male undergraduates showed a more romantic orientation to love than female undergraduates on a scale designed to measure "romantic" versus "conjugal" orientation toward love, in which one component of the romantic view was the belief that differences in social background were of minimal importance when choosing a marriage partner.

In a related study, Fengler (1974) found that among those university students who showed "high involvement in courtship" (e.g., "going steady," dating frequently, closer proximity to marriage), the college men were more likely than the college women to receive high scores on "romantic idealism." A person receiving a high score on the romantic idealism scale would oppose choosing a marital partner on pragmatic grounds, believing that "personal feelings should not be compromised by considerations of background, parental obligations, economic factors and occupational and domestic skills" (Fengler, 1974, p. 136). Fengler interpreted his findings in terms of traditional gender role-expectations regarding marriage, in which women were expected to choose a spouse who would be a good economic provider, whereas men instead could focus on more personal/emotional factors—an interpretation consistent with the functionalist perspective.

In summary, findings from several studies of undergraduates from the 1950s to the 1970s have indicated gender differences in beliefs about love that accord well with a functionalist interpretation. This conceptual framework has some further provocative implications. The findings discussed above are consistent with traditional gender-role expectations regarding marriage in North American society, where the husband has traditionally been the sole or main economic provider. Given the number of women employed outside the home today, one would expect some college women's attitudes toward love and marriage to reflect a desire for economic self-sufficiency and independence. According to a functionalist perspective, college women whose personal goals are more career-oriented should be less pragmatic toward love and more romantically idealistic, compared to college women adhering to more traditional gender-roles. In other words, the functionalist interpretation leads to the prediction that career-oriented college women should be more similar to college men in their attitude toward romantic love, with both of these groups differing from college women who continue to follow traditional gender role expectations.

## Falling In and Out of Love

Hill, Rubin, and Peplau (1976) have emphasized another difference between college women's and college men's orientations toward love that clearly relates to the preceding gender differences and the functionalist interpretation. Specifically, they proposed that " (a) men tend to fall *in* love more readily than women, and (b) women tend to fall *out of* love more readily than men" (p. 160, emphasis added). Their rationale for these statements closely parallels the functionalist explanation for gender differences in attitude toward love that we have emphasized.

Because a young woman's years of "marriageability" are limited, she must presumably be selective and discerning in choosing a prospective marital partner to ensure that he is right for her and perhaps the best available to her. Accordingly, she cannot permit herself to fall in love too quickly, lest her judgment be clouded, nor can she sustain a romantic relationship once she has decided that her partner is not truly suitable for her. Considerable evidence suggests that in contemporary North American society, college men do indeed show greater readiness than college women to become romantically involved with a heterosexual partner.

In surveying over 1000 white college students in the Philadelphia area, Kephart (1967) found that nearly twice the percentage of males as females indicated being "very easily attracted" to members of the opposite sex—a result replicating similar findings observed in previous work on heterosexual relationships. Similarly, in Kanin, Davidson, and

Scheck's (1975) research, male university students reported that they became aware of "being in love" earlier in a relationship than female students, suggesting a less cautious approach to romantic love on the college men's part. A final illustration comes from Hill et al.'s (1976) longitudinal study of 231 dating couples recruited from Boston area colleges. In an initial questionnaire, the college men attached greater importance than the college women to "the desire to fall in love" as a reason for becoming involved with their partner. Findings like these bear on P. T.'s case noted at the outset of the chapter; he worried that he might be effeminate because he fell in love so easily. From the evidence available, however, the readiness to fall in love is apparently an experience more typical of men than women in our society, at least for undergraduates.

Hill et al.'s (1976) longitudinal study also supports the notion that "women fall out of love more readily than men." About 45 percent of their college couples broke up during the two-year period of their study. Data from these break-up couples yielded several gender differences in apparent willingness to terminate a romantic relationship. The college women cited more problems as having contributed to the break-up than did the college men. Compared to their male counterparts, the college women also placed greater emphasis on issues of personal compatibility, such as differences in interests, intelligence, and ideas about marriage, as well as their desire to be independent, and their interest in someone else. These college women also appeared to take the lead in ending the relationship, even if they were the more highly involved partner. Hill et al. (1976, pp. 155-156) presented the example of a break-up between David and Ruth. Although allegedly more emotionally involved in the relationship than David, Ruth played the "break-upper" role and noted in retrospect: "I don't think I ever felt romantic [about David]—I felt practical. I had the feeling that I'd better make the most of it because it won't last long."

Thus, from Hill et al.'s research, it appears that college women are more likely to terminate a premarital, romantic relationship that does not live up to their expectations or compares unfavorably to alternatives. There is, however, a notable exception to this dictum that Hill et al. (1976) fail to mention. With a subsample of 63 college couples from the same longitudinal study, Stewart and Rubin (1974) observed that for college men but *not* college women, strength of power motivation correlated negatively with love and liking for the partner and positively with anticipated problems in the relationship, including differences in interests, conflicting ideas about marriage, and the prospect of being interested in someone else. Moreover, after two years, college couples in which the male partner was high in power motivation were less likely to have gotten married and more likely to have broken up than college couples in which the male member was less motivated toward power. In contrast, the college women's standing on power motivation was unrelated to stability of the romantic relationship. On the face of it, it appears that power motivation in college men renders them prone to terminate close relationships with members of the opposite sex.

## Styles of Love

Like us, Lee (1973) believes that the meaning of love differs for different individuals. Based on the literature concerning love and on interviews with English and Canadian respondents actually in love— including people not in university—he identified six different styles of love. *Storge* is a "companionate" or friendship type of love, in which the lovers develop a close, long-lasting, and deeply caring friendship with one another. *Ludus* is a playful, noncommital, and permissive style of love, in which love is viewed mainly as a game one tries to win. *Mania* is an obsessive style of love characterized by strong, disruptive emotions, such as excitement, jealousy, anxiety, and depression. *Agape* is an altruistic style of love epitomized by concern and charity toward one's partner. *Eros* is a romantic style of love involving an "immediate, powerful," and physical attraction based on the partner's physical appearance. Finally, *pragma* is a logical or practical style of love, in which one's choice of partner is carefully planned and deliberated. Using Lee's (1973) typology, Lasswell and Lasswell (1976) developed questionnaire scales to assess a respondent's style(s) of love.

Particularly pertinent to this chapter, two sets of investigators have employed the Lasswells' measure of Lee's styles of love to explore gender differences in samples of students and other adults. With a large sample of respondents from two California universities and from other contexts, including several racial-ethnic groups and age ranges, Hatkoff and Lasswell (1979, p. 224) reported that "males were very much more ludic than females. . . and also more erotic. . . . Females were slightly more manic, storgic and pragmatic." Similarly, with a racially and ethnically heterogeneous sample of over 800 University of Miami students, using an adaptation of the Lasswells' questionnaire, Hendrick, Hendrick, Foote, and Slapion-Foote (1984) found gender differences on several styles of love. The clearest gender differences occurred on the storge and pragma styles of love. Of ten items measuring storge (i.e., friendship love), the college women scored higher than the college men on eight of them. Of the nine items defining pragma, college women scored as more pragmatic than college men on most items. These college women also tended toward a more manic style of love than college men; whereas college men displayed stronger tendencies than college women for ludic and erotic styles of love.

Thus, the two preceding studies are highly consistent with one another as regards the existence and nature of gender differences in styles of love in college student samples. From this research, college women appear to be more prone to storgic and pragmatic styles of love than college men, whereas college men's styles of love are more ludic and erotic than college women's. The strong and consistent difference between college women and college men regarding the pragmatic style of love is, of course, consistent with the gender differences in attitudes toward love and proneness to fall in and out of love noted in the preceding sections. As with the latter, researchers have stressed the importance of sociocultural factors (e.g., gender-role socialization, norms concerning choice of marital partner) for understanding these gender differences in styles of love.

## The Experience of Romantic Love

In the preceding sections on gender differences, we have presented considerable evidence that female college students in contemporary North American society have typically adopted a more pragmatic orientation toward love than male college students, as exemplified by attitude toward love, readiness to fall in and out of love, and styles of love. We and others have suggested that this general pragmatism is a product of the system of mate selection in our society that strongly encourages women to be discerning in accepting romantic partners and prospective mates.

A pragmatic orientation, however, does not preclude experiencing romantic love as an intense and satisfying emotional experience. Indeed, it could be argued that a careful choice of romantic partner would help to ensure a rewarding love experience and appreciation of the partner's virtues. Whether for this or some other reason, there is evidence to suggest that college women experience romantic love more deeply and intensely than college men and regard their partners more highly as well.

Some of this evidence comes from our own research. Among those who indicated only a single love experience in the locus of control study (Dion & Dion, 1973), female college students described their love experiences as having been more intense than did the male college students. Further, among those who indicated being or having been in love in this study, the college women indicated feeling more euphoric while in love than the college men. Similarly, in the self-esteem study (Dion & Dion, 1975), among those who indicated being or having been in love, college women reported being more euphoric while in love than the college men and also described their romantic love experiences as being more rewarding in general. Moreover, the college women tended to express greater trust and admiration for their romantic partners than did the college men. The college women also indicated stronger liking for their partners and also tended to show greater love for them on the Rubin scales.

Nor are these findings due to sex differences in locus of control or social self-esteem, dimensions shown above to be correlates of romantic love. For example, like the majority of studies that have reported no sex differences in I-E Scale scores (Phares, 1976, p. 44), we also found no association between sex of subject and their classification as internal or external in our locus of control study (Dion & Dion, 1973, p. 52). Similarly, in our self-esteem study, women's and men's social self-esteem scores did not differ (Dion & Dion, 1975, p. 54, note 12). Moreover, on a wide variety of standard self-esteem measures, there is little evidence of any sex differences from childhood to early adulthood (Deaux, 1976; Maccoby & Jacklin, 1974, pp. 152-153).

Other researchers have found differences between college women's and college men's love experiences that closely parallel our findings. For example, with a sample of 373 Boston University undergraduates, Black and Angelis (1974) reported that female college students rated both a heterosexual, romantic partner and a platonic, same-sex friend more highly on Rubin's love and liking scales than did the male college students. In a questionnaire survey of over 700 undergraduates at a large midwestern state university, Kanin et al. (1975) asked respondents to describe the emotional reactions they experienced in *one* love affair, either an ongoing one or a previous one. The college women were more likely than the college men to report emotional and euphoric experiences traditionally associated with romantic love, such as having trouble concentrating, feeling giddy and carefree, as well as a general feeling of well-being. Also, these college women were more likely to idealize their romantic partners. In particular, comparing college men and college women who rated themselves as being "extremely in love," the women assessed their partners more favorably on four of five personality traits and indicated that they could not have a better relationship with anyone else, whereas the men scored higher only on the item that said that their partner's personality could not be better. Kanin et al. (1975) concluded that *once in love,* it is women rather than men who show the "stereotypic romantic reactions."

Similar findings from three other studies by different investigators deserve mention. In his previously described self-actualization study, Dietch (1978) found that among those reporting at least one love relationship, sex of respondent was clearly the strongest predictor of scores on the B-love scale, with the college women showing considerably higher B-love scores than the college men. According to Dietch, high B-love scores reflect reports of a deep and fulfilling romantic relationship characterized by honesty and empathy for one's partner. Because Dietch (1978, p. 630) found neither male-female differences in self-actualization scores nor an interaction between sex and "involvement in a love relationship," the gender difference in B-love scores cannot be attributed to an inadvertent confounding of sex and self-actualization.

In research on styles of love, Lee (1973) employed a card-sort technique in which respondents selected cards from a large pool to describe their experiences. He observed an interesting gender difference: Men selected cards indicating that their female partners were more "deeply in love" than they themselves were, whereas women's card selections suggested that their male partners were "holding back" emotionally (Lee, 1973, p. 252). In another study in which undergraduates gave open-ended descriptions of various emotional experiences including love, Schwartz and Shaver (1984) reported that college women were more prone to indicate feeling warm, loved, and secure and to have said "I love you" in accounts of their love experiences.

Taken together, the results indicate that once in love with a partner they consider appropriate for an exclusive commitment, college women become more emotionally involved in the experience and find it more personally rewarding than do college men. This gender difference is probably the product of several factors. As noted above, it may be due to the greater care that college women show in selecting and accepting romantic partners. Also, as argued in the next section, it may reflect greater adeptness and responsiveness on the part of college women to close intimacy with another person. A cautionary note is also in order: Almost all the research on gender differences in romantic love that was discussed above has had students in college or university as the subjects. As a consequence, the generality of the observed gender differences to nonuniversity samples remains to be established in future research.

Another issue that warrants attention concerns the joint contribution of gender and personality to the experience of love. In our previous studies (Dion & Dion, 1973, 1975), we found only a few gender × personality interaction effects upon respondents' subjective reactions to love. Certainly, further research on correlates of love should continue to explore the possibility of gender-personality interactions. To cite one possibility, the separate and joint contributions of gender-role orientation (i.e., masculine, feminine, and androgynous) and gender (i.e., male versus female) to understanding the phenomenology of love is a potentially interesting direction to explore in the future.

Finally, the congruency of gender-role orientation between members of a couple also has a bearing on the compatibility of their relationship. Ickes (in press) has described a program of research on individuals' gender-role orientation and their initial interaction in both same-sex and mixed-sex dyads. This research indicates that owing to the distinctive behavioral styles associated with each gender-role orientation, differences in gender-role orientation between members of a dyad can lead to problems in initial interactions and incompatibilities in heterosexual relationships.

## Conceptual Issues and
## Directions for Future Research

The findings discussed in this chapter indicate that there are indeed individual differences in the phenomenology of romantic love. An important task is therefore to explain why these differences exist. The pattern of correlates found to date suggests that *responses to intimacy* underlie the relation between personality and the experience of romantic love. Previously, we have argued that as intimacy is an integral component of romantic love, individuals' reactions to intimacy (for example, responses to another's self-disclosure) should contribute to our understanding of love (Dion & Dion, 1978).

Certain personality dimensions seem to be characterized by orientations to others that might well deter, or at least make more difficult, the development of intimacy; in contrast, other dimensions seem likely to facilitate this process. Specifically, individuals exhibiting a strong need for personal control (internal locus of control) appear to be resistant to social influence. With increasing personal involvement in a romantic relationship, a person becomes more emotionally vulnerable. Thus for internals, increasing intimacy may heighten conflicts centering around the vulnerability associated with interdependence. Similarly, more defensive persons may feel anxious and conflicted about the interdependence that accompanies romantic love. These conflicts may make it harder for them to fully trust and confide in another person, thereby delaying or inhibiting the development of intimacy. On the other hand, dimensions such as self-actualization or genuine self-acceptance (high self-esteem and low defensiveness) should be associated with a greater capacity to experience intimacy. These persons would be expected to have no ambivalence about giving or receiving personal disclosure and to welcome the opportunity for emotional closeness.

The importance of intimacy as an essential feature of romantic dyadic relationships has been well articulated by Shaver and Buhrmester (1983) in their discussion of the psychological benefits provided by different types of groups (including dyads). In their conceptual framework, romantic love represents "the extreme of intimacy," in particular, *psychological intimacy*. Shaver and Buhrmester suggest that relationships characterized by a high level of psychological intimacy have several features, including the absence of defensiveness, the presence of reciprocal self-disclosure, emotional supportiveness, and nurturance. The personality differences in the experience of love discussed here seem to reflect differences in dealing with these various aspects of psychological intimacy.

The concept of psychological intimacy is also pertinent for understanding the gender differences in the experience of love discussed at the end of the previous section. In several studies, women's reports of their personal experience of romantic love suggest more affective involvement, including greater euphoria, more "self-actualized" love, and more favorable evaluations of their partner. These findings are consistent with research on gender differences in the quality of reported social interaction and peer relationships. For example, compared with men, women's friendships with same-sex peers are characterized by higher levels of psychological intimacy (Shaver & Buhrmester, 1983; Dion, 1985; Reis, in press). Based on college students' records of their ongoing peer interactions, Wheeler, Reis, and Nezlek (1983, p. 951) concluded that in encounters with both same- and opposite-sex peers, women "contribute meaningfulness and emotional closeness to an interaction."

As discussed in this chapter, the phenomenology of romantic love largely concerns the beliefs and personal experiences of young adults. It has been suggested that the formation of intimate relationships may be the central developmental task during this phase of the life span (Erikson, 1963). One intriguing question concerns, therefore, the developmental antecedents of the capacity for psychological intimacy in early adulthood.

Researchers studying close relationships from a developmental perspective have proposed that differences in adult love relationships may relate to earlier attachment processes. Shaver, Hazan, and Bradshaw (1984) compared and contrasted features of the infant's attachment to the caretaker and love relationships in adulthood. Components of adult love relationships were derived from college students' descriptions of either their own personal experiences or what they believed characterized others' "typical" experiences of love. Of particular relevance for this discussion, Shaver and his associates suggested that there may be different types of adult love relationships that parallel Ainsworth and her colleagues' (1978) typology of attachment styles in infancy: securely attached, anxious/ambivalent, and avoidant styles. Applied to adult relationships, these general attachment styles can be regarded as reflecting different responses to close intimacy with another person. For example, our finding that highly defensive persons avoid increasing intimacy with another person may be an adult manifestation of an avoidant style of infant attachment.

Another example of a developmental approach to close relationships can be found in Hindy and Schwarz (1984). These researchers examined the correlates of a type of relationship they refer to as "anxious romantic attachment" based on Ainsworth's idea of anxious attachment in infancy. Of interest for this discussion, these authors hypothesized that persons susceptible to this type of love experience are more likely to have encountered inconsistency of parental affection and love in the context of early family relationships. In an initial study, they found that undergraduate men who showed a greater tendency toward anxious attachments in adult heterosexual relationships perceived their parents as having been more "love inconsistent."

To conclude, the research reviewed in this chapter clearly demonstrates that there are personality correlates of romantic love and individual differences in the phenomenology of love. Love truly does mean different things to different people. Perhaps because both adult romantic love and infant attachment involve establishing a bond of close intimacy with another person in a dyadic unit, there are interesting and provocative analogues between these phenomena. Accordingly, we believe that exploring the developmental antecedents of adult love relationships will extend our knowledge of why people experience love differently.

In focusing on the personality, gender, and developmental correlates of heterosexual, romantic love, we are obviously *not* denying the importance of other processes (e.g., role-related processes) or units of analysis, such as the dyadic approach (see Ickes, in press). We are arguing that an individual's personality, gender, and developmental history cannot be ignored when trying to understand love.

Finally, the research reviewed in this chapter may have some useful implications. In their discussion of "styles of loving," Lasswell and Lasswell (1976) noted that individuals may expect their partners to share their views about love. They described a case study to illustrate some of the problems that can arise when this expectation is violated and suggest how a counselor might assist such a couple by helping them to understand that people may hold different views of love. Furthermore, they point out the need to reassure members of a couple with different perspectives on love that they are both "valid." Similarly, knowing how individuals' personality, gender, and developmental history relate to different orientations and experiences of love should prove helpful to psychologists and related professionals who counsel couples.

## NOTES

1. These items were drawn from a more comprehensive questionnaire on sexual behavior designed in the late 1960s by Marvin Dunnette and his students, then at the University of Minnesota.

2. The other three factors were as follows: circumspect love (subtle, cautious, passive); passionate love (sensual, active, physical, emotional); and impetuous love (fast, impulsive, adventurous, and sudden).

3. The items constituting these dimensions based on a factor analysis of respondents' adjective ratings of love were as follows: rewarding love (long, rewarding, tender, active, spiritual, direct, deep, and relaxed); steady love (steady, relaxed, and tender); circumspect love (slow, slowly-developing, and cautious); and straightforward love (logical, direct, and understandable). In addition, there were two other dimensions: emotional love (emotional, physical) and impulsive love (impulsive, adventurous). The items making up the seventh dimension, rational love, have already been described in the text.

4. Shostrom (1974) has also suggested the possibility of deriving scores for ten further subscales from the POI, beyond the I and Tc Scale scores. However, given the considerable overlap in items defining these subscales, critics (Bloxom, 1972; Tosi & Lindamood, 1975) have noted that the subscales cannot be considered statistically independent and that intercorrelations among the subscales are accordingly difficult to interpret.

## REFERENCES

Ainsworth, M.D.S., Blehar, M. C., Waters, E., & Wall, S. (1978). *Patterns of attachment: A psychological study of the strange situation.* Hillsdale, NJ: Lawrence Erlbaum.

Beigel, H. B. (1951). Romantic love. *American Sociological Review, 16,* 326-334.

Bills, R. E., Vance, E. L., & McLean, O. S. (1951). An index of adjustment and values. *Journal of Consulting Psychology, 15,* 257-261.

Black, H., & Angelis, V. B. (1974). Interpersonal attraction: An empirical investigation of platonic and romantic love. *Psychological Reports, 34,* 1243-1246.

Bloxom, B. (1972). Review of the POI. In O. K. Buros (Ed.), *The seventh mental measurements yearbook* (Vol. 1, pp. 290-292). Highland Park, NJ: Gryphon Press.

Burhenne, D., & Mirels, H. L. (1970). Self-disclosure in self-descriptive essays. *Journal of Consulting and Clinical Psychology, 35,* 409-413.

Cook, T. D., & Campbell, D. T. (1979). *Quasi-experimentation: Design and analysis for field settings.* Chicago: Rand McNally.

Coppinger, R. M., & Rosenblatt, P. C. (1968). Romantic love and subsistency dependence of spouses. *Southwestern Journal of Anthropology, 24,* 310-319.

Crowne, D. P., & Marlowe, D. (1964). *The approval motive.* New York: John Wiley.

Damm, V. J. (1969). Overall measures of self-actualization derived from the Personal Orientation Inventory. *Educational and Psychological Measurement, 29,* 977-981.

Deaux, K. (1976). *The behavior of women and men.* Monterey, CA: Brooks/ Cole.

Dietch, J. (1978). Love, sex roles, and psychological health. *Journal of Personality Assessment, 42,* 626-634.

Dion, K. K., & Dion, K. L. (1975). Self-esteem and romantic love. *Journal of Personality, 43,* 39-57.

Dion, K. K., & Dion, K. L. (1976). *Models of heterosexual attraction.* Canada Council Research Grant. (Available from the authors, Department of Psychology, University of Toronto, Toronto, Canada, M5S 1A1.)

Dion, K. K., & Dion, K. L. (1978). Defensiveness, intimacy, and heterosexual attraction. *Journal of Research in Personality, 12,* 479-487.

Dion, K. L. (1985). Sex, gender, and groups: Selected issues. In V. O'Leary, R. K. Unger, & B. Strudler-Wallston (Eds.), *Women, gender, and social psychology* (pp. 293-347). Hillsdale, NJ: Lawrence Erlbaum.

Dion, K. L., & Dion, K. K. (1973). Correlates of romantic love. *Journal of Consulting and Clinical Psychology, 41*, 51-56.

Dion, K. L., & Dion, K. K. (1976). Love, liking, and trust in heterosexual relationships. *Personality and Social Psychology Bulletin, 2*, 187-190.

Dion, K. L., & Dion, K. K. (1985). *Self-actualization and romantic love.* Manuscript in preparation, University of Toronto.

Elkins, G. R. (1978). Attitudes toward love, irrationality, and locus of control. *Psychological Reports, 43*, 246.

Erikson, E. H. (1963). *Childhood and society* (2nd ed.). New York: Norton.

Fengler, A. P. (1974). Romantic love in courtship: Divergent paths of male and female students. *Journal of Comparative Family Studies, 5*, 134-139.

Ford, L. H., Jr., & Hersen, M. (1967). Need approval, defensive denial, and direction of aggression. *Journal of Personality and Social Psychology, 6*, 228-232.

Fox, J., Knapp, R. R., & Michael, W. B. (1968). Assessment of self-actualization of psychiatric patients: Validity of the Personal Orientation Inventory. *Educational and Psychological Measurement, 28*, 565-569.

Fromm, E. (1939). Selfishness and self-love. *Psychiatry: Journal for the Study of Interpersonal Processes, 2*, 507-523.

Hatkoff, T. S., & Lasswell, T. E. (1979). Male-female similarites and differences in conceptualizing love. In M. Cook & G. Wilson (Eds.), *Love: An international conference* (pp. 221-227). New York: Pergamon.

Hattie, J., Hancock, P., & Brereton, K. (1984). The relationship between two measures of self-actualization. *Journal of Personality Assessment, 48*, 17-25.

Hendrick, C., Hendrick, S., Foote, F. H., & Slapion-Foote, M. J. (1984). Do women and men love differently? *Journal of Personal and Social Relationships, 1*, 177-195.

Hill, C. T., Rubin, Z., & Peplau, L. A. (1976). Breakups before marriage: The end of 103 affairs. *Journal of Social Issues, 32*, (1), 147-168.

Hindy, C. G., & Schwarz, J. C. (1984, July). *Individual differences in the tendency toward anxious romantic attachments.* Paper presented at the Second International Conference on Personal Relationships, Madison, WI.

Hinkle, D. E., & Sporakowski, M. J. (1975). Attitudes towards love: A re-examination. *Journal of Marriage and the Family, 37*, 764-767.

Hobart, C. W. (1958). Incidence of romanticism during courtship. *Social Forces, 36*, 363-367.

Ickes, W. (in press). Sex-role influences on compatibility in relationships. In W. Ickes (Ed.), *Compatible and incompatible relationships.* New York: Springer-Verlag.

Jones, S. C. (1973). Self and interpersonal evaluations: Esteem theories vs. consistency theories. *Psychological Bulletin, 79*, 185-199.

Kanin, E. J., Davidson, K. R., & Scheck, S. R. (1975). A research note on male-female differentials in the experience of heterosexual love. In J. R. DeLora & J. S. DeLora (Eds.), *Intimate life styles: Marriage and its alternatives* (pp. 25-31). Santa Monica, CA: Goodyear.

Kephart, W. M. (1967). Some correlates of romantic love. *Journal of Marriage and the Family, 29*, 470-474.

Knapp, R. R. (1965). Relationship of a measure of self-actualization to neuroticism and extraversion. *Journal of Consulting Psychology, 29*, 168-172.

Knox, D. H., Jr. (1970). Conceptions of love by married college students. *College Student Survey, 4*, 28-30.

Knox, D. H., Jr., & Sporakowski, M. J. (1968). Attitudes of college students toward love. *Journal of Marriage and the Family, 30*, 638-642.

Lasswell, T. E., & Laswell, M. E. (1976). I love you but I'm not in love with you. *Journal of Marriage and Family Counseling, 2*, 211-224.

Lee, J. A. (1973). *Colours of love.* Toronto: New Press.

Lester, D., Edge, W. R., Kawich, E. J., & Lee, R., III. (1983). Correlates of rational attitudes toward love. *Psychological Reports, 53*, 190.

Levenson, H. (1974). Activism and powerful others: Distinctions within the concept of internal-external control. *Journal of Personality Assessment, 38,* 377-383.

Maccoby, E. E., & Jacklin, C. N. (1974). *The psychology of sex differences.* Stanford, CA: Stanford University Press.

MacLeod, R. B. (1947). The phenomenological approach to social psychology. *Psychological Review, 54,* 193-210.

Maslow, A. H. (1945). *The S-I inventory.* Palo Alto, CA: Consulting Psychologists Press.

Maslow, A. H. (1968). *Toward a psychology of being.* Princeton, NJ: Van Nostrand.

Maslow, A. H. (1970). *Motivation and personality,* (2nd. ed.). New York: Harper.

Munro, B. E., & Adams, G. R. (1978). Correlates of romantic love revisited. *The Journal of Psychology, 98,* 211-214.

Pam, A., Plutchik, R., & Conte, H. R. (1975). Love: A psychometric approach. *Psychological Reports, 37,* 83-88.

Phares, E. J. (1965). Internal-external control as a determinant of amount of social influence exerted. *Journal of Personality and Social Psychology, 2,* 642-647.

Phares, E. J. (1976). *Locus of control in personality.* Morristown, NJ: General Learning Press.

Reis, H. T. (in press). Gender effects in social participation: Intimacy, loneliness, and the conduct of social interaction. In R. Gilmour & S. Duck (Eds.), *The emerging field of personal relationships.* Hillsdale, NJ: Lawrence Erlbaum.

Rogers, C. R. (1959). A theory of therapy, personality, and interpersonal relationships, as developed in the client-centered framework. In S. Koch (Ed.), *Psychology: A study of a science* (Vol. 3, pp. 184-256). New York: McGraw-Hill.

Rosenblatt, P. C. (1974). Cross-cultural perspectives on attraction. In T. Huston (Ed.), *Foundations of interpersonal attraction.* (pp. 79-95). New York: Academic.

Rotter, J. B. (1966). Generalized expectancies for internal versus external control of reinforcement. *Psychological Monographs, 80* (1, Whole No. 609).

Rubin, Z. (1969). *The social psychology of romantic love.* Doctoral dissertation, University of Michigan, Ann Arbor.

Rubin, Z. (1970). Measurement of romantic love. *Journal of Personality and Social Psychology, 16,* 265-273.

Rubin, Z. (1974). Lovers and other strangers: The development of intimacy in encounters and relationships. *American Scientist, 62,* 182-190.

Schon, D. A. (1963). *Displacement of concepts.* London: Tavistock.

Schwartz, J. C., & Shaver, P. (1984). *A prototype approach to emotion structure.* Paper presented at the American Psychological Association Convention, Toronto, Canada.

Shaver, P., & Buhrmester, D. (1983). Loneliness, sex-role orientation and group life: A social needs perspective. In P. B. Paulus (Ed.), *Basic group processes.* New York: Springer-Verlag.

Shaver, P., Hazan, C., & Bradshaw, D. (1984, July). *Infant-caretaker attachment and adult romantic love: Similarities and differences, continuities and discontinuities.* Paper presented at the Second International Conference on Personal Relationships, Madison, WI.

Shostrom, E. L. (1964). An inventory for the measurement of self-actualization. *Educational and Psychological Measurement, 24,* 207-218.

Shostrom, E. L. (1974). *EdITS manual for the Personal Orientation Inventory.* San Diego, CA: Educational and Industrial Testing Service.

Steck, L., Levitan, D., McLane, D., & Kelley, H. H. (1982). Care, need, and conceptions of love. *Journal of Personality and Social Psychology, 43,* 481-491.

Stewart, A. J., & Rubin, Z. (1974). The power motive in the dating couple. *Journal of Personality and Social Psychology, 34,* 305-309.

Tosi, D. J., & Lindamood, C. A. (1975). The measurement of self-actualization: A critical review of the Personal Orientation Inventory. *Journal of Personality Assessment, 39,* 215-224.

Valecha, G., & Ostrom, T. (1974). An abbreviated measure of internal-external locus of control. *Journal of Personality Assessment, 33,* 369-376.

Wall, J. (1970). Relationship of locus of control to self-actualization. *Psychological Reports, 27,* 282.

Walster, E. (1965). The effect of self-esteem on romantic liking. *Journal of Experimental Social Psychology, 1,* 184-197.

Warehime, R. G., & Foulds, M. L. (1971). Perceived locus of control and personal adjustment. *Journal of Consulting and Clinical Psychology, 37,* 250-252.

Warehime, R. G., & Foulds, M. L. (1973). Social desirability response sets and a measure of self-actualization. *Journal of Humanistic Psychology, 13,* 89-95.

Warehime, R. G., Routh, D. K., & Foulds, M. L. (1974). Knowledge about self-actualization and the presentation of self as self-actualized. *Journal of Personality and Social Psychology, 30,* 155-162.

Wessman, A. E., & Ricks, D. F. (1966). *Mood and personality.* New York: Holt.

Wheeler, L., Reis, H., & Nezlek, J. (1983). Loneliness, social interaction, and sex roles. *Journal of Personality and Social Psychology, 45,* 943-953.

Ziller, R. C. (1973). *The social self.* New York: Pergamon.

Ziller, R. C., & Grossman, S. A. (1967). A developmental study of the self-social constructs of normals and the neurotic personality. *Journal of Clinical Psychology, 23,* 15-21.

Ziller, R. C., Hagey, J., Smith, M.D.C., & Long, B. H. (1969). Self-esteem: A self-social construct. *Journal of Consulting and Clinical Psychology, 33,* 84-95.

# Jealousy and Social Behavior

**10**

## A REVIEW OF PERSON, RELATIONSHIP, AND SITUATIONAL DETERMINANTS

ROBERT G. BRINGLE
BRAM BUUNK

**Robert G. Bringle** is Associate Professor of Psychology at Purdue University at Indianapolis. His research interests include interpersonal processes, evaluation of social and health programs, cognitive development, and the social psychology of aging.

**Bram Buunk** is a faculty member in the Department of Psychology at the University of Nijmegen, The Netherlands. His research interests are mainly in the area of close relationships, and include topics such as marital satisfaction, friendship, jealousy, alternative lifestyles, sex roles, and cross-cultural perspectives.

Jealousy must have aroused the interest of men and women long before recorded history provided accounts. Through the arts we see the recurrent examination of its perplexing and volatile nature. However, social scientists have largely ignored it as a topic of investigation. Prior to the mid-1970s, most discussions in the social sciences focused on clinical analyses of pathological jealousy. Clanton and Smith (1977) note that the popular literature during this time included a steady "trickle" of articles, typically in women's magazines, that discussed jealousy as a natural part of being in love. However, these articles virtually ceased to appear during the late 1960s and early 1970s, "as though writers, editors, and publishers sensed that jealousy was changing somehow" (Clanton & Smith, 1977, p. 15).

During the period between 1974 and 1977 several significant events occurred that marked the beginning of a new era of interest in jealousy and empirical investigations of it. Lay articles reappeared, but the theme

**AUTHORS' NOTE:** Preparation of this report was supported by a grant from the Netherlands Organization for the Advancement of Pure Research (Z.W.O.) to Bram Buunk and support for a sabbatical leave from the Psychology Department at New Mexico State University and Department of Social Psychology at the University of Nijmegen to Robert Bringle. We wish to thank Ann Peplau, Walter Stephan, and George Levinger for comments on an early draft of the manuscript.

had changed to one of questioning the appropriateness of jealousy in personal relationships. Clanton and Smith (1977) published their book, *Jealousy,* which drew together thoughts on jealousy from popular literature and the social sciences. During this same period, several research programs were independently initiated by social scientists. Finally, a 1977 APA symposium on sexual jealousy provided an overview of this early research.

The purpose of the present chapter is to introduce personality and social psychologists to the role of jealousy in personal relationships. We will do this by presenting a summary of research conducted primarily since the mid-1970s. In addition, we wish to provide an appraisal of what has been studied, provide some integration of available conceptual approaches, and indicate areas that hold promise for future research and theory development.

## CONCEPTUALIZATIONS OF JEALOUSY

In contrast with some historical discussions of jealousy, which view it as a unique emotion or constellation of emotions, most contemporary conceptualizations of jealousy focus on situational antecedents to define it. Definitions that focus on situational antecedents have the advantage of allowing jealousy-evoking situations to be differentiated from envy situations. Constantine (1976) and Bryson (1977) view jealousy as due to a threat from an agent to a person's relationship with someone. In contrast, envy is a negative reaction that is precipitated when someone else has a relationship to a person or object. Envy may include the desire to possess the object, or it may be limited simply to begrudging the other person's possession of it. Bryson (1977) also contrasts jealousy and envy with rivalry, which is defined as occurring when two persons are both attempting to establish a relationship with a mutually desired object or person. It is important to acknowledge that although these three situations may be conceptually distinct, they are often concurrently present and become intertwined in a stream of social events. Thus, for example, your partner having an affair may be a jealousy-evoking event because it presents a threat to all or part of your relationship with him or her, but it may also evoke "sexual envy" (e.g., "I begrudge each of them for having a good time") and rivalry (e.g., "I am concerned about my sexual performance in comparison to his").

For purposes of the present discussion we offer the following definition. *Jealousy is an aversive emotional reaction that occurs as the result of a partner's extradyadic relationship that is real, imagined, or considered likely to occur.*

## MEASUREMENT OF JEALOUSY

### Individual Differences

Virtually everyone agrees that there are individual differences in people's responses to jealousy-evoking events, and several scales have been designed specifically to assess person variability. Bringle, Roach, Andler, and Evenbeck (1979) developed a 20-item Self-Report Jealousy Scale (SRJS-I) to measure *dispositional jealousy*. It presents romantic, work, social, and family situations that respondents rate in terms of the degree to which each one would cause them to feel "jealous." The scale has been revised and, in addition to other changes, the Self-Report Jealousy Scale-II (SRJS-II) uses a response format anchored by "pleased" and "upset" rather than "jealous" (Bringle, 1982).

Buunk (1978, 1982a) has also measured the intensity of jealous reactions by presenting specific jealousy-evoking events to respondents. His scale asks respondents to indicate how they would feel when their partner exhibited each of the following five behaviors toward another person: having a long-established sexual relationship, being in love, sexual contact, a short sexual relationship, and flirting. To guard against the possible social undesirability of the label "jealousy," Buunk uses a response scale anchored by "very unpleasant" and "very pleasant."

Hupka and his colleagues (Hupka & Bachelor, 1979; Rusch & Hupka, 1977) measure individual differences with a 27-item scale that presents predominantly romantic stimuli accompanied by a Likert-type response format. A similar approach is used in the 28-item Interpersonal Jealousy Scale (Mathes & Severa, 1981) and a 31-item scale developed by Tipton, Benedictson, Mahoney, and Hartnett (1978).

White (1981a, 1981c) has used a 6-item Chronic Jealousy Scale to measure individual differences in the global, general tendency to be jealous and a 6-item Relationship Jealousy Scale to measure differences in levels of jealousy in a particular relationship. The response formats vary from item to item, with some referring to intensity, some referring to frequency, and some including a reference to "jealousy."

In general, investigators have offered minimally acceptable evidence concerning their scales' psychometric characteristics. Evidence for reliability has included assessments of internal consistency (all scales) and temporal reliability (SRJS-I and II). In addition, a variety of evidence has been offered in support of each scale's validity. Construct validity has been developed through correlations with other characteristics (Bringle et al., 1979; Bringle & Williams, 1979; Buunk, 1981a, 1981b, 1982a; Hupka & Bachelor, 1979; Mathes, Roter & Joerger, 1982;

Mathes & Severa, 1981; White, 1977, 1981e), comparisons with a therapist's rating or ratings by one's partner (Hupka & Bachelor, 1979; White, in press), and convergent and discriminate validity (Mathes, Roter et al., 1982; White, 1984). Mathes, Phillips, Skowran, and Dick (1982) used a behavioral measure to validate the Interpersonal Jealousy Scale. They confronted college students with a rival seeking permission to date their girlfriend or boyfriend. Judges then rated the responses in terms of displayed threat and possessiveness.

These scales differ in numerous ways. For example, they differ in the specificity of the underlying construct being measured. The Self-Report Jealousy Scale (I and II) and the Chronic Jealousy Scale are intended to measure global tendencies toward jealousy across a variety of situations, partners, and relationships. In contrast, Bunnk's scale, the Interpersonal Jealousy Scale, and the Relationship Jealousy Scale all refer to a particular relationship and partner. Hupka's scale includes some general and specific items. The formats differ in that some scales include the word "jealous" as part of the stimulus items (White's scales), some as part of the response format (SRJS-I, some of White's items), and some in neither (Buunk's, Hupka's, and Mathes's scales and the SRJS-II).

Differences in the construction and intended use of these scales make comparisons difficult. Two studies that examined subsets of them found relatively high convergence (Mathes, Roter, et al., 1982; White, in press).

## Situational Differences

One approach to the assessment of situational differences uses scales designed to measure individual differences and then collapses the data matrix across individuals rather than situations. Bringle, Renner, Terry, and Davis (1983) used this procedure to examine the relative importance of situational and person differences, and Bunnk (1978) used his scale to examine how aspects of the partner's behavior related to the intensity of jealousy. A more detailed approach to analyzing situations was taken by Buunk (1980b). In this study he referred respondents to a specific jealousy-evoking situation that had occurred in the past, i.e., the partner's most intensive involvement in an outside sexual affair. He was able to establish the relative contributions of the person and the relationship to the intensity of jealousy.

Bryson (1977) examined situational differences with a scale not originally designed to measure individual differences. He presented subjects with a videotaped vignette in which an old boyfriend or girlfriend shows up at a party. The attractiveness of the interloper was varied and viewers of the scene reported the likelihood that each of 36 actions and feelings would have occurred if they had been in the situation.

## Differences in Reactions

Investigators have also examined the variability of jealous reactions. However, the studies conducted so far are not very comparable because of differences in the stimulus presented. Teismann and Mosher (1978) had couples role-play a jealous situation and compared their verbal interchanges with couples who role-played a nonjealous situation (e.g., conflict with parents or roommates), using Raush, Barry, Hertel, and Swain's (1974) Coding System for Interpersonal Conflict.

Buunk (1982b) measured the feelings and coping behaviors of persons whose partners had actually had an extradyadic relationship. Bryson (1976) reported a factor analysis of 24 behaviors and 24 feelings for which respondents indicated how "characteristic" each was when they were "jealous." Factor scores from this scale or responses to individual items can be used to analyze affective responses and coping strategies that people anticipate using when jealous (Bryson, 1977). In addition, this scale allows examination of individual differences in specific emotional and behavioral reactions.

## Conclusions

With few exceptions (Jaremko & Lindsey, 1979; Mathes, Phillips et al., 1982; Teismann & Mosher, 1978), all measures have been of the self-report type. In general, we advocate increased use of behavioral measures of jealousy. Concerning self-report measures, we would discourage procedures that ask people only how jealous they are in general. We strongly recommend measuring individual differences by presenting respondents with several specific, well-defined jealousy-evoking situations. The response format can vary depending on the use of the scale. If an overall assessment of jealousy is desired, one can sum across responses that measure how positive or aversive the emotional reaction is on each item. This procedure allows for the assessment of situational differences from the same data matrix. If a more detailed analysis of responses is desired, then the response format can be expanded to include specific types of emotional, cognitive, or behavioral reactions. As previously mentioned, we view jealousy primarily as an aversive emotional reaction to the partner's involvement with a third person, and our suggestions for measurement are consistent with this definition.

THE NATURE OF JEALOUSY:
COGNITIONS, EMOTIONS, AND BEHAVIORS

Studies examining the nature of the jealous response have included analyses of the nature of the threat, the different physiological and affective responses evoked by the threat, and the coping strategies used to deal with the jealousy-evoking situation. In analyzing these aspects of jealousy, researchers have relied on cognitive theories of emotion (e.g., Lazarus, 1968; Schachter, 1964). Lazarus's theory has been particularly useful because it differentiates the initial appraisal of how threatening an event is (primary appraisal) from the subsequent appraisal of how to react affectively and behaviorally to the event (secondary appraisal; see Hupka, 1981; White, 1981c).

## Nature of the Threat

There are several examples of nonempirical speculations concerning what makes a jealousy-evoking event threatening. Clanton and Smith (1977) point to the feeling of being excluded and the fear of losing the partner. According to Walster and Walster (1977), there are two kinds of threats mentioned in discussions of jealousy: wounded pride and fear of losing one's property.

Mazur (1977) has made a distinction between five types of jealousy, all of which represent a different kind of threat: (1) possessive jealousy, characterized by the perception that one's property rights are violated; (2) exclusion jealousy, being left out of a loved one's important experience; (3) competition jealousy, competing with the partner as the result of feeling inadequate; (4) egotism jealousy, an inability to expand one's ego awareness and role flexibility; and (5) fear jealousy, the fear of being lonely or rejected. Based primarily on clinical work with jealousy, Constantine (1976) has suggested that jealousy always involves the perception that some valued aspect of the relationship has been lost, such as one's "face" or status, need gratification, control, predictability, territory, and amount of time spent with the partner.

Buunk's research (1980b, 1981a) has explicitly attempted to test some of these theoretical ideas. In his study, all respondents had a partner who had been involved in at least one extramarital sexual relationship during the past two years. The following threatening aspects of such involvements were mentioned most often: (1) affective deprivation—getting less attention than before; (2) the perception that the partner enjoyed certain things more with the other person; (3) feeling excluded from the activities of the partner; and (4) uncertainty. The first three of these perceptions can be interpreted as indicative of people feeling that their spouse is doing certain things with another person that belonged originally to the exclusive domain of their own relationship. Another frequently mentioned perception—the unpleasant feeling of no longer being the only one for the partner—is similar. Thus, the notion of having an exclusive domain breached seems to be a central component of the threat. It is noteworthy that, in this sample, fear of losing the partner turned out to be of minor importance. It is possible that the majority of persons in this sample felt secure with the future of their relationship and did not see the behavior as leading to its destruction.

In addition to assessing the ways in which the partner's jealousy-evoking behavior has disrupted the relationship, the jealous person will also be concerned with explaining *why* the partner engaged in the behavior. Buunk's research (1978) shows that virtually everyone who is jealous is compelled to identify causes for the partner's behavior. Only a few studies have attempted to identify and examine the motives atributed to the partner. White (1981b) used both judges' ratings and factor analysis to identify the following four motives: sexual attraction, nonsexual attraction to the rival, dissatisfaction with the relationship, and desire for greater commitment. Only commitment failed to produce significant correlations on measures of the subject's jealousy, the partner's jealousy, perceived threat in the relationship, and anger to hypothetical jealousy-evoking incidents. Buunk (1984) found that intensity of jealousy was correlated with variations in the perception that the partner's behavior was due to deficiencies in the marital relationship or to aggressive intentions on the part of the partner, and among women, to pressure by the third person.

Because of the jealous person's concern with causes of the partner's behavior, attribution theory may provide a conceptual framework for integrating past research and suggesting directions for new research. Kelley and his associates (Kelley, 1979; Orvis, Kelley, & Butler, 1976; Passer, Kelley, & Michela, 1978) have suggested that behavior in personal relationships is evaluated in terms of how positive or negative and how stable the partner's *attitude* is perceived to be. Concerning jealousy, we feel that it is an aversive emotional reaction because it implies a nonpositive attitude on the partner's part concerning at least some aspects of the current relationship. How negative the inferred attitude is will depend upon subsequent attributions and will influence the intensity of jealousy.

Concerning the temporal *stability* of the attributions, we hypothesize that in most instances stable attributions will result in more upset and negative affect than unstable attributions. This is expected because stability can imply that the behavior is chronic or that the cause is resistant to change. There are two qualifications to this hypothesis. First, attributions to unstable causes can imply an unpredictable and chaotic environment. When this is the case, it too may be aversive. However, even here a stable attribution is being made ("It will happen again"); what is upsetting is not knowing when, how, and with whom. The second qualification is that in some cases a stable cause may be adapted to more easily than an unstable cause. For example, when one has learned over time that the partner is just a flirt who does not intend to threaten the relationship, then it is possible to adapt. However, it is important to note that in this example there is no perceived threat. If the stable characteristic to which the jealous person had to adapt was the partner's need for sexual variety, then this would represent a more severe stressor, and prolonged adaptation for most people would be quite costly.

A final factor that influences attributions is the degree to which the attribution is *ego-involving*. The most damaging attribution concerning the partner's behavior is one that implicates the self. Self-blame, attributing undesirable characteristics to the self, or identifying aspects of one's own behavior that caused the partner to engage in extradyadic relationships has more serious implications than being able to attribute the cause to a less ego-involving source (e.g., idiosyncratic circumstances).

An important issue that relates to attributions and jealousy, as well as to coping strategies, concerns the possibility of attributional conflict within the couple. According to Kelley's (1979) analysis of typical conflicts in couples over attributions for undesirable events, one would expect the jealous person to explain the jealousy-evoking event mainly in terms of stable personal characteristics and attitudes of the partner (e.g., "You did it because you are selfish and don't really care about me"). On the other hand, the perpetrator would often give excuses or justifications and emphasize a positive attitude toward the partner (e.g., "In those circumstances I simply went too far, but I love you more than anyone else"). No research has yet confirmed that such attributional conflicts do occur in the case of jealousy. Instead, the only relevant available research suggests striking similarity in the ways both partners explain the extradyadic sexual behavior (Buunk, 1984). In this study, most respondents had engaged at least once in the same behavior as their partner (i.e., extramartial sex), which probably increased their empathy with and understanding of the partner's motives. Moreover, as research by Taylor and Koivumaki (1976) has shown, the closer the relationship, the more people interpret the other's behavior in the same way as their own.

## Physiological and Affective Responses

In theoretical analyses of jealousy it has been emphasized repeatedly that jealousy is a *complex* emotion that consisted of a variable constellation of basic emotions, such as anger, fear, and sadness (e.g., Ankles, 1939; Walster & Walster, 1977). Important questions for research therefore include the following: (1) Are any particular basic emotions, or combinations of emotions, characteristic of jealousy? (2) Are there different types of jealousy, each characterized by different emotional profiles? And (3) does the type of emotional reaction that occurs depend on the person or the situation? Hardly any empirical work has been carried out on these issues.

In Bryson's (1976) factor analytic investigation of jealous reactions, three of the factors—emotional devastation, intropunitiveness, and anger—contain predominantly affective reactions. However, Bryson presented no percentages and did not make clear which emotional reactions are more or less characteristic of jealousy. Buunk (1978) found that emotional pain was the most frequently mentioned affective response. In fact, his respondents were two times more likely to mention this feeling than anger when they were jealous. Similar results were obtained in a later study (Buunk, 1980b). Future work should be devoted to ascertaining the exact emotional content of the jealous reaction.

## Coping Strategies

It is not always clear which activity or sequence of activities elicited by a jealousy-evoking situation should be defined as coping strategies. Such strategies are not limited to deliberate, conscious attempts to modify the threat inherent in the situation or to behaviors that are visible to others. For example, redefinition (Constantine, 1977), cognitive reappraisal, and some defense mechanisms are purely cognitive processes that are often viewed as part of coping strategies. In fact, sometimes it is possible for someone to engage in cognitive reappraisal for the purpose of *not* expressing or revealing affective responses that were initially elicited. For the purpose of the present discussion, *coping strategy* will refer to any of those cognitive and behavioral activities that result from a jealousy-evoking event and that can be viewed as goal-directed attempts to change or influence the self, others (including the partner), the relationship, or the circumstances.

A number of different typologies of coping strategies have been developed theoretically and empirically. These typologies typically are based on characteristic behavior patterns or communication styles and can be fitted into four broadly defined coping strategies distinguished by Constantine (1977): isolational, antagonistic, redefinitional, and resolutional. Most of White's (1981a) coping strategies (i.e., denial, derogation, introspection, and relationship improvement) are quite similar to Constantine's categories. The same is true for the three coping strategies empirically derived by Buunk (1982b): avoidance, reappraisal, and communication.

The results of other factor analytic studies are only partially comparable with studies just mentioned because they have included not only items referring to coping behaviors, but also items referring to affective reactions in jealousy situations. A factor analysis of 48 feelings and behaviors conducted by Bryson (1976) produced seven interpretable factors: (1) emotional devastation, (2) reactive retribution, (3) arousal, (4) communication, (5) intropunitiveness, (6) confrontation, and (7) anger. Although most of these factors are interpretable in terms of Constantine's typology, the first, fifth, and seventh are not. As pointed out earlier, these are primarily emotional responses and not coping strategies.

Instead of specifying the course of action, other typologies have emphasized the *goals or outcomes* of coping. For example, in his cross-cultural survey Hupka (1981) mentioned three functions of jealous behavior: prevention of loss of the partner, punishment of the partner or rival, and compensation. Rodgers and Bryson (1978) have distinguished two different goals of coping in a jealousy-evoking situation: self-esteem maintenance versus relationship maintenance. Other typologies have not been clearly based on either behavioral patterns or goals. For example, Clanton and Smith (1977) mentioned four different coping strategies in a jealousy-evoking situation, two of which seem to describe behavioral strategies (leave the relationship, deny or tolerate the jealousy-evoking behavior) whereas two others are described in terms of their preferred outcomes (induce partner to stop or modify the behavior, work on one's own jealousy). The four long-term coping strategies found in a factor analytic study by Buunk (1981a)— increasing independence, accepting jealousy, building trust, and communication—also seem to include outcomes as well as behaviors.

As will be clear from the foregoing, past theoretical and empirical work has confounded three issues: (1) the activity, (2) its goals, and (3) its outcome or consequence. We view these as conceptually independent issues. A particular behavior may be enacted to accomplish a particular goal and have various outcomes. Subsequent research needs to deal with the problem of the relationship between the outcomes that are sought when one is jealous, the relative importance of these outcomes, which activities are used to attain the outcome, and the outcomes that, in fact, result from the activity.

Furthermore, it is reasonable to expect that there will be individual differences in the selection of coping strategies, which will be referred to as *coping styles*. Indeed, Buunk (1982b) found that women with low self-esteem were inclined to avoid their husband when he had an extramarital relationship. Furthermore, people with higher neuroticism scores seemed to deal with jealousy by avoiding the issue or by attempting to reappraise the situation, but not by communicating with the spouse or rival. Bringle and Williams (1979) found that sensitizers (individuals who approach threatening stimuli) and nonscreeners (individuals who do little stimulus screening and therefore maintain diffuse and complex stimulus environments) reported a greater diversity of behavioral reactions when jealous. These few findings suggest that more research on the relationship between personality characteristics and coping styles will be beneficial.

## Conclusions

Not much attention has been devoted to the nature of the jealous response and available research does not provide very definitive answers. This is despite the fact that some very basic questions deserve attention. For example, it has yet to be determined which affective, cognitive, and behavioral responses are characteristic of jealousy. A related question concerns whether there is only one typical response that can manifest itself in several ways or several clearly distinctive types of jealousy. Furthermore, we wonder whether the nature of the threat, affective response, and coping strategies are not more closely interrelated than the foregoing discussion suggests. Possibly, specific types of threats go together with specific affective responses and coping strategies.

### ANALYSIS OF THE INTENSITY
### OF JEALOUS REACTIONS

Different paradigmatic perspectives have been adopted in analyzing the intensity of jealous reactions. This section will review work that has considered intensity of jealousy and issues related to it from the point of view of the person, situation, relationship, culture and subculture, and demographic characteristics.

## Jealousy as It Relates to
## Characteristics of the Person

There is good reason to assume that there are personal characteristics that influence the intensity of the jealous reaction. Because of the assumption that some of these characteristics are stable, researchers have hypothesized relationships between personality dimensions and aspects of jealousy. An extension of this reasoning is represented in *dispositional jealousy,* which views jealous reactions as having, in part, temporally consistent qualities that can be meaningfully studied in terms of personality characteristics (Bringle, 1981a, 1981b; Bringle & Evenbeck, 1979; Bringle et al., 1983; Bringle et al., 1979).

### Self-Concept

In discussions of jealousy, one of the most frequently mentioned aspects of the jealous person is the self-concept, viewed as both a cause for jealousy and a locus of consequences resulting from it. Typically, *self-esteem* is the component of the self-system that is implicated (e.g., Mead, 1977; Rodgers & Bryson, 1978; White, 1981b).

Using the SRJS-I, which is designed to measure the dispositional nature of jealousy, rather consistent and moderate negative relationships have been obtained with self-esteem (Bringle, 1981a; Manges & Evenbeck, 1980; Jaremko & Lindsey, 1979). Using other measures of jealousy, studies have either obtained similar effects (Aronson & Pines, 1980; Hupka & Bachelor, 1979), weak and inconsistent findings (Buunk, 1982a; White, 1977, 1981c, 1981e), or null findings (Mathes & Severa, 1981).

In contrast to self-esteem, the *self-concept* has received little attention. When considering the self-concept, it is important to note that the interaction of self-concept and relationships is not limited to primary, romantic relationships, but extends to all relationships with significant others. This is consistent with the view that the self-construct system is intimately dependent upon current social interactions, as well as past interactions. Concerning past interactions, Bringle and Williams (1979) found continuity between parents and offspring on dispositional jealousy and jealous feelings. In addition, they found familial continuity between jealousy and screening-nonscreening for parents and female offspring. With regard to current relationships, White (1981d) has shown that the effects of self-esteem on jealous reactions are mediated by perceived inadequacy in a particular relationship.

## Attitudes

Another personal characteristic that can influence jealousy is attitudes. Buunk's (1978, 1980b) research has shown that permissiveness of one's sexual attitudes on such issues as exclusivity and extradyadic relationships is related to the intensity of jealous reactions. White (1981c) also found attitudes toward exclusivity related to Chronic Jealousy and Relationship Jealousy. Jealousy was also found to be related to attitudes toward women for all subjects by Bringle et al. (1977) and for males by White (1981e). White (1981e) failed to find a relationship between jealousy and romanticism. Hupka and Bachelor (1979) failed to find a relationship between jealousy and attitudes toward premarital sexual permissiveness, trust in people, and a competitive attitude.

## Arousability

Based on theoretical traditions such as Schachter's (1964) theory of emotion, which posits arousability as a necessary condition for an emotional response, it is reasonable to expect that high arousability will lead to intense responses to potentially jealousy-evoking situations (Bringle & Williams, 1979; Walster & Walster, 1977). Several personality variables that are conceptually related to arousability have consistently produced moderate correlations with jealousy. These include repression-sensitization (Bringle & Williams, 1979; White, 1984), anxiety (Bringle, 1981a; Jaremko & Lindsey, 1979), neuroticism (Buunk, 1981a; Mathes, Roter et al., 1982), and screening-nonscreening (Bringle & Williams, 1979).

## Other Personality Correlates

Numerous other personality correlates have been considered in jealousy research. Jealous persons were expected to be more external in their locus-of-control orientation and this was confirmed by Bringle (1981a) using two different measures of locus of control. White (1984) found the same relationship using three different jealousy scales. Jeremko and Lindsey (1979), however, failed to confirm this hypothesis.

Dogmatism is characterized as a response to a threatening environment that results in a person being anxious, rigid, and self-deprecating, and feeling inadequate. Because of previous results, it was hypothesized and confirmed that jealous persons would be relatively dogmatic (Bringle, 1981a). Other studies have found jealous persons to be more feminine (Bringle et al., 1977), insecure (Mathes, Roter et al., 1982; Mathes & Severa, 1981, females only), and susceptible to reward, coercive, and legitimate power (Manges & Evenbeck, 1980) than less jealous persons. Intensity of jealous reactions has not correlated with Machiavellianism (Bringle, 1981a; White, 1984).

## Jealousy as It Relates to Characteristics of the Situation

Several studies have explored how specific situational cues influence jealous reactions. Both Bryson (1977) and Buunk (1978) found that a socially undesirable third person—one who is unattractive or disliked— evoked more jealousy than a socially desirable person. One explanation for this is based on balance theory (Heider, 1958). That is, this situation is upsetting because it is aversive to one's self-concept to have one's partner attracted to someone who is unlikeable. A second explanation for this effect refers to the jealous person's attributions. Specifically, it is upsetting to realize that the partner is attracted to someone who does not seem to have very compelling qualities. This leads to the inference that the partner must be quite vulnerable or predisposed to engaging in extradyadic relationships because the threshold needed to evoke the behavior appears to be so low.

Concerning other situational and contextual factors, Buunk (1978, 1980b) found that jealousy is much less intense when the jealous person is having or has had an extradyadic relationship. His research also showed that the nature of the extradyadic relationship is important, with sexual involvement eliciting higher levels of jealousy. However, when and why a sex-only versus nonsexual (friendship) versus both friendship and sexual extradyadic relationship differ is yet to be determined. Other important issues include whether or not the other person is known, how much is known about the extradyadic relationship, the degree of intimate self-disclosure about the primary relationship by the partner in the extradyadic relationship, the visibility of the extradyadic relationship to others, who initiated the relationship and who was most active in developing and maintaining it (the partner or the other person), and the characteristics of the other person (e.g., age, marital status, physical characteristics). Finally, there is the instance in which the rival relationship is homosexual. To our knowledge, the dynamics of this situation remain uninvestigated.

## Jealousy as It Relates to Characteristics of the Relationship

Most theorists agree that characteristics of the relationship influence the intensity, frequency, and management of jealousy. Indeed, several studies have touched on this issue by looking for correlations between jealousy and, for example, marital satisfaction, love, dependency, and relative involvement. However, there seems to be some confusion about the exact definition of the concepts used in these studies and about the relationships among these concepts. It has become clear to us that most concepts can easily be subsumed under three major independent properties of interdependence distinguished by Kelley (1979): correspondence of outcomes, degree of dependence, and mutuality of dependence. Therefore, the following discussion is organized around these concepts.

## Correspondence of Outcomes

According to Kelley (1979), outcome correspondence will be a function of the degree to which the behavior of the other person is rewarding and the degree to which coordination of behavior results in mutually rewarding outcomes. All of the different conceptualizations and operationalizations of marital satisfaction (Spanier & Lewis, 1980) refer to this construct. Satisfaction has produced moderately negative correlations with jealousy (Bringle, Evenbeck, & Schmedel, 1977, Buunk, 1980b). However, the relationship between jealousy and marital satisfaction has not always been identified. In a study of married men, Hansen (1983) found no correlation between the two variables. He also reported that men with a satisfactory marriage more readily accepted their spouse's involvement in a hobby.

## Degree of Dependence

The degree of dependency in a relationship reflects the degree to which the partners in that relationship control and influence each other's outcomes (Kelley, 1979). Attachment (Kitson, 1982), love (Rubin, 1974), cohesion (Olson, Sprenkle, & Russell, 1979), and a low comparison level for alternatives (Thibaut & Kelley, 1959) are all variables that refer to a high degree of dependency. On the basis of Kelley's theorizing it can be predicted that the amount and intensity of jealousy will covary directly with the degree of dependency on the relationship. Many studies, using different indices of dependency, confirm this prediction. Buunk (1980b) reports jealousy to be negatively related to the number of extramarital relationships the respondent has had. Bringle, Evenbeck et al. (1977), and Buunk (1982a) found jealousy negatively related to a measure of relationship dependency. Hansen (1983) reports a substantial correlation between jealousy and the desperate efforts people make to help their marriage succeed. Instead of interpreting this last variable as reflecting high marital satisfaction, as Hansen does, we prefer to see it as a measure of dependency. Studies using Rubin's love scale have established a positive correlation between love and jealousy (Buunk, 1981b; Mathes & Severa, 1981; Mathes, Roter et al., 1982; White, 1984). Mathes and Severa (1981) found a strong negative correlation between jealousy and the desire for the partner to maintain a separate identity—a variable that can be seen as reflecting a low degree of relationship cohesion.

## Mutuality of Dependence

The variables reflecting dependency discussed in the previous section have been presented as applying to a particular person in the relationship, independent of the perception of the partner's appraisal of similar issues. However, it can be assumed that a person compares his or her dependency in the relationship with that of the partner. This estimate reflects his or her relative dependency. The relative dependencies estimated by each member of the couple can be compared to determine the degree of correspondence between them. For example, White (1981d) found that the majority (61 percent) of persons concurred with their partner's estimates. White reasoned that the person who is relatively more dependent—more involved in the relationship—would be more jealous and more likely to intentionally induce jealousy (White, 1980). His research supported this hypothesis. Bringle et al. (1983) found that relative dependency correlated with jealousy among dating, but not among married, couples.

The issue of relative dependency is closely related theoretically to the issue of equity in interpersonal relationships. In terms of equity theory, partners in a relationship can be characterized as being overbenefited, underbenefited, or equitably rewarded (Bunnk, 1980b; Walster, Walster, & Berscheid, 1978). It will be the overbenefited partner who is motivated to put more effort into the relationship and who will be more jealous. Indeed, White (1981c) found relative involvement-effort positively related to chronic and relationship jealousy.

## The Relationship Between Person
## and Situational Determinants of Jealousy

Figure 10.1 presents several possible patterns for three persons responding to three different jealousy-evoking situations (adapted from Argyle & Little, 1976). The two graphs in the top row (trait and behaviorist) show patterns that would occur if jealousy were due only to person factors or only to situational factors, respectively. Either pattern would be unusual in reality, though not impossible (Argyle & Little, 1976).

However, there are two other reasonable possibilities concerning the relationship between person and situational determinants of jealousy,

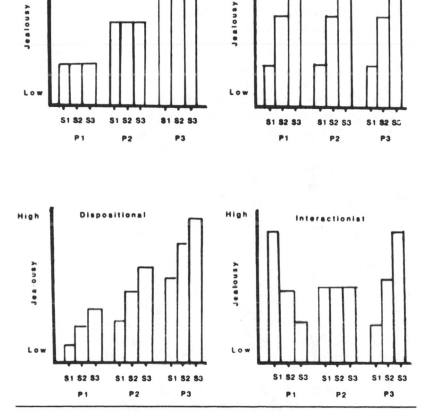

Figure 10.1    Four models of behavior. Adapted from "Do personality traits apply to social behavior?" by M. Argyle and B. Little. In N. S. Endler and D. Magnusson (Eds.), *Interactional psychology and personality*, 1976. New York: Hemisphere. Adapted by permission.

and these offer mutually exclusive predictions. The dispositional prediction is that the person and situation main effects will *both* be significant, but their interaction will not be substantial. The interaction prediction is that the interaction will explain the most variance, *and* the main effects will be nonsignificant. Bringle et al. (1983) tested these four hypotheses. The findings failed to support any one hypothesis unequivocally over the others. The interaction term explained 16 percent of the variance, persons explained 15 percent, and situations explained 11 percent. The implication of these results is that no one paradigmatic approach to studying jealousy should be emphasized, and the study of jealousy should balance the perspectives of the person, situation, and relationship to give the clearest picture of the phenomenon.

## Jealousy as It Relates to Characteristics of the Culture and Subculture

Although jealousy seems to exist in all cultures, a global cross-cultural review reveals that culture influences jealousy in many ways. First, as Hupka (1981) has extensively described, culture specifies which extradyadic sexual and nonsexual behaviors with persons of the opposite sex are permissible and which constitute a violation of the integrity of the primary relationship. Depending on the culture, these rules are likely to be quite specific in terms of place, timing, contextual factors, and the kind of third person that evokes jealousy.

In addition, as Hupka (1981) has shown, certain features of a society appear to be related to the frequency of jealousy. Hupka's research identifies three factors associated with level of jealousy: (1) the value attached to personal property; (2) the degree to which the attainment of sexual gratification is subject to restrictions; and (3) the meaning of marriage and progeny for an individual's status. Finally, culture influences jealousy by designing appropriate ways of coping, such as fighting, debating, killing, divorcing, or requiring financial compensation.

Even within Western culture, there seem to be important differences between countries and social groups in defining which extradyadic behaviors constitute a threat on the primary relationship. For example, "swingers" seem to accept quite easily their partner's extramarital sex when it occurs in their presence, is to a certain extent under their control, and is not accompanied by emotional involvement (e.g., Gilmartin, 1977). Couples in so-called "sexually open marriages" seem to develop different ground rules specifying the circumstances under which extramarital sex is permissible. For example, Buunk (1980c) found that couples use such ground rules as permitting an extradyadic relationship only when the partner agrees with it, knows the third person, or is not too aware of it. According to Pines and Aronson (1981), in the Kerista commune, jealousy would only arise if a commune member would have sex outside the group, but jealousy is nearly absent among the polygamous commune members themselves. Ludwig (1982) reported that male homosexuals experienced much lower levels of jealousy than heterosexuals if their partner engaged in sexual behavior with others.

These examples, as well as Hupka's (1981) cross-cultural review, illustrate how one's culture and subculture contribute to the definitions of jealousy-evoking behaviors. Furthermore, no culture or subculture is able to give people complete freedom for extradyadic relationships. In all cases there seems to be a strong need to structure the relationships with tacit or overt rules concerning jealousy-evoking incidents. Nevertheless, it is apparent in all cultures and subcultures that regardless of the nature of the structuring through norms, violations still occur.

## Jealousy as It Relates to Demographic Characteristics

### Age

A study of jealousy by Bringle and Williams (1979) included both students and their parents and, therefore, sampled a wide range of ages. They found that although age was uncorrelated with dispositional jealousy (the intensity of expected reactions to a wide variety of jealousy-evoking events), there were negative correlations between age and the following variables: variety of emotional responses when jealous, the variety of behavioral responses when jealous, and the frequency of jealousy. Although the effects were modest, they do raise questions about the relationship of jealousy to age, cohort, length of relationship, or some combination of these factors. It is easy to speculate that changes in sexual norms and lifestyles during the past thirty years could have created cohort differences. The "sexual revolution" and new-found freedoms have increased the ambiguity, uncertainty, and instability of interpersonal relationships. However, how this has influenced jealous responses will remain a matter of speculation because there are no baseline data against which to evaluate these changes (Bernard, 1977; Bringle & Williams, 1979).

### Familial Influences

There are numerous commentaries on jealousy (see Bringle & Williams, 1979) in which it is assumed that adult jealousy is the result of sibling conflict (whether it be jealousy, envy, or rivalry is probably unimportant to the thesis). Although there are numerous studies on sibling rivalry, there is *no evidence* that early conflict is related to adult reactions. The available studies on sibling conflict (see Bringle & Williams, 1979) all report that sibling conflict is more common in children from small families and in children in earlier ordinal positions. Thus, if the original thesis is correct that adult jealousy has its roots in sibling conflict that is, in part, related to familial structural characteristics, then one would expect correlations between jealousy and such variables as family size and birth order. Bringle and Williams (1979) found no support for these speculations. A null finding for birth order was also reported by White (1981e).

## Gender Differences

In the clinical and anthropological literature, different answers have been given to the question of which gender is more jealous. Years ago, Freud (1946) assumed women to be the jealous sex. On the other hand, several authors have maintained that men are more jealous than women because of their stronger concern for sexual competition, which sometimes has been assumed to have a genetic basis (Kinsey, Pomeroy, Martin, & Gebbard, 1953; Westermarck, 1922). Despite these assumed differences, research has not consistently shown one sex to be more frequently jealous or more intensely jealous. In a study of college students (Mathes & Severa, 1981) males were found to be significantly more jealous. However, other studies based on student samples have not revealed significant sex differences (Bringle et al., 1979; Bringle & Williams, 1979; White, 1981a, 1981b, 1981d), and studies in other social groups have found women to be significantly more jealous (Bringle, Evenbeck et al., 1977; Buunk 1978, 1981a). These findings suggest that the degree and direction of sex differences in the intensity of jealousy are dependent upon the nature of the population being investigated.

Many qualitative sex differences have been postulated. For example, Clanton and Smith (1977) suggested that men are more apt to deny jealous feelings, but that men would also be more apt to focus on sexual activity, be competitive, blame others for their jealousy, and express their jealous feelings through rage and violence. Women, according to Clanton and Smith, are more apt to acknowledge their jealousy, focus on the emotional involvement between their partner and the third party, be possessive, and blame themselves. Research offers some support for these speculations. First, concerning the nature of the threat, several studies suggest that males feel especially threatened by the sexual aspect of their partner's involvement with a third person (Buunk, 1980a; Francis, 1977; Teisman & Mosher, 1978) and males are more concerned with status and competition (Francis, 1977; White, 1981a).

On the other hand, females seem to feel that the loss of time and attention is especially threatening (Francis, 1977; Teismann & Mosher, 1978), and they focus more than males on the consequences of their partner's behavior for the relationship (White, 1981a). Other studies, however, do not unequivocally confirm this picture of the self-esteem-oriented male and the relationship-oriented female. For example, jealousy has been found to be somewhat more related to self-esteem among males than females (Buunk, 1980b; White, 1981a), whereas in other studies the opposite result has been obtained (Buunk, 1982b). Similarly contradictory results have been reported concerning the correlation between dependency and jealousy (Buunk, 1980b, 1982a; Mathes, Roter et al., 1982; White, 1981a). Furthermore, jealousy was found to be negatively related to marital happiness more strongly for males than for females (Bringle, Evenbeck et al., 1977; Buunk, 1981a).

Some findings have been reported on sex differences in coping strategies. First, men seem more apt to repress and deny the awareness of potentially jealousy-evoking situations whereas women are sometimes unreasonably suspicious (Francis, 1977; White, 1981c). Second, men's coping strategies seem more directed toward maintaining their self-esteem, whereas women seem more likely to use strategies aimed at improving the relationship (Buunk, 1980b, 1981a; Shettel-Neuber & Bryson, 1978; White, 1981c). Third, males are more inclined to undertake direct action and confront the partner or rival, whereas females are more inclined to avoid, blame themselves, and be depressed (Bryson, 1976; Buunk, 1978, 1982b).

To conclude, there is some research evidence regarding quantitative and qualitative sex differences in jealousy, but the evidence has the following serious limitations: The effect-size of the differences is small; many findings have not been replicated or have been replicated only in a few studies; and there is contradictory evidence on several issues. There has been no systematic, integrated attempt at understanding sex differences in jealousy; typically, these differences assume an ancillary status while other issues receive the primary attention. Regarding many aspects of sex differences, well-conceived studies are still needed.

## CONCLUSION

Ten years ago there was no social psychological research on jealousy. Today, this is no longer true. The study of jealousy has established itself as a research topic with its own identity, issues, concepts, controversies, and future (see Clanton, 1981). Social scientists are accumulating a research base to which they can refer in commenting on questions related to jealousy.

The research to date has drawn heavily upon other research and theory from social psychology, personality, marriage and family relations, communications, and clinical work. As the endeavor progresses, we would expect that each of these areas in turn will also benefit from the study of jealousy. In this way, the study of jealousy will enrich our knowledge of intrapersonal, interpersonal, and societal processes.

# REFERENCES

Ankles, T. M. (1939). *A study of jealousy as differentiated from envy.* Boston: Bruce Humphries.

Argyle, M., & Little, B. R. (1976). Do personality traits apply to social behavior? In N. S. Endler & D. Magnusson (Eds.), *Interactional psychology and personality.* New York: John Wiley.

Aronson, E., & Pines, A. (1980). *Exploring sexual jealousy.* Paper presented at the annual meeting of the Western Psychological Association, Honolulu.

Bernard, J. (1977). Jealousy in marriage. In G. Clanton & L. Smith (Eds.), *Jealousy.* Englewood Cliffs, NJ: Prentice-Hall.

Bringle, R. G. (1981a). Conceptualizing jealousy as a disposition. *Alternative Lifestyles, 4*(3), 274-290.

Bringle, R. G. (1981b). Viewing jealousy from a personality perspective. In E. Aronson (Chair), *Exploring sexual jealousy: An interdisciplinary approach.* Symposium presented at the meeting of the American Psychological Association, Los Angeles.

Bringle, R. G. (1982). *Preliminary report on the revised Self-Report Jealousy Scale.* Unpublished manuscript.

Bringle, R. G., & Evenbeck, S. E. (1979). The study of jealousy as a dispositional characteristic. In M. Cook & G. Wilson (Eds.), *Love and attraction: An international conference.* Oxford: Pergamon.

Bringle, R. G., Evenbeck, S. E., & Schmedel, K. (1977, Fall). *The role of jealousy in marriage.* Paper presented at the meeting of the American Psychological Association, San Francisco.

Bringle, R. G., Renner, P., Terry, R., & Davis, S. (1983). An analysis of situational and person components of jealousy. *Journal of Research in Personality, 17,* 354-368.

Bringle, R. G., Roach, S., Andler, C., & Evenbeck, S. (1977). *Correlates of jealousy.* Paper presented at the meeting of the Midwestern Psychological Association, Chicago.

Bringle, R. G., Roach, S., Andler, C., & Evenbeck, S. (1979). Measuring the intensity of jealous reactions. *Catalog of Selected Documents in Psychology, 9,* 23-24.

Bringle, R. G., & Williams, L. J. (1979). Parental-offspring similarity on jealousy and related personality dimensions. *Motivation and Emotion, 3,* 265-286.

Bryson, J. B. (1976). *The nature of sexual jealousy: An exploratory study.* Paper presented at the meeting of the American Psychological Association, Washington, DC.

Bryson, J. B. (1977). *Situational determinants of the expression of jealousy.* Paper presented at the meeting of the American Psychological Association, San Francisco.

Buunk, B. (1978). Jaloezie 2. Ervaringen van 250 Nederlanders. *Intermediair, 14*(12), 43-51.

Buunk, B. (1980a, July). *Attributions and jealousy.* Paper presented at the meeting of the 22nd International Congress of Psychology, Leipzig.

Buunk, B. (1980b). *Intieme relaties met derden. Een sociaal-psychologische studie.* Alphen a/d Rijn: Samsom.

Buunk, B. (1980c). Sexually open marriages. Groundrules for countering potential threats to marriage. *Alternative Lifestyles, 3,* 312-328.

Buunk, B. (1981a). Jealousy in sexually open marriages. *Alternative Lifestyles, 4,* 357-372.

Buunk, B. (1981b). Liefde, sympathie en jaloezie. *Gedrag,* (4), 189-202.

Buunk, B. (1982a). Anticipated sexual jealousy: Its relationship to self esteem, dependency and reciprocity. *Personality and Social Psychology Bulletin, 8,* 310-316.

Buunk, B. (1982b). Strategies of jealousy: Styles of coping with extramarital involvement of the spouse. *Family Relations, 31,* 13-18.

Buunk, B. (1982c, July). *Jealousy: Some recent findings and issues.* Paper presented at the 1st International Conference on Personal Relationships, Madison, WI.

Buunk, B. (1984). Jealousy as related to attributions for partner's behavior. *Social Psychology Quarterly, 47,* 107-112.

Constantine, L. L. (1976). Jealousy: From theory to treatment. In D.H.E. Olson (Ed.), *Treating relationships.* Lakeview, IL: Graphics.

Constantine, L. L. (1977). Jealousy: Techniques for intervention. In G. Clanton & L. G. Smith (Eds.), *Jealousy.* Englewood Cliffs, NJ: Prentice-Hall.

Clanton, G. (1981). Frontiers of jealousy research. *Alternative Lifestyles, 4*(3), 259-273.

Clanton, G., & Smith, L. G. (Eds.). (1977). *Jealousy.* Englewood Cliffs, NJ: Prentice-Hall.

Falbo, T., & Peplau, L. A. (1980). Power strategies in intimate relationships. *Journal of Personality and Social Psychology, 38,* 618-628.

Francis, J. L. (1977). Toward the management of heterosexual jealousy. *Journal of Marriage and Family Counseling, 3,* 61-69.

Freud, S. (1946). *Collected papers* (Vol. 18). London: Hogarth.

Gilmartin, B. G. (1977). Jealousy among the swingers. In G. Clanton & L. G. Smith (Eds.), *Jealousy.* Englewood Cliffs, NJ: Prentice-Hall.

Hansen, G. (1983). Marital satisfaction and jealousy among men. *Psychological Reports, 52,* 363-366.

Heider, F. (1958). *The psychology of interpersonal relations.* New York: John Wiley.

Hupka, R. B. (1981). Cultural determinants of jealousy. *Alternative Lifestyles, 4*(3), 310-356.

Hupka, R. B., & Bachelor, B. (1979, April). *Validation of a scale to measure romantic jealousy.* Paper presented at the meeting of the Western Psychological Association, San Diego.

Jaremko, M. E., & Lindsey, R. (1979). Stress coping abilities of individuals high and low in jealousy. *Psychological Reports, 44,* 547-553.

Kelley, H. H. (1979). *Personal relationships: Their structure and processes.* Hillsdale, NJ: Lawrence Erlbaum.

Kinsey, A., Pomeroy, W. B., Martin, C. F., & Gebhard, P. H. (1953). *Sexual behavior in the human female.* Philadelphia: Saunders.

Kitson, G. C. (1982). Attachment to the spouse in divorce: A scale and its application. *Journal of Marriage and Family, 44,* 379-394.

Lazarus, R. (1968). Emotions and adaptation: Conceptual and empirical relations. In W. J. Arnold (Ed.), *Nebraska symposium on motivation.* Lincoln: University of Nebraska Press.

Ludwig, S. (1982). *An investigation of jealousy among homosexuals and heterosexuals* Paper presented at the meeting of the Midwestern Psychological Association, Minneapolis.

Manges, K., & Evenbeck, S. (1980). *Social power, jealousy, and dependency in the intimate dyad.* Paper presented at the meeting of the Midwestern Psychological Association, St. Louis.

Mathes, E. W., Phillips, J. T., Skowran, J., & Dick, W. E. (1982). Behavioral correlates of the interpersonal jealousy scale. *Educational and Psychological Measurements, 42,* 1227-1231.

Mathes, E. W., Roter, P. M., & Joerger, S. M. (1982). A convergent validity study of six jealousy scales. *Psychological Report, 50,* 1143-1147.

Mathes, E. W., & Severa, N. (1981). Jealousy, romantic love and liking: Theoretical considerations and preliminary scale development. *Psychological Reports, 49,* 23-31.

Mazur, R. (1977). Beyond jealousy and possessiveness. In G. Clanton & L. G. Smith (Eds.), *Jealousy.* Englewood Cliffs, NJ: Prentice-Hall.

Mead, M. (1970). Jealousy: Primitive and civilized. In F. Lindenfeld (Ed.), *Radical perspectives on social problems. Readings in critical sociology.* London: MacMillan.

Mead, M. (1977). Jealousy: Primitive and civilized. In G. Clanton & L. G. Smith (Eds.), *Jealousy.* Englewood Cliffs, NJ: Prentice-Hall.

Olson, D. H., Sprenkle, D. H., & Russell, C. E. (1979). Circumplex model of marital and family systems: I. Cohesion and adaptibility dimensions, family types, and clinical applications. *Family Process, 18,* 3-27.

Orvis, B. R., Kelly, H. H., & Butler, D. (1976). Attributional conflict in young couples. In J. H. Harvey, W. J. Ickes, & R. E. Kidd (Eds.), *New directions in attribution research* (Vol. 1). Hillsdale, NJ: Lawrence Erlbaum.

Passer, M. W., Kelley, H. H., & Michela, J. L. (1978). Multidimensional scaling of the causes for negative interpersonal behavior. *Journal of Personality and Social Psychology, 36,* 951-962.

Pines, A., & Aronson, E. (1981). Polyfidelity: An alternative lifestyle without jealousy? *Alternative Lifestyles, 4*(3), 373-392.

Rausch, H., Barry, W., Hertel R., & Swain, M. (1974). *Communications conflict and marriage.* San Francisco: Jossey-Bass.

Rodgers, M. A., & Bryson, J. B. (1978). *Self esteem and relationship maintenance as responses of jealousy.* Paper presented at the meeting of the Western Psychological Association, San Francisco.

Rubin, Z. (1974). From liking to loving: Patterns of attraction in dating relationships. In T. Huston (Ed.), *Foundations of interpersonal attraction.* New York: Academic.

Rusch, P. A., & Hupka, R. B. (1977). *Development and validation of a scale to measure jealousy.* Paper presented at the meeting of the Western Psychological Association, Seattle.

Schachter, S. (1964). The interaction of cognitive and physiological determinants of emotional states. In L. Berkowitz (Ed.), *Advances in experimental social psychology* (Vol. 1). New York: Academic.

Shettel-Neuber, J., & Bryson, J. B. (1978). Physical attractiveness of the "other person" and jealousy. *Personality and Social Psychology Bulletin, 4,* 612-615.

Spanier, G., & Lewis, R. (1980). Marital quality: A review of the seventies. *Journal of Marriage and Family, 42,* 825-839.

Taylor, S. E., & Koivumaki, J. H. (1976). The perception of self and others: Acquaintanceship, affect and actor-observer differences. *Journal of Personality and Social Psychology, 33,* 403-408.

Teismann, M. W., & Mosher, D. L. (1978). Jealous conflict in dating couples. *Psychological Reports, 42,* 1211-1216.

Thibaut, J. W., & Kelley, H. H. (1959). *The social psychology of groups.* New York: John Wiley.

Tipton, R. M., Benedictson, C. S., Mahoney, J., & Hartnett, J. J. (1978). Development of a scale for the assessment of jealousy. *Psychological Reports, 42,* 1217-1218.

Walster, E., & Walster, G. (1977). The social psychology of jealousy. In G. Clanton & L. G. Smith (Eds.), *Jealousy.* Englewood Cliffs, NJ: Prentice-Hall.

Walster, E., Walster, G., & Bersheid, E. (1978). *Equity: Theory and research.* Boston: Allyn & Bacon.

Westermarck, E. (1922). *The history of human marriage.* New York: Alterton.

White, G. L. (1977, Fall). *Inequity of emotional involvement and jealousy in romantic couples.* Paper presented at a meeting of the American Psychological Association, San Francisco.

White, G. L. (1980). Inducing jealousy: A power perspective. *Personality and Social Psychology Bulletin, 6*(2), 222-227.

White, G. L. (1981a). Coping with romantic jealousy: Comparison to rival, perceived motives, and alternative assessment. In E. Aronson (Chair), *Exploring sexual jealousy: An interdisciplinary approach.* Symposium presented at the meeting of the the American Psychological Association, Los Angeles.

White, G. L. (1981b). Jealousy and partner's perceived motives for attraction to a rival. *Social Psychology Quarterly, 44,* 24-30.

White, G. L. (1981c). A model of romantic jealousy. *Motivation and Emotion, 5,* 295-310.

White, G. L. (1981d). Relative involvement, inadequacy and jealousy: A test of a causal model. *Alternative Lifestyles, 4*(3), 291-309.

White, G. L. (1981e). Some correlates of romantic jealousy. *Journal of Personality, 49,* 129-147.

White, G. L. (1984). Comparison of four jealousy scales. *Journal of Research in Personality, 18,* 115-130.

# 11

# Personal and Social Resources and the Ecology of Stress Resistance

## STEVAN E. HOBFOLL

Stevan E. Hobfoll is a Senior Lecturer in Psychology at Tel Aviv University in Israel. He is involved in research on social support and stress resistance, especially as they involve major life stressors. He has also worked on selection of mental health paraprofessionals and interpersonally-oriented physicians and their development as effective interventionists.

Stressors impinge on all of us; daily problems and massive crises are the milestones we use to measure our lives. Major accidents, life-threatening illnesses, job loss, and death of loved ones befall each of us within a lifetime and almost no one remains untouched for even a few years by crises. Fortunately, our efforts to meet these daily challenges and occasional crises are also formidable because numerous coping resources are available to us.

Social scientists have responded to the challenge of studying stress resistance because of the omnipresence of stressors and the potential preventive and therapeutic advantages of unravelling the process of combating stress. Some very complex models of stress resistance have been proposed (Antonovsky, 1979; Dohrenwend & Dohrenwend, 1981; Lazarus, 1980), but research has usually focused on how a single resource, or pair of resources, aids the individual in times of stress. Thus, although the models have been quite sophisticated, their research applications have bowed to the parsimony demanded by the early stages of any scientific investigation.

Before going on, some definitions of the terms that will be used frequently in this chapter are offered. Surprisingly, there is as yet no accepted stress lexicon. For the purposes of this chapter, *stressors* are

AUTHOR'S NOTE: Work on this chapter was made possible, in part, by grants provided by the Faculty of Health Sciences, Ben Gurion University of Negev, and the Center for the Absorption of Sciences, Israel Ministry of Absorption. Comments on earlier versions of this chapter by Dr. Giora Kenan, Professors Ron Shuval and Phillip Shaver, and two anonymous reviewers are gratefully acknowledged.

defined as objective events that signify loss or that potentially threaten the individual and the things he or she values. *Stress* is defined as the perceived imbalance between the demand these stressors make and the response capabilities of the person in question (Cox & Mackay, 1978; McGrath, 1973). This response capability is dependent on both the *resources* available to the individual and his or her assessment of the adequacy of these resources. *Resources* have been defined as personal (internal), social (external), and behavioral characteristics possessed by, or available to, the individual that tend to limit the detrimental effects of stressors (Antonovsky, 1979; Cobb, 1976; Dean & Lin, 1977). These resources, in other words, are the key to health. To the extent that they are perceived as inadequate, the physical and emotional health of the person under stress is likely to deteriorate. This deterioration, termed *strain*, may be measured in terms of physical illness, psychopathology, or signs of emotional distress. The process of combating the link between stressors and strain is called *stress resistance*.

The major thrust of this chapter will be to review selectively the research on stress resistance from an ecological perspective, a perspective that considers both the individual and the situation in which the process of stress resistance takes place (Kelly, Snowden, & Muñoz, 1977; Moos, 1984). I will first briefly explore how researchers have operationalized stress to date. Studies that examine personal and social resources, and the ways in which these resources aid stress resistance, will be discussed next. Following this, more recent attempts to gain an interactive understanding of these two resource domains will be delineated.

This will lead to presentation of a model of "ecological congruence." The goal of this model is to encourage more complex lines of research addressing the interface of the person and the environment. I will argue that the model of ecological congruence opens the door for considering multidimensional models that are not so all-encompassing as to be unresearchable given the present state of the art. Although not overly complex, the model raises research questions about stress resistance in real-life contexts and therefore promises to maximize the applicability of research findings.

The chapter is not intended to be a general review of the voluminous literature on stress resistance. For this reason, not every available line of research will be addressed in detail. Moreover, I have no intention of implying that social support, for instance, is more important in stress resistance than, say, coping behaviors (Lazarus & Folkman, 1984) or material wealth. The same points that I will make by focusing on control-related variables and social support could have been made by focusing on wealth and a strong physical constitution. Because control-related variables and social support are two important stress resistance resources, and because they have been studied in an ecological context, they will serve to illustrate the ecological perspective.

## CONCEPTUALIZING STRESS

### Stressful Life Events

Stress has typically been operationalized as the accumulation of life events, especially undesirable ones, that confront individuals over a particular period of time (Brown, Bhrolchrain, & Harris, 1975; Myers, Lindenthal, & Pepper, 1974; Weissman & Paykel, 1974). To this end, stressful life-event scales have been developed that require respondents to indicate which of a wide variety of stressors they have encountered during, say, the past year. Such measures have come under increasing criticism (Brown, 1974; Dohrenwend, Dohrenwend, Dodson, & Shrout, 1984; Kessler, 1983), the principle objection being that they are confounded with symptoms; in fact, many of the "events" themselves are the result rather than the cause of stress. Marital problems and changes in sleeping habits—typical items listed—may be either stressors or the consequences of stress. Given the modest correlations typically found between stressful life-event scores and psychological strain (Rabkin & Streuning, 1976), it is easy to see how this partial confounding alone might have produced the relationships.

When considering stress resistance, another problem with life-event scales emerges that further confounds the stress-distress relationship. Specifically, it has been argued that if a resource limits the magnitude of the deleterious effect of stressors on strain, then the resource aids stress resistance (Antonovsky, 1979; Dean & Lin, 1977). To examine such effects, events are averaged across individuals to arrive at summary statistics. The "rub" is that the summary nature of this method makes it impossible to say what is being affected. Does the effect of the resource cut across all stressors? Does it affect certain specific classes of stressors, such as loss or exit events (Weissman & Paykel, 1974)? Does it add to the situation's stressfulness for still other stressors (Hobfoll, in press a)? Do the stressors need to be of a particular magnitude for the resource to be effective? Are resources so robust as to protect the individual immediately upon event occurrence, as well as months later? Because we cannot pinpoint what is being affected—what the nature of the stressor is—we cannot infer the mechanism by which the resource has operated.

**Single Case Designs**

An alternative strategy that has been suggested is to investigate stress resistance for a single stressor (e.g., cancer, job loss). Such designs have been termed case studies, and their most powerful application is in longitudinal research, which includes a comparison group that has not experienced the stressor (Kessler, 1983). This solves a number of problems. For one thing, a known stressful event can be chosen that is objectively evaluated as being a stressor for most people. This avoids problems of individual differences in perceptions of what constitutes a stressful event—a problem that occurs when subjects are asked to check off event occurrence from a list of events (Brown, 1974; Dohrenwend et al., 1984). Potential confounding of stressors with psychological attributes of the people who experience them (Dohrenwend et al., 1984) may also be avoided by selecting events that occur more randomly and that individuals are unlikely to have brought upon themselves (Hobfoll & Walfisch, 1984).

Tasks and emotional demands related to specific events can also be delineated. This makes for a more sophisticated discussion of "resources to need fit" for that specific event (Mitchell & Hodson, 1983). The meaning of "resource to need fit" will be discussed in detail later. For now, let me say merely that I am implying a lock-and-key relationship between needs and resources. Certain resources are seen as meeting demands related to specific needs.

In addition, by studying single events we can observe how related tasks and demands change over time and in response to our actions. In this regard, Wilcox (in press) has emphasized that the study of single events allows for an examination of the *process* of stress resistance, emphasizing that coping is a multistage process. The successive stages bring changing demands and tasks. A good analogy is the Olympic decathalon which, unlike the individual event categories, involves a broad repertoire of strengths and skills: speed and stamina, strength and agility. The athlete must be powerful enough to throw the shot-put and graceful enough to pole-vault.

The disadvantage of the single-event design is that generalizability to the stress resistance conferred by a given resource in the face of other stressors is limited. Given the difficulty of defining the attributes of a particular stressor, we are threatened with the possibility that we must study every conceivable type of event. In this regard, a number of categorization dimensions have been suggested (Abramson, Seligman, & Teasdale, 1978; Hobfoll & London, in press; Hobfoll & Walfisch, 1984; Kanner, Coyne, Schaefer, & Lazarus, 1981; Pearlin, Lieberman,

Menaghan, & Mullan, 1981; Pearlin & Schooler, 1978). Still more headway needs to be made in categorizing events; meeting this challenge may be a prerequisite for progress in stress-resistance research.

## When Stress Demands a Response

I would argue that another important issue concerns whether the term "stress"—however it is measured—is overly diluted. Our stress models may have more validity in situations where the stressors are of a more serious nature than those usually studied (Murrel & Norris, 1984). Mischel (1984) argues that when not stressed toward performance limits, our personal characteristics—and I would add social characteristics also—are not good predictors of what we will do. In day-to-day behavior, stereotypic patterns and role-consistent repertoires are acted out by most people in accordance with habit and situational demands. Traits and characteristics of people become relevant when the environment challenges the individual to react outside this stereotypic range. Consistency (with traits), writes Mischel (1984), was "found in extreme situations that require cognitive and self-regulatory competencies that exceed the person's available competence" (p. 362). One of the most accepted definitions of stress says, in fact, that it is a state in which the individual perceives that normally practiced modes of behavior and resources are inadequate for handling environmental demands (McGrath, 1973).

The importance of this issue may be most apparent when we consider that we have attempted to construct a psychology of the stress-resistance process expecting internal and external resources to moderate stress across most individuals in most situations—for all ecologies. To the extent that Mischel is correct, the resources we have explored should be expected to be relevant only when specific situations evaluated as posing clear and meaningful threats are investigated. The accumulation of stressful life events and most of the single, undesirable events available for study in typical community or student samples may, for most subjects, not achieve levels that press individuals to abandon stereotypic and role-related behavior.

## STRESS-RESISTANCE RESOURCES

### Personal Resources

A number of personal resources have been cited as aiding stress resistance. Persons with these internal resources have been portrayed as able to meet the challenge of stress. Because of their inner strengths such people are believed to be less vulnerable to the effects of stress on physical and psychological strain and functioning.

Variables that relate to mastery or control have been a major focus of research. A number of control-related variables have been examined, and the findings have generally been encouraging, if not always straightforward (Folkman, 1984; Taylor, 1983; Thompson, 1981). Kobasa's (Kobasa, 1982; Kobasa, Maddi, & Courington, 1981) concept of hardiness, for example, has received widespread attention and she herself has carried out a number of exemplary studies of stress resistance. Hardiness is seen as composed of three elements: commitment, control, and challenge. Although Kobasa has looked consistently at hardiness in combination with other variables, her emphasis is distinctly on the hardiness concept. Kobasa et al. (1981) write:

> Hardy persons have considerable curiosity and tend to find their experiences interesting and meaningful. Further, they believe they can be influential through what they imagine, say and do. At the same time they expect change to be the norm, and regard it as an important stimulus to development. These beliefs and tendencies are very useful in coping with stressful events. Optimistic cognitive appraisals are made; challenges are perceived as natural enough, meaningful and even interesting despite their stressfulness and in that sense are kept in perspective. Also, decisive actions are taken to find out more about the changes, to incorporate them and to learn from their occurrence whatever may be of value for the future. In these ways hardy persons transform stressful events into less stressful ones. (pp. 368-369)

Kobasa's studies indicate that hardy persons have better physical and psychological health when faced with stressful events than individuals who do not score as hardy (Kobasa et al., 1981; Kobasa & Puccetti, 1983). Accepting this general trend, however, we still have learned little about how hardiness works. Although Kobasa's findings suggest that hardiness contributes to stress resistance in general, we cannot be sure. She has focused primarily on men, most of them from the middle class, in executive work settings. She notes in one study that job-related stressors were most common for her subjects (Kobasa & Pucetti, 1983). How specific is hardiness to aspiring men in challenging work settings? By relying on accumulated stressful event surveys as measures of stress level, the data are entangled in averages, exemplifying a pattern mentioned earlier.

Another question concerns whether the nature of Kobasa's subjects' coping *behavior* was actually what would be expected of the hardy individual. Whether these men exhibited curiosity, believed themselves to be influential in the face of stressors, accepted the transitional strains that resulted from stress, and made optimistic appraisals is a conjecture. We know that this was their *attitude* toward themselves, but not whether it was functionally significant. Did they *act* hardy or *believe* themselves to be hardy?

Moreover, whereas one may wish to conclude that hardiness aids stress resistance, even if we need now to unravel the operating mechanism, this conclusion is extreme in light of the study designs employed. Intuitively, the description of the hardy person seems most relevant for the aspiring male middle executive. It is hard to see what relevance "curiosity," "personal influence," and "decisiveness" have, or what "value" may be gained, when one's child unexpectedly dies, one's spouse (the family breadwinner) becomes unemployed, or one is brutally raped. Certainly, the healthy individual may grow from any and all experiences (Maslow, 1968), and meaningfulness may be found even in a Nazi death camp (Frankl, 1959), but it is more likely that hope, religious faith, or belief in the all-knowingness of God, the State or some benefactor will contribute to successful outcomes in such extreme cases. We must be very careful as researchers not to overgeneralize our findings when our research designs are so limited. Hardiness may be less relevant than summary statements based on studies using stressful-event scales seem to imply, and may be more applicable to executive men than women and other groups who have even less say in their fate (Ganellen & Blaney, 1984).

Another measure of control employed in the search for factors limiting the effects of stress is locus of control. Persons with an internal locus of control are described as feeling in control of their environment. Unlike those with an external locus of control, internals believe that their successes and failures are self-determined and are not the by-products of blind chance or the results of powerful others' actions (Johnson & Sarason, 1978; Lefcourt, Miller, Ware, & Sherk, 1981).[1] Another tack researchers have taken is to consider people's learned helplessness (Abramson et al., 1978). Those high in learned helplessness are comparable to externals. As the term implies, such individuals have learned that the environment is not affected by their actions, so they cease to believe that their behavior can influence what happens to them in the future. Studies of each of these concepts have shown that the negative effect of stressful events is reduced among those who feel in control, whereas those who do not feel in control are more negatively affected (Barthé & Hammen, 1981; Lefcourt et al., 1981; Johnson & Sarason, 1978).

These studies, taken together, indicate that people with a sense of control are less worn by the demands of harsh periods of their lives than those who see their fate as resting in others' hands. So we may feel safe in assuming that control is a good thing and begin to advise clinicians and educators to adopt control-enhancing interventions and curricula. But we can do this only by ignoring a large body of research on denial (Breznitz, 1983a). This "denial" among researchers of the relevance of denial to our understanding of stress resistance stems from the tendency to aggregate our thinking about life stress as if stress were a unidimensional entity. Expanding along the dimensions of time, stressfulness of the event, and potential for affecting change will illustrate the multidimensionality of stress, and the need to consider the ecology of stressful events as it pertains to control.

To take control, one must confront the environment. The implication is that control requires vigilance and is incompatible with denial. However, in the early, most devastating period of a massive life crisis, a little denial appears to be related to more successful coping (Lazarus, 1983). Vigilance, on the other hand, may result in a poorer outcome.

Self-deception, in the form of denying the seriousness of the problem, may be an especially valuable initial strategy in the coping process. This may be most apparent when there is little the individual can do to alter events. Burn and polio victims, for instance, who deny the seriousness of their illness may fare better in the long run than those who immediately confront reality (Hamburg, Hamburg, & de Goza, 1953; Visotsky, Hamburg, Goss, & Lebovits, 1961). Lifton (1964), in his study of victims of the atomic holocaust at Hiroshima, suggests that denial may facilitate a "psychic closing off" of the unbearable impinging reality. Others have noted that initial deniers have better recovery rates following heart attacks, whether expressed in terms of returning to work, sexual functioning, psychological distress, or decreased mortality (Hackett, Cassem, & Wishnie, 1968; Stern, Pascale, & McLoone, 1976).

Opposite findings regarding the detrimental effect of denial can also be found in the literature (Janis, 1974). It may be, however, that denial has time-related effects, perhaps being positive in the early stages of a massive crisis, when the person's resources "are insufficient to cope in a more problem-focused [controlled] way" (Lazarus, 1983, p. 24). Only later may control become more beneficial, when the degree of threat is felt to be less and control-related behavior can be effective.

If time, degree of stressfulness, and controllability are not considered, important distinctions get lost in the general notion of stress. Even more worrisome, if these dimensions are not considered, many important questions cannot even be asked. Lazarus's (1983) thinking on the effect of denial versus control demands the employment of longitudinal research strategies centered on a given event whose time of occurrence is known for each subject. Longitudinal case studies will thus be the best bet for investigating the changing demands and the effectiveness of responses intended to meet those challenges. The point also needs to be made that we must study the full range of the process. Stress resistance begins when the individual is confronted with the threat (Hobfoll & London, in press; Hobfoll & Walfisch, 1984) and continues long after the threat itself no longer exists and the stressor is only the memory of a past experience (Antonovsky, 1979).

## *Which Personal Resources Do We Study?*

Before leaving the issue of personal resources, it might be useful to ask why research has focused to such an extent on the control-denial continuum in the first place. Sarason (1980) writes that we wish to believe we are "masters of our own fate," but that this belief is an illusion in light of the vicissitudes of life's course. Antonovsky (1979) suggests that this trait is, in any case, only relevant for a small proportion of middle-class people whom society allows some degree of choice. I have argued further that among the working class, women especially may have to use other resources because the avenues of control are often closed to them (Hobfoll, in press, b). Thus, the control we have over events in our lives is, at best, partial, and for many segments of society control is impossible.

By expanding our focus of attention beyond the control-denial axis, we bring to light other relevant personal resources; for example, self-esteem. Persons high in self-esteem are less likely to attribute negative traits to themselves when burdened with tribulations and may thus be relatively resistant to stress (Hobfoll & Walfisch, 1984; Pearlin & Schooler, 1978). A sense of hope (Breznitz, 1983b) or meaningfulness (Antonovsky, 1979; Frankl, 1959) may also ensure more successful adjustment. Still another trait, resourcefulness, may facilitate stress resistance, even in the absence of control (Rosenbaum & Palmon, 1984). Resourcefulness has been defined as the ability behaviorally and cognitively to regulate internal responses that interfere with smooth execution of target behaviors (Rosenbaum & Palmon, 1984). The theorists who developed each of these concepts emphasized context and environment in detailing their theoretical perspectives.

## Social Resources

Supportive social interactions have also been conceptualized as contributing to stress resistance. Caplan (1974) suggested that the existence of loving and caring relationships provides a sort of protective web around the individual. Early theorists implied that both the instrumental actions of supportive persons and the feelings elicited in the recipient of such supportive efforts resulted in a buffering of the effects of stressful life events (Cobb, 1976; Dean & Lin, 1977).

Very quickly, research on social support mushroomed (Gottlieb, 1983). Yet this research has not seemed so much to move forward as to gain breadth, a fact that has, in part, been blamed on methodological problems and lack of clear definitions of social support (Thoits, 1982). However, I would argue that the area has suffered from perseveration around a single question in a single limited study design due to a disegard for the ecology in which social support transpires.

In this regard, researchers have examined whether social support has a buffering or a direct effect on mental and physical health (Cobb, 1976; Wilcox, 1981; Williams, Ware & Donald, 1981). The buffering hypothesis would be supported if social support were more effective for people under high stress than for those under low stress. A direct effect would be suggested if social support contributed to general well-being independent of stress level. Evidence in support of both possibilities has been obtained, and it would appear that both buffering and direct effects actually occur (Wilcox, 1981).

Again, the lack of regard for process mechanisms and the lumping of stressors into a single category may have been the culprits limiting so much of social support research to this one—albeit important—question. Pearlin (in press) remarks that after all this research we still do not have a good idea under which conditions social support is a successful mediator. It has even become unclear whether social support is necessarily a positive element in stress resistance. In this regard, some researchers have recently noted cases in which social support increases strain (Hobfoll & London, in press; Rook, 1984).

In recent papers (Hobfoll, in press a, in press b), I have attempted to delineate the personal-environmental characteristics that contribute to the effects of social support. The key issues, I argue, concern potential limiting circumstances, limiting personal characteristics, and the interaction of circumstances with individuals' traits. Circumstances that may limit the positive effect of social support include environments or contexts in which support cannot be delivered, for example during disasters; family tragedies that deeply affect all potential support providers; and situations in which for logistical reasons the victim is separated from supportive contacts. Personal characteristics may limit the contribution of social support in cases where the individual has high self-esteem and is therefore less in need of support (Pearlin et al., 1981). In contrast, individuals who are very much in need due to depression or psychiatric problems may not be able or willing to access or benefit from supportive interactions (Coyne, Aldwin, & Lazarus, 1981; Tolsdorf, 1976).

At times the environment and the individual's traits interact to short-circuit the social support process. This may be seen in the case of stressful events that the individual perceives as reflecting poorly upon himself or herself. In this vein, such events as illness and divorce may be experienced with embarrassment. Teichmann (1978) has shown that high trait-anxious people are especially sensitive to embarrassing situations and are more likely to withdraw in such situations than to seek social contact. Others have also found that personality is related to attitudes toward seeking help and the degree to which individuals view receipt of help as demeaning (Nadler & Mayeless, 1983).

Again, one senses that research on social support as an aid in stress resistance—like research on control-related resouces—occurred in the absence of a broader theoretical framework. Social support research has not benefited from a substantial literature on the nature of interpersonal relationships and personality or interpersonal relationships and mental health (Hansson, Jones, & Carpenter, 1984; Jones, in press). I would argue that the reason social support research in particular, and stress resistance research in general, remains atheoretical is that interested researchers and theorists originally identified the problem of "stress" outside of the context of person-environment fit. When research on stress resistance followed, it tended to be conceptualized within the stress models already espoused. As a result, generalizations concerning the negative effects of stressors and the shielding effect of resistance resources have been made, but information about the specific relationships or the mechanisms that determine these relationships is lacking. Inquiry into the specific relationships between stressors, resources, and strain requires attention to *interactive models* that consider individuals, their relationships, and their environments.

## Personal Resources and
## Social Support Viewed Together

Examination of the interactive effects of control-related variables and social support on stress resistance has provided insights that single or additive models could not (Kobasa & Puccetti, 1983; Lefcourt, Martin & Saleh, 1984; Sandler & Lakey, 1982). The application of an interactive model is more realistic, but it is not yet what I would call ecological, because stress is still interpreted as a monolithic entity measured via summary stressful-event surveys. This precludes investigation of how these personal and social resources interact with different environmental demands.

Interaction studies have found that people who have an internal control orientation benefit more from social support than those with an external control orientation (Lefcourt et al., 1984; Sandler & Lakey, 1982). For people low in internal control, social support was found in one case to have a decidedly negative effect (Kobasa & Puccetti, 1983). Kobasa (1982) argues that social support may have a different meaning for persons who have different orientations toward their work and social interactions. Lefcourt et al. (1984) conclude that control-related variables may have a smaller moderating effect on stress than earlier research suggested. Rather, it is the combination of an internal style of coping and an efficient, positively directed exploitation of social support that most likely leads to positive outcomes.

The interactive personal and social resource model provides a better understanding of stress resistance than single or additive resource models. However, the lack of attention to the environment still leads to the making of overly general statements about stress and to no small amount of confusion. Lefcourt el al. (1984) do note in their discussion that differences were found in their study regarding "*achievement* locus of control" for honors as compared to non-honors students, and they acknowledge the importance of resource-context fit. However, findings for "*achievement* locus of control" are later discussed as if a general locus of control scale has been used and are related to the ways in which this control would affect stress in general. Might the limited magnitude of the findings be related to their limited context—a survey of college students, about stressors experienced in their relatively guarded environment, using an achievement-focused measure? When Lefcourt et al. (1984) looked at "*affiliation* locus of control," opposite findings were noted! This leads one to suggest that the type of control may be relevant to and interact with social support in a different manner depending on social-ecological context. Disregarding context, the authors can only conclude that the effect of locus of control on coping is "complex" (Lefcourt et al., 1984), but such conclusions do not add to predictive ability or bring us closer to application.

## THE MODEL OF ECOLOGICAL CONGRUENCE

In recent papers I have attempted to address the problems surveyed above by developing a naive model of interaction between the individual and the environment as it relates to the stress resistance (Hobfoll, in press a, in press b). The model is naive in the sense that its purpose is only to draw attention to the components of the person-environment interaction in the process of confronting stressors; it provides no specific hypotheses. To build a building one needs structural components, connective material, and tools. Likewise, the model of ecological congruence outlines the factors that need to be considered when studying the process of stress resistance.

The general model is presented in Figure 11.1. The components to which the model refers are resource, need, strain, time, values (of self and others), and perception. These components are seen as constituting a contextual aggregate that determines the "valence of effect."

Following Figure 11.1 let us begin with the *resource dimension*. Resources may or may not be related, but already at this juncture the possibility of their interrelatedness should be considered. So too, researchers must consider whether the chosen resource could be a by-product of a more comprehensive one or an artifact of another more relevant to the issue. Wilcox (1981), for instance, cautioned that self-esteem and social competence might account for the effects associated with social support.

At the next step of the model, the *valence of effect* is considered. Just because we have called social support by this favorable-sounding name does not mean that we can assume it is *de facto* supportive. Social scientists should be alert to the need in all science for openness to unexpected outcomes. Social psychology has focused on the fact that researchers may unintentionally bias their experiments to form a self-fulfilling prophesy rather than a scientific test (Rosenthal, 1964). If we do not, for example, consider the possibility that control might in some circumstances increase strain and sabotage effective coping, we will probably not construct the experiment that will reveal this obtainable outcome.

Moving forward, we come to the *strain dimension*. Why might a given resource affect health behavior, whereas another resource is more closely related to anxiety or depression? To answer this question we must consider both the person and the *need dimension* presented in the following step in the diagram. Regarding the person, his or her strengths and weaknesses need to be evaluated. Regarding the *need dimension*, the model emphasizes that situations "press" the individual in certain directions. So, for example, a man may be biologically vulnerable to hypertension, and a situation may press him to withhold displays of anger—a behavioral pattern related to hypertension (Spielberger et al., in press).

Also implied by the model is a relationship between needs and available resources. Referring again to Figure 11.1, we see that resources may meet, not meet, or even interfere with tasks and emotional demands that stem from the individual's needs. Again using the example of hypertension, the personal tendency not to express anger (this tendency being a personal resource) may decrease conflict (i.e., meet some needs)

Resources, among them:

Resource Dimension
1. social support
2. personality resources
3. coping strategies
4. financial resources

will tend to

Valence of Effect
a. reduce
b. not affect
c. increase

Strain Dimension
1. psychological distress
2. physical symptoms

to the extent that the resource

Valence of Effect
a. meets
b. does not meet
c. interferes with

Need Dimension
1. task demands
2. emotional demands

of the individual at a given point in time in relation to

Values Dimension
1. personal values
2. cultural and family values
3. environmental constraints

in relation to the existant

Perception Dimension
1. degree of threat
2. assessment of need
3. availability/suitability of potential support

and perception of

as seen by the individual.

Time Dimension
1. the individual's own life
2. the elapsed time since the stressor event

Figure 11.1 Model of ecological congruence. Adapted from *Stress, social support, and women* by S. Hobfoll (Ed.), in press. Washington, DC: Hemisphere.

but prevent release of unhealthy tension (i.e., interfere with other needs; Spielberger et al., in press).

Next is the *time dimension*. Time in an individual's life refers to his or her personal history and developmental stage. The loss of a breast has different meanings for young single women as compared with elderly women (Taylor, 1983). Prior successful experience with stressors may have inoculated the individual, whereas a series of failures may have created a fragile background on which new stressful events are cast (Meichenbaum, Tark, & Burstein, 1975; Ruch, Chandler & Harter, 1980).

Elapsed time since the stressful event is also germane. A crowd of protective friends may aid initial resistance, whereas a push toward self-sufficiency may be the best help a friend can give at another stage. My colleagues and I have found, for example, that social support is most effective at the time of the stressor event (Hobfoll & Walfisch, 1984), but only when the messages inherent in the social interactions are indeed supportive (Hobfoll & London, in press). In times of disaster or war, social interactions may initially result in an undesirable "pressure cooker" effect at the stage when everyone is panicked (Hobfoll & London, in press).

The Jewish ritual of grief is explicit on the matter of time. No comforting is permitted until the burial (which must be performed as early as possible), in order to encourage a full awareness of the event. The funeral can be postponed only until immediate family—those who need to receive or give support—arrive. Friends and family are then obliged to offer intense support to the mourner in the first week, tradition encouraging the most intimate supporters to visit first. After the week of intensive mourning, the bereaved must return to their work and responsibilities, but are denied social contact as explicitly "joyous occasions" (e.g., dances and parties). At six months the individual who has lost a spouse is already encouraged to seek intimate relations with the opposite sex, and marriage is encouraged. The time sequence revolves around the changing needs of the individuals involved to regain control over their lives and return to independent functioning. Social support by intimates and the community is intended to be the instrument that ensures the enactment of this time sequence. This process, codified thousands of years ago, is strikingly consistent with modern psychological thinking about the grief process (Schoenberg, Carr, Paretz, & Kutscher, 1970).

The values of the individual, family, group, and culture are depicted in the *values dimension* of Figure 11.1. Following this, the individual's perception of threat and his or her needs is depicted in the *perception dimension*. These two dimensions are seen as very much related.

Research on coping behaviors has emphasized perception (Moos, 1984, Lazarus, 1980), but values have been relatively ignored. More precise predictions of the effect of resources may follow from an awareness that values pervade people's responses to their environment, and that perceptions color the phenomenological experience of the event and our choices for coping with it. Millions of women's perceptions of the stressfulness of pregnancy, for instance, depend on values decreed by the Vatican. Individuals' background and training create cognitive sets that affect perceptions of the stressfulness of the event and how alternative coping strategies are viewed (Lazarus & Folkman, 1984; Meichenbaum et al., 1975).

## Ecological Congruence Applied to Research

Some examples will illustrate how the concept of ecological congruence can be applied. In a recent study, we (Hobfoll & Leiberman, in press) attempted to address each of the dimensions presented in the model. Pregancy outcome was chosen as a stressor that would be accepted by most women as a potentially threatening and at the same time valuable event (*perception dimension*). It was further assumed that a healthy, uncomplicated outcome would be considered desirable by all women (*value dimension*). These two dimensions were not measured, but the assumptions are important in describing what we expected to be the phenomenological context of the event.

For this event it was hypothesized that self-esteem and social support would be important internal and external resources, respectively, both of which might aid women in meeting the emotional and task demands that follow both normal and complicated pregnancies. Because we expected that intimacy with spouse would be a vital supportive resource, we chose this as the support variable to be measured (*resource dimension*). The demands revolve around the woman's adjustment to an abrupt change in routine upon arrival of a healthy newborn and more extreme emotional and task demands in caring for an unhealthy infant or caring for an infant when the woman is weakened following a complicated delivery. Our interest was thus directed toward emotional reactions of women, principally postpartum depressive feelings (*strain dimension*).

Time defined as life stage was not included in the study design, because these women were generally at a similar developmental stage, but *time since the event* was considered critical. Self-esteem, an integral personal resource, was expected to contribute to immediate stress resistance, at event occurrence (within hours after the event), and following a period of three months. Social support was also expected to aid initial stress resistance. However, it was anticipated that social support would not aid stress resistance independent of self-esteem after three months had passed, even if stress continued. This is important because the buffering hypothesis predicts that social support would continue to limit psychological distress in the case of chronic stress. Our thinking, based on the ecology of social support in stress resistance, argued otherwise. We believed that by this time supportive interactions would decrease and the individuals would be expected to cope on their own.

By considering multiple resources, we were able to formulate predictions other than ones based on the buffering hypothesis. Specifically, a substitution hypothesis was proffered predicting that either self-esteem or social support would be effective if available at the time of the event, but that little would be added by availability of both resources. This prediction is based on the argument that in situations where a number of resources are effective, they may substitute for one another.

In order to examine *valence of effect*, a related condition was sought—one that might have a different ecology and therefore be affected differently by resources. It was decided that spontaneous abortion might be an appropriate condition for this case. Specifically, spontaneous abortion before third trimester was chosen as an event that is usually accompanied by little support. On one hand, this may be a very emotionally painful event. However, many women may be hospitalized only overnight and miss just one or two days of work. Often, relatives and friends are not informed of the abortion and supportive interactions are limited by what in some ways is a nonevent. In this case, it was predicted that social support would not independently aid stress resistance, either under high initial stress or under lower stress three months later.

The results supported the hypotheses. Women high in self-esteem (which did not change between initial reactions and follow-up three months later) were less likely to experience depressive emotionality than women lower in self-esteem. This was true whether the stressor was strong (chronic or acute) or weak (originally acute stressor which had subsided over the three months). Social support, on the other hand, was independently effective only for initial stressors. Also, as predicted, only in the case of spontaneous abortion did social support not have an independent initial effect on depression. Regarding the substitution hypothesis, either self-esteem or social support was effective in reducing initial depression. At that time, having both resources was not superior to having just one, but having neither resource exposed women to quite extreme depression levels.

An interactive interpretation that considers resources, type of strain, demands, time, and values is proffered. This is illustrated in Figure 11.2. Women high in what we called "trait self-esteem" (*resource dimension*) withstood the deleterious effects of stress independent of the situation, because trait self-esteem is part of the individual and relatively resistant to change (*time dimension*; Pearlin et al., 1981). Social support acted to increase state self-esteem (i.e., a temporary rise in self-esteem), but this inoculation was time-limited (*time dimension*). Our society values individuals "standing on their own two feet" (*values dimension*), so that the effectiveness of social support declined as the supporter expected the victim to return to normal functioning (and individuals expected this of themselves). Those low in trait self-esteem could not, in any case, remain convinced by supportive messages that they were all right, because they basically felt that they were not. For them, social support offered a temporary inoculation during a critical risk period. Those without social support or self-esteem were in double jeopardy. Not only did they attribute events to their own failure, their lack of support was a poignant reminder of their loneliness and inadequacy.

Pearlin et al. (1981) also report a study of stress resistance that is consistent with the model of ecological congruence. Studying unemployment, they hypothesized that depression could be limited by social support, self-esteem, and mastery. But they were much more specific than this. A particular coping process was tested in which social support was expected to limit decreases in self-esteem, which in turn would be prerequisite to increases in depression. Social support aimed directly at the worries and concerns of being unemployed (ecologically congruent support) was expected to be the most important supportive element. The authors argued that self-esteem could be viewed as an intervening variable between the stressor and depression only if it could be shown that depression did not cause a decrease in self-esteem. To prove this point, they turned to a different type of event—loss of a loved one—which they expected to affect depression and not self-esteem. That is, the different ecologies of the two events would lead to different stress-resistance processes. If this could be shown to be the case, it could be argued that changes in self-esteem led to changes in depression and were not caused by changes in depression. The authors' predictions were verified.

The role of social support in boosting self-esteem was also illustrated by examining changes in the relationship between social support, self-esteem, and depression over time since the event. Viewing Pearlin et al.'s approach within the model of ecological congruence, we can see how an acknowledgement of the demands, time, perceptions, and values of individuals in two situations were used to further understanding of

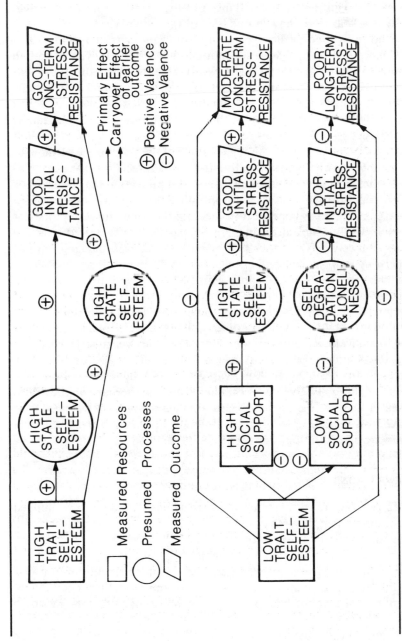

**Figure 11.2** An interactive process interpretation of the ecology of stress resistance.

283

causal order in the stress-resistance process. Much more complicated designs and analyses have borne less fruit (Kessler, 1983).

Studies by George Brown and his colleagues (Brown et al., 1975; O'Conner & Brown, 1984) offer another illustration of awareness of an interactive ecological approach. Most recently, Brown (1984) has attempted to find the specific factors that aid resistance to specific stressors. In particular, he has identified paradoxical cases in which usually effective coping resources are counterproductive. For example, self-esteem in women may result in greater depression because self-esteem was the very thing "that gave some of the women the confidence to get into the conflictual situation in the first place" (p. 14).

Rather than selecting the kind of social support that may be effective in general, Brown has searched for specific intimate relationships, which he argues are most important in meeting the needs involved in stress resistance following a stressful event. He has also concentrated on actual support received (O'Conner & Brown, 1984), conceptualizing support as a behavioral process and not just as an attitude or belief. His search for risk factors that predispose women to depression shows a keen regard for the ecology of the urban environments he has explored and of the potential for alienation among women who become isolated at home with young children. Brown argues that intensive personal interviews lasting many hours are necessary if we are to uncover the true nature of the stress process and resistance resources. This approach is very different from the North American one, which has centered on brief questionnaires. To the extent that an ecological model is applicable to research on stress resistance it is clear that more emphasis will need to be placed on measuring *process*, a direction in which North American mainstream psychology has been slow to move.

## CONCLUSIONS

In general, stress-resistance researchers have adhered to an implied dichotomy. People with good resources will cope effectively with stressors whereas those without them will succumb to stress. This dichotomy denies the context in which the coping saga unfolds. The model of ecological congruence calls attention to the notion not of a dichtomy, but of *relative fit*. In so doing, the model presents a more complex picture of the possible outcomes of attempts at stress resistance.

Figure 11.3 illustrates the implications of this distinction. The dichotomous model is presented in the first and last resource-environment interaction (ll.3A and 11.3D). In the best of situations, individuals

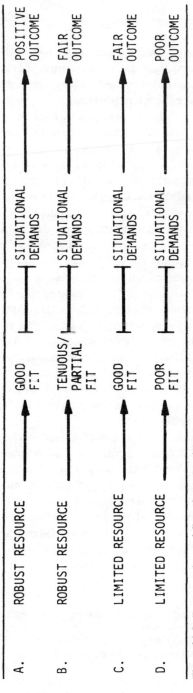

**Figure 11.3** Resource-demand fit and stress resistance.

possess a generally efffective resource that is robust or multipurpose (see Antonovsky, 1979). Mastery is such a resource, because it is effective in a variety of situations and is carried with the individual as part of his or her "personal luggage." Even in isolation from significant others, one is left with this key asset. If the demands of the stressor are ecologically congruent with the exercise of this resource (i.e., the situation is one in which control can affect the environment), the most positive resolution would be expected. This is depicted in Figure 11.3A.

In the worst situation (Figure 11.3D), the individual does not possess a robust resource and the resources he or she does possess do not fit the task-emotional demands. Thus, denial (denial being a limited resource) of a lump noticed in the breast might delay turning to medical examination and result in an irrevocable spread of cancer.

Two other intermediate possibilities emerge, however, when fit to the environment is considered. In the first (Figure 11.3B) the resource is a robust one, but fit with the situational demands is tenuous. So, for example, hope (Breznitz, 1983b) may be a very robust resource, but its effect may be limited in situations that demand direct action. Another possibility is that the resource is a limited one, but may fit the given situation (Figure 11.3C). Denial may be such a resource, as it may be effective in limiting the overwhelming initial stress involved in confrontation with massive stressors. However, over time it would limit effective coping, which must in the long run be based on a realistic assessment of the threat.

Our choice of instruments and emphasis on variables related to control and social support implies that we believe them to be what Antonovsky (1979) called "general resistance resources." Surely, certain styles of coping are usually more effective than others. However, whereas some researchers have chosen to attempt to isolate a single resource that is effective in the widest variety of situations, others have directed their efforts in recognition that stress resistance is most relevant when discussed in the context of the kind of demand structure inherent in the situation. Lazarus and Folkman (1984), supporting the latter position, write:

> Coping thoughts and actions are always directed toward particular conditions. To understand coping and to evaluate it, we need to know what the person is coping with. The more narrowly defined the context, the easier it is to link a particular coping thought or act to a contextual demand . . . to speak of a coping process means speaking of change in coping thoughts and acts as a stressful encounter unfolds. Coping is thus a shifting process in which the person must, at certain times, rely more heavily on one form of coping, say defensive strategies, as the status of the person-environment relationship changes. (p. 142)

Although the concept of general resistance resources may be appealing, it tends to lead toward a division of the world of copers into haves and have-nots. We tend to idolize the steadfast matador in the ring or the Lone Ranger moving from town to town. The matador, however, faces a bull who has already been caused by others to lose much blood, and these others are ready to enter the ring if the bull should get the upper hand. The Lone Ranger always had Tonto. Nor do I use the analogies frivolously: We as researchers tend to look for the simple "silver bullet" that will explain the phenomena we are investigating. Hardiness is attractive, partly because it fits with the way in which stories like the Lone Ranger—and for those a little older, Flash Gordon—taught us to want to see ourselves. These concepts pervade Judeo-Christian culture, of which psychologists are a part. No one is saying that these concepts are without merit, but heavy emphasis on them retards progress toward the more interactive (others have called it transactional) approach that this chapter is meant to illustrate.

I have attempted to clarify the distinction between ecologically and nonecologically-oriented research. This required discussion of the demands inherent in research based on a multidimensional and interactive view of coping resources. A model of ecological congruence was presented that, it is hoped, will help guide future research on stress resistance. The model should encourage discussion of more suitable research designs and the testing of more specific hypotheses. Perhaps we can soon begin to answer the question, "In what context do which resistance resources have which effects?"

## NOTE

1. The chapter is conceptually rather than chronologically organized. As a result, there are places where researchers may be criticized on points that they themselves have recognized and improved upon in later investigations. I have tried in such cases to cite both the researchers' earlier and later studies. Because of the chapter's conceptual organization, the subsequent study may not be discussed until some pages later.

## REFERENCES

Abramson, L. Y., Seligman, M. E., & Teasdale, J. P. (1978). Learned helplessness in humans, critique and reformulation. *Journal of Abnormal Psychology, 87*, 47-74.

Antonovsky, A. (1979). *Health, stress, and coping.* San Francisco: Jossey-Bass.

Barthé, S., & Hammen, C. (1981). A naturalistic extension of the attribution model of depression. *Personality and Social Psychology Bulletin, 7*, 53-58.

Breznitz, S. (1983a). (Ed.) *The denial of stress.* New York: Free Press.

Breznitz, S. (1983b). The noble challenge of stress. In S. Breznitz (Ed.), *Stress in Israel* (pp. 265-274). New York: Van Nostrand.

Brown, G. W. (1974). Meaning, measurement, and stressful life events. In B. S. & B. P. Dohrenwend (Eds.), *Stressful life events: Their nature and effects* (pp. 217-243). New York: John Wiley.

Brown, G. W. (October, 1984). *Social support and depression.* Paper presented at the First Gerald Caplan Lecture, Harvard University School of Public Health, Boston, Massachusetts.

Brown, G., Bhrolchrain, M., & Harris, T. (1975). Social class and psychiatric disturbance among women in an urban population. *Sociology, 9,* 225-254.

Caplan, G. (1974). *Support systems and community mental health.* New York: Behavioral Publications.

Cobb, J. (1976). Social support as a moderator of life stress. *Psychosomatic Medicine, 38,* 300-314.

Cox, T., & Mackay, C. (1978). *Stress.* Baltimore: University Park Press.

Coyne, J. C., Aldwin, C., & Lazarus, R. S. (1981). Depression and coping in stressful episodes. *Journal of Abnormal Psychology, 90,* 439-447.

Dean, A., & Lin, N. (1977). The stress buffering role of social support: Problems and prospects for future investigation. *Journal of Nervous and Mental Disease, 165,* 403-417.

Dohrenwend, B. S., & Dohrenwend, B. P. (1981). Socioenvironmental factors, stress and psychopathology. *American Journal of Community Psychology, 9,* 128-165.

Dohrenwend, B. S., Dohrenwned, B. P., Dodson, M., & Shrout, P. E. (1984). Symptoms, hassles, social support, and life events: Problems of confounded measures. *Journal of Abnormal Psychology, 93,* 222-230.

Folkman, S. (1984). Personal control and stress and coping processes: A theoretical analysis. *Journal of Personality and Social Psychology, 46,* 839-852.

Frankl, V. E. (1959). *Man's search for meaning.* New York, Beacon.

Gannellen, R. J., & Blaney, P. H. (1984). Hardiness and social support as moderators of the effects of life stress. *Journal of Personality and Social Psychology, 47,* 156-163.

Gottlieb, B. H. (1983). Social support as a focus for integrative research in psychology. *American Psychologist, 38,* 278-287.

Hackett, T. P., Cassem, N. H., & Wishnie, H. A. (1968). The coronary care unit: An appraisal of its psychological hazards. *New England Journal of Medicine, 279,* 1365-1370.

Hamburg, D. A., Hamburg, B., & de Goza, S. (1953). Adaptive problems and mechanisms in severely burned patients. *Psychiatry, 16,* 1-20.

Hansson, R. O., Jones, W. H., & Carpenter, B. N. (1984). Relationship competence and social support. In P. Shaver (Ed.), *Review of personality and social psychology* (Vol. 5). Beverly Hills, CA: Sage.

Hobfoll, S. E. (in press, a). The limitations of social support in the stress process. In I. G. Sarason & B. R. Sarason (Eds.), *Social support: Theory, research, and application.* The Hague: Martinus Nijhof.

Hobfoll, S. E. (in press, b). Stress, social support and women: An ecological, life-span perspective. In S. E. Hobfoll (Ed.), *Stress, social support, and women.* Washington, DC: Hemisphere.

Hobfoll, S. E., & Leiberman, J. R. (in press). Personality and social resources in immediate and continued stress resistance among women. *Journal of Personality and Social Psychology.*

Hobfoll, S. E., & London, P. (in press). The relationship of self concept and social support to emotional distress among women during war. *Journal of Social and Clinical Psychology.*

Hobfoll, S. E., & Walfisch (1984). Coping with a threat to life: A longitudinal study of self concept, social support, and psychological distress. *American Journal of Community Psychology, 12,* 87-100.

Janis, I. L. (1974). Vigilance and decision making in personal crisis. In G. V. Coelho, D. A. Hamburg, & J. E. Adams (Eds.), *Coping and adaptation* (pp. 139-175). New York: Basic Books.

Johnson, J. H., & Sarason, I. G. (1978). Life stress, depression and anxiety: Internal-external control as a moderator variable. *Journal of Psychosomatic Research, 22,* 205-208.

Jones, W. (in press). The psychology of loneliness: Some personality issues in the study of social support. In I. G. Sarason & B. R. Sarason (Eds.), *Social support: Theory, research and application.* The Hague: Martinus Nijhof.

Kanner, A. D., Coyne, J. C., Schaefer, C., & Lazarus, R. S. (1981). Comparison of two modes of stress measurement: Daily hassles and uplifts versus major life events. *Journal of Behavioral Medicine, 4,* 1-39.

Kelly, J. G., Snowden, L. R., & Muñoz, R. F. (1977). Social and community interventions. *Annual Review of Psychology, 28,* 323-361.

Kessler, R. (1983). Methodological issues in the study of psychological stresss. In H. B. Kaplan (Ed.), *Psychosocial stress: Trends in theory and research* (pp. 267-341). New York: Academic.

Kobasa, S. C. (1982). Commitment and coping in stress-resistance among lawyers. *Journal of Personality and Social Psychology, 42,* 707-717.

Kobasa, S. C., Maddi, S. R., & Courington, S. (1981). Personality and constitution as mediators in the stress-illness relationship. *Journal of Health and Social Behavior, 22,* 368-378.

Kobasa, S.C.O., & Puccetti, M. C. (1983). Personality and social resources in stress resistance. *Journal of Personality and Social Psychology, 45,* 839-850.

Lazarus, R. S. (1980). The stress and coping paradigm. In L. A. Bond & J. C. Rosen (Eds.), *Competence and coping in adulthood* (pp. 28-74). Hanover, NH: University Press of New England.

Lazarus, R. S. (1983). The costs and benefits of denial. In S. Breznitz (Ed.), *The denial of stress* (pp. 1-30). New York: Free Press.

Lazarus, R. S., & Folkman, S. (1984). *Stress, appraisal, and coping.* New York: Springer.

Lefcourt, H. M., Martin, R. A., & Selah, W. E. (1984). Locus of control and social support: Interactive moderators of stress. *Journal of Personality and Social Psychology, 47,* 378-389.

Lefcourt, H. M., Miller, R. S., Ware, R. S., & Sherk, D. (1981). Locus of control as a modifier of the relationship between stressors and moods. *Journal of Personality and Social Psychology, 41,* 357-369.

Lifton, R. H. (1964). On death and death symbolism: The Hiroshima disaster. *Psychiatry, 27,* 191-210.

Maslow, A. H. (1968). *Toward a psychology of being.* New York: Van Nostrand Reinhold.

McGrath, J. E. (1973). A conceptual formulation for research on stress. In J. E. McGrath (Ed.), *Social and psychological factors in stress* (pp. 10-21). New York: Holt, Rinehart & Winston.

Meichenbaum, D., Turk, D., & Burstein, S. (1975). The nature of coping with stress. In I. G. Sarason & C. D. Spielberger (Eds.), *Stress and anxiety, Vol. 2.* (pp. 337-360). Washington, DC: Hemisphere.

Mischel, W. (1984). Convergences and challenges in the search for consistency. *American Psychologist, 39,* 351-364.

Mitchell, R. E., & Hobson, C. A. (1983). Coping with domestic violence: Social support and psychological health among battered women. *American Journal of Community Psychology, 11,* 629-654.

Moos, R. H. (1984). Context and coping: Toward a unifying conceptual framework. *American Journal of Community Psychology, 12,* 5-36.

Murrel, S. A., & Norris, F. H. (1984). Resources, life events and changes in positive affect and depression in older adults. *American Journal of Community Psychology, 12,* 445-464.

Myers, J. K., Lindenthal, J. J., & Pepper, M. D. (1974). Social class, life events and psychiatric symptoms: A longitudinal study. In B. S. Dohrenwend & B. R. Dohrenwend (Eds.), *Stressful life events: Their nature and effects* (pp. 191-205). New York: John Wiley.

Nadler, A., & Mayeless, O. (1983). Recipient self esteem and reactions to help. In J. D. Fisher, A. Nadler, & B. M. DePaulo (Eds.), *New directions in helping, Vol. I* (pp. 167-188). New York: Academic.

O'Conner, P., & Brown, G. W. (1984). Supportive relationships: Fact or fancy? *Journal of Social and Personal Relationships, 1,* 159-175.

Pearlin, L. I. (in press). Social structure and social supports. In S. Cohen & L. Syme (Eds.), *Social support and health.* New York: Academic.

Pearlin, L. I., Lieberman, M. A., Menaghan, E. G., & Mullan, J. T. (1981). The stress process. *Journal of Health and Social Behavior, 22,* 337-356.

Pearlin, L. I., & Schooler, C. (1978). The structure of coping. *Journal of Health and Social Behavior, 19,* 2-22.

Rabkin, J. G., & Streuning, E. L. (1976). Life events, stress, and illness. *Science, 194,* 1013-1020.

Rook, K. S. (1984). The negative side of social interaction: Impact on psychological well-being. *Journal of Personality and Social Psychology, 46,* 1097-1108.

Rosenbaum, M., & Palmon, N. (1984). Helplessness and resourcefulness in coping with epilepsy. *Journal of Consulting and Clinical Psychology, 52,* 244-253.

Rosenthal, R. (1964). Experimenter outcome orientation and the results of psychological experiments. In A. Haber & R. P. Runyon (Eds.), *Research problems in psychology* (pp. 73-84). Reading, MA: Addison-Wesley.

Ruch, L. O., Chandler, S. M., & Harter, R. A. (1980). Life change and rape impact. *Journal of Health and Social Behavior, 20,* 248-260.

Sandler, I. N., & Lakey, B. (1982). Locus of control as a stress moderator: The role of control perceptions and social support. *American Journal of Community Psychology, 10,* 65-80.

Sarason, S. (1980). Individual Psychology: An obstacle to comprehending adulthood. In L. A. Bond & J. C. Rosen (Eds.), *Competence and coping in adulthood* (pp. 6-27). Hanover, NH: University Press of New England.

Schoenberg, B., Carr, A. C., Paretz, D., & Kutscher, A. H. (1970). *Loss and grief.* New York: Columbia University Press.

Spielberger, C. D., Johnson, E. H., Russell, S. F., Crane, R. J., Jacobs, G. A., & Worden, T. J. (in press). In M. A. Chesney & R. H. Rosenman (Eds.), *Anger and hostility in cardiovascular and behavioral disorders.* New York: Hemisphere/McGraw-Hill.

Stern, M. J., Pascale, L., & McLoone, J. B. (1976). Psychosocial adaptation following acute myocardial infarction. *Journal of Chronic Disease, 29,* 513-526.

Taylor, S. E. (1983). Adjustment to threatening events: A theory of cognitive adaptation. *American Psychologist, 38,* 1161-1173.

Teichman, Y. (1978). Affiliative reactions in different kinds of threat situations. In C. D. Spielberger & I. G. Sarason (Eds.), *Stress and anxiety* (Vol. 5, pp. 131-144). Washington, DC: Hemisphere.

Thoits, P. (1982). Conceptual, methodological, and theoretical problems in studying social support as a buffer against life stress. *Journal of Health and Social Behavior, 23,* 145-159.

Thompson, S. C. (1981). Will it hurt less if I can control it? A complex answer to a simple question. *Psychological Bulletin, 90,* 89-101.

Tolsdorf, C. C. (1976). Social networks, support, and coping: An exploratory study. *Family Process, 15,* 407-417.

Visotsky, H. M., Hamburg, D. A., Goss, M. E., & Lebovits, B. Z. (1961). Coping behavior under extreme stress. *Archives of General Psychiatry, 5,* 423-448.

Weissman, M. M., & Paykel, E. S. (1974). *The depressed woman: A study of social relationships.* Chicago: University Press of Chicago.

Wilcox, B. L. (1981). Social support, life stress and psychological adjustment: A test of the buffering hypothesis. *American Journal of Community Psychology, 9,* 371-387.

Wilcox, B. L. (in press). Stress, coping and the social milieu of divorced women. In S. E. Hobfoll (Ed.), *Stress, social support, and women.* Washington, DC: Hemisphere.

Williams, A. W., Ware, J. E., & Donald, C. A. (1981). A model of mental health, life events, and social supports applicable to the general population. *Journal of Health and Social Behavior, 22,* 324-336.

# 12

# Personality and Health

## SPECIFYING AND STRENGTHENING
## THE CONCEPTUAL LINKS

## SUZANNE C. OUELLETTE KOBASA

**Suzanne C. Ouellette Kobasa** is Associate Professor in the Doctoral Program in Psychology, Social/Personality Subprogram, Graduate School and University Center, City University of New York. Her research interests include health psychology, adult personality, and the psychology of religion.

> I told jokes, I tried to sound savvy about medicine, I tried hard to be interesting. . . .
> I wanted my doctor to see that I was unique, different from the other patients, that I had a personality.
>
> —A young female lawyer hospitalized for cancer surgery

A number of autobiographical and biographical accounts portray the experience of illness as a stripping away of personal distinctiveness, a dehumanizing process in which one's individuality is traded for membership in an unenvied class defined by a medical diagnosis. Consider the case of Paul Tsongas, a former senator from Massachusetts who developed cancer while pursuing a very busy political and family life. His recent book (1984) contains a number of provocative moments in which his existence as a patient with unpredictably emerging lumps completely overshadowed his other ways of being. His formerly crucial identities as an unusual vote-seeker who disliked and avoided the Washington social scene, or a uniquely self-reflective politican who constantly tried to balance family and work commitments, lost some of their salience as he described his illness experience. Having lymphoma appeared to rob him of what Gordon Allport might have called the "Paulian quality of Paul." In attempts to be the good patient for oncologists, in public appearances foiled by distracting thoughts about his cancer, and in numerous other illness-related episodes that will be familiar to anyone who has known someone with a serious medical problem, Tsongas seemed to be without some of that "dynamic organization within the individual of those psychophysical systems that determine his unique adjustments to his environment" (Allport, 1937, p. 48).

This depiction of illness challenges the researcher intent on identifying the place and function of personality in health and illness phenomena. How is one to find valid and reliable personality indicators within such reports, provided by the actual victims of illness as well as those who treat them (e.g., Bigwood, 1976; Vachon, 1982)? Facilitated either by personal motives or pressures from the medical setting and its protagonists to conform, being sick appears to blur the differences between individuals. Blurring, however, is not eradication. The challenge to the personality researcher is to look a little harder than he or she may need to in other behavioral arenas.

One way of looking harder has the researcher redefining the illness experience as a distinctive and powerful occasion for observing personality. By reconstructing struggles with illness as testing grounds or projective tests for personality, for example, one stands a chance of observing behaviors that are critically revealing of persons as distinctive individuals. Illness typically confuses and threatens one's usual ways of thinking and feeling about oneself and the world. As such, it calls forth from the person attempts to reorder experience and instill meaning as he or she hears the cancer diagnosis, or the lab result of excessively high cholesterol. These behaviors, in turn, draw upon basic motives, needs, and general orientations toward the environment. Although any autobiographical account by Paul Tsongas might have revealed the influence of personality variables such as Murray's (1938) *need for affiliation,* Tsongas's description of how he copes with illness makes its salience in his psychological organization especially clear.

Another way of looking a little harder involves the researcher asking about more than isolated, inside-the-skin, predisposing personality variables. To understand something as complicated as another's health or illness, one needs to observe personality as it emerges in the distinctive and varied situational and sociocultural contexts of one's subjects. The Tsongas case is again illustrative. A personality psychologist could argue that Tsongas's predisposition to what Jung called an *attitude of introspection* underlies his various responses to his illness. Relating this construct of introspectiveness to contextual observations, however, provokes more convincing explanations. For example, pairing the attitudinal data with situational and sociocultural information such as Tsongas's membership in a warm and loving young family, the role demands associated with being a U.S. senator, and a physician's willingness to see him on Sunday in an otherwise empty office building suggest a number of viable ways of explaining behaviors ranging from his first response to the word "cancer" to his decision not to run for reelection.

In this chapter, I will argue for the viability and value of attempting to meet the challenge of "finding" personality in health and illness phenomena. I recognize that making my case will not be easy. I begin with a brief review of what troubles me most about the dominant trends in the existing literature on personality and health. This opening describes what is missing from personality psychology's contribution to health research and where we may have gone wrong in the past. The next section has a more optimistic tone: In it, I elaborate on those two research strategies noted above—the recasting of illness experiences as appropriate subject matter for personality psychology and the technique of searching for personality in context. I discuss each strategy as representative of a promising perspective for future research on personality and health. The first perspective calls for a broadening of the personality psychologist's approach to include matters of illness behavior as well as illness itself. The second perspective offers a contextual framework for conceptualizing health and illness phenomena as essentially both intraindividual *and* social in nature.

To illustrate the usefulness of both perspectives I draw from my own ongoing research with the personality construct *hardiness*. The third and penultimate section of the chapter provides some examples of current attempts to put these perspectives to work in studies of pregnant women and of hardiness interventions designed to increase stress resistance. To ensure the viability of both perspectives, I make a closing case for the importance of theory in research on personality and health. The final section describes an existential theory of personality that I believe is especially well-suited to meet the challenges described in this chapter.

## CRITIQUE OF EXISTING
## PERSONALITY AND HEALTH LITERATURE

Many contributions to the very busy research area of health psychology begin by citing Galen's observations that certain persistent mood states and behavioral styles characterize persons at risk for serious disease. This second-century reference gives historical sophistication to many current attempts to replace the limited biomedical approach with a broader biopsychosocial model of health and illness.

There is something ironic about this frequent use of Galen. His work essentially is turned into a statement about the link between cancer and personality. The contemporary research that uses Galen as an introduction, however, is quite likely not to involve the subject matter of personality, but rather other psychological concerns, such as isolated moods (e.g., state anxiety) or seemingly universal cognitive processes (e.g., the tendency to make causal attributions). Although health psychology is described accurately as a research endeavor to which all of the subdisciplines of psychology—personality, social, developmental, community, educational, and so on—might contribute, the dominant emphasis is currently far from distinctively personological. The quantitative and qualitative differences between the contributions of personality psychology and social psychology are especially striking. In 1978, Taylor wrote a very informative and—judging from the reactions of my graduate students—inspirational paper in which she outlined what the available theories and methodologies of social psychology have to offer all five problem areas within medical practice. She described the variety of social psychological applications to concerns about etiology, prevention of disease, management of health and illness, treatment, and health-care delivery. No comparable piece exists in the personality literature.

One might counter the charge that personality has been neglected by pointing to the large number of investigations devoted to identifying and understanding the link between coronary heart disease and Type A, a constellation of psychological characteristics thought to include competitiveness, time urgency, extreme job involvement, and hostility (see Carver & Humphries, 1982, and Mathews, 1982, for reviews). This rebuttal offers little consolation, however, to the personality researcher attempting to continue in the traditions of Allport and Murray. Although summaries of Type A findings in the popular media refer to the Type A *personality,* the majority of researchers in the area deliberately avoid use of this term and the related phrase, personality type. These researchers define Type A as a *behavioral pattern* and emphasize the situational characteristics that elicit it. As the review by Matthews makes clear, the focus in this research has been essentially twofold: If investigators are not preoccupied with developing the best possible way of measuring Type A, they are busy varying situational characteristics such as the degree of control allowed subjects in an experiment. Matters that would be of interest to the personality psychologist, such as the psychological processes that underlie Type A or the early life determinants of Type A, have received significantly less theoretical and empirical attention.

Bringing together the work on Type A with other seemingly personality-related endeavors, I am struck by a number of problems or gaps in existing research. I wish to consider two of these here: (1) the lack of theoretical development and the associated restriction of investigations to single personality variables, and (2) the excessive emphasis on links between personality and illness etiology.

## Weak Theorizing and
## Variable-Based Research

There have, of course, been opportunities for the elaboration of formal theories of personality and health. Taking the example of behaviors enacted in response to an illness, one can cite two preliminary formulations of the role of personality that derived from two radically different psychological sources. Consider the social learning theory conceptualization of internal-external locus of control (the extent to which people view events as dependent on their own behavior or on external determinants such as luck, fate, or powerful others), and the early formulation of locus as a *generalized* expectancy that shapes behavior most definitively when people confront ambiguous and unusual demands (Rotter, 1954). Defined as such, locus of control emerged as a personality construct especially well-suited to the understanding of responses to illness. In fact, data from tuberculosis patients provided some of the earliest evidence for the criterion validity of the internal-external dimension (Seeman and Evans in 1962 supported locus of control theory by finding that hospitalized patients with an internal locus of control are more likely to desire and have knowledge about tuberculosis than their external counterparts).

Consider also the essential link between personality and responses to illness that began to be forged in an early classic of personality theorizing. For Murray, illness experience was a particular form of *press*, one "against which the will of the individual must contend" (1938, p. 311). Bringing his perspective to childhood episodes of illness, Murray defined changes in health status as crucial influences upon the developing need structure of the child. A child with a serious illness who is confined to bed, for example, may undergo a strengthening of his or her basic need for succorance; but that child may also discover in himself or herself an attraction to self-reflection and other forms of mental activity. Murray portrays another's experience of illness as illustrative of both that person's characteristic ways of adjusting to the world and changes in these adjustments.

Although promising, neither the social learning nor Murray's formulation provoked sustained theoretical effort. Murray's comments on personality and health took up only a few pages of his lengthy work; and, to my knowledge, apart from a handbook chapter by Mages and

Mendelsohn on the impact of cancer (1979), there have been no substantial and widely recognized attempts at personality and health theorizing in Murray's full personological tradition. With regard to the locus of control tradition, one finds much more activity but also disappointments concerning both empirical and theoretical efforts.

There are numerous studies linking locus of control to all of the following: knowledge about health and illness, health promotion or risk-reduction behaviors, coping with illness, reactions to medical interventions, and behavior in health care settings (Strickland, 1982; Wallston & Wallston, 1982, provide good reviews of this work). Although establishing that there is some kind of relationship between this variable and health and illness, the studies taken together shed doubt on the magnitude and consistency of this relationship. Moreover, they contain methodological shortcomings, such as inappropriate controls and retrospective designs, which interfere with the drawing of firm conclusions. It is the conceptual shortcomings, however, that require the most comment in the context of this chapter.

The vast majority of locus of control studies, those having to do with health and illness phenomena as well as more general investigations, represent variable-based rather than person-based research. As Carlson (1975) and other commentators on the current state of personality psychology have noted, such research necessarily restricts the advancement of theory. A focus on variables often leads to a preoccupation with measurement strategies at the expense of conceptual clarification. In studies of control and patients' responses to medical procedure, for example, researchers have told us more about what scales to use to measure control than about *why* control might be an important issue to consider. The lack of theoretical elaboration threatens both our understanding of the relevant underlying psychological processes and our explanation of why control, or any other psychological variable, affects recovery from surgery (e.g., Newman, 1984).

Another problem with variable-based research lies in its fostering of the mistaken view that personality can be understood in terms of some single dimension. Personality, as descriptive of persons, needs to be assessed through a number of different variables. If locus of control matters for health, it probably does so in relation to other components of personality. In my own work with personality and stress-resistance, for example, control emerges most clearly as a significant buffer of the debilitating effects of stress when considered as part of a personality constellation that also includes the dimensions of commitment and challenge (e.g., Kobasa, 1982).

The Wallstons (Wallston & Wallston, 1982) close their review of the often less than convincing research on locus of control and health with the comment that future investigations should observe subjects' control as it interacts with specified aspects of the subjects' situation (suggesting, for example, that an internal locus of control may lead to improvement in health in the face of some controllable illnesses, although worsening health if brought to uncontrollable illnesses). This is good advice, but for those interested in elaborating the role of locus of control as a personality construct, additional suggestions are also in order.

In moving from a variable- to a person-based approach, one would want to check whether or not one's construct of control is in itself combining a number of different personality characteristics in need of consideration as distinct dimensions; if it is, one's assessment procedures and theory would have to allow for appropriate discriminations. A second suggestion would underline the need to consider control alongside other personality constructs defined as important individual difference variables in one's chosen approach to persons. Although discussed here with special relevance to locus of control, these suggestions also apply to the other single variables that characterize current personality and health research. The list includes trait anxiety, neuroticism (as assessed through the Eysenck Personality Inventory), Type A, and coping styles such as vigilance versus avoidance.

## The Excessive Emphasis on Etiology

Health and illness phenomena refer to a broad range of behavioral concerns: why someone becomes ill, how and when they choose to seek formal care, how satisfied they are with the care they receive, and so on. The dominant trends in personality and health research, however, belie this breadth. Many personality studies focus narrowly on illness etiology—on the role of personality in the causation of illness. Beginning with Alexander in the thirties (see, for example, Alexander, 1950), continuing through the contemporary psychodynamic researchers like Schmale and Engel (e.g., Schmale, 1972), and emerging in more behaviorial form in work such as that on locus of control (e.g., deHaas & vanReken, 1979), investigators often have been concerned with disease as a dependent variable and with personality as its likely determinant. One hears a note of irony in these studies: Although attempting to correct traditional biomedical approaches to health, psychological researchers often find themselves focusing on that very part of the health and illness continuum that they accuse physicians of overemphasizing. In effect, personality emerges simply as a new kind of germ.

With this focus on etiology, researchers have failed to appreciate the multitude of ways in which personality may be related to health and illness. Taking a small example from my own work, there is much that we might want to know about the relationship between personality and the propensity to associate formal physical illness labels or diagnoses with perceived symptoms (e.g., to attribute stomach pains to an ulcer). An analysis of data collected from Canadian and American lawyers (e.g., Kobasa, 1982) demonstrates a link between the stress-buffering of personality hardiness and a decrease in reports of specific physical symptoms, and a second link between these lowered symptom reports and a decrease in reports of formal illness episodes.

A closer look at the path analysis, however, shows that not all of the variance in illness is explained by symptoms. In fact, there is a strong suggestion in the data that there are notable differences between individuals in their willingness to associate formal illness labels with symptoms; differences having to do with hardiness and other personality characteristics. A larger data set, involving more subjects and additional information on subjects' medical backgrounds, might be analyzed to address this and other health-related issues that go beyond the concern with strict causality of illness.

With this focus on etiology, researchers have also failed to meet Murray's challenge to see illness as an occasion for possible personality change, or at least for the shaping of personality by new and unusual demands from the environment. Conceptualizing personality as essentially static, these researchers cut short that continuous psychosocial process that is illness. This limitation has serious implications for what health-care professionals are able to learn, and not learn, from personality research. Personality explanations of illness etiology are too often reductionistic in ways that are potentially damaging to the individuals involved. They foster what has been called "blaming the victim" (e.g., Sontag, 1978). Additionally, the new labels for patients suggested by these personality explanations (hysterical, excessively dependent, impulsive, etc.) allow health-care professionals to minimize their own influence on the well-being of those they treat. Personality labels, like medical diagnostic categories, can have the unfortunate consequence of letting physicans turn patients into passive and fixed entities. One does not have to interact with patients thought of in this way, one has only to tell them what to do. It is revealing that personality and illness etiology studies are often done with social groups occupying lower segments of the status hierarchy, or patient groups that are unpopular with physicians (note, for example, how many of these studies have involved illnesses that strike only women).

## TWO PROMISING PERSPECTIVES
## FOR FUTURE RESEARCH

### Elaborating the Connections
### Between Personality and Health

An obvious correction to the excessive emphasis on personality and etiology is a turn to other health and illness phenomena. Indeed, I began this chapter with comments about someone who was already ill in order to promote a shift of focus. Where, however, should the focus now move? One important source of new directions is the discussion of the distinction between illness and illness behavior.

Several good cases have been made for appreciating the difference between these two concepts. In drawing the contrast, medical sociologists like Mechanic (e.g., 1972, 1977) and other health researchers have restricted the term "illness" to refer only to objective symptoms with a physiological basis (examples include white cell count, observed tissue damage, and recorded blood pressure readings). Illness behavior, on the other hand, "refers to the varying perceptions, thoughts, feelings, and acts affecting the personal and social meaning of symptoms, illness, disabilities and their consequences (Mechanic, 1977, p. 79). Mechanic calls us to consider the acts, thoughts, and feelings displayed as a person begins to experience signs of physical distress, decides whether or not to stay home from work, chooses whom to consult for help, describes symptoms to a health-care professional, follows or fails to follow medical advice, and responds to the demands of health-care institutions. This takes us far beyond the acts, thoughts, and feelings associated with becoming ill, the typical subject matter of the personality psychologist interested in health.

### Why the Neglect
### of Illness Behavior?

Mechanic's discussion introduces a variety of new outcome variables for health research. Why is it, however, that when one looks at the kinds of studies of illness behavior that exist in the literature, one finds relatively few investigations with a personality emphasis? Studies linking illness behavior with matters such as life situation factors (e.g., attitudes of family members), aspects of the treatment regimen (e.g., complexity of drug administration), demographic characteristics (e.g., age), and quality of doctor-patient interactions far outnumber personality studies. One reason for the neglect may have to do with an attitude of defensiveness or self-protection on the part of personality psychologists.

A number of presentations of the illness/illness behavior distinction (e.g., Cohen, 1979) serve as serious critiques of much personality and health research. Presenters argue that personality psychologists' failures to appreciate the distinction allow them to draw mistaken conclusions about the relationship between psychological and social realities (e.g., personality characteristics and stressful life circumstances) and health and illness phenomena. Most of these mistaken conclusions, it is said, serve to exaggerate the importance of the psychological or nonbiomedical realties in illness etiology: Personality psychologists may have thought they were identifying some causal relationship between a psychological style such as repression-sensitization and cancer, or between a social loss such as the death of a spouse and mortality, but all they were really doing was observing connections with illness behavior. The tie was not between, for example, repression and growth of the tumor, but rather between repression and the cancer patient's ways of interpreting symptoms and coping with his or her illness. These presentations of illness behavior amount to alternative explanations, or grounds for dismissal, of personality and health connections. In the face of these, the reluctance of personality psychologists (e.g., Kobasa, 1979) to refer to illness behavior is somewhat understandable.

## What is There To Learn from Illness Behavior?

At this point in the development of biopsychosocial studies of health and illness, it seems appropriate to lessen antagonisms between different behavioral and social science perspectives, and to recognize that personality may be related to *both* illness and illness behavior. In attending to illness behavior, personality psychologists meet opportunities to make a number of improvements over prior work. Two of these are discussed below: (1) doing person- rather than variable-based research, and (2) considering patterns or constellations of behaviors as they change over time, rather than static relationships between single variables.

Although Mechanic sometimes cautions *against* the use of personality approaches to illness behavior (e.g., Mechanic, 1983), his initial formulation of illness behavior attributed to personality an influential role in shaping what people do as they recognize symptoms, seek out care, comply with medical advice, and so on. In an article written specifically to clarify the health-care implications of illness behavior, "suggesting how understanding illness behavior may provide strategies for care and rehabilitation different from those suggested by traditional medical concepts" (1977, p. 79), Mechanic gave center stage to issues that are definitive of a personality orientation in the Allport and Murray tradition. Alongside the more typically sociological concerns such as comparison processes, economic assets, and social support resources, he discussed the patients' search for meaning, motivations, needs, and defensive techniques. He portrayed the relationships and interactions between these psychological factors as crucial in shaping persons' responses to illness and the likelihood of their success in various rehabilitation efforts.

Mechanic appears to be challenging personality researchers to take personality more seriously than they often do. Indeed, the majority of studies that he criticizes focus on only single personality traits. He is probably correct that it is only in looking at personality in more complex and thorough ways that one will observe its significant impact on illness behavior.

These more complex ways include allowing for behavioral inconsistency. For example, it is probably unrealistic to expect that the degree of personal control a person displays immediately upon hearing his or her cancer diagnosis is the best predictor of both behaviors in the crisis hospital setting and behaviors years later while the cancer is in remission. Having cancer and being treated for it probably modify a characteristic such as control and its salience in one's personality. Prediction requires that this modification be taken into account.

Another way of recognizing complexity involves the personality psychologist's approach to outcome variables. Too many existing studies examine only a single and narrow aspect of illness behavior, such as whether the person keeps scheduled appointments or takes all the medication prescribed. Given what we know from clinicians' reports about patients, however, *patterns of illness behavior* appear to be the more likely correlates of personality. To understand these patterns, we need to take into account at least all of the following: the nature of the illness, the stage of its course, the distinctive meaning that the illness has for the patient, and the specific others with whom the patient interacts around his or her illness. Leventhal's ongoing research on issues such as "common sense representations of illness danger" (e.g., Leventhal, Meyer, & Nerenz, 1980) provides a good model for this new research emphasis.

## Looking at Personality
## and Health in Context

Having considered the variety of *what* the personality psychologist interested in health might look at, we can now turn to a concern with *how* he or she might do this looking. In this section of the chapter, I argue for the value of a contextual model that presents as appropriate subject matter not only intraindividual processes, but also the dyads, small group settings, social institutions, and broader cultural contexts to which individual processes are related. Health and illness phenomena are essentially social. This characterization holds whether one is concerned with behaviors that follow upon the news of an illness, like those cited in the introduction, or with matters such as how a person stays healthy in the face of situations thought to be detrimental to health, whether a person complies with medical recommendations, and how being sick impacts on a person's effectiveness at work and in other parts of life. In order to appreciate the connections between all of these health phenomena and personality, the researcher has to understand the possible relevance of contexts such as doctor-patient interactions, the family relationships of the patient, the patient's work setting, and note their impact on the well or sick person.

### *Context as a Corrective*

The mistakes we made in using personality variables as labels might have been harder to make if we had recognized the social and cultural restrictions placed on our subjects. We might not have expected consistency in a behavior such as symptom reporting if we were aware of the varying constraints placed on motives by different interpersonal interactions. A young woman who generally strives to present herself as competent may minimize her symptoms to her spouse. She feels compelled to offer him some explanation for why she is not feeling on top of her work and why she hasn't hosted a fancy dinner party. This same young woman may maximize her symptoms when in the hospital. She has come to see that competence is evaluated by the important others in the medical setting in terms of how little one complains (Lorber, 1975; Taylor, 1979).

We might also have provided more complex descriptions and explanations of illness behavior if we had recognized how personal and immediate situational factors interact with larger social contexts. For example, in my search to understand why some subjects were less likely than others to associate diagnoses of physical illness with their somatic complaints, it was helpful to note that such subjects were more likely to be lawyers than business executives, army officers, or priests. Lawyers as a group, those I studied as well as those written about by others (e.g., Mayer, 1967), describe themselves as being healthier than members of other occupations. In my interviews, staying free of physical illness emerges as part of their job description. The questionnaire data justify relating variance in illness reports to personality and stressful life event scores. In combination with the interview data, however, they also call for a fuller explanation that draws on factors from the social context within which lawyers work. The struggle here is not to determine which is the more important explanation—the one provided by personality or the one by occupation, but how to combine the explanations meaningfully.

## An Early Example of the Importance of Context

An early psychological study of patients' responses to cancer provides a good illustration of the conceptual value of conceiving of personality and health phenomena within a series of related social contexts. The crucial data are from conversations between Morton Bard, then a visiting lecturer to Scandinavian medical settings, and a Scandinavian patient (Bard, 1966). Bard's observations offer support for Sanford's claims for the greater articulation of personality and social systems. Bard's example makes clear that it is only in moving back and forth from what is observed about personality to what is found at various sociocultural levels that the investigator begins to understand the health phenomena at hand. Personality and social realities in isolation provide incomplete formulations.

Based on his observations of general social heterogeneity, differences in fundamental values between patients and physicians, and patient dissatisfaction with medical care in his own cultural setting in North America, Bard went to the largely homogeneous societies of Scandinavia expecting to find minimal discrepancies between physicians and patients on basic attitudes, and therefore strong rapport. The widespread similarities were indeed there: The majority of Scandinavians placed great emphasis on values such as self-reliance, stoicism, and social responsibility. Virtually universal within the cancer treatment setting were the beliefs that patients had a right to the truth about their medical condition and the assumption that patients coped with the truth, no matter how stressful or threatening.

For the most part, these cultural factors were reflected in patient behavior. Many patients presented themselves as independent and stoical. There were, however, some patients who showed unusual distress in response to their illness. Bard observed the Scandinavian physicians as they approached these "mangagement problems" with their typical value stance and engaged in a rather massive denial that real problems existed. When Bard interviewed these same patients himself, however, something other than denial emerged. In conversations with him, Scandinavian patients actively expressed the depth of their emotional upset. He observed adaptational strategies that reminded him of coping behaviors observed in New York, including some very non-Scandinavian ways of behaving.

When patients had the opportunity to talk with someone holding different value assumptions, they appeared freer to express their idiosyncratic concerns. Further, they were then better understood. Bard suggested that both by knowing something about the culture and by being sensitive to the power of personality differences—all within the distinctive two-person interaction defined by a particular American and a particular Scandinavian—one built theories and planned better interventions. According to Bard, it was only from a combined psychological and sociocultural stance that "it is possible to really assist the patient in achieving autonomous solutions to adaptive requirements" (p. 998).

## A Current Example of Context

Bard's example demonstrates the value of context for understanding how someone copes with illness. A contextual perspective, however, can also usefully inform a number of different health and illness phenomena, including those having to do with illness onset. A relatively new research area in which the value of elaborating both intraindividual and sociocultural issues is especially clear is that involving Type A and women's health (see Baker, Dearborn, Hastings, & Hamberger, 1984, for a review).

Findings from physiological studies show interesting gender differences in stress reactivity, and reports from laboratory social-psychological studies mention women's distinctive responses to interpersonally competitive situations. The power of these results is most clear, however, when viewed from the perspective promoted by field studies of Type A. What we learn from our laboratory and personality questionnaire studies needs to be supplemented by sociocultural information. Especially striking is the observed relationship between job status and the health-debilitating impact of Type A (e.g., Haynes & Feinleib, 1980). Not all women are put at significant risk for coronary heart disease by Type A—only women who work in low-status jobs. Looking at personality in relation to social systems, one finds that it is not being Type A, but being Type A while also being confronted with numerous stressors from work and home, and lacking the rewards and power of high-status jobs, that is bad for women's health.

## RECENT DIRECTIONS IN HARDINESS RESEARCH

The proposed focus on personality as linked to many health and illness phenomena, and as viewed in context, informs two of my ongoing research efforts. The first seeks to expand the perspective of hardiness research beyond illness onset and stress-resistance. The second recognizes the importance of context for the success of stress intervention attempts.

### The High-Risk Pregnancy Study

Most of my health psychology research has been concerned with illness rather than illness behavior. Its basic point has been to demonstrate the influence of personality characteristics on stress-related illness. My general hypothesis has been that under highly stressful life-event conditions, persons with personality hardiness (a combination of commitment, control, and challenge) are significantly less likely to suffer illness-provoking arousal and activation than are persons without hardiness (i.e., persons who report alienation, powerlessness, and threat in the face of change). The research to date has portrayed hardiness as facilitating an active, optimistic, and self-determined form of coping with stressful life events that renders them less threatening to the organism. Confirmation of the hardiness hypothesis (e.g., Kobasa, Maddi, & Courington, 1981; Kobasa, Maddi, & Kahn, 1982) came with the demonstration that hardy and nonhardy subjects under high stress differed from each other on medical or biological status (as seen in self-reports of illness, doctors' medical records, and clinical test results). The studies stopped, as it were, with the observation of whether or not subjects became physically ill.

My current work allows me to look beyond illness onset and to consider more complex relationships between personality and health. In a study that is now in its pilot stages, we are observing women as they live through a pregnancy that has been labeled as "high-risk." All of these women face the threat of a severely premature birth experience. For one or more obstetrical or gynecological reasons, they now find themselves coping with a highly stressful health and illness event. In this study, change in health status moves from being confined to the last box in a research model to equally important placement in the first box; that is, health status becomes an independent as well as dependent variable.

The questions raised in this study include the following: How do personality characteristics such as hardiness, stressful life experiences from work and home, earlier coping experience, and support from others at work and home influence a woman's psychological and biological well-being during pregnancy? How do they influence the outcome of the pregnancy, including its length? How do they affect women's efforts to cope with the highly technical and highly physician-controlled dimensions of their obstetrical care?

Additionally, with the collaboration of Milton Viederman, a liaison psychiatrist who has had extensive experience with interviewing and counseling medical patients, I am using this study as an opportunity to ask about personality change in the face of poor health. High-risk pregnancy certainly qualifies as a strong form of Murray's press. Following Murray's suggestion, I hope to examine both the hardiness that women bring to the struggle and the changes in hardiness and other personality characteristics that may emerge through the course of pregnancy and later.

## Hardiness Intervention
## and Its Social Context

Having found that hardiness buffers the negative effects of stressful life events in both retrospective and prospective studies with several different subject groups (Kobasa, 1982), Sal Maddi and I, aided by our students at both the University of Chicago and City University of New York, have turned to questions of application. Given the health-protecting effect of hardiness in the lives of persons under stress, it seems worthwhile to consider ways of increasing hardiness.

A series of pilot studies involving Chicago telephone company executives (Maddi & Kobasa, 1984) provide grounds for optimism. Preliminary results demonstrate that executives identified as being under high stress and low in hardiness and suffering stress-related symptoms (typically, high blood pressure as well as general strain) benefit significantly from group counseling sessions designed to enhance hardiness and its associated coping style. When compared with controls, our hardiness-group subjects show increases in hardiness and decreases in symptoms at the end of two months of weekly intervention meetings and several months later.

It is hoped that investigations of these intervention strategies will correct, or at least avoid, a number of the problems in personality and health research noted earlier in this chapter. One of these problems is the tendency to define personality variables as static in their impact on health. Although our interest in stress-resistance puts us in the camp of those personality psychologists who emphasize illness onset, our interest in intervention keeps us from viewing personality as unchanging in response to environmental influences, a too frequent assumption of members of this camp. Another problem at stake is the failure to specify environmental influences. It is hoped that the following makes clear that the demands of a contextual model shape our research on hardiness intervention.

Contextual concerns certainly are helping shape our intervention attempts with executives. Although we focus on individual issues such as attitudes toward the company and perception of personal efficiency, we also find that we spend a good deal of our counseling efforts talking with executives about the telephone company—that is, about how best to engage in hardiness coping within this distinctive work setting at this point in its history. More than our interviews and questionnaires from individual group members inform these discussions. Our success at helping others cope, and at systematically evaluating our efforts, appears crucially to rely on our organizational observations that began in 1977, and on our continuous contact with informants and "gatekeepers" from various parts of the organization.

Context looms as even more important as we plan to take hardiness intervention outside of the single setting of the phone company and bring it to other occupations. Although each of the groups we have studied (executives, lawyers, army officers, priests) provides support for the general hardiness and stress-resistance hypothesis, there are also interesting differences between the groups. For example, lawyers report more hardiness and less stress-related strain and illness than do executives, and lawyers differ even more strongly from army officers and priests. Given these results, the design of intervention strategies may be enhanced through learning more about how and why lawyers are different. Sociocultural matters such as lawyers' occupational climate, role expectations, and professional socialization may suggest more organizationally sophisticated ways of promoting change.

In my earlier discussion of lawyers' reluctance to give illness labels to their symptoms, I referred to their particular perception of stress and health. Lawyers and the public at large appear to view lawyers as thriving under stress. They are reputed never to get sick, to live very long lives, and to perform best under great pressure. In the well-documented socialization experience of law school (e.g., Barry & Connelly, 1978), young lawyers appear to meet a strenuous pace that characterizes the rest of their professional lives.

Thinking about personality and health in terms of our series of situational and sociocultural contexts, we can conceive of several ways in which this stress ideology or mythology might function to promote lawyers' stress resistance. The individual lawyer may develop greater stress resistance as a result of attempts to live up to the expectations of the profession and the public. For example, the social context defined by this ideology may easily draw out the challenge component of hardiness. It may be easier to learn to think about change as positive if one works within a setting that defines the taking on of new challenges every time a client walks into one's office as an essential part of the attorney's role. It may be that law school is a training ground for later coping with stress. Within its radical initiation, law students may actually learn stress management techniques such as dealing efficiently with time. It may also be the case that the law profession provides structures and processes that reinforce the excercise of stress resistance throughout the lawyer's career. Finally, it may be that individuals who decide to go to law school, and make it through, have hardier personalities.

Learning more about the viability of each of these explanations and, equally important, the relationships between them should provide some important directives for personality and social system intervention for stress resistance.

## THE CRITICAL ROLE
## OF THE APPROPRIATE THEORY

The suggestions offered for better specifying and strengthening the conceptual links between personality and health assume the availability of sophisticated methodologies and a broad-based theory of personality and human behavior. Elsewhere (Kobasa, 1985), I discuss prospective-longitudinal methods as holding special hope for the personality researcher seeking to avoid mistakes of the past and advance the field. I would like to conclude this chapter with some remarks about theory. In what follows, I argue for the appropriateness of an existential theory of personality for the formulation of hypotheses that are in the spirit of the two promising perspectives for future research discussed above.

Existentialism (e.g., Kobasa & Maddi, 1977) has already proven itself a useful guide in my own health psychology research. In at least two ways, it emerges as distinctively relevant to the conceptualization of stress. Existentialism's emphasis on persons as beings in the world (e.g., Heidegger, 1962)—who do not carry around a set of static internal traits, but rather continuously construct personality through their actions—suits the personality in situation emphasis of the stress phenomenon (see Mischel, 1973). Additionally, existentialism portrays life as always changing and therefore as inevitably stressful. Unlike many other approaches to stress that are essentially pessimistic, existentialism allows for successful coping; that is, for outcomes other than debiliation and illness. In the hardiness research, it supports the formulation of hypotheses about how persons can rise to the challenges of their environments, turning stressful life events into opportunities for well-being and personal growth.

I am hopeful about what an existential theory of personality has to offer future research in health psychology. Although existentialism places radical emphasis on subjectivity and individual autonomy, it describes the exercise of freedom, responsibility, decision making, and other human capabilities as inevitably taking place within environments that are both interpersonal and physical. From an existential perspective, one has to ask about the behaviors of a specific individual, but also about the immediate and distant others and the factual circumstances to which those behaviors relate. Existentialism requires the contextual perspective argued for in this chapter.

An existential theory of personality also highlights aspects of human behavior that are crucial in matters of health and illness. It emphasizes the human search for and creation of meaning. As such, it has special relevance for the better understanding of those who are ill. Remember the case of Paul Tsongas. What intrigues the psychologically oriented reader of his book are not the personality characteristics that may have predisposed him to cancer, but rather his attempts to reestablish and discover who he is and what is important to him. The focus in existentialism on psychological processes, such as the setting of goals and the evaluating of priorities, makes it well-suited to the explication of the choices of someone like Tsongas.

A final reason for my endorsement of an existential theory of personality has to do as much with ideology as with science. Every theory of personality has a particular view of what the good life is and associated prescriptions for how it might be best lived. In choosing a theory, the researcher has to be aware of, first, what these underlying assumptions are; and second, the degree to which they are responsive to the human and social needs that his or her research addresses.

Existentialism defines autonomy or the freedom of individuality as essential to well-being. It also makes clear that, because human nature is essentially social, one needs to ensure that one person's exercise of freedom facilitates—rather than inhibits—the same exercise in another. These assumptions and associated goals strike me as fitting given the current state of health care. One does not have to look very hard to find forces of dehumanization and failures to recognize personal integrity in many of our modern health-care settings. In the face of these, existentialism offers a socially responsive guide to psychological research and the promise of needed intervention.

# REFERENCES

Allport, G. W. (1937). *Personality: A psychological interpretation.* New York: Holt.

Alexander, F. (1950). *Psychosomatic medicine.* New York: Norton.

Baker, L. J., Dearborn, M., Hastings, J. E., & Hamberger, K. (1984). Type A behavior in women: A review. *Health Psychology, 3,* 477-498.

Bard, M. (1966). Clues to the psychological management of patients with cancer. *Annals of the New York Academy of Sciences, 125,* 995-999.

Barry, K. H., & Connelly, P. A. (1978). Research on law students: An annotated bibliography. *American Bar Foundation Research Journal, 4,* 751-804.

Bigwood, G. F. (1976). Emotional reactions to cancer. *Lahey Clinic Foundation Bulletin, 25,* 24-29.

Carlson, R. (1975). Personality. In M. R. Rosenzweig & L. W. Porter (Eds.), *Annual review of psychology* (Vol. 26). Palo Alto, CA: Annual Reviews.

Carver, C. S., & Humphries, C. (1982). Social psychology of the Type A coronary-prone behavior pattern. In G. S. Sanders & J. Suls (Eds.) *Social psychology of health and illness.* Hillsdale, NJ: Lawrence Erlbaum.

Cohen, F. (1979). Personality, stress, and the development of physical illness. In G. C. Stone, F. Cohen, N. E. Adler, & Associates (Eds.), *Health psychology: A handbook.* San Francisco: Jossey-Bass.

deHaas, P. A., & vanReken, M. K. (1979). *Menstrual cycle symptoms as a function of health locus of control.* Paper presented at the Association for Women in Psychology Conference, Dallas, Texas.

Haynes, S. G., & Feinleib, M. (1980). Women, work, and coronary heart disease: Prospective findings from the Framingham Heart Study. *American Journal of Public Health, 70,* 133-141.

Heidegger, M. (1962). *Being and time.* New York: Harper & Row.

Kobasa, S. C. (1979). Stressful life events, personality, and health: An inquiry into hardiness. *Journal of Personality and Social Psychology, 37,* 1-11.

Kobasa, S. C. (1982). The hardy personality: Toward a social psychology of stress and health. In G. S. Sanders & J. Suls (Eds.), *The social psychology of health and illness.* Hillsdale, NJ: Lawrence Erlbaum.

Kobasa, S. C. (1985). Longitudinal and prospective methods in health psychology. In P. Karoly (Ed.), *Measurement strategies in health psychology.* New York: John Wiley.

Kobasa, C. S., & Maddi, S. R. (1977). Existential personality theory. In R. Corsini (Ed.), *Current personality theories.* Itasca, IL: Peacock.

Kobasa, S. C., Maddi, S. R., & Courington, S. (1981). Personality and constitution as mediators in the stress-illness relationship. *Journal of Health and Social Behavior, 22,* 368-378.

Kobasa, S. C., Maddi, S. R., & Kahn, S. (1982). Hardiness and health: A prospective study. *Journal of Personality and Social Psychology, 42,* 168-177.

Leventhal, H., Meyer, D., & Nerenz, D. (1980). The common sense representation of illness danger. In S. Rachman (Ed.), *Medical psychology* (Vol. 2). New York: Pergamon.

Lorber, J. (1975). Good patients and problem patients: Conformity and deviance in a general hospital. *Journal of Health and Social Behavior, 16,* 213-225.

Maddi, S. R., & Kobasa, S. C. (1984). *The hardy executive.* Homewood, IL: Dow Jones-Irwin.

Mages, N. L., & Mendelsohn, G. A. (1979). Effects of cancer on patients' lives: A personological approach. In G. C. Stone, F. Cohen, N. Adler, & Associates (Eds.), *Health psychology: A handbook.* San Francisco: Jossey-Bass.

Matthews, K. A. (1982). Psychological perspectives on the Type A behavior pattern. *Psychological Bulletin, 91,* 293-323.

Mayer, M. (1967). *The lawyers.* New York: Harper & Row.

Mechanic, D. (1972). Social psychological factors affecting the presentation of bodily complaints. *New England Journal of Medicine, 286,* 1132-1139.

Mechanic, D. (1977). Illness behavior, social adaptation, and the management of illness: A comparison of educational and medical models. *Journal of Nervous and Mental Disease, 165,* 79-87.

Mechanic, D. (1983). The experience and expression of distress: The study of illness behavior and medical utilization. In D. Mechanic (Ed.), *Handbook of health, health care, and the health professions.* New York: Free Press.

Mischel, W. (1973). Toward a social learning theory reconceptualization of personality. *Psychological Review, 80*, 252-283.

Murray, H. A. (1938). *Explorations in personality.* New York: Oxford University Press.

Newman, S. (1984). Anxiety, hospitalization, and surgery. In R. Fitzpatrick, J. Hinton, S. Newman, G. Scambler, & J. Thompson, *The experience of illness.* New York: Tavistock.

Rotter, J. B. (1954). *Social learning and clinical psychology.* Englewood Cliffs, NJ: Prentice-Hall.

Sanford, N. (1965). Will psychologists study human problems? *American Psychologist, 20*, 192-202.

Schmale, A. H. (1972). Giving up as a final common pathway to changes in health. *Advances in Psychosmatic Medicine, 8*, 20-41.

Seeman, M., & Evans, J. W. (1962). Alienation and learning in a hospital setting. *American Sociological Review, 27*, 772-783.

Siegel, R. E. (1968). Galen's system of physiology and medicine. New York: Karger.

Sontag, S. (1978). *Illness as metaphor.* New York: Farrar, Straus & Giroux.

Strickland, B. R. (1982). Internal-external expectancies and health-related behaviors. *Journal of Consulting and Clinical Psychology, 46*, 1192-1211.

Taylor, S. E. (1978). A developing role for social psychology in medicine and medical practice. *Personality and Social Psychology Bulletin, 4*, 515-523.

Taylor, S. (1979). Hospital patient behavior: Reactance, helplessness, or control? *Journal of Social Issues, 35*, 156-184.

Tsongas, P. (1984). *Heading home.* New York: Knopf.

Vachon, M.L.S. (1982). Stress and burnout among medical students and physicians. *University of Toronto Medical Journal, 60*, 3-6.

Wallston, K. A., & Wallston, S. B. (1982). Who is responsible for your health? The construct of health locus of control. In G. S. Sanders & J. Suls (Eds.), *The social psychology of health and illness.* Hillsdale, NJ: Lawrence Erlbaum.